# Fundamentals of Teaching English to Speakers of Other Languages in K–12 Mainstream Classrooms

*Hanizah Zainuddin*

*Norchaya Yahya*

*Carmen A. Morales-Jones*

*Eileen N. Ariza*

 **KENDALL/HUNT PUBLISHING COMPANY**
4050 Westmark Drive    Dubuque, Iowa 52002

# Contents

# *Foreword*

In April 2002, I attended the annual TESOL Conference in Salt Lake City as did thousands of other professionals—all educators and teachers of English as a second or foreign language. There, in the Salt Palace, the city's magnificent conference center, I ran into one of my colleagues—Eileen Ariza, a friend and former student, and one of the authors of the present work. Wild with enthusiasm (as she usually is), Eileen cornered me while she spoke of their manuscript in progress. This work, prepared by a team of four experts, each contributing a distinct area of expertise, was sorely needed, she explained.

Given the elimination or reduction of many bilingual programs in various parts of the country and an increasing trend to integrate limited or non-English speakers of other language backgrounds into regular mainstream classrooms, we both tried to imagine our public school colleagues addressing—in addition to ethnic diversity, diverse learning styles and strategies, and possibly learning disabled students—now, a smattering of English-language learning students. These are pupils, of course, whose native language is Spanish, Greek, Thai, or some other tongue—whose special needs are now being added as well to the mainstream classroom mix. Quite a task!

While interesting and diverse, any teacher who finds him or herself in such a classroom situation indeed faces an overwhelming challenge, especially those teachers with little or no prior preparation or experience in teaching English as a Second Language (ESL). Yes, I agreed! Teachers in these situations need help—all they can get. At this point, I happily consented to review this work, designed to assist the mainstream teacher in this specialty area.

When I later read the manuscript, I was pleased to see it that was truly a work of praxis—an attempt to combine theory and concept with implementation. In their plan to provide both theoretical concepts and applications, the authors designed the book with several important components: research and challenges, points to remember, lesson plans and examples of activities, and an accompanying workbook. Together, these components provide the users—both experienced and inexperienced teachers of ESL—with a wealth of information in addition to practical examples. Most importantly, they attempt to help teachers recognize the differences between limited language proficiency and learning disabilities, an easy and common confusion often made by the uninitiated, with important consequences for the learners.

In a number of states, elementary teachers are required to hold an endorsement in ESL, given the increasing number of limited English-speaking populations in their area. This book aims to teach them what they need to know to enhance the English-language learning process. And, of course, it is especially valuable for teachers in other areas who have never had ESL training and for ESL pull-out teachers, an even larger contingent of potential users, whether in schools with bilingual education programs or not.

The work draws, wisely, from a variety of disciplines and integrates these with specific purposes in mind: teaching in a multicultural education setting, principles and practices in ESL, teaching the four skill areas, organizing and planning language instruction, and a final chapter on teaching ESL through content areas. As a result, the materials often found only in separate texts are brought together in a single work. The result is a practical compendium of the fundamentals of teaching ESL, conveniently assembled.

I enthusiastically recommend this work and I sincerely hope that mainstream teachers who use it will find it an important tool in easing them through some very compelling and worthwhile challenges.

Alvino E. Fantini, Ph.D.
Senior Faculty
Master of Arts in Teaching Program
School for International Training
Brattleboro, Vermont

# *Preface*

## Organization

**Fundamentals of English Language Teaching and Content-Based Instruction** is organized into five parts. **Part I** defines the term *multicultural education* and provides ideas for modifying classroom instruction by incorporating multicultural components into the curriculum. This section also offers the reader valuable insights into how variations in cultures do not necessarily indicate deficiencies in the learners' experiences but provides the knowledge base for teachers to comprehend the multifaceted nature of culture in language learning and teaching.

**Part II** gives a brief overview of first and second language acquisition theories with specific examples to clarify each. The impact of Stephen Krashen's five hypotheses on the field of second language teaching is highlighted. In addition, this section exposes the reader to the historical development of methods of teaching English to speakers of other languages (TESOL). The theoretical underpinnings of the communicative language teaching approach are discussed. Salient aspects in planning classroom tasks that are communicative in nature are emphasized. Specific ideas and examples for teaching English to speakers of other languages (ESOL) from a communicative perspective are described and discussed. This section ends with a discussion on the paradigm shift in grammar instruction and the benefits of teaching grammar with a communicative focus.

**Part III** emphasizes the integration of language and content when planning for English language instruction. Capitalizing on the importance of teaching English from a communicative perspective, various integration approaches are described. In addition, this section provides a framework for planning interdisciplinary, content-based thematic units of instruction. Each step provides examples taken from actual units. Bloom's Taxonomy, including helpful tables, is introduced and discussed in detail. Gardner's model of multiple intelligences is also discussed at length. A wealth of ideas for activities to employ in developing multiple intelligences using Gardner's model are provided.

**Part IV** explores research and its application for teaching listening, speaking, reading, and writing skills to English language learners (ELLs). Specific examples of activities to employ for teaching as well as ways to assess listening and speaking are described in respective chapters. A specific chapter is devoted to the teaching of vocabulary, complete with specific suggestions for teaching vocabulary for multiple levels of proficiency. The last two chapters of this section give a description of the historical movements and perspectives on first and second language reading and writing research. These chapters also stress the close connection between reading and writing and offer a variety of instructional strategies for multiple-level learners that facilitate the development of various language arts skills and critical thinking in content-based learning. This section ends with a discussion of a variety of reading and writing assessments including students' self-assessment of their attitudes and strategies for learning to read and write.

**Part V** addresses teaching ESL through specific content areas. This section, written by content area experts, provides the reader with a rationale for teaching ESOL through the content area as well as a wealth of concrete ideas on how to do so. These ideas are of significant value for teachers who are seeking for specific ways to teach ESOL in content areas such as art, music, drama, science, social studies, and mathematics. In addition, Part V contains a chapter on addressing the needs of the exceptional education ESL learners with helpful insights for the exceptional student educator. A chapter devoted to using technology with English learners is included. Two appendices have been added to supplement the knowledge base contained in Part I. Appendix A provides valuable information about cultural characteristics of specific cultural groups such as Spanish, Islamic, and Arabic speakers; Haitian students; Asian Americans; and Native Americans. Appendix B highlights "Interesting Insights" on beliefs that signify good and bad luck in specific cultures.

## Audience and Purpose

Although many texts exist for teachers of English language learners, this book offers a knowledge base to aid teachers to be effective in today's classrooms, where students of multiple cultures and ethnic groups speak a variety of languages and learn through a range of styles. The general education teacher must know how to reach all students, regardless of the students' prior knowledge, home language, or cognitive capacity. Today's teachers are far more responsible for issues that were unheard of in earlier educational eras.

Teachers of today need to know how to offer critical content that is cognitively demanding, yet modified to the ability of the student's language proficiency. In addition to the multitude of tasks and traditional issues attended to by the classroom teacher, teachers must be skilled in offering alternative assessments as well as standardized assessments; know how to interpret the students' cultural background and prior educational and life experience; and offer affective comfort so that learning can take place in a non threatening environment.

This book seeks to offer an inclusive overview of pertinent topics for teachers who are responsible for giving comprehensive instruction to all students. The authors discuss culture, multicultural education, technology, exceptional education (both gifted and learning disabled), and instructional strategies to present modified critical content. The primary goal is to include information about the English language learner for the purpose of helping all teachers, regardless of training, to acquire an in-depth knowledge of the issues vital to the understanding and teaching students of English.

## Features of the Book

The book's pedagogy is perhaps its best feature because it umbrellas several attractive features of the book that make it a reader-friendly text or a reference book.

- Each chapter opens with a list of important key issues such as research, problems faced by English language learners (ELLs), strategies and skills, and assessments that later are fully discussed in the chapter.

- The key issues are followed by classroom vignette that expose readers to strategies and techniques of teaching language skills used by teachers. The narrative and illustrative features of the "real-life" scenarios allow readers to visualize the applications of important ideas used in classrooms.

- "Points to Remember" which summarizes and highlights the main ideas of the chapter, concludes every chapter. This feature not only recycles, but restates, the most important points in the chapter, making it easier for students to focus on the main issues in the chapter.

- The workbook that accompanies this text is comprised of a collection of challenge sheets. In every chapter students are challenged to answer three levels of questions: they are to recall/research information from the text, apply their knowledge based on ideas given in the text, and evaluate strategies and techniques presented in the text. These challenge sheets are perforated, making it easy for students to submit completed tasks to the instructor.

- The inclusion of instructional applications and/or activities in each chapter is yet another attractive feature of this book. Less experienced preservice teachers are given specific ideas to incorporate in designing their own lessons.

■ The book covers the most salient aspects of teaching. It addresses multicultural education; cultural issues; teaching language skills such as listening, speaking, reading, writing, and vocabulary; content area teaching such as math, social studies, art, science, technology, music, and drama; and the simultaneous teaching of subject matter content and language skills using scaffolding techniques.

# *Acknowledgments*

The authors would like to thank all those involved in making this project come to fruition, especially those who have provided valuable comments on the earlier manuscript. A special thank you to Ana E. Erazo for supplying her drawings to print on pages 92 and 93.

# *About the Authors*

**Hanizah Zainuddin** received her Ph.D. from Indiana University, Bloomington in 1995 and is currently an Assistant Professor of TESOL at Florida Atlantic University, Boca Raton. Her areas of interest include second language writing, contrastive rhetoric, and teacher education. She also has extensive experience teaching English as a second language to adults and adolescents inside and outside of the United States.

**Noorchaya Yahya** received her Ph.D. in Rhetoric and Linguistics from Indiana University of Pennsylvania. Currently, she is an Assistant Professor at Florida Atlantic University, where she teaches TESOL methods courses. She has taught ESL for more than 10 years at institutions of higher teaming both inside and outside of the United States. She is currently involved in the training of preservice teachers for ESOL certification in Florida. Her research interests lie in the areas of second language writing, teacher education, and second language acquisition.

**Carmen A. Morales-Jones** received her Ph.D. in Curriculum and Integrative Studies from Florida State University, Tallahassee, in 1975. Her career encompasses the teaching of ESL and French at the Laboratory School of the University of Puerto Rico, as well as teacher training at Florida Atlantic University in the area of language acquisition (language arts for elementary education majors, foreign languages for foreign language majors, and English as a second language for elementary preservice teachers and inservice teachers). Currently, she coordinates the TESOL program at Florida Atlantic University and teaches numerous courses in this program. Her research interests are in the areas of teacher training and second language acquisition.

**Eileen N. Ariza** received her Ed.D. in Multilingual/Multicultural Education from the University of Massachusetts, Amherst, and her MAT in TESOL, Spanish as a Second Language, and her Bilingual/Multicultural Endorsement from the School of International Training in Brattleboro, Vermont. A Teaching Fellow for many years at Harvard University's English Language Institute, she is now an Assistant Professor of TESOL in Florida Atlantic University's teacher education program, where she prepares both prospective and current teachers in the undergraduate and graduate programs for Florida-mandated ESOL endorsement. Ariza has spent time in more than 50 countries, and has taught English as a foreign and second language in eight countries to students ranging from preschoolers to the elderly. Her primary research interests are in ESOL and bilingual teacher preparation in the United States and overseas.

# *About the Contributors*

**Joseph M. Furner**, Ph.D. is an Associate Professor of Mathematics Education at Florida Atlantic University in Jupiter, Florida. His research interests are related to math anxiety, the implementation of the *NCTM Standards*, ESOL issues as they relate to math instruction, the use of technology in mathematics instruction, math manipulatives, and children's literature in the teaching of mathematics. Prior to teaching at the university level, Dr. Furner taught middle school mathematics in New York and at the American School in Mexico City, Mexico.

**Toni Fuss Kirkwood** is an Associate Professor of Social Studies and Global Education in the Department of Teacher Education, Florida Atlantic University. Prior to her appointment to the Florida Atlantic University, she spent 22 years in the Miami Public Schools as a classroom teacher, social studies coordinator, and Director of the Office of Multicultural Affairs. Her research interests are in the areas of global, international/comparative education, and minority issues in education.

**Susanne Lapp** is an Associate Professor of Reading/Language Arts at Florida Atlantic University. She holds a Doctorate in Curriculum and Instruction from the University of Cincinnati in Cincinnati, Ohio. Prior to joining the faculty at Florida Atlantic, she taught reading and language arts at the University of Texas-Pan American. Her research interests include multicultural literacy, educational technology, and assessment.

**Joan Lindgren** received her Ph.D. in Curriculum & Instruction from the University of Florida in 1993, and is an Assistant Professor of science education at Florida Atlantic University. Prior to her position at FAU, she taught in the School of Education at Frostburg State University in Maryland, and worked as a public school teacher in Florida for over 15 years. Besides an interest in the learning of science by English language learners, her research interests include writing to learn through science, gender issues in science classrooms, and teacher self-efficacy beliefs regarding the teaching of science.

**Catherine A. Matsuno** received her M.A. degree in Educational Leadership from the University of Hawaii at Manoa. A long-term resident of Honolulu, Matsuno serves as a social studies teacher and technology instructor at Sacred Hearts Academy. Matsuno also serves as a faculty member at Chaminade University, Honolulu, in the Master of Education program. As an adjunct in this program, she teaches preservice and in-service teachers to incorporate technology into the curriculum. Her passions are technology and reading.

**Barbara Ridener**'s experiences include teaching elementary, middle, and secondary grades in Florida. She holds a Bachelor's degree in Elementary Education and a Master's in Secondary Mathematics Education, both from the University of Central Florida. In 1995, she received her Ph.D. in Mathematics Education from the University of Georgia and taught mathematics preservice courses in both Pennsylvania and Florida. Currently a market manager for Texas Instruments, Inc., Barbara Ridener is responsible for developing efforts to partner with teacher educators to effectively train preservice teachers to use classroom technology. Her research interests include how calculators affect teaching and learning mathematics, integrated curriculum, and ways by which preservice teachers come to understand teaching.

**Timothy A. Rodriquez** is an Assistant Professor at Findlay University in Findlay, Ohio. He received his Ph.D. from the University of Iowa, specializing in reading and bilingual education. Prior to teaching at Findlay, Dr. Rodriquez was a visiting professor at Florida Atlantic University, Jupiter campus.

**Cynthia Wilson** received her Ph.D. in Special Education from Florida State University in 1988 and has been at Florida Atlantic University since 1993. Her research interests include teacher preparation for preservice teachers and professional development for in-service teachers. Her primary focus is to improve the literacy achievements of at-risk students and students with mild disabilities by training teachers to implement effective teaching practices. Dr. Wilson is involved in the FAU Urban Professional Development Schools where she works directly with an urban elementary school as faculty liaison to teachers. Her involvement at the school includes teaching courses and facilitating workshops for both preservice and in-service teachers on site; supervising field experiences, student teachers, and graduate interns; and providing unique professional development opportunities for classroom teachers.

**Margarita Bianco-Cornish** is a doctoral student at Florida Atlantic University, Department of Exceptional Student Education. She received her Master's Degree in Special Education from Florida International University and has 15 years experience in both general education and special education. Her major teaching and research interests are in the areas of gifted students with learning disabilities and teacher preparation programs.

# Part I

# Multicultural Issues in Teaching English as a Second Language

# Chapter 1

## *Multicultural Education*

---

### KEY ISSUES

❏ Multicultural education

❏ Goals of multicultural education

❏ Negative cultural diversity

❏ Multicultural curriculum

❏ Parent-school collaboration in multicultural curriculum

It's 5 p.m. on a Friday evening. Fall semester is over and Alex and Joe, teacher education students, have just turned in their final language arts project to their professor. The halls of the university seem deserted except for the curious sounds and unfamiliar languages coming from the large reception room at the end of the hall. Beautiful music, laughter, and the terrific smell of exotic food beckon Alex and Joe to peer inside the room. To their surprise, they discover approximately 20 international students gathered in the room for an end-of-semester party. Through the crowd of students, they identify a familiar face. Fan, a classmate from their statistics class, appears and invites them to come in and join the party. The university Multicultural Club is celebrating the end of finals and the beginning of the winter break. Although everyone appears very happy, Alex and Joe are hesitant. Both Alex and Joe's families have been in the United States for several generations, and therefore have never identified themselves as being multicultural. Alex explains to Fan that neither of the young men feels like he could fit into the club. Fan laughs out loud and tells her classmates that they would fit perfectly into the club, "You two guys need to learn a whole bunch of things about being multiculturally aware!"

## Defining Multicultural Education

The notion of multicultural education begins with the individual and seeks to prepare that person for harmonious existence within a pluralistic society (Baker, 1983) and involves several important goals (Solomon, 1996):

1. Encourage individuals to become aware of themselves, their cultural group, and their place in the world at large.
2. Promote an appreciation of other cultures.
3. Encourage individuals to maintain the lifestyles, values, and beliefs of any ethnic and/or cultural groups they choose.

Multicultural individuals maintain an appreciation of their culture while developing an appreciation of other cultures. Becoming aware of oneself, one's culture, and/or other cultures provides an effective formula for functioning successfully within the larger society.

The two young men featured in the earlier vignette needed to understand that multicultural education and awareness are not merely associated with individuals from other countries, but are integral to their own personal development and their relationship to other individuals and society as a whole. As future teachers, it is essential that Alex and Joe develop greater multicultural sensitivity and awareness because their classrooms will increasingly reflect the multicultural, multilingual nature of our diverse society.

## Background of Multicultural Education

Banks (1988) states that multicultural education embraces the notion that all Americans have come from many races and ethnic groups and these individuals and groups have helped to create and establish the United States. As a result, their contributions must be welcomed and celebrated and these individuals must feel represented in America.

Bank's philosophy on multicultural education rings true as researchers predict that the minority population will soar by the year 2050. The present percentage of Latinos will triple, the Asian population will more than triple, the African-American population will increase by 3%, and the non-Hispanic white population will drop from 76% to 53% (Carger, 1997).

Across the nation, minority students are gradually making academic gains in the classroom. Hispanic and African-American students trail whites in high school graduation rates, according to the American Council on Education. The completion rate for whites was 81.9% in 1995 while African-American and Hispanic completion rates were 76.9 % and 58.6%, respectively (Adair, 1997).

As the demographics of American society change and educators begin to instruct students from diverse language and literacy communities, they must also be prepared to handle any negative reaction to cultural diversity.

Negative cultural diversity occurs when individuals and groups regard each other suspiciously. This negative reaction to cultural diversity creates an unhealthy social dynamic with dominant and subordinate cultures competing for economic, social, and political power.

To guard against negative cultural diversity, teachers must encourage all students to understand that cultural diversity means that societal groups coexist in harmony. All people feel that they have equal access to the resources of the nation (civil rights, political power) and they must feel that they are represented equally. Everyone regards the other person with tolerance and appreciation of individual differences.

## Creating a Multicultural Curriculum

The American multicultural mosaic must be reflected appropriately in instructional materials and school life. Because of the changing demographics in American schools, teachers need to learn to appreciate and attend to new voices, languages, and educational needs of their students.

Generally, classrooms in the United States have made attempts at exposing students to multicultural themes by setting aside special days, weeks, and months to celebrate a variety of holidays and customs. Noteworthy in their efforts, teachers and administrators must strive to go beyond *exposing* students to short-term multicultural celebrations and instead strive to *integrate* multicultural themes into their everyday school curriculum.

Creating and establishing a multicultural curriculum, in many cases, involves reshaping the social climate of the school. Teachers and administrators must find effective ways to instill a multicultural atmosphere in the school. Recognition of deep cultural values (such as family values, health issues, family structures, and male/female roles) instead of the typical surface cultural values (such as clothing, music, and food) must be explored.

Multicultural curriculum should:

- Create an atmosphere of cultural diversity and positive attitudes for people from all backgrounds and cultures.
- Create a classroom atmosphere of equal opportunity for all students.

- ■ Establish a non threatening atmosphere for learning so that students can explore creative activities and succeed in school.
- ■ Encourage students to become more culturally literate.

Additionally, schools must open their doors and welcome the support of parents and the school community. Involving parents and the school community helps to extend the goals of multicultural education (Carger, 1997).

## Involvement of Parents and the School Community

- ■ Motivates cross-cultural interaction and encourages parents and community members to explore new education and academic ground.
- ■ Encourages parents to integrate new information into their childrearing practices and incorporate new ideas about education into their family networks.
- ■ Supports parents' confidence in actively participating in their students' school experiences and helps them realize that school success is possible.

The classroom environment where students learn should encourage children to become more tolerant and just individuals and members of society.

## Sample Activities for the Multicultural Curriculum

### Activity I

**Topic**

Pictures that Create a Thousand Words

**Age Level**

Lower/Upper Elementary Grades

**Activity**

To increase language and literacy development, young children should be exposed to a wealth of images and pictures that will enhance their knowledge of the world around them and develop their communicative efforts.

1. Teachers instruct their students to begin collecting pictures from a variety of media including photos, magazine articles, and newspaper clippings.

2. To increase durability, the pictures are then attached to stronger backing ($3 \times 5$, $4 \times 6$ or $5 \times 8$-inch cards).

3. These cards can now be used in a number of language and literacy activities including:

   ■ Discussion starters based on popular themes including sports, hobbies, families, foods, and customs.

   ■ Theme-based writing assignments using the aforementioned themes.

   ■ Attribute matching where students locate common attributes among the pictures and discussing the criteria for selection and non selection.

   ■ Role-playing situations and other dramatic play activities.

Children should be encouraged to discuss how the visual images impact their cultural understanding of others as well as their own cultural backgrounds.

## Sample Activities for the Multicultural Curriculum

### Activity 2

#### *Topic*

Intergenerational Storytelling: Recalling Stories that Shaped Our Lives

#### *Age Level*

Upper Elementary Grades

#### *Activity*

Intergenerational support for learning is invaluable for children. Encouraging parents, grandparents, siblings, and caregivers to share common life experiences with students helps to enhance cultural understanding and communication for the entire community.

Sharing common stories helps students connect their past and provides them with an opportunity to understand and interpret historic, social, and political events through the experiences of family members.

■ Family members are asked to gather together at school and complete a series of questions on significant events in their lives. Members either record their experiences on paper or share them orally through tape recordings.

- Family members are then encouraged to share these experiences with their children in small-group discussions.
- Students are encouraged to ask more detailed information from family members regarding specific cultural, and social issues.
- After the story-telling, students are encouraged to create books that detail some of the stories that were shared among their families. These books are referred to throughout the year as classroom discussions focus on some of the historic, social, or political experiences of family members.

Story-telling activities enhance students' respect for other cultures as well as their own culture. They gain additional respect for their family experiences and begin to see how historic, social, and political issues may be personally relevant for themselves, their families, and/or their classmates. Through story-telling activities, students and their families learn the importance of valuing diverse perspectives as well as their own.

## Sample Activities for the Multicultural Curriculum

### Activity 3

**Topic**

Multicultural Newspaper (Our Worldwide Voices)

**Age Level**

Upper Elementary Grades

**Activity**

Establish a classroom or school newspaper that highlights and features the languages spoken in your classroom/school. The newspaper should be written, edited, and published by students in the classroom/school. The newspaper will feature articles and creative writing (poetry, short stories, etc.) submitted by students and published in the students' native languages and translated into English. The newspaper can be copied and read by all students in the classroom or school. A copy of the newspaper may also be available in the school library where parents, community members and other visitors can enjoy the newspapers' contents.

Teachers may also use the newspapers in the classroom to work on a number of language/ literacy skills and strategies.

## *Skills*

- Mechanics in the English language (spelling and grammar skills)
- Researching skills: computer/Internet; library resources: checking out books, interlibrary loan

## *Strategies*

- Teach students about different forms/purposes of writing: expository versus narrative writing.

## *Multicultural Activities*

- Students locate and identify the countries where these languages are spoken and their proximity to the United States.
- Students may also compare the orthographic representation of written pieces and identify similarities and differences between the various languages represented in the newspaper.

## Points to Remember

❑ Multicultural education begins with the individual and prepares that individual for harmonious existence within a pluralistic society (Baker, 1983).

❑ Multicultural education

A. Encourages individuals to become aware of themselves, their cultural group, and their place in the world at large.

B. Promotes an appreciation of other cultures.

C. Encourages individuals to maintain the lifestyles, values, and beliefs of any ethnic and/or cultural groups they choose.

❑ The multicultural population in the United States is expected to increase by the year 2050. The present percentage of Latinos will triple, the Asian population will more than triple, the African-American population will increase by 3%, and the non-Hispanic white population will drop from 76% to 53% (Carger, 1997).

❑ Negative cultural diversity occurs when individuals and groups regard each other suspiciously, which creates an unhealthy social dynamic with dominant and subordinate cultures competing for economic, social, and political power.

❑ To discourage negative cultural diversity, students must understand that cultural diversity means that societal groups coexist in harmony.

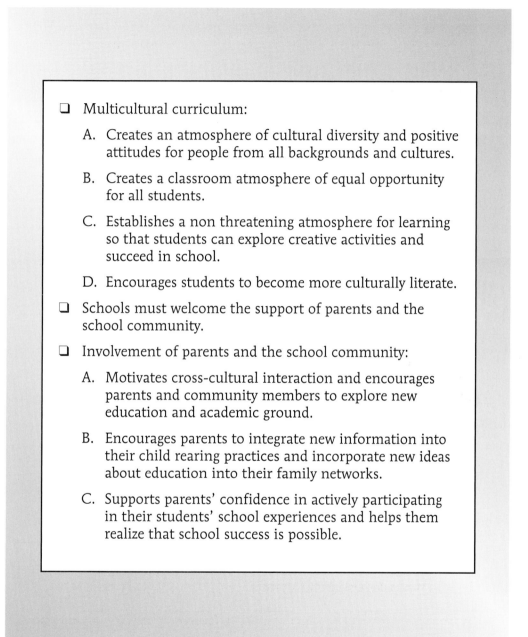

❑ Multicultural curriculum:

A. Creates an atmosphere of cultural diversity and positive attitudes for people from all backgrounds and cultures.

B. Creates a classroom atmosphere of equal opportunity for all students.

C. Establishes a non threatening atmosphere for learning so that students can explore creative activities and succeed in school.

D. Encourages students to become more culturally literate.

❑ Schools must welcome the support of parents and the school community.

❑ Involvement of parents and the school community:

A. Motivates cross-cultural interaction and encourages parents and community members to explore new education and academic ground.

B. Encourages parents to integrate new information into their child rearing practices and incorporate new ideas about education into their family networks.

C. Supports parents' confidence in actively participating in their students' school experiences and helps them realize that school success is possible.

# Chapter 2

## *Culture in the Classroom*

## KEY ISSUES

❑ Learning styles

❑ Cultural styles

## Effects of culture in the classroom

Ms. Whelan chats with her colleagues in the front doorway of the bilingual colegio in Mayaguez, Puerto Rico, where she is doing her internship. The bell rings and children charge noisily through the halls, each clamoring to be the first in line to go home. Marco, in his hurry to be first, accidentally slams his full weight into Ms. Whelan, almost knocking her down. Angrily, she admonishes him, "Can't you say 'excuse me' when you bump into someone?" He ignores her and just stands there looking at the floor. Even angrier because he ignores her, Ms. Whelan repeats her words, "Don't you know you are being rude? Excuse yourself when you bump into someone! Look at me when I am talking to you!" But Marco still keeps his head down, ignoring her outburst. Ms. Whelan leaves the school with a very bad impression of Marco's manners.

Sang Li has recently arrived from Korea and is assigned to Mrs. Cannon's class. Mrs. Cannon explains the activity the students are to do, and then asks, "Does everyone understand the assignment?" The students answer in unison, "Yes, Mrs. Cannon," and begin to work diligently. After a few minutes, the teacher notices that Sang Li is looking over Peter's shoulder and copying what he has written. She quickly says, "Sang Li! Do your own work. Cheating is not allowed!" Sang Li hangs his head and turns red with shame.

In the previous scenarios, each child is from a different culture, and each culture has different values. Nowhere is this more evident than in the classroom. In the first scenario, Marco does not say, "Excuse me," because in his culture, it is impolite to look at an adult in the eyes when being chastised, and he is too ashamed to answer. The typical American child is raised hearing,"Look at me when I am talking to you," and is encouraged to look directly into the adult's eyes when spoken to. In the Puerto Rican and Haitian cultures (as well as others), children are taught to never look at an adult in the eyes, as it is a sign of insubordination.

In the second scenario, Sang Li is looking over Peter's shoulder to see how to do the assignment. Not only does Sang Li not understand the directions, but in Korea, students are expected to work together cooperatively.

By learning about students' cultures, the classroom teacher can provide better instruction because learning styles are directly related to cultural values. If teachers are aware of the values that individual cultures hold dear, they are better equipped to reach and teach the diverse children in today's multicultural classrooms.

## A Historical Overview of Culture

When research on culture and the phenomenon of culture shock became prominent in the 1950's, renowned researchers such as Edward Hall, Kalvero Oberg, and others launched their landmark findings that are benchmarks still referred to by scholars today. A more recent definition of culture was coined by Saravia-Shore and Arvizu (1992) who refer to *"culture"* as a "dynamic, creative, and continuous process that includes behaviors, values, and substance shared by people that guides them in their struggle for survival and gives meaning to their lives" (p. xviii). Others describe *"culture"* as an unconscious or conscious pattern of behaviors that reflect the societal beliefs and values shared by the people who are members of the group (Goodenough, 1981; Kohls, 2001; Saville-Troike, 1978).

When references are made to the word "culture," people often think of the arts, music, and theater. When speaking of a person being "cultured," this description might be used when an individual likes opera, has good manners, and is well read. However, in this book, the reference to "culture" implies the learned behavior patterns and attitudes of people in their societies.

Oberg (1960) first explained culture as the "environment, which consists of man-made physical objects, social institutions, and ideas and beliefs." He also said that parents are not consciously responsible for the culture they transmit to their young. By means of this culture, "the young learn to adapt themselves to the physical environment, and to the people with whom they associate" (p. 180).

After individuals learn their culture, it becomes a sure, familiar way of life and they function automatically within this cultural system, using the appropriate actions to get what is desired from the environment. This process manifests itself as a "value" of that particular system.

## Ethnocentrism

The term *ethnicity* refers to the sense of belonging to a cultural group. Tiedt and Tiedt (1998) explain that ethnicity includes the national or linguistic background with which the individual is affiliated. At this point, it is important to mention the problem of "stereotyping" individuals instead of "sociotyping" (Bennet, 1990, 1993). According to Bennet, *stereotyping* can happen when false and exaggerated characteristics of a group are attributed to the individual, but *sociotyping* involves an accurate generalization about cultural groups as a whole.

Oberg further explains that people accept their culture as the best and only way of doing things and that this attitude, called *ethnocentrism,* is normal and understandable. Being ethnocentric is presuming that one's culture, race, ways of life, and nations form the center of the world. Typically, individuals of any cultural entity identify strongly with the rest of the group, and when a negative comment is made against the group (or country, or family, and so on), the individual is indignant and takes the affront personally. It is this attitude that begets stereotypes, which is the tendency to attribute all individual peculiarities as national characteristics.

People from the United States can be described as nationalistic, patriotic, and even ethnocentric. Picture it this way: Most Americans are raised hearing how lucky they are to be Americans, that the United States is the greatest nation in the world, the best country in the world, and so forth. If the United States is the superior country, doesn't that imply that every other country is inferior? This is, by definition, *ethnocentrism.*

Each individual's cultural viewpoint is based on meaningful context from internalized patterns buried in the unconscious. The blueprints for social existence control thought and speech patterns, conceptual and motor habits, and emotional responses (Condon, 1974). These behavioral traits are accepted as common, normal behavior, and any behavior outside of the norm is considered somewhat deviant. This unconscious ethnocentrism stems from an individual's inability to see beyond his own perception of reality.

Condon further explains that different cultural groups inhabit different orders of reality, each determined by a specific cultural heritage. Those who are not conscious of differing world perceptions, or that perceptions are shaped in different ways by different societies, are bound to be engaged in misunderstandings with members of other societies, even when speaking the same language.

It is unlikely that an individual is fully cognizant of the depth and strength of his own cultural patterns until he has the opportunity to experience a cross cultural interaction that threatens, challenges, or violates his cultural values. As the saying goes, "you can't ask a fish to describe water."

Members of a cultural group are aware of the obvious cultural values and assumptions, but often are ignorant of their own cultural values until they are challenged. Culture is an integral part of language (Kramsch, 1993). Edward Sapir (Whorf, 1956) believed that culture determines the contents of human actions and thoughts, while language formulates them (p. 178). Today, proponents of multicultural education believe that language and culture are intertwined, and practices that build on students' language skills and cultural backgrounds should be reflected in the school curriculum.

## The Role of Culture

Culture plays the role of ensuring that members conform to socially acceptable actions, and cultural groups use laws as external restrictions to enforce appropriate behavior. However, within this framework, an allowance for diversity, and a certain amount of freedom of individual choice exist.

An individual's culture provides a safe haven because common behaviors and familiar surroundings allow automatic responses and a relaxed state. The world is predictable and the individual is firmly oriented. Words and actions do not need to be translated, and the appropriate response to almost every encounter is internally ingrained. Within one's own culture, a common frame of reference exists for acceptable behavior.

In their own cultures, people have learned what to do and do not need to make radical decisions as to what type of behavior is expected of them. When individuals come into contact with other cultures, they undergo an acculturation process and the original patterns of behavior and language are interchanged (Miranda & Umhoefer, 1998; Padilla, 1980).

## Points to Remember

❑ Each society has its own set of values and belief system.

❑ Cultural values often influence learning styles.

❑ By learning about students' cultures, teachers can better provide instruction.

❑ "Culture" refers to a loosely unified set of beliefs, customs, values, and ideas belonging to a society. Within the society, there is individuality and a continuum of behaviors.

❑ Ethnocentrism is the belief that one's culture, people, nation, society, or ways are the best. Your way is the only way.

# Chapter 3

## *Language Determines Culture*

## KEY ISSUES

❏ The relationship between language and culture

❏ Cultural misunderstandings

❏ Deep culture and surface culture

❏ Assumptions about culture

Señora Salazar, the director of a growing school in a fairly large city in Colombia, decided that her new "bilingual" school needed to offer a more authentic experience if the students were to become bilingual. The current teachers of the colegio were native-born Colombians with excellent English skills; however, parents were complaining that none of the teachers were native English speakers. To look for teachers willing to teach overseas, Señora Salazar began advertising in the United States for teachers to direct and teach in her bilingual program. Three young women with Master's degrees and a collective total of 12 years living and teaching ESOL accepted the challenge and decided to go to work in Colombia. After 8 months at the position, the director of the colegio had become rude and intolerant of the North American teachers, continuously made nasty remarks, and decided that she hated Americans. One teacher quit under threat of arrest, and the other two shortly began to think of ways to get out of their situation. After the North American teachers left, the director hired British teachers, with the same disastrous results.

What had gone wrong? The young women were experienced language teachers, familiar with culture shock, and knowledgeable about adapting to other cultures. They applied their skills to their working situation and nothing seemed to be appropriate. When they left, it was under volatile auspices.

Language and culture are inseparable. The director of the school wanted the English language taught without any American culture traits. However, language is a mirror of its speakers' attitude and ideas (Chaika, 1989; Kramsch, 1993) and it is impossible to teach the language in a vacuum. Speakers of different languages have different perceptions of the world (Whorf, 1956) according to their own cultural perceptions.

The North American teachers who went overseas to teach took their American values with them. By only seeing through their "American" cultural lenses, problems rapidly arose.

In the vignette, the first North American teacher to leave was the only one who had a working knowledge of Spanish. She was placed in the position of translating, from her perception, everything to her colleagues. If she misinterpreted, no one would know, so it was uncertain what, if any, misinterpretation had taken place.

The cross-cultural miscommunications mounted quickly, both in professional and personal areas. Señora Salazar did not understand why the American teachers had to make decisions collectively; she expected the American hired as director to make all the decisions and direct the other two teachers. Additionally, the American teachers were shocked when the director would not hire a fluent English speaker because she was not attractive enough. The director explained that the students would not accept the teacher if she was of a lesser status (which included beauty, dress, manners, and social class) than they.

Other cultural differences were soon evident to the North Americans. They could not accustom themselves to the attitude of unimportance of time. They would decide on time frames and deadlines to implement educational strategies, and these were totally disregarded. The North American teachers were more informal in their dress and manner in the classroom. They would sit on the desk, talk to the maid who served them morning coffee, and would not hesitate to state their opinions if they disagreed with the director. To the director, all of these behaviors denoted their lack of proper decorum and total lack of respect for tradition and ritual, resulting in daily discord. Inevitably, the teachers left believing that the director was a cruel person with a dictatorial style, and that she was abusive to the overworked Colombian teachers. The director, however, was left with the feelings that North Americans were rude, disrespectful to authority, and lazy.

It is easy to see what went wrong after examining the typical cultural values that are being challenged on both sides. Egalitarianism, time values, and discomfort with being deferential are traits within the American value system, whereas the Colombians value more formality, respect for traditional roles, and less pressure on time and schedules. It is clear, then, that language learning cannot be successful without cultural learning. Conversely, when people from other cultures arrive in the United States, they bring their own cultural baggage that inevitably results in misunderstandings.

## Deep Culture and Surface Culture

In school situations, teachers often decide to highlight different cultures in an effort to incorporate the mosaic of ethnic diversity. Hispanic Month or Black History Month will be declared, or perhaps a cultural festival will be held. Although these ideas may be entertaining, they only highlight the surface culture that is visible at first glance. These activities do not touch the roots of deep culture that are perceptible when serious challenges are made to the belief system of individuals.

Frank Gonzalez (1978) wrote the following comprehensive list of descriptions of surface and deep culture. By studying both categories, it is easy to see why a simple fiesta or cultural celebration merely touches on the shallow components of culture.

### Assumptions About Culture

1. **Culture is universal.** All people have culture and, therefore, share in a common humanity.
2. **Culture is organized.** There is a coherence and structure among the patterns of human behavior.
3. **Culture is stable, yet changeable.** It is dynamic and manifests continuous and constant change.

### Elements of Surface Culture

| | |
|---|---|
| **Food** | food and culinary contributions |
| **Holidays** | patriotic holidays, religious observances, personal rites and celebrations |
| **Arts** | traditional and contemporary music, visual and performing arts, and drama |
| **Folklore** | folk tales, legends, and oral history |

History         historical and humanitarian contributions, and social and
                political movements

Personalities   historical, contemporary, and local figures


## Elements of Deep Culture

Ceremony                 what a person is to say and do on particular
                         occasions

Courtship and Marriage   attitudes toward dating, marriage, and raising a
                         family

Esthetics                the beautiful things of culture: literature, music,
                         dance, art, architecture, and how they are enjoyed

Ethics                   how a person learns and practices honesty, fair
                         play, principles, moral thought, etc.

Family ties              how a person feels toward his or her family,
                         friends, classmates, roommates, and others

Health and Medicine      how a person reacts to sickness, death, soundness
                         of mind and body, medicine, etc.

Folk Myths               attitudes toward heroes, traditional stories,
                         legendary characters, superstitions, etc.

Gesture and Kinesics     forms of nonverbal communication or reinforced
                         speech, such as the use of the eyes, the hands,
                         and the body

Grooming and Presence    the cultural differences in personal behavior and
                         appearance such as laughter, smile, voice quality,
                         gait, poise, hair style, cosmetics, dress, etc.

Ownership                attitudes toward ownership of property,
                         individual rights, loyalties, beliefs, etc.

Precedence               what are accepted manners toward older persons,
                         peers, and younger persons

Rewards and Privileges   attitudes toward motivation, merit, achievement,
                         service, social position, etc.

| | |
|---|---|
| **Rights and Duties** | attitudes toward personal obligations, voting, taxes, military service, legal rights, personal demands, etc. |
| **Religion** | attitudes toward the divine and the supernatural and how they affect a person's thoughts and actions |
| **Sex Roles** | how a person views, understands, and relates to members of the opposite sex and what deviations are allowed and expected |
| **Space and Proxemics** | attitudes toward self and land; the accepted distances between individuals within a culture |
| **Subsistence** | attitudes about providing for oneself, the young, and the old and who protects whom |
| **Taboos** | attitudes and beliefs about doing things against culturally accepted patterns |
| **Concepts of Time** | attitudes toward being early, on time, or late |
| **Values** | attitudes toward freedom, education, cleanliness, cruelty, crime, etc |

Source: Gonzales, Frank. *Mexican American culture in the bilingual education classroom.* Unpublished doctoral dissertation, The University of Texas at Austin, 1978.

## Points to Remember

- ❏ Language and culture are inseparable.
- ❏ Language determines culture
- ❏ Cultural miscommunication occurs because people perceive concepts through their own cultural lens.
- ❏ Surface culture and deep culture are very different. Surface culture is the superficial outer layer of a culture and is noticed as the way people dress, talk, look, and the foods they eat.
- ❏ Deep culture is the underlying value and belief system of a society and may not be recognized until values are seriously challenged.

(Gonzalez, 1978)

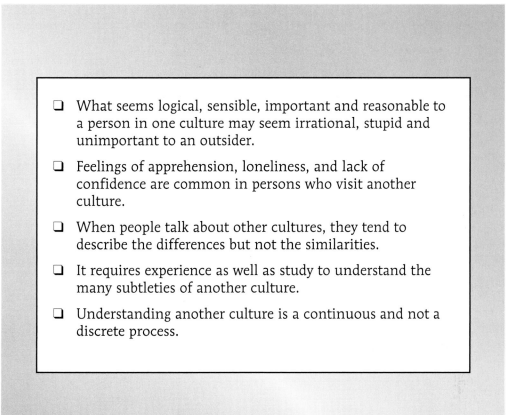

❏ What seems logical, sensible, important and reasonable to a person in one culture may seem irrational, stupid and unimportant to an outsider.

❏ Feelings of apprehension, loneliness, and lack of confidence are common in persons who visit another culture.

❏ When people talk about other cultures, they tend to describe the differences but not the similarities.

❏ It requires experience as well as study to understand the many subtleties of another culture.

❏ Understanding another culture is a continuous and not a discrete process.

# Chapter 4

## *Examining "American" Values*

### KEY ISSUES

❏ The term "American"

❏ Looking at "American" values

Four teachers from Massachusetts, Jane, Mary, Paula, and Cathy, decided to take a trip to explore the culture and history of Mexico and visit some local schools. Victor, the first teacher they met, asked the ladies where they were from. "We are American," they answered, to which Victor took great offense. He insisted he was American, too, which the teachers from Massachusetts did not understand. "Aren't you Mexican?" they asked. He insisted that Mexico was a part of the Americas and, therefore, he called himself American.

Tomoko, a new student from Japan, was very quiet in Mrs. Silva's fifth-grade classroom. Mrs. Silva never knew if Tomoko understood what was being taught because she never raised her hand to answer questions, and when asked if she understood, she always smiled and said, "Yes, teacher." After the first formative assessment, Mrs. Silva was surprised to discover that Tomoko failed miserably. "Why didn't you tell me you did not understand?" she asked. Tomoko just smiled, which, to the teacher was an inappropriate response.

Mrs. Silva happened to mention Tomoko's behavior to the ESOL specialist in the school. He explained that in Tomoko's culture, silence is a virtue. The student is not expected to question the teacher and if the student does not understand, she will try to figure it out at home or ask a classmate later. A smile does not always indicate happiness; it can mean embarrassment or nervousness. The individual in Tomoko's culture is not supposed to stand out—that is negative behavior.

Mrs. Silva reflected on how these cultural expectations were contrary to what she expected in the American classroom. The other children clamored to answer the questions to show they were the smartest and knew the answer. If they did not understand a concept, they often interrupted the flow of the class to ask for further explanation. After learning a little about Tomoko's culture, Mrs. Silva was able to adjust her "American" expectations to understand the norms under which Tomoko is operating. Mrs. Silva also vowed to gently teach Tomoko about expectations in her new American classroom.

In this book, the word "American" is used to refer to the people of the United States only for its facility. No offense is intended to citizens of Central America, South America, Mexico, or Canada, as it is realized that they, too, are from "The Americas."

Before looking at other cultures, there is a need to take a critical look at the American system. Once identifying characteristics of the United States, it will be easier to understand why Americans criticize others. The United States is a country with tremendous diversity as a result of the influx of immigrants from countries all over the world who bring their cultural traits and customs to their new country. Regional diversity is also very influential in lending to the flavor of the country. For example, the South is famous for its hospitality, charm, and southern cooking, while the North is famous for its history, educational institutions, and seafood. However, in spite of the individuality, American mainstream values are pervasive; they share the same government, educational and economic system, and receive the same mass media exposure. Over time, a sort of acculturation takes place and a degree of "Americanization" occurs. Eventually, the traditional culture is less prominent and segments of mainstream values are absorbed.

The irony of a value system is that often individuals are not aware of their values until they are challenged. Only when people compare and contrast themselves with people from another culture do they realize what their cultural values are.

Every group has individuals who do not conform, and are therefore, not "typical" representatives of their group. Although care must be taken not to stereotype cultural groups, each culture has a set of mainstream values by which the majority abides. Different societies are often recognized by their general overarching traits.

Many anthropologists have depicted a set of values pertaining to American culture, as observed by outsiders. Table 4-1 lists observable traits (according to Kohls, 2001, 1984) attributed to the majority of Americans and a "contrasting value" that can be observed in non-Western cultures.

## Table 4-1
## Observable American Traits and Contrasting Values

| American Values | Contrasting Cultural Value |
|---|---|
| 1. Personal control over the environment. Man can determine the direction of his life. | Fate: Life's plan is our destiny that cannot be altered by willpower. |
| 2. Change and progressiveness are good. The past is something to learn from and improve upon. | Tradition, rituals, customs, and the old tried and true ways are honored. |
| 3. The importance of control over time. Time should not be wasted, but should be saved. Schedules are important. For example, invitations say 2:00 until 4:00, and the party will end at 4:00. | Time is unimportant. There is no rush. The "mañana" syndrome is present (i.e., "tomorrow" the work will be finished, but there is no specification *which* tomorrow.) |
| 4. Egalitarianism: the ideal of equality. "All men are created equal" and all races and creeds must enjoy equal rights under the law. | Hierarchy, status, class differences, and rank determine importance in life. Someone is always superior or inferior to another. |
| 5. Individualism and promotion of one's own benefit and needs. Individuality is more important. Privacy is honored. | Group orientation; the individual acts for the good of the family, to uphold the family, group, or the nation, and any acts that bring dishonor to the "group" disgrace everyone. One must "save face" at all cost. |
| 6. Future orientation: live for what is to come and live for today. (America is basically a very young, progressive country that looks toward future growth.) | Past orientation: follow the path of your ancestors and traditional ways. |

**Table 4-1** *(continued)*
**Observable American Traits and Contrasting Values**

| American Values | Contrasting Cultural Value |
| --- | --- |
| 7. Self-help: honoring the "self-made" man. One can create his own luck and fortune with hard work and can rise from poverty to riches. | Birthright inheritance: people are born into their place in life. Individuals may not have a penny, but if they are born royalty, position and status are afforded. |
| 8. Informality. Newcomers can become confused by the apparent lack of formality and "casual" attitude when dealing with Americans. Ritual and formality do exist, but are not easy to discern. | Formality: addressing people by titles, last names, and observing formal rituals. Formal address is even included in language forms and functions (e.g. *tu* is informal, and *usted* is the formal way to say *you* in Spanish). |
| 9. Directness, frankness, and candid honesty are valued. It is better not to "beat around the bush"; one should "get right to the point." This trait is reflected in writing as well. | Indirectness and "saving face" so as not to hurt or embarrass anyone is of prime importance. |
| 10. Action and work orientation. As an example look at the saying, "Idle time is the devil's workshop." It reflects the moral value placed on work. The employee must find something to do, even if the job is finished. Some kind of action must be taken or the employee is seen as lazy. | "Being" orientation: One is not defined by a career or by what one does. |
| 11. Materialism: The tangible items are more important than intangible ideals. | Spiritualism and intellectual pursuits are valued. |

American values stem from historical, political, and religious beliefs throughout a long period of time. It can be a challenge to ascertain whether the values an individual displays result from the country, the ethnic group, the family, or from the individual himself. Whatever the case, it is easy to see why cross-cultural clashes can occur. However, with prior knowledge of cultural characteristics, teachers can better understand the behavior of students and their parents.

## Points to Remember

❑ Some people are offended because people from the United States use the word "American" to describe themselves. "American" can refer to Latin Americans, Central Americans, South Americans, Mexicans, and North Americans. The term is used because no easier or more appropriate word exists to describe people from the United States.

❑ Once people understand their own cultural values, they can understand why other cultures may be so "different"; not wrong, just different. Every culture functions well within its own system.

❑ Cultures have mainstream values but need to avoid stereotypes. Individuals are different within their own culture.

❑ American values, and values of every culture, stem from historical, political, and religious beliefs over a long period of time.

# Chapter 5

## *Culture Shock: Reaction to an Unfamiliar Environment*

## KEY ISSUES

❏ Culture Shock

❏ Symptoms

❏ Acculturation and recovering from culture shock

Anne, an American student studying to be a teacher, realized the benefit of learning another language. She thought it would make her more marketable, and she would be able to understand children better by knowing what they were going through trying to learn in another language. She had studied Spanish I and II and felt she had a strong language foundation. She memorized vocabulary and grammar, and felt ready to take the challenge of studying at a Mexican university. Upon arriving at the university, she was shocked to find that everyone spoke Spanish to her and she didn't understand anything. She could not even use the telephone because the dialing system and money were different, and she was unable able to understand the language without face to face contact.

In trying to register for classes, Anne was shocked to find that no one spoke English. She thought, "Don't they realize I am here to <u>learn</u> Spanish; I don't know it yet?" She was also surprised in class to learn that her instructors were going to teach her Spanish through Spanish. How could that be? She hadn't considered that because in the United States, her Spanish teachers taught her Spanish through English!

Anne suffered terribly. She had a horrible headache every evening from trying to think in Spanish all day long. Uncharacteristically, she cried at the least provocation, got angry when she got lost on the subway, and was horrified when men she didn't even know would pay for her bus fare. She quickly realized that there was no way she was going to transfer credits from the Mexican university to her home college as she had planned. She knew it would be impossible to get all A's and this would ruin her perfect grade point average. She longed for someone to speak English to but became irrationally angry when men would try to practice their English by talking to her. What was wrong with her?

After several months, Anne finally became more adjusted to her situation. When she reentered the United States 8 months later, she attended a seminar on "Culture Shock." After discerning that culture shock was the reason for her discomfort, she understood what had happened to her and wished that she had known about this phenomenon before leaving the United States. She also knew this experience would make her a better teacher because she would have great compassion for any student new to the American culture.

In discussing culture shock, reference is again made to older research because it is the groundwork upon which more recent literature is based. Because an individual's cultural patterns are so deeply ingrained, both consciously and unconsciously, an instinctive reaction toward the unfamiliar is likely to occur when he or she encounters a new culture. This adjustment process is not limited only to a move overseas, but can happen during any geographic relocation, even in a person's own country. Moving from the familiar to the new, moving from the North to the South, from urban to rural, or from the East Coast to the West Coast can cause culture shock. The superficial environment might be the same, but any cross-cultural contact can be sufficient cause to provoke emotional discomfort.

The term "culture shock" refers to "a removal or distortion of many of the familiar cues a person encounters at home and the substitution of them for other cues which are strange" (Hall, 1959, p.156). The individual reacts to cultural stimuli that possess no recognizable significance. Culture shock is described as an occupational disease, or silent sickness, which is precipitated by the anxiety that results from losing all our familiar signs or signals of social intercourse. These signs or cues include the thousands of ways in which we orient ourselves to the situation of daily life (Furnham & Bochner, 1982; Gordon, 2001; Juffer, 1984; Nolan, 1990; Oberg, 1959). Physical manifestations of culture shock are easy to see, especially in children. Thus, it is easy to understand why they may pass through a silent stage, refusing to speak or respond positively in new cultural situations. It is assumed that few people escape without experiencing culture shock altogether and that people do not realize that they are handicapped by culture shock until the phenomenon has passed because the symptoms are difficult to isolate. Adults, who can control and make rational sense of their environment, can suffer drastically from culture shock. Imagine the plight of a child who did not choose to leave the home country, and now is in a strange classroom, listening to the babble of a foreign language. The prospect can be terrifying.

Familiar signs, symbols, and cultural rules that people learned as children are the internal blueprints used to decipher everyday cues that guide them to respond appropriately. Words, gestures, facial expressions, customs, and norms are the unconscious props that dictate their behavior. An unconscious level of comfort is maintained because there is no threat to their beliefs. However, when an individual is suddenly transplanted, no matter how exciting the situation may be, he or she can feel discomfort because, "No matter how broadminded or full of goodwill you may be, a series of props have been knocked from under you, followed by a feeling of frustration and anxiety" (Oberg, 1960, p.177). People react to the frustration of a new culture in much the same way; only the degree to which culture shock affects individuals differs greatly.

Some classic reactions of culture shock in Oberg's model are:

- A feeling of helplessness;
- A desire for dependence on long-term residents of one's own nationality;
- Fits of anger and irritability over delays and minor frustrations;
- Depression;
- Loss of appetite;
- Poor sleep;
- Impatience or curtness with the nationals;
- Delay and/or refusal to learn the host language;
- Great concern over minor pains; and
- A terrible longing to be back home.

Disgust with the host country, its food, its citizens, its customs; and a constant comparing of how bad the new place is compared to the home country may be evident. These negative feelings impede and delay adjustment to the new environment. Students new to the classroom may manifest any number of negative reactions, and the problems are compounded by lack of expertise in English.

Another way to look at this uncomfortable phenomenon is to call it "language shock" (Smalley, 1963) and recognize the accompanying emotional distress (Bennet, 1993; Paige, 1993b). In this framework, language is the primary determinant of culture shock and the study of language itself may cause culture shock for some people. Until the cues of the new culture are learned, individuals remain culturally and linguistically disoriented (p. 49) as adults are reduced to the level of being a child again, stripped of their primary means of personal interaction—language. Language learners feel insecure about how to participate in language discourse, such as knowing when it is appropriate to interrupt in a conversation, or when to ask questions (Mauraner, 1994). Further, new language learners are subjected to making constant mistakes and being corrected. They find themselves responding to intelligent and educated people as if they were children because of their incapability of responding as educated, intelligent adults. The newcomer's education and intelligence are not recognized by the host country, which can be a blow to self-esteem and adult status.

Children who are developing their primary language as well as acquiring the new language are not subjected to the loss of status, but they suffer with the inability to express themselves in interpersonal relations. Additionally, where the adult might have the cognitive concepts and abilities that can transfer to the second language, the child may lack the prior knowledge to transfer to English, which can result in a tremendous cognitive burden. Not only does the child have to learn English to survive, but he then must learn academic concepts through the foreign language. It is much easier to acquire the decoding skills necessary in reading the native language first and then transfer that knowledge, than it is to learn to read in a foreign language with no previous reading skills (Chamot & O'Malley, 1996a; Cummins, 1984).

Children may also manifest their cultural discomfort and anxiety with physical symptoms such as upset stomachs, headaches, and malaise as the body responds to cultural disorientation. Trying to function all day long through another language is physically and mentally exhausting, and as a result, students may be unable to resist an overwhelming desire to sleep. An exhausted head on the desk may irritate the teacher, but would be better met with understanding and compassion.

Researchers have given different names to the stages of culture shock, but all agree on these basic four:

1. **Honeymoon stage.** This stage includes a euphoric feeling of fascination with novelty. Experiencing the country for the first time, feelings of enthusiasm, admiration, and enchantment are prominent while the individual experiences friendly, and cordial, yet superficial relationships with host nationals. The similarities of the new culture with those from home are salient because the individual has not had to deal with the realities of functioning in daily life. The newcomer may overly depend on another newcomer with good English skills and knows how to maneuver within the country. This stage can last for a few days or weeks to six months, depending on the circumstances.

2. **Hostile or aggressive stage** as a reaction to crisis. Immersion cause initial differences to become salient; daily activities become insurmountable problems. The individual struggles with a different language, concepts, and values he is unaware of or does not understand. Familiar cues, symbols, and signs no longer evoke the same responses, which may lead to feelings of inadequacy, frustration, anxiety, and anger. In an attempt to rationalize the adjustment problem, the individual is very critical of the new culture, its people and ways, and may describe the people of the new country, as well as the country itself, in derogatory terms. At this point, the newcomer may seek solace in associating with others who reject the environment that is causing such discomfort: "the ways of the host country are bad because they make us feel bad"(Oberg, 1969, p.77) and the home country becomes "irrationally glorified." If an individual can make it through this dismal period, he can overcome culture shock. If this stage of crisis is not tolerable, the individual will often return to his home country before adaptation is possible.

3. **Recovery.** At this stage, the individual reconciles with the language and begins to understand the cues of the culture. Humor returns, and helping newly arrived people who are struggling may offer feelings of confidence, as the "old-timer" can speak and get around.

4. **Adjustment.** Finally, the host culture is accepted in a meaningful way as the customs of the country are seen as just another way of living. Living and working in the new culture with a minimum of anxiety and moments of strain make life acceptable. Understanding of the new language is clearer, and the individual accepts and enjoys the food, drinks, customs, and habits of the new country.

## Acculturation and Recovering from Culture Shock

The teacher plays a pivotal role in facilitating a child's adjustment to the new culture. Learning the new culture and understanding how it operates is one antidote to culture shock. A good way to get over culture shock is to try to get to know the people of the country, the customs, and the culture. Learn what culture shock is and realize that it will pass. Of course, this is difficult if one does not have facility with the language of the host country.

The key to success in the new culture entails the acquisition of behaviors, skills, and norms appropriate to function within the cultural paradigm. It is like trying to play a game where one player does not know the rules. Can you imagine the chaos and ambiguity he or she would feel while trying to interpret everyone else's actions? Eventually the player would become frustrated and probably ask himself/herself what the point in playing was, as it certainly was not fun.

How can the teacher help students overcome culture shock while respecting their native culture? Teachers wield a powerful influence on the attitudes of their students. They can deflect focus from the mainstream or more extroverted children in the class who often tend to monopolize classroom time by focusing attention on the English language learner. To highlight the favorable aspects of each child's culture, the teacher must express positive value in whatever appears "foreign" to the native English speakers. Demonstrating a positive attitude toward music, food, clothing, and other manifestations of the new culture is within the power of the classroom teacher. This attitude helps the children learn how to respond with an open mind. With a little imagination, teachers can plan instruction so that all students can integrate their cultural histories into reading, writing, art, social studies, or any other subject across the curriculum.

Music from a variety of heritages can be highlighted and appreciated. Food and traditional dress can be incorporated as superficial exhibitions of culture, but it is also more meaningful to make the students aware of the feelings, values, and belief systems of their classmates. Developing lessons that spark questions, discussions, and critical thinking will allow the mainstream students to experience a new cultural dimension, while highlighting the affective aspects of the multicultural children.

Alma Flor Ada (1993) recommends home-school interaction to validate the child's culture. Teachers who make visits to the homes of children gain valuable insight and information. Most parents from other countries have a deep respect for the teacher. By knowing the parents and the child's home situation, the teacher can further assist in the child's learning. Additionally, the teacher can aid the parents by explaining the important roles they play in the education of their children in the American school system. Paraprofessional teacher assistants, parent volunteers, and other bilingual personnel provided by the school systems can lend support by interpreting for the teacher in these meetings. However, the child should not act as interpreter as it may disrupt familial hierarchy by usurping parental authority.

Classrooms that embrace and value multiculturalism by using dialogue journals, providing the children with buddies, engineering study groups, sharing cultures, and fostering feelings of being "at home" in the classroom will smooth the transition for the newcomers.

## Points to Remember

❏ Culture shock is a distortion of many of the familiar cues encountered at home and is substituted for other cues that are inexplicable.

❏ Learning another culture is like trying to play a game with the wrong set of rules. Children experiencing culture shock may manifest cultural discomfort with physical symptoms such as headaches, upset stomachs, and an overwhelming desire to sleep.

❏ Learning a foreign language is physically exhausting.

❏ Four basic stages of culture shock are:

A. Honeymoon stage: Euphoria with the idea of being in a new culture.

B. Hostile or aggressive stage: The honeymoon is over and daily activities become insurmountable problems.

C. Recovery: The individual reconciles with the language and begins to understand the cues of the new culture.

D. Adjustment: Life is now acceptable and the anxiety and strain of life in the new culture diminishes.

Teachers can help students overcome culture shock by understanding the symptoms, embracing multiculturalism, incorporating the home culture into daily lessons, reaching out to the families, and making positive parental contact.

# Chapter 6

## *Differences in Verbal Communication*

### KEY ISSUES

❏ Participation structures

❏ High involvement/high considerateness
conversational patterns

❏ Directness/indirectness in speech

❏ Saving face

❏ High context/low context culture

*"To know another's language and not his culture is a very good way to make a fluent fool of one's self."*
**—Winston Brembeck**

Ms. Saidi's class consists of seven Koreans, two Japanese, one Italian, one Greek, one Arab, two Venezuelans, and two Spaniards. The Asians indicated in their preclass conferences with the teacher that they wished to improve their speaking skills. Ms. Saidi's instructional plans included much time for opportunities to practice meaningful conversations. She decided to start the class with a half-hour cooperative learning project wherein the students would be in mixed groups of four for maximum cross-cultural exposure. As the activity got underway, Ms. Saidi circled the classroom and listened in on the discussions. Although each student had a task to complete, the Asians were not conversing with the rest of the individuals in the groups. Ms Saidi wondered what was wrong.

Cultural differences can interfere with student participation within classroom activities. **Participation structures** (Hancock, 1997; Jarvis & Robinson, 1997; Philips, 1983) describe the interactions of students in the classroom, and each culture has its own rules about when and how to speak, and even what to speak about. Some students are only comfortable with whole-class activities, and others function better in small-group or individual formats of instruction rules. Many cultures are based upon cooperation for the good of the whole, and group instruction reflects this background. In other words, culture influences communication, which can (and often does) create misunderstandings. It is up to the teacher to notice which formats are best for individual students.

Individuals from some cultures appreciate heated discussions about politics and other potentially volatile topics, while other cultures participate in a more reserved style of conversing. Generally speaking, Americans shy away from controversial topics and may even "agree to disagree". Italian or a Germans (for example) who like a lively discussion might actually be angry that an American will not argue.

According to Deborah Tannen (1990), a sociolinguistic researcher who wrote a book called *You Just Don't Understand,* people from some cultures value "high-involvement" conversational patterns, while others might follow a "high-considerateness" pattern. She explains that typically, people from conversationally "high-involvement" cultures tend to talk and interrupt more, expect and are not bothered by people who interrupt them and speak louder and quicker than those individuals from conversationally "high-considerateness" cultures. She names cultures such as Russian, Italian, Greek, Spanish, South American, Arab, and African (p. 207) as belonging to the "high involvement" category. People from cultures that follow a "high considerateness" conversational pattern speak one at a time, do not interrupt while others are speaking, listen politely to the speaker, nod, show interest, and make positive sounds that indicate they are paying attention. The conversational partners are more hesitant, and individuals are likely to avoid confrontational or heated discussions. Tannen characterizes the Asian cultures (such as Chinese, Korean, and Japanese) as belonging to the "high-considerateness" profile of conversational style. American conversational patterns are also "high considerateness"; however, there is so much regional, ethnic, and environmental diversity that it is easy to see the differences along the cultural continuum.

The conversational clash can occur when Americans are speaking with people from other cultures and may not know how to interrupt or interject a comment. Additionally, American culture values small talk, while most Asians (and other cultures) value silence, which might lead them to believe that Americans talk too much. While the American is not comfortable with long periods of silence in the conversation, the Asian will take more time to answer. This can carry over into the classroom, when more wait time is necessary as the English learner may be slower to answer for a multitude of reasons (processing the questions, thinking of how to translate, cultural conversational style, etc.). It is imperative that the teacher allow more wait time, and appear to be comfortable doing so. Teachers can set the tone of the class and if they demonstrate patience, the students will learn patience as well.

Another consideration in verbal conversation is the directness or indirectness in speech. In "mainstream" American culture, directness is typically valued more than indirectness, yet there is a continuum within these qualities as well. The Californian may consider the New Yorker as too direct (or rude), while the New Yorker may consider the Southerner as too slow. The English language reflects a positive attitude toward directness by its expressions: "Get to the point." " Don't beat around the bush." "The bottom line is...," Yet people from other cultures may consider Americans rude because in their own cultures, they do not directly disagree. In Japanese, for example, there are many ways to say "no" or disagree without actually saying no. To disagree or point out a mistake would be very rude. Being direct is such an important value in the American culture that courses are offered to teach people (especially women) how to be assertive, direct, and to say "no."

If students from non-American cultures are in the classroom with a teacher who does not realize the implication of indirect communication, great misunderstandings can occur. Not embarrassing or shaming another person ("saving face") is an objective of indirect cultural conversation patterns cherished by many cultures (Asian, Latin American, Native American), without regard to "high-involvement" or "high-considerateness" styles.

By being aware of ingrained cultural conversational patterns, the teacher can better control classroom discussion and verbal interactions as some students may monopolize conversations and discussions. The teacher can orchestrate the activities so that all students can have their turn sharing thoughts and opinions and answering questions. This is especially important when non-native English speakers are in the classroom with native English speakers. While it might take more time for the language minority students to gather thoughts and decide what and how to say what is on their minds, the native English speaker does not have this linguistic hurdle and has blurted out the answer.

The teacher can develop techniques to ensure that everyone has a chance to answer. Two simple ways to guarantee that everyone has participated are methods such as the following: 1) Write the names of all the students on slips of paper and put the slips into a bowl. One by one, randomly select a name and direct a question to the individual whose name was drawn. If the student cannot answer the question, put the slip of paper in a different bowl to be drawn later. Names of students chosen to answer go back into another bowl to be started over again. 2) Place an object (such as an eraser or stuffed animal) on the table where students are clustered. Before speaking, the student must pick up the object. No one can speak without picking up the object. This system also buys more time for the language minority speaker to prepare to speak.

## High- and Low-Context Cultures

Anthropologist Edward Hall introduced the idea of **high-** and **low-context** cultures. He explains the difference by saying "words and sentences have different meanings depending on the context in which they are embedded" (1983, p. 59 & 1976, p. 91). High-context (HC) communication or message is one in which most of the information is either in the physical context or internalized in the person; very little is in the coded, explicit, transmitted part of the message. Information about procedure is rarely communicated; members are supposed to know how to perform in various situations, but the rules of cultural performance are implicit.

A low-context (LC) communication is just the opposite; the mass of the information is vested in the explicit code. Information is abundant, procedures are explained clearly, results and expectation are discussed frequently, and instructions are followed as given. American culture, according to Hall, is in the middle of the scale that measures context, while Japanese are very high context, and Germans and Swiss are very low context. Simply put, in high-context cultures, people do not have to speak very much and they know what others mean, think, and expect. The culture is static and because customs are long-lived, the culture is unified. In low-context cultures, individuals need to be very specific, explain what is expected, and almost go overboard in training because the culture is fast changing. The low-context culture is unstable and is progressively changing over time, while the high-context culture might maintain its hold on its high-context position too long. These types of communication reflect thinking patterns as well, based on high- or low-context cultural modes.

Some researchers believe that cultural traits reflect the hemisphere in the brain that corresponds to the definition of high-context and low-context cultures. Based on this theory, Dr. Carmen Judith Nine-Curt developed a chart of hemispheric traits that is interesting to compare:

| Low-Context Left Hemisphere Societies (Anglo) | High-Context Right Hemisphere Societies (Puerto Rican, Hispanic Caribbean) |
|---|---|
| 1. Speech, verbal | 1. Nonverbal, spatial, musical |
| 2. Logical, mathematical | 2. Artistic, symbolic |
| 3. Linear, sequential ordering, monochronic | 3. Simultaneous, polychronic |
| 4. Emotionally controlled, detached, uninvolved | 4. Emotionally involved, empathetic |
| 5. Task, work oriented | 5. Family oriented |
| 6. Worldly, active, dominant | 6. Spiritual, quiet, receptive |
| 7. Analytic, precise | 7. Synthetic, intuitive, imprecise |
| 8. Detailed, specific | 8. Holistic, gestalt |
| 9. Reading, writing, naming | 9. Creative, facial recognition |
| 10. Perception of significant order | 10. Perception of abstract figures |
| 11. Recognition of complex motor sequence | 11. Recognition of complex figures |

Taking a cue from these findings, teachers can begin to understand why some classroom behaviors may be reflections of cultural values. Students from a variety of cultures will behave according to how they are taught within their culture, and the home values can conflict with school values. However, if teachers are aware of the systems under which other cultures operate, they can adjust instruction to address the needs of their students more appropriately.

## Points to Remember

❑ Based on cultural norms, "participation structures" describe the interactions of students in the classroom, when and how to speak, and what to speak about.

❑ People from cultures with "high involvement conversational patterns talk and interrupt more, expect and are not bothered by people who interrupt them while speaking, and speak louder and quicker than those individuals from conversationally "high considerateness" cultures. Cultures such as Russian, Italian, Greek, Spanish, South American, Arab, and African are examples of the high involvement category.

❑ "High considerateness" conversational patterns are found in the Chinese, Korean, Japanese, and even American cultures. Individuals from these cultures do not interrupt while others are speaking, listen politely to the speaker, nod, show interest, and make positive sounds that indicate they are paying attention to the speaker.

❑ Directness in speech is valued in the American cultures. "Don't beat around the bush," "Get to the point," and "The bottom line is...," are indicators of the values placed on direct speech.

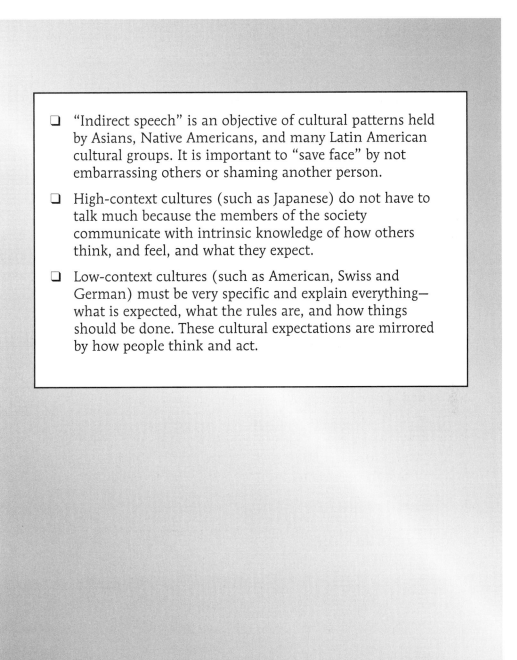

❑ "Indirect speech" is an objective of cultural patterns held by Asians, Native Americans, and many Latin American cultural groups. It is important to "save face" by not embarrassing others or shaming another person.

❑ High-context cultures (such as Japanese) do not have to talk much because the members of the society communicate with intrinsic knowledge of how others think, and feel, and what they expect.

❑ Low-context cultures (such as American, Swiss and German) must be very specific and explain everything—what is expected, what the rules are, and how things should be done. These cultural expectations are mirrored by how people think and act.

# Chapter 7

## *Nonverbal Communication*

## KEY ISSUES

- ❏ Proxemics
- ❏ Kinesics
- ❏ Paralinguistics
- ❏ Haptics
- ❏ Oculesics
- ❏ Monochronic time
- ❏ Polychronic time

Mariela was a first grader who recently arrived from Cuba. Her family settled in northern Florida, where there was a very small Hispanic community. Her father believed that his children would have a greater opportunity to learn English if they were immersed in a majority English-speaking community. When Mariela started school, her teacher spoke in a soft manner to Mariela, so that even though she did not understand what the teacher was saying, the teacher's voice sounded nice. But several times Mariela approached her teacher and the teacher kept backing away from her. Mariela left school that day broken-hearted and went home crying to her mother. "Mami, la maestra no me quiere!" (Mommy, the teacher doesn't love me.)

Atsama was a Chinese girl from Thailand whose family was transferred to Vermont. When Atsama started school, she noticed that she was smaller than her classmates and everyone kept saying what a "doll" she was. The teacher thought Atsama was so cute that she couldn't resist patting the little girl on her head. Atsama immediate recoiled from the teacher's touch. Later, when it was story time, all the children sat on rugs on the floor, while the teacher sat in a chair with her legs crossed, ready to read to the children. Atsama would not sit with the children and insisted on standing. The teacher could not help thinking the child had problems interacting with people, while the child was shocked and insulted at the teacher's behavior.

Mr. Omiya, a 52 year-old gentleman from Japan, came to Boston to study English for the summer. The teacher, Ms. Whelan, a fun-loving young woman who had lived in many countries, was well aware of the cultural values of her students. In addition to presenting practice in reading, writing, listening, and speaking English, Ms. Whelan inundated the class with cross cultural experiences and opportunities that would broaden their knowledge base of foreign cultures (especially that of the United States). The dialogue journals the students wrote revealed precious reflective sharing, and Ms. Whelan thought Mr. Omiya was stepping out of his cultural patterns when he allowed her to hug him at the end of the summer, during the graduation ceremonies. However, Ms. Whelan began to realize just how deeply ingrained his cultural patterns were when she read Mr. Omiya's last journal entry:

Dear Professor,
I wish to give thanks to you for all you have shown and taught us this summer. You are wonderful teacher I will never forget. I go now to meet my son at airport. I have not seen him for four years and I wish to embrace him. However I cannot. I must only bow because I am Japanese man.
Yours truly,
Mr. Tsuneyoshi Omiya

If nonverbal communication is akin to speaking without words, what were the nonverbal cultural misinterpretations in the preceding scenarios? In the first scene, Mariela is hurt because she tries to get close to her teacher, and it appears to her that her teacher shuns her. In reality, individuals unconsciously maintain a certain personal distance between themselves and others. This is referred to as **proxemics** (discussed further in this chapter) a term coined by Hall to describe the use of space as it relates to different cultures. People in Arab and Hispanic cultures are more comfortable standing closer to one another than are Americans, who typically stand farther apart from each other (from 18 inches to 4 feet, according to Edward Hall in *Hidden Dimensions,* 1966). To "invade" the personal space of an American signifies a certain intimacy or aggression.

Little Mariela, being from a "warm" culture in which individuals touch one another frequently and stand closer together, wanted to be physically closer to her teacher, but she was making her American teacher uncomfortable. Teachers in the United States are often advised not to touch their students, and this teacher in particular was not a physically demonstrative person. Mariela did not understand the teacher's reluctance to embrace her, and was hurt by her coldness and supposed rejection.

Atsama is from a spiritual Buddhist family whose members believe that the head, which houses the soul, must not be touched. Additionally, when the children were sitting on the floor, the bottom of the teacher's shoe was facing them, which is an insult to Thais (and to people from Saudia Arabia, and others). They consider the foot the dirtiest part of the body. Atsama was insulted by the teacher's body language, and the teacher was confused by Atsama's strange reaction.

Finally, Mr. Omiya, who is aware of his cultural constraints, longs to embrace his son, whom he has not seen for 4 years, but cannot because his life-long cultural patterning is stronger than the values he learned in the summer he spent learning English and American culture.

**Kinesics** (the study of body language) includes facial expressions, posture, gestures, body movements, eye contact, or any ritual, that conveys messages or meaning for a culture. The Japanese bow is an example of kinesics. From the American standpoint, a bow is just a hello or good bye gesture. However, to the Japanese (and some other Asian cultures), a bow can be quite complex because a deeper meaning can be conveyed by the bow. The lower-status individual must begin the bow, and must bow lower than the higher-status person. When the individuals bowing are equals in society, the bow is simultaneous and of the same depth.

Body posture can convey different meanings. The American informality and friendliness stance can appear rude to more formal cultures. However, teachers should take care when judging body language; the message the teacher believes is being conveyed may not be the same truth as seen from the student's cultural context.

From the previous scenarios, we learn that it can be dangerous to attempt to read someone's behavior based on our own frames of reference. Although emotions such as happiness, sadness, anger, hatred, embarrassment, shame, and love are universal, the ways they are expressed are as individual as the culture itself. Take a smile, for example. In the American culture, a smile usually appears friendly, but it can signify affection or disguise feelings. Americans smile at strangers, and they are just being polite. People from Russia think that is unusual, inappropriate, or even suspicious. If an American smiled at a Russian who did not return the smile, the American would probably think the Russian rude. In some Asian cultures, a smile can be used for completely inappropriate reasons, according to the American perception. A smile can cover pain, embarrassment, and sadness for Asians.

Sadness, grief, and pain are expressed openly in some cultures and are borne silently in others. Some individuals mourn openly (e.g., Arabs, Iranians, and Irish) while others are more stoic (Chinese, Japanese, and some individuals within any culture) and do not display their grief for the world to see.

***Paralinguistics*** is the set of vocal, non-verbal utterances that carry and augment meaning. How people speak, and use pitch, intonation, grunts, and so on help to clarify what they are trying to say. Intonation can infer sarcasm, humor, disbelief, emotion, and any other type of meaning.

***Haptics*** is the art of how people use touch to communicate. Touching indicates different meanings in different societies. In the American, German, English, and other white Anglo-Saxon cultures, individuals are usually not touch-oriented. Arab, Jewish, Eastern European, and Mediterranean cultures have been characterized as cultures wherein individuals frequently touch each other.

Displays of friendship or feelings of love are expressed quite diversely as well. In the Philippines, girls walk hand-in-hand, and boys can embrace unselfconsciously, but boys and girls will not been seen holding hands (unless they live close to the American military bases, ironically). Young Korean men are quite comfortable sitting with their arms innocently around one another (while only the American teacher will watch with discomfort).

In the United States, heterosexual males usually do not touch one another. Men will shake hands and maybe slap each other on the back, but even some male family members will not touch each other. Females are allowed to openly display affection and may kiss cheeks or hug upon greeting or when saying good bye. Males and females will show affection publicly (depending on the individuals). In certain cultures, such as in France, it is perfectly acceptable for men to kiss each other on the cheeks; in other cultures, it is acceptable for men to kiss on the lips.

Because facial expressiveness can mean different things to different cultures, people should not try to interpret the faces of others as they would interpret the faces of people from their own cultures. Emotions are shown in different ways by every cultural group, and even by individual families within those cultural groups. There is no single standard of measurement for everyone.

## More about Proxemics

In his book *The Hidden Dimension* (1966), Edward T. Hall states that people from all cultures have patterns of interaction between themselves and others. All individuals have a zone of personal space surrounding their bodies. American and Northern Europeans stand farther apart from each other and touch each other less than do people from cultures such as Greek, Latin American, Arab, Turk, and individuals from African countries. Americans touch one another more than do Japanese adults; however, Japanese have more tactile contact with babies and children than do Americans. The continuum is relative when comparing all cultures.

## Gestures

Gestures are not universal. What is common and polite in one culture can be considered rude in another. Snapping fingers at a waiter can be considered appropriate in one culture, and not acceptable in another. The "OK" symbol in the United States holds different meanings in other countries. It stands for money in Japan and in Brazil means something vulgar.

In the United States, people beckon others to come by putting the palm up and wiggling the fingers toward themselves, or they hold the palm up and wiggle the crooked pointer finger toward themselves. This is how animals are called in the Philippines, and the gesture is rude in Korea and in some parts of Latin America as well. People are called by cupping the fingers, palms facing toward the other person, and waving the hands downward.

In many Spanish-speaking countries, tapping the flexed elbow with the palm of the opposite hand means someone is cheap; wiggling the pointing finger (straight up) side-to-side in front of one's body means no; and animals are measured with the arm out to the side horizontally with the hand extended, palm parallel to the floor (the way people's height is measured in the United States).

Gestures considered vulgar or obscene in non-American cultures are: the American hitchhiking (thumb out) signal in New Zealand and Australia; and using two fingers to make "horns" on someone's head (which accuses someone's wife of cuckolding her husband) in Spanish-speaking countries.

# Eye Contact

**Oculesics** is the study of eye movement and position. Eye contact is frequently misunderstood. Americans acknowledge each other's presence by making brief eye contact, although it is considered rude to stare. In more intimate settings (such as a classroom or at a friend's party), eye contact can be made and held longer, especially if the individual wants to get to know someone. In a store or an airport terminal where people are just passing through, people would be less likely to make eye contact. Too much eye contact makes Americans feel uncomfortable, and too little eye contact indicates untrustworthiness or a lack of attention or interest. Navaho Indians attribute eye contact as a severe indication of disapproval and, therefore, individuals do not look directly at each other.

Studies show that American babies are attracted to their mother's eyes, and the mother's gaze is often focused lovingly on her baby. Experiments demonstrate that babies respond by smiling when shown a pair of eyes (Hall, 1976). In Japan, however, babies are often carried on their mother's back, thereby providing less eye-to-eye interaction. As a result, Japanese adults are not prone to place emphasis on eye contact to gather conversational meaning from one another. One's gaze during a conversation in Japan might be on the neck of one's conversation partner. Compare this to the American who shows interest in his conversation partner by the proper gaze, but feels distrust for the individual who does not look him in the eye. The classic misunderstanding of encoding or decoding cultural meaning incorrectly occurs when the Haitian or Puerto Rican child, who is taught that it is disrespectful to look at an adult's eyes, does not look at the American teacher's eyes and is accused of being rude.

For North Americans, winking the eyes can indicate teasing or flirting. Nigerians wink at their children when they want the children to leave the room, and a friendly wink in India may be perceived as an insult (Hall, 1986). A Colombian might wink one eye if he does not understand something or wants something explained, and a Filipino might raise the eyebrows to indicate "yes."

Condon (1976) offers an illustration of the cultural significance of widening the eyes.

| Significance | Intention | Culture |
| --- | --- | --- |
| Really! | Surprise, wonder | Anglo |
| I resent this. | Anger | Chinese |
| I don't believe you. | Challenge | French |
| I don't understand | Call for help | Hispanic |
| I'm innocent. | Persuasion | Black American |

Hall (1959) says the use and thought of time, **chronemics**, is a powerful element of culture. Polychronic time and monochronic time are expressions that describe cultural views of time, its importance, and how it is used. It appears that a continuum of time exists with monochronic time (doing one thing at a time) on one end of the spectrum and polychronic time (doing many things at once) on the other. Cultures are oriented in either direction. Individuals probably possess both inclinations depending on the situation, so it can be said the individuals have the overwhelming predisposition toward one tendency or another.

**Monochronics** (e.g. , American, British, Canadian, and German individuals) think in terms of linear sequential, time-ordered patterns with a beginning, middle, and ending. For example, a party invitation will specify the beginning and ending of the event (e.g., from 2:00 to 4:00). The guests know the party will be over at 4:00 and are usually conscious not to linger. They arrive on time or a few minutes early. If they are late, they apologize. The individuals in the culture know when they are late and feel self-conscious because the pattern of being on time is ingrained. The need to have closure in all aspects of life is evident in work, school, relationships, and daily activities.

**Polychronic** individuals (largely Latin American, African, Middle Eastern, and Southern European cultures) tend to think about and involve themselves in a number of activities simultaneously. They may feel overloaded, which may result in procrastination because they are trying to do too much. Polychronics follow a time orientation not dictated by the clock or schedules. Everyone knows that an invitation to dinner at 7:00 does not really mean 7:00. Depending on the culture, it could mean 8:00, 9:00, or even 10:00. Problems arise only when the monochronic is in the polychronic culture (or vice versa). and does not know the rules. That is when people start labeling others as "lazy," and "never on time," or "neurotic about arriving early."

The use of time tells a subliminal story. If the telephone rings in the middle of the night in the United States, it can signal an emergency. Being late for an appointment indicates lack of interest. In Latin America, a long wait for an appointment may not be unusual, but to a North American, being kept waiting is an insult. In other cultures such as those in some villages in Africa, or in the culture of the Sioux Indians, time starts when everyone is ready, and there may not even be a word that indicates late or waiting (Porter, 1972). Time can be informal (after a while, later, some time ago) or time can refer to exact points (at "2:00 P.M. today," or "yesterday at 6:30"). The misunderstanding occurs when individuals operate on different concepts of time.

# Points to Remember

❏ Every culture has its own way of depicting the following domains of nonlinguistic communication:

❏ Paralinguistics: Sounds that accompany language and vocalizations that replace speech.

❏ Kinesics: The study of body motion, gestures, unconscious body movement.

❏ Oculesics: Eye contact and motion to indicate meaning.

❏ Haptics: Location, frequency, and contexts in which people touch.

❏ Proxemics: The unconscious use and organization of personal space.

❏ Chronemics: Perception and use of time.

❏ Monochronic time: Doing one thing at a time, in a linear fashion.

❏ Polychronic time: Doing many things at a time.

❏ All cultures operate on their own systems of communication, and these beliefs will be manifested within the everyday context of the classroom.

❏ Knowledge of nonverbal communication specific to other cultures will help teachers to understand the students they teach, and well as students' parents.

❏ Educators must be careful not to make the mistake of judging people's emotions by using their own cultural indicators.

❏ Not everyone shows grief, anger, happiness, and embarrassment, or other emotions in the same manner.

# Chapter 8

## Teaching and Learning Styles: A Reflection of Cultural Backgrounds

### KEY ISSUES

- ❏ Cultural learning and teaching styles
- ❏ Field-dependent/field-independent learners
- ❏ Curriculum that facilitates learning
- ❏ Teacher strategies for culturally diverse classrooms

Ms. Peters teaches a first-grade bilingual class and adores the beautiful children she sees in front of her. She has spent many years learning Spanish, and this is her first bilingual class. Her 34 children are almost all from Puerto Rico, with the exception of one child who is from Peru. She has no teacher's assistant yet, but she has invested a lot of time in organizing and planning for instruction, so she feels well-prepared. She chooses an assignment to get to know her children. "Niños, vamos a hacer algo muy divertido. Hagan un dibujo que muestre lo que hicieron durante sus vacaciones este verano." (Children, we are going to do something that is a lot of fun. Make a drawing that shows what you did during your vacation this summer.) The children began a barrage of questions, "Pero que hacemos? Usamos las crayolas o los marcadores? Teacher, usted me puede ayudar a dibujar un barco? No se' que hacer. (But what do we do? Do we use the crayons or the markers? I don't know what to do. Teacher, can you help me draw a boat?) "Wow!" thought Ms. Peters. "So many questions for such an easy assignment."

**A**ll individuals have their own learning styles and approaches to educational experiences. Age, cultural environment, and the family's beliefs and training mold the child into a certain type of learner, which is reflected by his or her cognitive behavior in the classroom. When home beliefs are incongruent with those of the teacher and culture of the American classroom, misunderstandings occur. As a general rule, Americans cherish individuality, independence, and self-reliance. Consequently, children are raised in a corresponding manner. For example, American babies are usually expected to sleep in their own rooms, away from their mothers, at a very early age. (Imagine the disbelief a newcomer to this country might feel upon learning Americans will let their dogs sleep in their beds, and yet the children are expected to sleep in their own rooms!)

In kindergarten, children are expected to know their telephone numbers, addresses, and how to call 911, and are taught how to care for themselves. They are encouraged to "be a big girl" while Mommy's gone, and not to cry. Role-play or videos might be used to teach children how to act appropriately in various hypothetical situations. For example, children learn how to ward off sexual predators and to distinguish inappropriate touch. The implication is that they will be alone, think for themselves, and make responsible decisions. Children in daycare situations, where independence is promoted, are encouraged to become self-reliant. Later, they often have more freedom of choice in matters such as choosing friends and making certain decisions at an earlier age.

On the other hand, parents of children from many other cultures (e.g., Hispanics, Asians, etc.), might be more inclined to "hover" over their children, doing *for* them, which promotes more dependence on the family members. Family interaction often consists of greater contact with grandparents and extended families.

Children who come from cultures that promote independence are often "field-independent," which suggests that their learning styles may be more analytical and independent. Gollnick and Chin (1998) mention that children who are less assimilated into the dominant society (with the exception of Asian Americans) may have the tendency to be global or "field-sensitive" learners. (Please refer to the chart of characteristics in the appendix.) Neither style is better; the point here is to highlight the comparisons because if the teachers are from the typical "American" culture, those cultural values will be manifested in their classroom expectations. Teachers and students who understand each other's expectations can expect fewer cultural collisions that disturb the educational process. Students can become bored, unresponsive, discouraged, or test poorly if they are uncomfortable in class (Felder & Henriques, 1995). However, if teachers misinterpret learning style data because they have lumped all students into one category, and then make instructional decisions based on incorrect assumptions, students can be hurt or limited in their school experience. For example, a student deemed field-independent might not be expected to contribute to cooperative learning activities, or a child labeled as field-dependent might not be chosen for a leadership role.

Students who have teachers from their same culture have little problem understanding the cues provided by the teacher and the appropriate interactional behaviors expected in the classroom. Those children and teachers from differing cultures do not know the rules of each other's "games" and have difficulty interpreting correct teacher-student interactions. Although not the panacea to end all classroom problems, effective teaching is more apt to take place if both the teacher and student are aware of the benefits of integrating appropriate instructional materials that correspond with culturally congruent teaching and learning styles (Smalley & Hank, 1995.)

Knowing that cultural patterns drive behavior, teachers who are aware that their children have differing cognitive styles are able to adapt their classrooms to include activities that incorporate all types of learning in their teaching. The teacher will begin to understand why some students experience problems when their natural learning styles are incompatible with the teaching style of the teacher. Various researchers have pointed out that Asian students tend to be highly visual learners (Erhman & Oxford, 1995; Reid, 1995b). Hispanics are generally auditory learners, and non-Westerners are more inclined to learn through tactile and kinesthetic modes.

Differences in cognitive styles also can be demonstrated by examining the impulsive/reflective dimension. Impulsive students are those who are the first to raise their hands to answer questions and the first to finish a test. Reflective learners may be slower, but often they make fewer errors. The teacher has the power to teach impulsive learners to be more reflective and to foster impulsive behaviors in the more reflective student (such as during a timed test).

Ramirez and Castaneda (1974) have determined characteristics of field-sensitive and field-independent learners. Individuals sensitive to their surroundings or to the social field may be more likely to choose careers such as teaching or social work, while the more field-independent learners might chose to work in more impersonal, abstract, or analytical professions such as the hard sciences or mathematics. However, with the guidance of the teacher, students can learn to become bicognitive, which means that they are able to function appropriately in any given situation, whether it is formal testing or cooperative learning. Cognitive learning and teaching styles are derived from early socialization patterns, which can be changed and modified. Learning strategies are teachable (Park-Oh, 1994; Sano, 1999) and will result in greater student achievement, increased motivation, and less anxiety. Field-sensitive instruction includes group projects, cooperative learning activities, culturally and ethnically relevant topics, and close interaction with the teacher. Field-independent instruction involves charts, diagrams, individual work, minimal teacher interaction, and analytical endeavors.

*Multicultural Education in a Pluralistic Society* (Gollnick & Chin, 1998) offers the following chart adapted from Ramirez & Castaneda (1974), which categorically depicts the differences in behavior between field-independent and field-sensitive students. Additional characteristics have added to the list.

| Field-Independent Behavior | Field-Sensitive behavior |
|---|---|
| *Relationship to Peers* | |
| Prefers to work independently. | Likes to work with others to achieve a common goal |
| Likes to compete and gain individual recognition | Likes to assist others |
| Is task-oriented; is inattentive to social environment when working | Is sensitive to feelings and opinions of others |
| Social atmosphere is secondary | |
| *Personal Relationship to Teacher* | |
| Rarely seeks physical contact with teacher | Openly expresses positive feelings for teacher |
| Is formal; restricts interactions with teacher to tasks at hand | Asks questions about teacher's tastes and personal experiences; seeks to emulate the teacher |
| *Instructional Relationships to Teacher* | |
| Likes to try new tasks without help from the teacher | Seeks guidance and demonstration from the teacher |
| Impatient to begin tasks | Seeks rewards that strengthen relationship with the teacher |
| Likes to finish first | Is highly motivated when working individually with teacher |
| Seeks nonsocial rewards | Teacher expresses approval |
| Teacher uses formulas, charts, and graphs to instruct | Teacher instructs primarily by modeling. |
| Learners prefer trial and error | Teacher provides personal rewards |
| | Teacher holds informal discussions in class |
| | Teacher is sensitive to students' problems |
| *Characteristics of Curriculum that Facilitate Learning* | |
| Emphasizes details of concepts | Explains performance objectives and global aspects of curriculum carefully |
| Parts have meaning of their own | Presents concepts in humanized story format |
| Teaches math and science concepts based on the discovery approach | Relates concepts to personal interests and experience of students |
| Emphasizes facts and principles | Approaches learning in a global perspective |
| Focuses on instructional objectives | Personalizes curriculum based on human needs of the learner |
| Encourages competition and independent achievement, which are approached analytically | |

While it is tempting to categorize individuals according to their ethnic group's cultural characteristics, it is important to keep in mind that reliability of all the learner style preference tests is questionable and often data are unsupported by research findings (Morgan & Ariza, 2002). However, mismatches of teaching and learning styles in the classroom often occur and it is up to the teacher to bridge the gap. Teachers often teach the way they were taught or teach in a way that reflects their own learning styles (Oxford, 1990). It is no surprise, then, that research shows a higher level of academic achievement when the teacher's instructional style is congruent with the student's learning style (Cornet, 1983; Dunn & Dunn, 1979; Dunn & Griggs, 1995; Oxford, Ehrman, & Lavine, 1991). Cornet (1983) and Marshall (1991) found that a teacher's instructional style can influence a student's learning style preference, as can factors such as age, prior knowledge, motivation, context, and age (Dunn & Dunn, 1979; Oxford & Ehrman, 1995; and Reid, 1987).

Cheng and Banya (in Reid, 1998) offer several ways for teachers to mitigate teaching/learning mismatches:

- Teachers should be cognizant of their own teaching styles as well as their students' learning styles, provide varied opportunities for students to discover their own learning styles, and take risks by experimenting with a number of instructional styles.

- Students need to be cognizant of their own learning styles, become more tolerant of ambiguity in the foreign language learning environment, and help themselves become more autonomous learners.

## Different Cultures; Clashing in the Classroom

*Mr. Cooper is the new teacher on the reservation. He has great respect for Native American cultures and appreciates the opportunity to work with the children of this nation. He has carefully introduced the concept of his lesson, and feels sure that his students understand what is being taught. He decides to test comprehension and directs a question to Running Bear, who does not know the answer. In an effort to help him, Mr. Cooper asks Sara, his brightest student, to help Running Bear by giving him the answer. Sara just puts her head down and does not answer. Mr. Cooper calls on one child after another, but no one will answer the question. Mr. Cooper is confused by his students' behavior. They are deliberately refusing to answer the simple question.*

In this situation, Mr. Cooper does not realize that Native Americans are more group-oriented than are Anglos, and the children must "save face" for their friend. They will not embarrass Running Bear by answering the teacher's question, even if they know the correct answer. No one wants to be singled out above the others because, like their elders, no one really directs because the group is the most important entity.

Although knowing about cultural learning styles and applying this information in the classroom can make instruction more effective for diverse learners, care must be taken not to simplify issues that are really quite complex. Bennett (1990) admonishes teachers to beware of thinking that merely understanding learning styles is a panacea for all the ills in the classrooms of today. Within the cultural paradigm, every family is unique, with its own set of traditions and values and finally, individuals have their own idiosyncrasies. Taking all of these factors into consideration, the teacher can then determine the most effective methods of reaching each child.

Ogbu (1988) explains that cultural differences of Anglo, mainstream teachers are often at odds with students from other cultures. Pajares (1992) found that teachers' cultural beliefs often clash with students' cultural beliefs, thus preventing learning. Conflicts can occur because the "way of life" of these students is discordant with the cultural values, beliefs, and norms of mainstream schools. As a result of research on culture and learning styles, advocates claim that the closer the congruence in the teacher's instructional styles and the student's learning style, the more academic success the student will have in the classroom. As an additional point of interest, Clarkson (1983) notes that women and minorities are more likely to be field-sensitive or field-dependent.

## Recommended Teacher Strategies

No matter what cultures teachers are from, they can get to know their students' preferred learning styles by daily observation and sensing what works best. Cox and Ramirez (1981, pp. 64–65) suggest that daily instruction techniques take into account the culturally reflected learning styles of the individual and offer a six-point plan to follow:

- Observe student behavior and note the changes from situation to situation. From this assessment, it is easy to determine the students' preferred way of learning.
- Design your teaching methods, strategies, incentives, materials, and situations so they complement student preferences.
- Execute the learning experiences as planned.
- Evaluate the learning experiences by determining if instructional objectives have been met, but also in terms of student behavior and task involvement.

■ Throughout the year, gradually plan and implement learning experiences that require behaviors that the students have previously shunned. Include one aspect of the unfamiliar behavior during each learning episode, focusing on the reward, the materials, the situation, or the task requirements. In this manner, the students have a scaffold to support the new learning experience with prior experience.

■ Continue the effort to provide familiar, comfortable, successful experiences while gradually presenting new ways for the children to learn.

## Points to Remember

❏ Teaching and learning styles reflect cultural backgrounds.

❏ Students who have teachers from their same culture have little problem understanding the cues provided by the teacher. Students will already be familiar with the appropriate interactional behaviors expected in the classroom.

❏ With proper instruction, field-dependent and field-independent students can learn to be bicognitive; that is, their learning styles can be expanded to function appropriately in any given situation.

❏ Teachers need to provide activities that incorporate all types of learning styles.

❏ Teachers need to be aware of their own cultural learning styles and preferences, as well as those of their students.

❏ *Stereotyping* can happen when false and exaggerated characteristics of a group are attribute to the individual, but *sociotyping* involves an accurate generalization about cultural groups as a whole. If teachers misinterpret the learning style data and make decisions based on incorrect assumptions, students can be hurt or limited in their school experience.

❏ Mainstream teachers are often at odds with their diverse students because they are unaware of the differing cultural values they bring to the classroom.

❏ Teachers need to plan curriculum and instruction to incorporate the learning styles of their students.

❏ If students are uncomfortable in class, they may become bored, unresponsive, or test poorly (Felder & Henriques, 1995).

# Part II

# *Principles and Practices in Second Language Teaching*

# Chapter 9

## *Teaching for Communication*

# KEY ISSUES

❏ Language as a complex system

❏ Native language acquisition theories
  ◆ Behaviorist
  ◆ Innatist
  ◆ Interactionist

❏ Principles in second language acquisition

❏ Krashen's monitor model

❏ Implications of Krashen's monitor model for the ESOL teacher

## What Is Language?

Language is the vehicle humans employ to express and communicate emotions and/or ideas by means of speech and hearing. Speech denotes the power of articulate utterances. Although animals can be said to have a "language" of their own, they do not have speech. However, language encompasses more than simply being able to communicate ideas and emotions orally. Thus, developing communicative competence requires mastery of all four language processes: listening, speaking, reading, and writing.

The following figure illustrates the complexity of language:

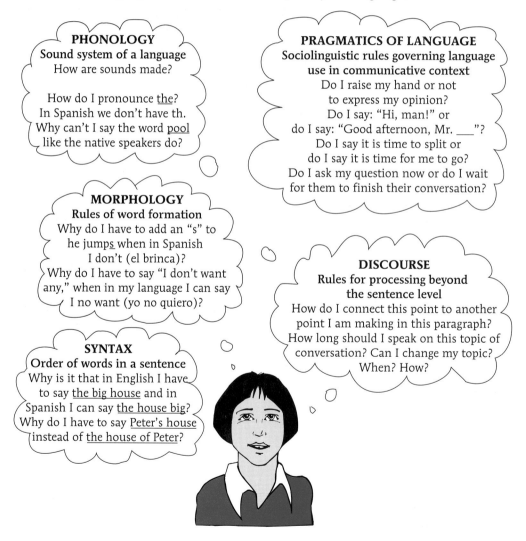

**PHONOLOGY**
Sound system of a language
How are sounds made?

How do I pronounce <u>the</u>?
In Spanish we don't have th.
Why can't I say the word <u>pool</u>
like the native speakers do?

**PRAGMATICS OF LANGUAGE**
Sociolinguistic rules governing language
use in communicative context
Do I raise my hand or not
to express my opinion?
Do I say: "Hi, man!" or
do I say: "Good afternoon, Mr. ___"?
Do I say it is time to split or
do I say it is time for me to go?
Do I ask my question now or do I wait
for them to finish their conversation?

**MORPHOLOGY**
Rules of word formation
Why do I have to add an "s" to
he jump<u>s</u> when in Spanish
I don't (el brinca)?
Why do I have to say "I don't want
any," when in my language I can say
I no want (yo no quiero)?

**DISCOURSE**
Rules for processing beyond
the sentence level
How do I connect this point to another
point I am making in this paragraph?
How long should I speak on this topic of
conversation? Can I change my topic?
When? How?

**SYNTAX**
Order of words in a sentence
Why is it that in English I have
to say <u>the big house</u> and in
Spanish I can say <u>the house big</u>?
Why do I have to say <u>Peter's house</u>
instead of <u>the house of Peter</u>?

# First Language Acquisition Theories

How do people acquire their native language? Through the years there have been numerous attempts to explain the phenomenon of language acquisition.

## Behaviorist Theory

B. F. Skinner (1957) based his explanation of acquisition of language on behavioristic principles. The basic elements in the behavioristic theory are stimulus, response, and reinforcement. Behaviorists hypothesized that children learned their first language through the same process of stimulus, response, and reinforcement. They also gave much importance to the processes of imitation and association. This theory made much sense because in observing the interactions of parents/caregivers and young children, it seemed apparent that children acquired their language as a result of this interaction.

**Stimulus:** Parents/caregivers talked to the young child using gesturing, demonstrating, showing, and telling.

**Response:** The child produced some form of utterance/speech.

**Reinforcement:** The parent/caregiver praised or demonstrated understanding. This reinforcement encouraged continuation of the behavior.

While this process is taking place, the child is imitating what he or she hears and associates meaning to the concrete examples to which he or she is exposed in everyday interactions. Behaviorists employed the term "tabula rasa" to describe the child's mind as a blank mental slate. Thus, children's language development comes as a result of imitating and associating the stimulus to which they are exposed and as it is reinforced by their parents/caregivers.

### Scenario:

Mother: The kitty is saying meow.

Child: Kitty meow.

Mother: Yes! The kitty is saying meow.

This scenario is repeated numerous times and eventually the child will say: "The kitty is saying meow."

There was a major flaw with the behavioristic theory because it could not explain how children would come up with novel (new) utterances (i.e., language [words] they had never heard before).

### *Scenario:*

Mother: Where did the ball go?

Child: It <u>goed</u> under the table.

Mother: You are right! It <u>went</u> under the table.

The child has never heard the word "goed," yet spoke it. However, if this sentence is analyzed, it makes perfect sense, the mother asked a question that requires the use of the past tense in the response; the child responded by using the past tense ending (ed) of a regular verb (such as jump<u>ed</u> or laugh<u>ed</u>), thus forming the past tense. This process would not make sense if the child were strictly responding following the behavioristic principles. In addition, in this example, the mother did not correct the child's grammatical error but simply reinforced the meaning of the response: "You are right." These and other concerns led to the realization that there had to be more to explaining language acquisition.

## Innatist Theory

Linguist Noam Chomsky (1957), engaged in a heated debate with Skinner, claimed the behaviorist theory was inadequate to explain observations of children's language development.

Noam Chomsky was a linguist with a genius mind for analyzing syntax. His early work on syntax and transformational grammar revolutionized the field of linguistics. As Chomsky studied the complexities of children's applications of grammatical principles and rules, he concluded that the only way to explain these was by assuming the possession of an "innate" ability to do so. He hypothesized that infants were born with a biological language acquisition device (LAD) or system that equipped them for linguistic analysis. Chomsky concluded that infants universally possess an innate "grammar template" or universal grammar that allows them to select out the many grammatical rules of the language they hear spoken around them, as they gradually construct the grammar of their own native language (Peregoy & Boyle, 2000). According to Chomsky (1957, 1959), children construct grammar through a process of hypothesis testing. For example, a child may hypothesize the rule that all past tenses of verbs are formed by adding-<u>ed</u>. Thus, when they are faced with the verb "to go" and the need to use it in the past tense, they say "goed" instead of went. Gradually, children revise their hypothesis to accommodate exceptions or the past tense of irregular verbs. Thus, Chomsky contended that children create sentences by using rules rather than by merely repeating what they have heard, as the behaviorists assumed. This is how the innatists explained the production of novel utterances.

### Scenario

The scene takes place in a home in Puerto Rico. The mother is American (native born and raised in the United States) and has always spoken to her daughter, Ana, in English. Ana is 3 years old and has always spoken to her mom in Spanish.

Mom: Ana, did you hang up your clothes?

Ana: Si, Mami. Ya yo la jangué. (Yes, Mom. I already hung it.)

### Analysis

Ana's response, though incorrect Spanish (novel utterance "jangué"), makes sense and is grammatically correct. She has applied the rule for the past tense of regular "ar" verbs in Spanish, drop "ar" and add an accented "é." She has also employed the correct ending for first-person singular ("yo"; "I"). In addition, Ana employed the appropriate feminine pronoun; "la" because "clothes" in Spanish is "ropa" and it is a feminine noun. She used the singular for "la" because the noun "ropa" in Spanish is a singular noun whether it refers to one piece of clothing or more than one. What Ana did, was apply the rules for Spanish grammar, but she created a novel utterance for a verb (to hang), which she did not know in Spanish. Ana's mother had never used the word jangué; thus, Ana had never heard this word.

This is the kind of analysis that Chomsky and his followers did do. They concluded that children acquired language with little help from their parents/caregivers. They diminished the role of the parents/caregivers to such an extent that their theory was unable to explain why people who are deprived of linguistic interactions are not able to fully develop language; those born deaf or who develop a hearing loss at a very young age are limited in their language development or are void of oral language. These observations, which were not fully explicable, led to further study of the complex process of language development.

## Interactionist Theory

Rooted in the cognitive psychology, with such proponents as Jean Piaget, Lois Bloom, and Dan Slobin, this theory embraces the view that language is directly related to cognitive development. In addition, cognitivists/interactionists place great importance on social interactions in the development of language. The interaction between nature (innate ability to acquire language) and nurture (the role of the social environment) is what allows language to develop.

Children's language develops over time, with many instances of the same or similar interactions. It would be nearly impossible for young children to produce language to which they have been exposed only once or twice. How many times do infants hear the words "bottle" or "daddy" before they actually produce those words? Thus, their ability to acquire the words, plus the numerous encounters with those words, account for the fact that eventually, after many approximations to those words (for example: ba; baba; da; dada;) the child, one day, says

### Table 9-1
### Comparison of Behaviorist, Innatist, and Interactionist Theories of Language Acquisition

| Acquisition Aspects | Behaviorist Perspective | Innatist Perspective | Interactionist Perspective |
|---|---|---|---|
| Linguistic Focus | Verbal behaviors (not analyzed per se); words, utterances of child and people in social environment | Child's syntax | Conversations between child and caregiver; focus on caregiver speech |
| Process of Acquisition | Modeling, imitation, practice, and selective reinforcement of correct form | Hypothesis testing and creative construction of acts Syntactic rules using LAD | Acquisition emerges from communication; scaffolded by caregivers |
| Role of Child | Secondary role: Imitator and responder to environmental shaping | Primary role: Equipped with biological LAD, child plays major role in acquisition | Important role in interaction, taking more control as language acquisition advances |
| Role of Social Environment | Primary role: Parental modeling and reinforcement are major factors promoting language acquisition | Minor role: Language used by others merely triggers LAD | Important role in interaction, especially in early years when caregivers modify input and carry much of conversational load |

Source: Peregoy & Boyle (2001) *Reading, Writing, and Learning in ESL, 3rd Edition.*

"bottle" and "daddy." It is not known, though, which factor in language development plays a greater role (i.e., is nature the most important factor or does nurture play the greater role?). More research is needed on both, the biological and social factors. However, it is important to acknowledge the importance of both factors. Language cannot develop fully without the child's innate ability and the sociolinguistic interactions that occur as the child grows and develops.

# Second Language Acquisition

Very few parents/caregivers are linguists, yet all normal children develop language. If first languages are acquired so naturally, what implications does this have for second language teaching? Should the same conditions present in first language acquisition be replicated for second language teaching? Would second language acquisition occur as naturally if the same conditions were present in the second language learner's classroom?

Stephen Krashen (1982) developed five hypotheses that have greatly impacted the teaching of foreign languages in the United States, as well as the field of teaching English to speakers of other languages (TESOL): (1) the acquisition vs. learning hypothesis, (2) the natural order hypothesis, (3) the monitor hypothesis, (4) the comprehensible input hypothesis, and (5) the affective filter hypothesis. Each one will be discussed below.

## The Acquisition vs. Learning Hypothesis

Krashen makes a distinction between acquiring language and learning language.

| **Acquisition** | **Learning** |
|---|---|
| Informal process | Formal process |
| "Picking up" | "Knowing about" |
| Unconscious process | Conscious process |
| Implicit | Explicit |

According to Krashen, in order for students to acquire a second language, teachers must focus on communication rather than on the rote memorization of rules (form).

For acquisition to occur, students must be immersed in meaningful and comprehensible contexts. It is not "knowing about" the language that helps develop communicative competency, it is using the language in meaningful interactions. Therefore, teachers must provide for these meaningful interactions to occur in the classroom.

Krashen contends that language that is simply "learned" is not the language that is spoken. Language "learning", or knowledge of grammatical rules, or use of much drill-and-pattern practice does not account for spoken language. For example, many students in the United States study foreign languages in high school. Years later, most are still able to conjugate a verb (in those languages) but are not able to speak the languages. The emphasis was placed on "learning about" the language and not in "using/speaking" the language in a natural way.

Krashen has been criticized for his claims that (1) only language that is acquired leads to fluent communication and (2) language that is "learned" cannot "turn into" spoken language. However, despite the criticisms, his insistence on the value of using the second language in meaningful communicative contexts has had a positive impact on the field of second language teaching.

## The Natural Order Hypothesis

According to Krashen, second language acquisition models first language acquisition. This means that there is a natural progression in the process of acquiring a second language that is similar to that of acquiring the first language. There are four stages or periods in first/second language acquisition:

1. Preproduction, comprehension, or silent stage or period
2. Early production
3. Speech emergence
4. Intermediate fluency

Children progress from not speaking at all (infant) to acquiring full command of the first/second language. According to Krashen, second language acquisition follows these four stages, so it is then understandable why second language learners usually go through a period when they do not speak, they are simply listening, "taking-in," getting their ears acclimated to the new sounds that surround them.

Krashen also indicates that grammatical structures and certain language structures are acquired in a predictable order. For example, in the English language, the concept of plural and the rule for forming the present progressive by adding "ing" are acquired earlier than the rule for forming the third-person singular by adding an "s." Also, vocabulary/words are acquired in a natural order: from no words at all (silent period) to one-to-two word sentences (early production period) to three-to-four word sentences (speech emergence period) to more complex sentences (Intermediate Fluency period). According to Krashen, errors are developmental and students will outgrow them as they are exposed to what is appropriate or correct.

## The Monitor Hypothesis

Krashen states that people produce language that they have "acquired," not language that they have "learned." However, he does assert that language learning is helpful in monitoring output. When the learners know the rules of the language, they can employ them to correct what they are thinking about saying (self-correct) or to correct what they have said (self-repair). In order for the monitor to work (or for the monitoring to take place), three conditions need to be present: (1) the learners need to have time to think about what they are about to say or have said, (2) the learners need to focus on "form", "how do I say it so that it is correct?"; and (3) the learners must have knowledge and be able to apply the rules. Second language learners who are literate in their first language and adult second language learners are more likely to use the monitor. In many instances, adult second language learners tend to over-monitor; therefore, it takes them longer to speak the second language.

The monitor is easier to employ in the written language because the learner has more time to go back, re-read, and edit processes that take additional time that is not "natural" when speaking at a normal pace.

## The Input Hypothesis

One of the most important elements in the successful acquisition of the second language is whether or not the input received by the learner is comprehensible. However, according to Krashen, the input not only needs to be "comprehensible input," but it also needs to be slightly beyond the students' current level of competency. This concept is represented as i + 1 (comprehensible input plus 1—slightly beyond the student's current level of proficiency). In order for the input to be comprehensible, teachers must present the material in ways that are not tied to language. That is, teachers must use visuals, objects, realia, manipulatives, gesturing, modeling, "parentese" (repeat, rephrase, slower speech) charts, graphs, and maps. In addition teachers must give positive feedback to the students to encourage their risk taking in the second language acquisition process. According to Krashen, vocabulary and grammatical structures must take into account i + 1 and should always be presented in meaningful contexts, not in isolation.

## The Affective Filter Hypothesis

Krahsen's fifth hypothesis addresses affective or social-emotional variables related to second language acquisition. Citing a variety of studies, Krashen concludes that the most important affective variables favoring second language acquisition are a low-anxiety learning environment, student motivation to learn the language, self-confidence, and self-esteem. Students are able to acquire the second language if they are in an environment where they feel accepted, where they are free to take risks and know that if they make mistakes, they will not be "ridiculed." When students feel uncomfortable, nervous, anxious, or afraid, their affective filter goes up as a defense mechanism and acquisition of knowledge is interrupted or stifled. A nonthreatening teaching/learning atmosphere is indispensable for language acquisition to take place. Krashen claims that, "People acquire second languages when they obtain comprehensible input and when their affective filters are low enough to allow the input in (Krashen, 1981).

## Implications of Krashen's Hypotheses for the Classroom Teacher

### Hypothesis #1: Acquisition vs. Learning

1. Thematic instruction: If students are totally immersed in a theme, they will have many opportunities to grasp the concepts and content. They will have numerous encounters with the same content/vocabulary/language structures, yet from different perspectives.

2. Teachers must avoid putting emphasis on rote memorization/drill for acquisition of learning to occur. For example, emphasis on rote memorization of spelling words should be avoided. Spelling words should be always taught in meaningful contexts and practiced in meaningful communicative activities.

3. Students must be provided numerous opportunities for employing/practicing the new concepts/language. Saying it once or writing it once will not allow for acquisition of knowledge.

4. Integrated curriculum also provides for numerous encounters with some of the same content because students not only learn about "mammals," for example, in science but they also learn about mammals in reading, as well as in social studies and mathematics. Thus, reinforcement of the acquired concepts and vocabulary, will take place throughout the entire school day. Students would have many opportunities to acquire the knowledge and develop second language competence throughout the entire school day for as long as the integration is taking place.

5. It was important to focus on the need to communicate; to create the "information gap" wherein students have a need to communicate with other students and/or the teacher. This provides for meaningful

communication. Cooperative groups are a positive vehicle for creating the environment conducive to this meaningful interaction among students. One student in the group has information that the others in the group need in order to fulfill their task. This is what is known as the "information gap." ("I have some information you need" thus it is necessary for us to communicate, so together, we have the total information we need.") This technique takes into account the way language develops (i.e., based on need).

## Hypothesis #2: Natural Order

1. Organize instruction from simple to complex taking into account the way language develops.

2. Respect the silent period. Teachers should not force students to speak until they are ready. In the meantime, teachers must engage students who are in the silent period in activities wherein they can respond nonverbally.

3. Allow mistakes because errors are developmental. One positive technique is to allow students to employ "invented spelling." If students know they will not be penalized for incorrect spelling, they will be more encouraged to write and will feel successful in their attempts.

4. Allow students to make mistakes in oral communication without the fear of being "corrected" each time they mispronounce a word or employ incorrect grammar/syntax. Teachers should simply make note of errors students are making and address these in lessons thus providing for meaningful practice.

## Hypothesis #3: Monitor Hypothesis

1. Teachers must allow "think time" so students can self-correct prior to speaking. Second language learners may need to "rehearse in their head" what they are going to say and how to say it before they can respond.

2. Teachers must provide numerous encounters with the same to allow students to grasp the concepts. If students develop the concept of how specific language "sounds," they will eventually produce accurate language.

3. Plan lessons employing the "discovery method," wherein students are provided many examples and much opportunity to be engaged in

discovering the knowledge instead of being told and required to memorize a set of facts. Discovery learning takes more time to plan but it is a much more effective teaching practice. If students are to employ the monitor, they must know how the output ought to be. By discovering the knowledge it is more likely to be retained and it will be easier to retrieve than if the students simply memorize something which they soon forget. If students discover grammar rules, for example, they are more likely able to apply them when trying to use the monitor.

4. Teachers must always model appropriate language and provide numerous opportunities for students to be exposed to appropriate models. Students may not always know why an utterance is produced in the appropriate way but if they have had much exposure to appropriate models, they will eventually be able to monitor their output effectively.

## Hypothesis #4: Input Hypothesis

1. Teachers must find ways to provide comprehensible input. One way is to employ means of presenting content that is not tied to language. Thus, the use of modeling, demonstrating, visuals (charts, graphs, gestures, pictures, models) and manipulatives is crucial.

2. Employing "parentese" (repeating, rephrasing, slowing down, simplifying language) is crucial.

## Hypothesis #5: Affective Filter

1. Teachers must create a nonthreatening teaching/learning atmosphere in the classroom.

2. Teachers must create a risk-safe environment where students will feel free to take chances, to try although they are not sure; and to make mistakes when producing language.

3. Teachers must create a warm, accepting classroom climate where students will not be worried about being criticized, or "put on the spot" for not being able to respond quickly and accurately.

4. Teachers must capitalize on what the students know rather than on what they do not know.

5. Teachers must create a teaching/learning environment where students encounter success rather than failure on a daily basis.

6. Teachers must provide positive feedback on a regular basis so students will be encouraged to engage in the lessons rather than remain disengaged due to fear of being criticized.

7. Teachers must provide many opportunities for cooperative learning and hands-on activities so students can interact with peers since this type of interaction is less threatening to them.

8. Teachers must continuously re-evaluate their attitude toward certain groups of students/people to ensure they are not displaying negative attitudes (either overtly with verbal comments, or nonverbally with gestures and body language such as facial expressions) toward students of certain cultural background.

## Points to Remember

❑ Communicative competence requires mastery of all four language processes: listening, speaking, reading, and writing.

❑ Aspects of language encompass phonology (sound system of a language), morphology (rules of word formation), syntax (order of words in a sentence), discourse (rules for processing beyond the sentence level), and pragmatics (sociolinguistic rules governing language use in communicative contexts).

❑ Behaviorists explained first language acquisition as a process of imitation of the care-giver.

❑ Behaviorists could not explain novel utterances.

❑ Innatists claimed that first language acquisition resulted from an innate ability.

❑ Innatists hypothesized that infants were born with a biological language acquisition device (LAD) that equipped them for linguistic analysis.

❑ Innatists could not explain how children/adults who were not exposed to language could not develop language.

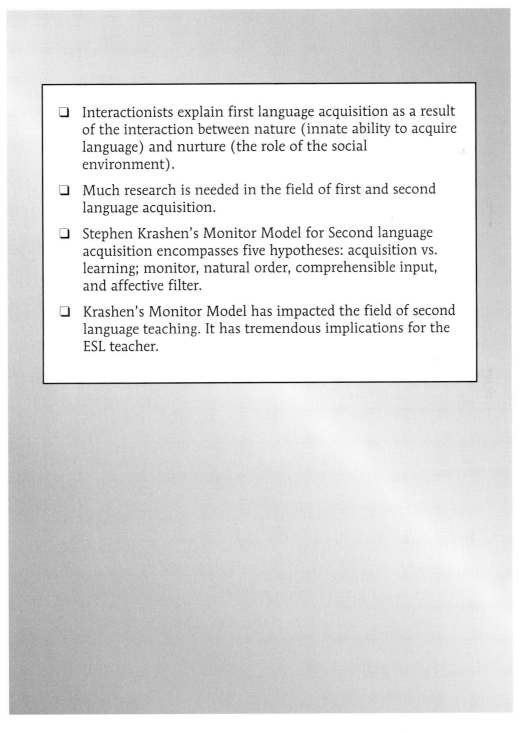

❏ Interactionists explain first language acquisition as a result of the interaction between nature (innate ability to acquire language) and nurture (the role of the social environment).

❏ Much research is needed in the field of first and second language acquisition.

❏ Stephen Krashen's Monitor Model for Second language acquisition encompasses five hypotheses: acquisition vs. learning; monitor, natural order, comprehensible input, and affective filter.

❏ Krashen's Monitor Model has impacted the field of second language teaching. It has tremendous implications for the ESL teacher.

# Chapter 10

## *Methods/Approaches of Teaching ESOL: A Historical Overview*

# Key Issues

❏ Historical overview of methods and approaches to teaching English as a foreign/second language

❏ The grammar-translation method

❏ The direct method

❏ The audio-lingual method

❏ Suggestopedia

❏ The silent way

❏ Total physical response

❏ The natural approach

❏ The communicative approach

For centuries, people have attempted to learn foreign/second languages through formal education. The methods and approaches employed have changed through the years, having been impacted by advancements in the theories and psychology of learning.

Basic assumptions about why and how people learn shape the way in which languages have been taught.

## The Grammar-Translation Method

The Grammar-Translation Method (also known as the Classical Method) was based on the belief that different kinds of knowledge were located in separate sections of the brain. Mathematic knowledge, for example, was thought to be located in one area, art in another, language in another, and so on. It was believed that studying different subjects was a good way of exercising the brain. Thus, learning another language provided the necessary mental exercise to develop the part of the brain believed to be earmarked for languages.

The main goal for learning a language was not for speaking and/or communication. The driving force was to exercise the mind and at the same time be able to read in that language. The languages taught in those early days were Latin and Greek, so another reason for studying foreign languages was to appreciate the classics in their original language. It must be pointed out that education was the privilege of an elite class, thus, it was a "mark of an educated person" to be able to read the classics.

The name of the method, Grammar-Translation captures the main emphases of this method (i.e. the study of grammatical aspects of language and the use of translation as a means of ascertaining comprehension). Communicating in the language was not a goal, so classes were taught primarily in the students' native language and the teacher made no effort to emphasize correct pronunciation of the language. Grammar study was the focus of the lessons, with much rote memorization of grammatical aspects such as verb conjugations and recitation of rules that described language functions. It was not surprising, then, that even students who spent several years studying a foreign language, were not able to speak that language. Much time was spent in learning about the language, not the language itself. Fortunately, this method is not widely used today in teaching English to English language learners. Yet, unfortunately, some aspects of this method are still employed to teach modern languages in the United States, primarily at the high school and university levels. Emphasis on reading and translating passages, conjugation of verbs, and explanation and memorization of grammatical rules still are observed in foreign language classrooms today.

# The Direct Method

The Direct Method is a complete departure from the Grammar-Translation method. This method dates back to 1884 when the German Scholar and psychologist F. Frankle provided a theoretical justification for the method by writing about the direct association between forms and meaning in the target language. It is also based on the work of Gouin, who in the 1880's observed children learning language in a natural setting (Freeman & Freeman, 1998).

The emphasis is on the direct associations the student makes between objects and concepts, and the corresponding words in the target language. The use of the native language, as in the Grammar-Translation method, is avoided; the use of the target language is emphasized at all times. In this method, the primary goals are for students to think and speak the language; thus, no use of the native language is allowed. Teachers employ objects, visuals, and realia to make the input comprehensible. Instruction revolves around specific topics. Aspects of grammar are taught inductively through the handling of the topic. For example, when studying different types of sports people practice, students are also introduced to verbs. The focus is not verbs and verb conjugations, but these are a logical way to expose students to these aspects of grammar. By much exposure and handling of the content, students inductively learn the appropriate use of different verbs that relate to sports. In addition, cultural aspects of the countries where the target language is spoken are also included in the lessons. For example, when studying Spanish, students would discuss the sports that are widely practiced in Spain or Mexico. This also brings in aspects of geography—where are these countries located? What aspects of language are related to directionality in describing the location, such as the names of the cardinal points (norte/north, sur/south, este/east, oeste/west)? How should these be used appropriately when referring to location (al norte de...; al sur de...; al este de...; al oeste de...)? In this process, vocabulary is emphasized and interaction among students and with the teacher was fostered, although it is limited to mostly asking and responding to questions. Reading and writing are also taught from the beginning.

The most widely known application of the Direct Method is practiced at the Berlitz language schools located throughout the world. Alhough the founder, Maximilian Berlitz, referred to the method as the Berlitz Method, the principles applied have been and continue to be those of the Direct Method. Berlitz classes are generally for highly motivated adults who need to speak a foreign language for business purposes. Although many techniques developed for the Direct Method have also been used in other methods, applying the Direct Method in noncommercial schools fell out of favor as early as 1920 (Richards and Rogers, 1986). The Grammar-Translation method dominated public school and university language teaching in the United States until World War II.

# Audio-Lingual Method (ALM)

The United States involvement in World War II brought a significant change in the teaching of languages in U.S. schools. It quickly became apparent that the Grammar-Translation Method had not produced people who were able to speak the foreign languages they had studied. The U.S. government asked the universities to develop foreign language programs that produced students who could communicate effectively in those languages.

Changes in the beliefs about how people learn impacted the teaching methodologies being developed. Based on the behavioristic psychology (refer to chapter 1), the Audio-lingual Method was developed.

In the audio-lingual method, the emphasis was on the memorization of a series of dialogues and the rote practice of language structures. The basic premises on which the method was based were that language is speech, not writing, and language is a set of habits. It was believed that much practice of the dialogues would develop oral language proficiency. The use of the native language was avoided.

The method became very popular in the 1960's. Language laboratories began to surge and students were required to listen to audio-tapes and repeat dialogues that captured aspects of daily living. In addition, specific structural patterns of the language studied were embedded in those dialogues. Students were required to participate in a number of practice drills designed to help them memorize the structures and be able to plug other words into the structure. For example, in a substitution drill, the structure might have been:

I am going to the <u>post office.</u>

Students were then required to substitute the word <u>post office</u> for other words such as supermarket, park, beach, drugstore, etc.

The belief was that students, through much practice, would form a "habit" and be able to speak the language when needed. Although the intent was to develop fluent and proficient speakers by providing much oral practice of the dialogues and the use of numerous drills to help in this endeavor, the reality was that language proficiency was not the outcome. Years later, students who studied with the Audio-lingual Method still remembered the dialogues but could not speak the foreign language they had studied. Thus, the method was not successful at accomplishing the main goal. It was too prescriptive; there was no opportunity provided for "true" communication to take place in the ALM classroom. Students had been taught a "script" and people do not speak following a particular script.

# Suggestopedia

Suggestopedia was developed by Bulgarian psychiatrist–educator Lozanov (1982), who wanted to eliminate the psychological barriers that people have to learning. It uses drama, art, physical exercise, and desuggestive–suggestive communicative psychotherapy as well as the traditional modes of listening, speaking, reading, and writing to teach a second language. The influence of the science of suggestology is clear in this method that calls class meetings "sessions" (Freeman & Freeman, 1998).

In this method, the classroom atmosphere is crucial. Creating a relaxed, nonthreatening learning environment is essential for its success. The goal is that students will assimilate the content of the lessons without feeling any type of stress or fatigue.

Classrooms are equipped with comfortable seating arrangements and dim lighting in an effort to provide an inviting and appealing environment. Soothing music is employed to invite relaxation and allow students to feel comfortable in the language classroom. The use of the native language is also allowed, especially to give directions and to create that welcoming atmosphere. Based on the belief that how students feel about learning will make a difference in the learning process, Suggestopedia takes into consideration the affective domain. It could be said that the philosophy of the little engine that could: "I think I can, I think I can, I know I can" (Piper, 1976) is one of the basic underlying principles of Suggestopedia. If the students feel they can learn, they will.

The use of drama, songs, and games provides for much practice, yet in a less threatening and more enjoyable fashion. As in the ALM, dialogues are employed, but they are presented in an enhanced fashion through creative dramatics. The rehearsing of roles provides the necessary practice, yet there is a purpose for practicing. When people are preparing for dramatic roles, they most likely spend much time rehearsing.

Despite the advancements over the Audio-lingual Method, Suggestopedia has not been widely adopted in the United States. It is impractical for large classes. In addition, current textbooks do not embrace this methodology; thus, making it difficult for teachers to apply the principles in regular classrooms.

# The Silent Way

Developed by Gattegno, the Silent Way requires that the teachers remain silent much of the time, thus its name. In this method, students are responsible for their own learning. Based on the belief that students are initiators of learning and capable of independently acquiring language, the Silent Way provides a classroom environment where this can take place. The teacher models once and the students are then given the opportunity to work together to try to reproduce what has been modeled.

Beginners are initially taught the sounds of the new language from color-coded sound charts. Next, teachers focus on language structures sometimes using colored, plastic rods to visually represent parts of words or sentences. As students begin to understand more of the language, they are taught stories using the rods as props. At all stages of the method, the teacher models as little as possible, and students try to repeat after careful listening with help from each other. The teacher leads them toward correct responses by nods or negative head shakes (Ibid).

The Silent Way is a fairly complex method that requires the teacher to receive extensive training in the use of the methodology. Students also need to be well versed in the use of the charts and the rods to participate effectively in the lessons. Since, according to research, teachers speak from 65% to 95% of the time in traditional classrooms, so it is difficult to find teachers who are comfortable with the required "silence" of the Silent Way, thus limiting the number of teachers available to teach employing this method.

## Total Physical Response (TPR)

The Total Physical Response (TPR) method was developed by psychologist James Asher (1974). This method is based on the principle that people learn better when they are involved physically as well as mentally. In TPR, students are required to respond nonverbally (physically) to a series of commands. As the teacher gives a command and the students respond physically, the teacher ascertains students' comprehension of the command. Initially, the teacher begins with simple commands such as:

Teacher:   Stand up! (teacher models)
Students:  Respond by standing up. (physical response not verbal)
Teacher:   Walk to the front of the room.
Students:  Respond by walking to the front of the room.
Teacher:   Turn around and walk back to your seats.
Students:  Respond by turning around and walking to their seats.
Teacher:   Sit down.
Students:  Respond by sitting down.

Once the students have practiced a number of times, the teacher simply gives the command and the students responds. Eventually the students will give the commands, thus developing oral proficiency.

In TPR, teachers can employ pictures, objects, and realia for students to manipulate as they respond nonverbally. For example, the students are studying a unit on "emotions." The teacher can pass out pictures of people displaying different emotions. Then, the teacher can give the following commands:

| | |
|---|---|
| Teacher: | Raise the picture of the girl who seems sad. |
| Student(s): | Raise(s) picture of sad girl. |
| Teacher: | Stand up if you have a picture of two boys who seem happy. |
| Student(s): | (who has/have that picture): Stand(s) up. |
| Teacher: | Place on the board the picture that shows a woman who seems surprised. |
| Student(s): | (who has/have that picture): Walk(s) up to the board and place(s) the picture on the magnetic board. |

Commands become more complex as the students continue to develop listening comprehension and knowledge of subject matter. For example, with the assistance of pictures, students can be asked to categorize modes of transportation by land, water, or air or they could be asked to rearrange pictures to show the life cycle of a butterfly.

Once students are able to respond to a series of commands and can give the commands themselves, the teacher can introduce the reading and the writing aspects of language. However, the emphasis in TPR is on listening comprehension until oral proficiency is developed.

TPR is an excellent method to employ with students who are in the preproduction/silent stage of language development. Students who are not yet speaking are able to be involved in lessons and respond nonverbally. Thus, these students begin to feel a sense of belonging and success as they participate in the lessons. The students benefit from the involvement in the lessons and the teachers are able to ascertain whether or not the students are developing listening comprehension.

TPR is somewhat limited within the confines of a classroom, however with the use of pictures, and other types of manipulatives a resourceful teacher can bring the outside world into the classroom. For example, a teacher may prepare a transparency of a picture that depicts many actions. Each student gets a copy of the picture (black & white acceptable for this type of activity). The teacher employs the transparency to demonstrate the actions following the commands given. Students imitate and follow along. This is an excellent way to introduce verbs and new vocabulary using TPR.

### Sample 1: Florida Waterbirds

### List of Commands:

1. Look up at the clouds.
2. Show me the clouds
3. Jump in the water.
4. Swim over to the blue heron.
5. Stand like the blue heron.
6. Flap your wings like a bird.
7. Let's count the birds in the picture
8. Wave to the pelican.
9. Squawk like a laughing gull.
10. Pet the flamingo.
11. Get out of the water.
12. Shake yourself off.
13. Wave "good-bye" to the birds.

## Sample 2: A Walk in the Field

### List of Commands:

1.  Walk up to the scarecrow
2.  Walk around the scarecrow.
3.  Wave "hello" to the scarecrow.
4.  Touch the scarecrow's hat.
5.  Wave "good-bye" to the scarecrow.
6.  Walk up to the ball.
7.  Pick up the ball.
8.  Put down the ball.
9.  Walk up to the pear tree.
10. Pick up two pears from the ground.
11. Place the pears in the basket.
12. Pick up one more pear.
13. Bite off a piece from the pear.
14. Chew the piece of pear.
15. Skip over to the other tree.
16. Get close to the trunk.
17. Step on and crush the leaves.
18. Look up!
19. Wave to the squirrel.
20. Peek in the hole in the trunk.
21. Walk past the scarecrow.
22. Wave "good-bye" as you leave the field.

Another excellent way to employ TPR is by the use of logical sequences of actions, also known as Gouin Series, such as driving a car or taking a picture. The following are two examples:

### *Driving a Car*

I take my car key in my hand.
I walk to the car.
I unlock the car door or I use my remote to unlock the door.
I open the car door.
I get into the car.
I close the door.
I put on the seat belt.
I place the key in the ignition.
I start the car.
I take off.

### *Taking a Picture*

I get the camera.
I open the film compartment of the camera.
I place the film in the camera.
I close the camera.
I check to see that the camera is ready.
I look through the lens of the camera.
I focus.
I take the picture.

These Gouin Series can be longer or shorter depending on how much language the teacher wishes to employ at one time. Initially, the teacher models the actions and the students pantomine the actions. As soon as the teacher feels the students can respond without imitating the actions, the teacher simply describes the action and the students respond by demonstrating the actions (*Curtain & Pesola,* 1994).

The following benefits of the Gouin series have been identified (Knop, in *Curtain & Pesola,* 1994):

1. It links language to action and visuals, leading to improved comprehension.
2. It teaches appropriate verbal and physical behavior, making it especially useful for teaching cultural behaviors.
3. It is easy to recall because it has multiple meaning reinforcers:
   - physical actions
   - visuals and props
   - logical sequence
   - appeal to several senses
   - beginning, middle, end

Gouin Series are also an excellent way of developing reading and writing skills. Once the students are able to say the series, the teacher can record the sentences on sentence strips. Students can then be introduced to the reading of the sentences. Students can illustrate the series and write the actions illustrated. Illustrations can be compiled in book form or can be displayed sequentially in the classroom.

### *Getting Ready for School*

I wake up at 6:00 a.m.    I get up and brush my teeth.    I get dressed.    I comb my hair.

I go to the kitchen.    I have breakfast.    I get my backpack.    I walk to the bus stop.

**Sample Gouin Series that has been illustrated and described in print.**

# The Natural Approach

Tracy Terrell (1977, 1982) developed this methodology based on Krashen's monitor model (discussed in detail in chapter 1). The main goal of this method is to develop immediate communicative competency. For this reason, most, if not all, classroom activities are designed to encourage communication. Terrell (1977) suggested that the entire class period be devoted to communication activities rather than to explanation of grammatical aspects of language. This method is based on Krashen's monitor model, so it should be easy to understand why the emphasis would be on providing the students with the opportunity to acquire language rather than forcing them to learn it, by emphasizing language form. In this method, the key to comprehension and oral production is the acquisition of vocabulary. Thus, much opportunity for listening/speaking (when ready) is afforded to students. Class time is not devoted to grammatical lectures or mechanical exercises. Any explanation and practice of linguistic forms should be done outside of class for the most part. Outside work is planned carefully and structured to provide the necessary practice with language forms. Although this was Terrell's position in his earlier writings, he seemed to amend his position in his last writings (1991). He suggests that there might be some benefit to providing form-focused instruction as a means of establishing form-meaning relationships in communicative activities. Teaching grammar for the sake of grammar instruction is not effective. However, clarifying it in context, using advanced organizers to tie it in with communicative activities, does have some value.

According to Terrell (1977), error correction is negative in terms of motivation and attitude; thus, he does not advocate the correction of speech errors in the process of oral language development. This position reflects Krashen's affective filter hypothesis, which purports that when students experience an embarrassing situation, the affective filter goes up, interrupting the language acquisition process. Thus, error correction would have a negative effect on the process.

The Natural Approach bases language acquisition on the natural order of native language development. Because native language development follows a progression (as discussed in Part II, chapter 9), during the silent period, students would be allowed to respond in their native language. The emphasis is on listening comprehension, so if students respond in their native language, they are demonstrating comprehension. At the same time, students can be exposed to a wide variety of topics and still be comfortable in the communication process.

It is imperative, in this method, that teachers provide comprehensible input at all times. The use of visuals (graphs, charts, pictures, objects, realia), gestures, demonstrations, motherese/parentese (slower speech, simpler language repetition, rephrasing, clear enunciation) is required. In addition, the use of yes/no type questions; either/or type questions; and questions that require short answers is strongly suggested in the beginning stages of second language acquisition. The use of total physical response (TPR) is employed particularly during the comprehension (silent/preproduction) stage.

## The Communicative Approach

The Communicative Approach to language teaching is based on several theoretical premises:

1. **The communication principle:** Activities that involve communication promote the acquisition of language.
2. **The task-principle:** Activities that engage students in the completion of real-world tasks promote language acquisition.
3. **The meaningfulness principle:** Takes place when learners are engaged in activities that promote authentic and meaningful use of language.

The main goal in this approach is for the learner to become communicatively competent. The learner develops competency in using the language appropriately in given social contexts. Much emphasis is given to activities that allow the second language learner to negotiate meaning in activities that require oral communication in the second language.

In the Communicative Approach, it is important to create an "information gap" between speakers. Thus, the need to communicate is authentic because, communication must take place to narrow the gap and accomplish the task ( i.e., "I/we have what you need and you have what I/we need to complete our task"). The task cannot be completed individually; partners must work together to successfully complete the assigned task.

Classroom activities must be varied and must include interactive language games, information-sharing activities, social interactions, need for impromptu responses, and the use of authentic materials, such as the newspaper for oral discussions on current events.

Savignon (1983, 1997) suggests designing the curriculum to include language arts (or language analysis activities), language-for-a-purpose (content-based and immersion) activities, personalized language use, theatre arts (including simulations, role-plays, and social interaction games), and language use "beyond the classroom" (including planning activities that take the learners outside the classroom to engage in real-world encounters.

The Communicative Approach embraces the principle of "learning by doing", encouraging the use of English from the beginning of instruction. Thus, language acquisition takes place as a result of using the second language in meaningful communication from the onset in the process.

Kagan (1995), one of the greatest proponents of cooperative learning in the classroom, has described how this strategy is very effective in ESL classrooms, particularly when employing the Communicative Approach. According to Kagan, language acquisition is fostered by input that is comprehensible, developmentally appropriate, redundant, and accurate. In cooperative groups, students need to make themselves understood, so they naturally adjust their input to make it comprehensible. This is a must in communicative settings. In cooperative groups, students receive repeated input from the members in the group, providing the necessary redundancy for language learning to move from short-term comprehension to long-term acquisition.

When analyzing the Communicative Approach, it could be said that peer output is less accurate than teacher output. However, Kagan states that in cooperative groups, frequent communicative output produces language acquisition far more readily than does formal accurate input. The same could be said of the Communicative Approach. Thus, the use of cooperative groups in a communicative approach environment should be strongly encouraged.

## Points to Remember

❑ In the Grammar-Translation Method (also known as the Classical Method), the emphasis was on teaching grammar and employing translation to ascertain comprehension.

❑ The Grammar-Translation Method did not produce speakers of the languages studied.

❑ In the Grammar-Translation Method, much use of the native language was employed since the goal was not on oral proficiency.

❑ In the Grammar-Translation Method, teachers did not necessarily have to be fluent speakers of the target language since the focus was not on communication.

❑ The Grammar-Translation Method dominated public schools and university language teaching in the United States until World War II.

❑ Today, unfortunately, there is still some evidence of the use of the Grammar-Translation Method in some public schools.

❑ The Direct Method was a complete departure form the Grammar-Translation method.

❑ The Direct Method did not allow for the use of the native language in the classroom.

❑ The Direct Method required the use of visuals in order to convey meaning in an effort to eliminate translation.

❑ The emphasis in the Direct Method was on developing proficient thinkers and speakers in the target language.

❑ The Direct Method takes its name from the emphasis in the "direct" use of the target language.

❑ The most widely know application of the Direct Method is practiced at the Berlitz language schools.

- ❑ The Audio-lingual Method (based on behavioristic psychology) emphasized the use of habit forming as a way to develop language proficiency.

- ❑ The main goal of the Audio-lingual Method was to develop fluent speakers of the languages studied.

- ❑ In the Audio-lingual Method, the emphasis was on the rote memorization of dialogues.

- ❑ In the Audio-lingual Method, the belief was that much oral, practice (dialogue memorization) would result in communicative competence.

- ❑ The Audio-lingual Method was unsuccessful since students could recite the dialogues but could not "communicate" in the target language.

- ❑ TPR stands for Total Physical Response.

- ❑ In TPR, students are actively engaged in the language acquisition process by responding nonverbally (physically).

- ❑ TPR is an effective method to employ while second language learners are in the silent (comprehension/preproduction) period.

- ❑ The TPR method allows teachers to ascertain comprehension way before second language learners are able to respond verbally.

- ❑ TPR is an effective method of including second language learners in lessons while in the silent period.

- ❑ TPR helps second language learners develop a sense of belonging and accomplishment while still in the silent period.

- ❑ Pictures, objects, and realia are effective to enhance and expand the use of TPR in the classroom.

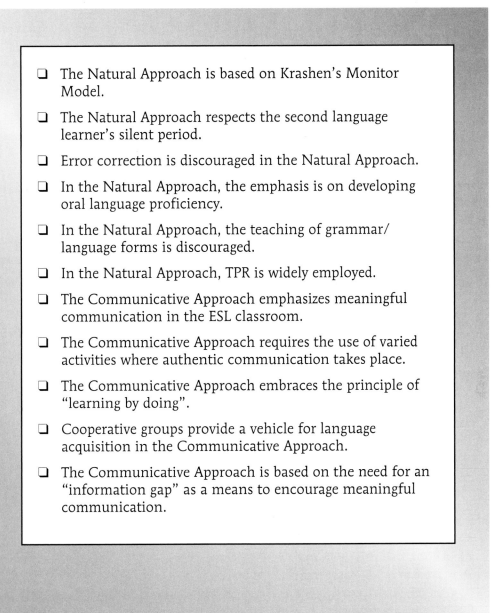

- ❏ The Natural Approach is based on Krashen's Monitor Model.
- ❏ The Natural Approach respects the second language learner's silent period.
- ❏ Error correction is discouraged in the Natural Approach.
- ❏ In the Natural Approach, the emphasis is on developing oral language proficiency.
- ❏ In the Natural Approach, the teaching of grammar/language forms is discouraged.
- ❏ In the Natural Approach, TPR is widely employed.
- ❏ The Communicative Approach emphasizes meaningful communication in the ESL classroom.
- ❏ The Communicative Approach requires the use of varied activities where authentic communication takes place.
- ❏ The Communicative Approach embraces the principle of "learning by doing".
- ❏ Cooperative groups provide a vehicle for language acquisition in the Communicative Approach.
- ❏ The Communicative Approach is based on the need for an "information gap" as a means to encourage meaningful communication.

# Chapter 11

## *Principles of Communicative Language Teaching*

## KEY ISSUES

❏ Principles underlying communicative language teaching

❏ Differences between traditional and current practices of language teaching

❏ The roles of learning goals, nature of input, setting and teacher and learner roles in communicative language teaching

❏ The changing views regarding grammar instruction

In a regular fourth-grade classroom, ESOL and non-ESOL students make up the class, which is taught by Ms. Williams, a monolingual English-speaking teacher. Some of the ESOL students speak Spanish or Vietnamese. Their proficiency levels vary. These fourth graders are learning about structures such as *more, less, most,* and *least*. In the past week, the students have been learning to use multiplication to solve real-life problems and learning about the basic food groups and their nutritional values. Ms. Williams plans to incorporate the mathematical concepts in her language arts lesson, which centers on the topic of food and nutrition.

Today the teacher has brought in a diagram of the Food Pyramid, picture cards of food, and some food labels. She wants the students to figure out their daily food intake and to create a balanced food plan for one day.

Ms. Williams begins the discussion by activating the students' background knowledge of everything they have eaten the day before. He asks them to look at their logs for the information they have recorded. As students reply, she lists their words on the board and sounds them out loud. She also pastes pictures of food that are listed on the board. She then asks students to count the number of servings they have eaten for each food. They are asked to find a partner and ask questions such as *"Did you eat more sweets than vegetables?"* or *"Did you eat less meat than fruit?"* *"What did you eat the most/least?"* Students are asked to reply by saying: *"I ate more X than Y"*, *" I ate less X than Y"*, or *"I ate X."*

Next, she shows them the Food Pyramid chart and talks about the different food groups and the amount of servings for each group. The teacher says, *"Last week, we learned that there are certain types of foods we should eat a lot of every day and foods we should eat less of. Can anyone tell me which food should we eat more of?"* Isabelle answers, *"Rice, we must eat more rice."* Ms. Williams replies, *"Yes, you're right, Isabelle."* Felipe raises his hand tentatively, *"Apple,"* and he points to pictures of fruits on the board. Ms. Williams sounds the words aloud for Felipe. She then points to the Food Pyramid chart and asks, *"What food group do apples and bananas belong to, Felipe?"* Felipe answers, *"Fruit."* Victor jumps in and says, *"meats."* Ms. Williams retorts, *"Do we need more meat than vegetables?"* Victor responds, *"No, more vegetables than meats. My father say meat is no good—they got many chemical inside their bodies and is no good for us."* Ms. Williams responds, *"Victor, I believe you are quite right. Yes, many farm animals are given hormones to make them grow faster and bigger. What do you think class?"* Discussion continues and Ms. Williams praises the students for their answers.

Ms. Williams continues to ask students for the name of the food group of the items they mentioned and discusses why they need different amounts of each. Then Ms. Williams passes out food labels to each pair of students. She asks the pair to state the amount of servings they would have if the food is eaten and if it exceeds the recommended daily servings.

Next she asks, "Teng, if we need 3 to 5 servings of vegetables each day, how much should we eat each week?" Teng answers, " *3 times 7 and 5 times 7, so we need about 21 to 35 servings each week.*" Ms. Williams says, "Nice job, Teng. *You're a math whiz!*" She then asks the class if there is another way to express the same idea. One student says, "we must eat 21 to 35 servings every week." *"Yes,"* says the teacher. Ms. Williams gives similar math problems for other students to answer and asks students to rephrase their statements.

Next, Ms. Williams breaks the students into small groups with mixed levels of English proficiency. She asks them to create a balanced food plan for one day and gives each group a Pyramid chart to fill in their information. She asks the less-proficient students to draw the pictures of food they select on their pyramid chart. She selects the more-proficient students to report orally to class the following information:

   a.   Foods they should eat more or less of
   b.   The number of servings of each food in their food plan

**H**ow would you characterize the classroom described in the vignette? Consider the following questions:

- What are the goals of language learning in this class?
- What areas of language are emphasized?
- Are students being drilled the language structures they need to learn?
- What is the role of content in language learning?
- What are students expected to do?
- What types of materials are used?
- How did the teacher use the materials to teach the structures?
- Are the students learning real-life language?
- What skills are they acquiring? Are they required to use these skills?
- How does the teacher respond to inaccuracies in language?

In the previous chapters, a plethora of language methods reveal the pendulum swing in our profession regarding the best way to teach and learn a second language. It is rather obvious that the early methods were strongly influenced by linguistic descriptions and contrastive analysis of languages and, hence, much of the teaching practices tend to emphasize linguistic analysis and overlearning of discrete linguistic rules. As educators gained more insights about how children acquire language naturally, they began to break away from drill and memorization to an emphasis on developing language learners' ability to communicate in the target language.

In the mid-1970s, many educators questioned the best way to promote second language acquisition based on what they have amassed from research on second language teaching and learning. Many researchers and educators realized that language learners who master and manipulate linguistic rules may not necessarily know how to use the language appropriately to perform the various linguistic functions typical of everyday social contexts. This distinction underscores a difference between linguistic competence and communicative competence. *Linguistic competence* refers to knowledge about language forms; *communicative competence* refers to knowledge that enables one to use language functionally and interactively. Hymes (1972) first introduced the term "communicative competence" which was later expanded by Canale and Swain (1980) and Bachman (1990). The term recognizes that social and cultural contexts of language use are just as important as the rules of language usage. Indeed, language learners must have communicative competence—knowing when to say what and how to whom to be successful at language learning. This principle of communicative competence provided impetus for the emphasis on communication as a goal for language learning. Canale (1983) identified four components that make up the communicative competence:

### Grammatical Competence

Focuses on the skills necessary to speak and write accurately using vocabulary, grammar, pronunciation, spelling, phonology, etc.

### Discourse Competence

Focuses on the skills to engage in conversations, which requires participants to connect sentences or stretches of discourse to form a series of meaningful, coherent discourse; also requires participants to become both sender and recipient of messages in spoken and written discourse.

### Sociolinguistic Competence

Focuses on using socioculturally appropriate language and discourse patterns in a variety of social settings. It requires understanding of social conventions, roles of participants, and purpose of interaction, which determines the appropriateness of forms (register) and meaning. For example, knowing how to make introductions, expressing opinions, complimenting, or declining an invitation require sociolinguistic competence.

### Strategic Competence

Focuses on manipulating language to achieve communication goals by utilizing verbal and nonverbal strategies. These strategies can be considered compensatory strategies that one can use to compensate for a breakdown in communication. Paraphrasing, repeating, avoidance, gesturing to convey a point, or modulating voice tone or volume to achieve effect are some examples.

In sum, language learners must be taught the social, cultural, and pragmatic features of language and be given tools for generating unrehearsed language beyond the immediate classroom task. In this new paradigm shift, educators are no longer overly consumed with developing learners' accuracy only, but help learners develop fluency. Many of the methods developed since the late 1970s reflect changing winds from a linguistic-structure approach to a Communicative Approach or communicative language teaching (Widdowson, 1990).

The emphasis on the term "approach" deserves special attention. The term "approach" focuses on how our beliefs, assumptions, and theoretical beliefs about the nature of language and language learning are compatible with classroom techniques. In other words, it is an umbrella term for a number of methods that may fall within the same theoretical and philosophical framework. For example, the Total Physical Response (TPR), Language Experience, and Natural Approach are considered communicative language teaching approaches because they all share fundamental ideas about the goal of language, which affects not only what is learned, what is expected of learners, and what actually happens in the classroom. In essence, these methods stress that language is an instrument of communication and, hence, its primary emphasis is on meaning rather than knowing structural forms. Fluency rather than accuracy is sought and, thus, errors in learning are natural developmental process. The learner negotiates and plays an active role in the process of learning. However, these methods may employ different techniques such as physical movements, personal experience, and natural language input through songs, poems, or stories to achieve the desired goal. Hence, the term "approach" implies a set of generalized beliefs, assumptions, and philosophical underpinnings instead of specific instructional procedures that reflect the approach. This position allows teachers to achieve some flexibility and at the same time, maintain a principled approach in their teaching Teachers do not slavishly adopt specific "methods" as a set of conventionalized procedures that fit all classroom contexts. Rather, effective teachers understand the value of undergirding their teaching with sound principles that enable them to decide what, why, and how they will design their instruction, how they will monitor their teaching effectiveness, and make necessary modifications. This kind of reflection allows teachers to gather new insights to make necessary modifications to their teaching plans.

Finnocchario and Brumfit (1982) summarize major differences between language approaches that focuses on form, namely the Audio-lingual methodology, and the approach that focuses on meaning, in this case, the Communicative Approach in table 11.1:

## Table 11-1
### A Comparison of the Audio-lingual Method and Communicative Language Teaching (Fonocchario & Brumfit, 1983)

| Audio-lingual Method | Communicative Language Teaching |
| --- | --- |
| Attends to structure and form more than meaning. | Meaning is paramount. |
| Demands more memorization of structure-based dialogs. | Dialogs, if used, center on communicative functions and are not normally memorized. |
| Language items are not necessarily contextualized. | Contextualization is a basic premise. |
| Language learning is learning structures, sounds, or words. | Language learning is learning to communicate. |
| Mastery or "overlearning" is sought. | Effective communication is sought. |
| Drilling is a central technique. | Drilling may occur, but peripherally. |
| Native-like speaker pronunciation is sought. | Comprehensible pronunciation is sought. |
| Grammatical explanation is avoided. | Any device that helps learners is accepted—varies according to their age, interest, experience, etc. |
| Communicative activities come only after plenty of rigid drills and controlled exercises. | Attempts to communicate may be encouraged from the very beginning. |

**Table 11-1** *(continued)*
**A Comparison of the Audio-lingual Method and Communicative Language Teaching (Fonocchario & Brumfit, 1983)**

| Audio-lingual Method | Communicative Language Teaching |
|---|---|
| The use of the student's native language is forbidden. | Judicious use of native language is accepted when feasible. |
| Translation is forbidden at early levels. | Translation is used when student needs it or benefits from it. |
| Reading and writing are deferred until speaking is mastered. | Reading and writing can start from the very first day, if desired. |
| The target linguistic system will be learned through the overt teaching of the patterns of the system. | The target linguistic system will be learned best through the process of struggling to communicate. |
| Linguistic competence is the desired goal. | Communicative competence is the desired goal. |
| Varieties of language are recognized but not emphasized. | Linguistic variation is a central concept in materials and methods. |
| The sequence of units is determined solely by linguistic complexity. | Sequencing is determined by any consideration of content function or meaning that maintains interest. |
| The teacher controls the learners and prevents them from doing anything that conflicts with theory. | Teachers help learners in any way that motivates them to work with the language. |
| "Language is habit," so error must be prevented at all costs. | Language is created often by the individual through trial and error. |
| Accuracy, in terms of formal correctness, is a primary goal. | Fluency and acceptable language are the primary goal: accuracy is judged not in the abstract but in context. |

**Table 11-1** *(continued)*
**A Comparison of the Audio-lingual Method and Communicative Language Teaching (Fonocchario & Brumfit, 1983)**

| Audio-lingual Method | Communicative Language Teaching |
|---|---|
| Students are expected to interact with the language system, embodied in machines and controlled materials found in language labs. | Students are expected to interact with other people, either in the flesh, through pair and group work, or in their writings. |
| The teacher is expected to specify the language that students are to use. | The teacher cannot know exactly what language the students will use. |
| Intrinsic motivation will spring from an interest in the structure of language. | Intrinsic motivation will spring from an interest in what is being communicated by the language. |

David Nunan (1991) has developed a list of key features of communicative language teaching. He describes the features of communicative language teaching as the following:

- Focuses on meaning through interaction in the target language
- Uses materials or texts that reflect authentic or real-world language
- Allows learners to rehearse language used outside the classroom by focusing on language forms or skills and the learning process
- Focuses on previous knowledge, experiences, or skills learners bring into the classroom as important contributors to language learning
- Plans a careful link between classroom language and real-world language

From these lists, significant features that are central to communicative language teaching can be extrapolated. These features are categorized into the following broad areas as shown in table 11.2:

---

### Table 11-2
### Summary of Key Areas of Communicative Language Teaching

*Goals*
Focus on meaning instead of discrete language forms; fluency and some level of accuracy are necessary in any Interaction; emphasis on language use also implies that specific skills may be developed in the process of learning.

*Inputs*
Focus on language that is relevant to real-life use; has a strong, real-world focus reflected by choice of topics, language functions, use of relevant personal or real-world knowledge, and the way members of the target language use language to communicate in different settings.

*Roles*
Focus on learners having an active, negotiative role; learners are both senders and receivers of input.

*Settings*
Provides opportunities for learners to use language through oral and written interaction with other people inside and outside the classroom boundaries; cooperative learning structures in either pair or group work expose learners to a variety of language input and pragmatic skills in interactive discourse.

---

What is abundantly clear in these lists is that there is an implicit agreement between them—the idea that language learning in the classroom can transfer to other uses of language in the real world. Hence, if the desired goal of a communicative approach is to provide learners with the transfer of skills and knowledge developed inside the classroom to its use in the outside world, then learners need exposure to the types of language encounter in real life. This links directly with Nunan's (1991) concept of language authenticity, which is important within the communicative language teaching framework because it influences how teachers select materials and design activities for interaction to achieve their learning or teaching objectives. The following discussion highlights the implications of authenticity, roles, and settings in language learning within a communicative language framework.

## Language Authenticity

Nunan (1989) defined authenticity as "materials that have not been specifically produced for the purposes of language teaching." This definition implies that any oral and written texts that are used by native speakers for social or transactional purposes are considered authentic texts. The rationale for selecting authentic materials includes: (a) they are much more interesting to learners; (b) they provide a "rich" source of input because they focus more on meaning than on form; (c) they have high face validity to learners because learners perceive these materials to be relevant, thereby increasing learners' intrinsic motivation; and (d) they expose learners to cultural concepts and skills through language use (Little, Devitt, & Singleton, 1994; Mitchell, 1994). Empirical research has also supported the use of authentic texts in language learning. Kienbaum, Russell, and Welty (1986) and Bacon Finneman (1990) suggest that authentic materials can increase intrinsic motivation, which will result in successful acquisition. Duquette, Dunnett, and Papalia (1987) also found that authentic materials expose learners to cultural awareness besides language, a desirable goal if language learners wish to participate in the target culture effectively and appropriately.

Equally important is what learners are asked to do with the material. In the Communicative Approach, learners must be actively engaged in "comprehending, manipulating, producing, or interacting in the target language" (Nunan, 1989, p.10); these tasks can help learners to use language for genuine communicative purposes, just as native speakers are "interested in meanings, and in getting things done" (Mitchell,1994, p. 37). In other words, selecting materials that contain real-life language use does not, in itself, make the task authentic; its authenticity is also contingent upon whether learners are asked to interact and become involved with the tasks in pursuit of a communicative outcome.

Nunan (1989) divides communicative tasks into two types: real-world and pedagogic. Real-world tasks resemble the type of interaction that occurs outside the classroom. Pedagogic tasks are those that are typically done in the classroom, but they enable learners to build necessary skills that are important for communication in the target language. In fact, the division between real-world and pedagogic is not so distinct. For example, will the students in the opening vignette be required to describe their diet outside of the classroom setting? The answer may perhaps be yes or no. But will students find themselves using language structures such as "more ... than..." or "less ... than..." in making comparisons in the real world? These structures are likely to occur. Thus, it is important for teachers to examine whether classroom tasks will equip and empower students to produce language they would need in the real world. To determine whether language tasks are authentic or not, teachers must also make judicious use of appropriate, authentic texts and activities that will guide students through a developmental process and give students adequate exposure to the language they will eventually need to function autonomously.

## Role of Teacher

In many traditional classrooms, the teacher controls what goes on and what learners will say and do. In the communicative classroom, the teacher does not control in the same way that teachers do in the traditional classrooms. Brown (1994) suggests that teachers play different roles to create an interactive classroom. Teachers must play the role of both a controller and a director. In order for interaction to take place, teachers must plan for interaction to take place. Specifically, they must know how to initiate initial response from learners, and how students will demonstrate performance skills. They must ensure the flow and direction of interaction and the production of desired responses. Teachers must also be the facilitator who advances the process of learning, helping students to overcome any "roadblocks" (Brown, 1994, p.161). They must provide necessary motivation for students to take risks in discovering and using language pragmatically. Teachers must also be a resource, giving advice and proper counseling to students when they ask for guidance. Brown explains that a communicative language teacher must be able to assume these roles to assist students with varying levels of proficiency, to move from "total dependence to relatively total independence" (p. 162).

## Role of Learner

When teachers ask students to communicate in a language in which they have partial control, they are asking them to take risks. This means that learners must be made to feel comfortable in order to experiment with language. Learners must also take responsibility for their own learning, and develop autonomy and skills in learning how to learn. In a communicative classroom, learners may sometimes have to learn and organize information on their own and become creative in experimenting ways of creating and using language. They are also required to be active by performing tasks in class, by interacting with fellow learners and the teacher, and by listening, reading, and practicing language. They may also be asked to organize what they have learned by making notes and charts, displaying them, and using these materials to communicate. In other words, there are plenty of opportunities for students to rehearse language and for learning about how to learn.

Learners in the process of learning must also learn to tolerate uncertainties and ambiguities. For example, learners may be encouraged to read or talk by comprehending the overall gist of the message as opposed to concentrating on every single word in the message. And if they do not understand, they should be willing to ask for help and error correction and ultimately learn from their errors. Learners must also learn to live with errors and not let errors become an impediment to their learning. In general, learners in a communicative paradigm must eventually learn how to take charge of their learning, with guided support.

To help learners become self-autonomous, teachers must create many opportunities for them to use language to express their ideas and opinions, and to react to different ideas and opinions. Teachers must also encourage learners to not be afraid of making mistakes as they are learning to improve their English and literacy skills. To achieve all of these goals, teachers must create a classroom environment where students and teachers respect differences in opinions and ideas and suspend judgments until different perspectives have been heard and understood. This is especially important when students are learning historical events, concepts, and issues in their textbooks and curriculum units from the perspectives of the dominant group. For example, in concepts related to the discovery of America, the role of the pioneers often reflects views of European Americans and often ignores or marginalizes the feelings and experiences of different indigenous groups in America or those who were brought to America by slavery. Such a classroom climate can create stereotypes about racial and ethnic groups and also can cause nonmainstream students to feel left out of the American story. Teachers must also provide models and guidance for learning how to learn through various discussion and shared reading and writing activities so that new English learners will be able to apply and transfer skills they have learned.

## Settings

According to Nunan (1989), " 'settings' refer to two specific things: (i) the classroom arrangements specified or implied in the task," (p. 91) which he refers to as "learning mode," and (ii) task that occurs in the classroom or outside the classroom which he refers to as "environment." Learning mode refers to whether learners are working individually or in groups or working at a self- or teacher-directed pace. In contrast, "environment" refers to where the actual learning takes place. Wright (1987:58) illustrates different ways in which learners are grouped within the classroom setting in figure 11.1.

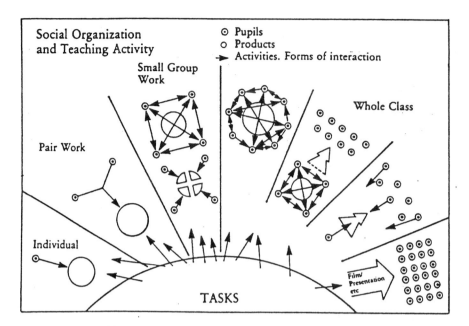

**Figure 11.1 Roles of Teachers and Learners**

Knerr and James (1991) advocate partner work and small-group work to maximize the opportunity for students to practice grammar, vocabulary, and language strategies that are presented in a whole class situation. These types of cooperative learning have become increasingly popular in second language instruction wherein each group member is given a specific role or information that must be shared with other group members before the student can complete the final product and receive a group reward. The cooperative and noncompetitive atmosphere for learning not only improves group relations between learners in the classrooms, but also improves their academic achievement by lowering their affective filter or anxiety, which is often associated with learning something new, be it language or content information. Other benefits of cooperative learning include:

- Developing a greater sense of accountability and responsibility for students' learning as well as for their group if the task creates a necessity for each member in the group to contribute to the whole.

- Exposing learners to natural exchanges as students engage in extended discourses that are more realistic as learners try to decipher the message amidst background noise, false starts, or listening to two people talking simultaneously.

- Encouraging learners to become communicators in a wide range of situations and to practice a full range of language strategies such hypothesizing, generalizing, disagreeing, summarizing, and clarifying (Long & Porter, 1985).

Knerr and James (1991, pp. 62–63) suggest the following ways for grouping learners on a specific task:

a. **Interest groups:** Particularly useful for longer and involved projects

b. **Homogenous ability groups:** A traditional method of grouping that allows learners to work at the learners' own pace as each group is given tasks that are tied to ability. A possible setback of this type of grouping would be the stigma associated with being a "slower" group and its impact on learning.

c. **Mixed-ability groups:** Learners of varying abilities are placed together on specific task. The advantage is that stronger students can help weaker students and, in turn, reinforce their own learning while weaker students benefit from the help of a peer in a more relaxed setting. Students can work with the same group to help group members attain familiarity with each other and to provide a stable source of support for new language learners who are still learning classroom routines.

d. **Random grouping:** Students are randomly selected to form a group by counting off; grouping by birthday, hobby, and so forth; placing names in a hat and having students to draw; or putting numbers or words in a box and pairing students with the matching item, and so on. Benefits of this type of grouping include the flexibility of students to work with different people on different tasks and thus expand their opportunity of getting to know one another and learn from other classmates.

e. **Topic- or task-driven grouping:** The jigsaw is a common type of cooperative group used in class. Each student is responsible for a portion of the topic or task. There are two subgroups in a jigsaw: home and topic. Members of the home group are given different assignments. For example, if a class is studying a unit on endangered animals, the teacher may divide the work into several topics: what animals are considered endangered and where they are found; what causes animals to be endangered, steps taken to protect endangered species; laws or regulations related to endangered animals, and so forth. Each member of the home group can be given a topic and a series of questions to guide his or her research and become an 'expert" in the topic. All members working on the same topic will get together to investigate their topic, and to help each other with any difficult words and other difficulties before seeking the teacher's help. After students have completed their assigned parts, they rejoin their home groups and share a piece of the jigsaw they were working on earlier. The members of the home group will then check to make sure that each member understands all the topics and can put all the information together into a product that can be presented in class.

f.  **Personality types:** Groups can be formed based on how well different personalities work together. Anyone who has been a classroom teacher can attest to the fact that there is a wide range of personalities that can influence classroom dynamics and learning. Some learners appear to be leaders; others are great motivators, listeners, focus setters, and so forth. For example, a group made up of students who tend to take charge and dominate others could actually restrict participation of linguistically less- proficient and quieter students. This type of grouping does not provide a low-anxiety environment for new language learners to feel safe in taking risks for fear of appearing foolish when they make mistakes. Likewise, a group of relatively shy and less talkative students or those who come from cultures where it is improper to speak extensively in the classroom may not actively participate in group tasks that require high levels of oral interaction. Successful group work often depends on how well members are able to focus on their task. It is instrumental to have a member who can guide all members to remain in focus and direct other members to keep the same pace until their task is completed. In addition, it is also important to remember that communication often requires a degree of empathy or the ability to understand the other person's feelings and thinking, or otherwise communication will suffer. If empathy is predictive of success in language learning, it is important to train or prepare learners to develop empathy and understand how different cultures express it. An unbalanced composition of students may not maximize opportunities for engagement of learners with diverse personality styles.

In many classrooms today, much of what students are learning goes beyond the confines of the classroom walls. In other words, teaching and learning can occur in natural settings found in individual communities. Many teachers who believe in the importance of teaching communicative language have included the use of resources in the wider community where learners can collect information on specific themes or topics that are being learned in class, adopt communicative roles that have relevance to their real-life, and interact with native speakers. For example, trips to a zoo, a library, a fire station, or a health facility can provide real-life language and situations that learners will find useful in helping them to learn, to become more interested in what they are learning, and become more confident about their interpersonal social skills.

# The Changing Role of Grammar in Communicative Language Teaching

Since the advent of communicative language teaching, the role of grammar in language learning, particularly in the classroom setting, has been challenged and has become the topic of many debates in the language teaching circles. Disagreements occur over whether grammar instruction is appropriate in a communicative classroom and what type of grammar instruction is appropriate. According to Celce-Murcia (1997), the role of "grammar is often misunderstood in the teaching field" (p. 1). Even if grammar was not eliminated, it was certainly neglected in many communicative classrooms. Celce-Murcia (1997) lists some commonly held misconceptions or "myths" about grammar and challenges these views:

## Myths about the Role of Grammar Teaching

1. **Grammar is acquired naturally; it need not be taught.** Although some learners are able to acquire second language grammar without any formal instruction in grammar, there are still learners who may not be able to acquire proficiency without direct instruction. The question, however, is not so much whether learners can or cannot become proficient without grammar instruction, but more importantly, if learners can become proficient at a faster rate. It is not surprising that some learners take longer than others to fully master the English grammatical system, just as native English speakers developed mastery over some structures of their language later in adolescent years (Chomsky, 1969). Unless more studies provide evidence for the effect of implicit teaching of grammar on language learning across age levels and different sociolinguistic contexts of learning, educators cannot simply rule out the potential benefits of teaching grammar on language proficiency for some groups of learners.

2. **Grammar is a collection of meaningless forms and arbitrary rules.** When people think of grammar, they automatically think of meaningless rules of language. However, grammar is not simply formulaic sets of rules. Grammar consists of arbitrary rules that embody morphosyntactic, semantic, and pragmatic interaction. For

instance, the passive construction can only be formed with transitive verbs, (i.e. a verb that needs an object such as *see, teach,* or *eat,* is composed of the *be* verb + the past participle and has a preposition *by* before the agent in the predicate). But passive construction has meaning; it shifts the status of the receiver, and so the focus from *I* shifts to the book as in *"Janet gave him the book."* and *"The book was given to him by Janet."* Are these rules arbitrary? Not really. Passives are used when the receiver is the theme, when the doer of the action is unknown, when the identity of the doer is obvious and, thus, unnecessary to mention, or when someone wishes to conceal the identity of the doer of the action. As such, the agent and object movement can be explained by the sense that the grammar conveys, which supports the view that grammar rules are not arbitrary. What does this mean to the English learner? To be a proficient language user, English learners must understand how to use the English passives accurately and appropriately.

3. **Grammar is boring.** Many people have the impression that grammar can only be taught by repetition and memorization of rules. However, this does not mean that there are no benefits of drills on language learning. If drills are used in a meaningful and purposeful way, the drill will not be monotonous and unmeaningful. For example, by asking students to reflect on what they typically eat, students can learn to use the structures for comparisons—*more, less, most, and least*—in an engaging way and not just provide mechanical responses.

4. **Students have different learning styles.** Not all students can learn grammar. There is no doubt that some students have a more analytical approach to learning and approach language learning tasks as "rule formers (p. 3). However, these learners may not necessarily be fluent language users. To date, there has been no research that shows that students are incapable of learning grammar. However, the fact that we can master our first language is a testimony of our ability to learn the grammar.

5. **Grammar structures are learned one at a time.** Although some teachers believe that grammar can be taught one structure at a time, there is no reason why students can not learn other structures before they master new ones that are taught. Thus, it is not surprising to hear English learners make errors in using the present progressive tense after they have acquired the simple present tense, just as it is common among children learning their first language to make errors such as *wented* even though they have acquired the past form of irregular verbs.

This regression is considered a natural phenomenon in language learning. "Unless learners internalize the distinct uses of the two tenses, it is expected that they will backslide between correct and incorrect language use."

6. **Grammar has to do only with sentence-level and subsentence-level phenomena.** Just as subject-verb agreement or word order determines the grammaticality at sub-sentence and sentence levels, respectively, there are grammar rules that are applied at the discourse level. The choice of using the definite article "the" after a noun phrase has been introduced the first time is discourse-governed, just as switching between past and present tense in a narrative may be explained by the whole discourse context. Consequently, it is necessary to explain grammar at both the sentence and intra-sentential and discourse levels.

7. **Grammar and vocabulary are areas of knowledge. Reading, writing, speaking, and listening are the four skills.** Learning rules of the language does not always guarantee that learners are able to use the newly learned grammar and vocabulary for communicative purposes. Many who have had the experience of learning a second or foreign language know that becoming proficient in a new language is a developmental process that takes a lot of practice. The question, then, is what kind of practice would speed up language acquisition? Ellis (1993) argues that grammar teaching within a communicative framework should aim at raising learners' awareness instead of practicing toward accurate productions. VanPatten and Cardierno (1993) support this view by arguing that students benefit more from the experience of processing linguistic input than by simply being given a grammatical explanation followed by practice in producing the target structures.

8. **Grammar provides the rules/explanations for all of the structures in a language.** Just as words and their meanings change over time, grammatical rules are not static either. Numerous examples can be found that were once frowned upon by language specialists and English teachers, such as nouns turning into verbs. These changes have now become commonplace in the English language today. Consider the following:

*We bus children to school where the teachers school them.*
*We pig out at the local eatery.*
*We horn our way into difficult situations and we weasel our way out of them.*

These examples demonstrate that grammar is subject to changes, presenting additional problems for the new language learners. It is imperative that teachers bear in mind that learning grammar is a process that requires learners to attend to linguistic analysis and descriptions as well as how speakers use grammar to accomplish their communicative endeavor.

9. **I don't know enough to teach grammar.** It is not uncommon to hear teachers admitting that they don't know enough about grammar, let alone teach it to their students. However, as native speakers of the language, most teachers have a sense for the meaningfulness and appropriateness of a grammar item in question but may not be able to describe or analyze the grammar structure per se. To give effective grammar instruction, teachers must be able to connect the form, meaning, and use of a particular grammar structure. Ultimately, an effective grammar instruction is one that teaches learners how to use their grammar rules to communicate specific meanings that are appropriate to the task at hand.

## When Is Grammar Teaching Helpful?

Students can benefit from grammar instruction in the following ways:

1. By knowing grammar, students may be able to notice "the gap" between their own productions and the input they receive.
2. Students can benefit from learning short, simple rules that they can easily recall and use for monitoring their output.
3. When students' attention is drawn to specific structures, they are also made aware of how things are said, which, in turn, serves as input for planning their future utterances.
4. Some students vary in their expectations of what good language instruction should be. Depending on their cultural and training backgrounds, some students expect grammar instruction and will become more receptive to try different activities if their grammar needs are met.
5. Older learners tend to benefit more from explicit grammar instruction because they have more experience and knowledge about language to analyze and break down language into smaller parts. Younger learners tend to prefer interactive activities from which they will get the opportunities to use particular grammatical structures.

# Strategies for Teaching Communicative Grammar

The following are some examples of communicative grammar activities that can help students bridge knowledge and practice of structures through meaningful content and situations. These activities can help students practice specific grammatical structures to develop communicative competence.

## Role-play

### Imperative Structure (Giving directions)

a.   Create an emergency situation and let the students work together in small groups or individually in giving instructions to the other students and teachers about what they should do. These situations can provide students practice for using language connected to routine school emergency activities such as how to prepare for a hurricane or a fire at the school.

### Contracted Be with impersonal pronoun it

b.   Play Santa. Give students one unusual/odd gift which they must accept graciously. These gifts can be household items such as can opener, rubber bands, dental floss, paper clips, a screwdriver, and so on. Items can be used more than once. Model the target pattern such as "Oh! It's a (noun). How nice!" Teachers should also point out the nuances of stress, intonation, and facial expressions when saying.

## Question/answers

### Present continuous:

a.   What ... Now? This game requires teachers to set up a hypothetical situation in a sentence and then ask each student prompt question, for examples:

It's 9 a.m. in Florida now. Jing-jing, what is your _____ (any family member) doing now?

It's about 8 in the morning in Madrid right now. Sabri, what is your brother doing now?

The student responds by using any of the following correct forms: *"He's eating breakfast,"* " *She's sleeping."*

Encourage students to begin their sentences with: *What do you think they are doing?* And begin their responses with *"I think ... is/are ..."* Teachers can use a map or hand drawn clocks to illustrate the time zones around the world.

### Future Tense

a.  Pretend that the whole class is going to make a visit to a fortune teller who sees, knows, and tells all!

First dim the lights. Then, the teacher can become the fortune teller by modeling the structures they will be using. The teacher could wear a bright colored scarf, spread a cloth over the table, and invite a student to step into his/her parlor. With the aid of a crystal ball (or any ball-shaped object), the fortune teller (the teacher) will answer any questions posed in the future tense. After modeling the role-play, the students can work in small groups of 4–5, with each group to choose their own fortune teller. Each student will then get a chance to talk about the future.

## Points to Remember

❑ The framework for understanding the communicative language teaching approach can be understood by conceptualizing four interacting aspects:
  - What is the goal of language learning?
  - In what does the goal interface with the types of input that will be used for teaching language?
  - What are the roles of teachers and learners?
  - How do these roles impact classroom organization and types of instructional activities?

❑ Communicative language competence requires learners to draw from four knowledge domains: grammatical, sociolinguistic, discourse, and strategic. Learners must have knowledge of grammar, pronunciation, spelling, and phonology and be able to use these forms of knowledge to transform a string of utterances into a coherent written or conversational discourse. Learners must also have knowledge of how speakers use language to express different things. At the same time, learners must develop effective strategies for problem solving and coping with difficulties in comprehension and communication so that they will maintain an interest and motivational levels in learning the language.

❑ Although grammar teaching has been largely ignored in language practices, there is a pedagogical rationale for including some level of explicit grammar instruction. When determining what type of grammatical instruction is most effective for each learner, teachers must bear in mind a few simple rules such as the brevity and simplicity of the rule, the age of the learners, the learner's previous language training and views about grammar instruction, and when to introduce grammar explanation.

# Part III

## Organizing and Planning for Second Language Instruction

# Chapter 12

## Integrating Language and Content

In the United States, Krashen's theory (1982) of second language acquisition has influenced the development of integrated instruction at all levels. Krashen suggests that a second language is more successfully acquired when the conditions are similar to those present in first language acquisition; that is, when the focus of instruction is on meaning rather than on form, when language input is at or just above the proficiency of the learner; and when there is sufficient opportunity to engage in meaningful use of that language in a relatively anxiety-free environment. This suggests that the focus of the second language classroom should be on something meaningful, such as academic content, and that modification of the target language facilitates language acquisition and makes academic content accessible to second language learners (Crandall, 1994).

# What Is Meant by "Integrating Language and Content"?

The language immersion program is one of the most effective innovations to emerge in second language education during the last three decades. In this method of second language instruction, the regular curriculum is taught through the use of the second language (L2). Thus, the second language is developed at the same time that the subject matter content is being taught. Although the primary focus of immersion programs is academic instruction, language development occurs because teachers are cognizant of the advantages of integrating both academic content and language. The first immersion programs were developed in Canada to provide English-speaking students with the opportunity to learn French, Canada's other official language. Since that time, immersion programs have been adopted in many parts of the United States.

There are numerous advantages in integrating second language instruction and academic content instruction. First, this mode of instruction is more effective than teaching the language in isolation. When the integration takes place, proficiency in the target language is not a prerequisite to academic development; rather, language acquisition results from using the second language to perform authentic communication functions. It is a known fact that language is acquired most effectively when it is employed for communication in meaningful and significant social situations. The academic content of the school curriculum can provide a meaningful basis for second language learning, assuming that the academic content is of interest or value to the students.

Second, students are able to acquire new vocabulary and language structures and patterns as they are immersed in important and interesting academic content. The second language learners are able to interact in meaningful communicative contexts. In this model, the second language learners acquire language at the same time that they acquire scientific knowledge or historical perspectives. Authentic classroom communication provides a purposeful and motivating context for acquiring the communicative functions of the second language. In the absence of meaningful communication, language is only learned as rote memorization, devoid of conceptual or communicative substance.

A third advantage of an Integrated Approach is that it addresses the relationship between language and other aspects of human development. Language, cognition, and social awareness develop concurrently in young children. Integrated second language instruction seeks to keep these components of development together so that second language acquisition is an integral part of social-cognitive development in school settings. Finally, knowing how to use language in one social context or academic domain does not necessarily mean knowing how to use it in others (Genesee, 1995). For example, evidence indicates that the way language is employed in particular academic domains, such as mathematics (Spanos, Rhodes, Dale, & Crandall, 1988), is not the same in other academic domains such as social studies (Short, 1994). For this reason, it is important for teachers to identify language concepts that are tied in to the subject matter content. Once these concepts are identified, teachers must introduce these employing second language acquisition strategies. In this fashion, the second language learner is not only acquiring the subject matter content but is also acquiring the language concepts so necessary for effective communication.

## Models of Integrated Approaches

### Experiential Learning

Experiential learning has been defined as the process whereby knowledge is developed through the transformation of the experience of the learner who is at the center of the learning process (Tarkington, 1996). The experiential base for learning requires that students take responsibility for deriving meaning from their experiences. The impact of experiential learning is affected by various factors, including the reality of the experience or the relevance to the student, the level of risk and uncertainty (how meaningful it is to the student), and student reflection, which derives the acquisition of knowledge from the experience. Experiential learning goes beyond having a common experience in the classroom and dictating a story (Language Experience Approach). It goes beyond an isolated experience; it involves the students in adventurous learning. The regular classroom imposes limitations to the regular classroom when teachers try to employ experiential learning. This approach can be employed in a classroom; however, it requires a creative and resourceful teacher who will set aside the traditional ways of teaching and transform the classroom into a "learning by living" type of environment. In this type of environment, students acquire knowledge instead of simply memorizing a set of facts.

Experiential learning is mostly associated with alternative schools because teachers require special training to develop the necessary strategies for helping students analyze the experiences they encounter (Crew, 1977). Although the regular classroom is limiting in and of itself, teachers who experiment with this approach to teaching, provide an excellent experience for their students, as students learn by experiencing. This is how language develops from the onset; thus, language develops naturally in the experiential learning classroom. It is an excellent way to provide the concrete knowledge so indispensable for second language learners. Incorporating well-planned field trips, in which students have an opportunity to interact with the environment, is one way of providing this type of "adventurous" learning. These field trips must go beyond simple "exposure" to be considered experiential learning.

## Content-based Language Learning

In content-based language learning, teachers use instructional materials, learning tasks, and classroom techniques from academic content areas as vehicles for developing language. The emphasis is on developing language while an academic subject area is employed. Language development takes precedence over the academic subject content, although the acquisition of science, social studies, and/or mathematics subject content takes place simultaneously. Language arts skills such as listening for details, or oral reporting and comparing/contrasting and/or organizing information by using charts, diagrams, or tables are developed by means of the subject matter content. New vocabulary is acquired and language interference problems are addressed because the input is chosen deliberately from the academic textual material to provide the appropriate context for this to happen. Oral language as well as reading and writing skills are emphasized in this type of approach. This approach is of much benefit for second language learners because language development is stressed at the same time that students are acquiring knowledge in academic subjects. For this method to be successful, second language acquisition strategies must be employed. The following strategies are essential: "parentese" (slowing down, rephrasing, repeating, simplifying language), making input comprehensible (through use of concrete objects, realia, pictures, demonstration, gesturing, use of charts, graphs, diagrams), organizing instruction from simple to complex, and scaffolding (building upon prior knowledge, connecting knowledge). For a wealth of ideas on how to apply this approach refer to Part V of this book.

## Sheltered English, or Specially Designed Academic Instruction in English (SDAIE)

In the Sheltered English, or SDAIE approach, second language learners are taught subject matter content entirely in English. The emphasis is on teaching subject matter content skills and concepts such as those specific to mathematics, science, social studies, and history. Students develop language skills while being engaged in cognitively demanding and grade-level appropriate material. Teachers must employ second language acquisition techniques in order to ensure comprehension. The name "sheltered" English is given because the teachers use sheltering techniques such as simplifying the language employed, adapting the textual material and introducing and reinforcing new vocabulary throughout the units of instruction.

Sheltered instruction is most effective for students who have already achieved intermediate English language proficiency. This type of program is found mostly in secondary schools. The second language learners may still receive English language support in an ESL pullout program. This would vary from school district to school district depending on district resources and student need.

## Language Experience Approach (LEA)

In the Language Experience Approach, the students, in a way, develop their own reading materials, which the teacher later employs to teach reading skills. It is an excellent approach to teaching reading, not only to second language learners but to native speakers of English as well.

The teacher becomes a facilitator of knowledge. Students are engaged in a common experience, and afterward they dictate a story. The teacher records the story on the board, experience chart paper, or a transparency.

The following scenario illustrates the approach:

On a table in front of her class, Ms. Ramirez has an electric skillet, a bottle of cooking oil, some plastic knives, and four ripe plantains, called "amarillos" in Puerto Rico. Today she is going to teach the children how to make "amarillo frito" (fried ripe plantain), or "maduros", as the Cubans call them.

Ms. Ramirez asks the students, "What do you think we are going to do today?" The students give various responses, including cooking. Then, Ms. Ramirez reiterates that they will be cooking, adding that they will be cooking "amarillos" and tasting them. She also explains that afterward they will be dictating a story to her about what they did and she will be writing it down.

The lesson continues, by Ms. Ramirez pouring some oil in the skillet as she describes what she is doing. While the oil gets hot, she demonstrates how to peel and cut the amarillos. Ms. Ramirez fries the amarillos and serves all the students a piece for them to taste. The students willingly participate in the lesson, taste the amarillos/maduros, and share their impressions with each other.

After the students have finished tasting the amarillos, the paper plates and napkins are thrown away, the cooking utensils are put away, and the second part of the lesson begins.

Ms. Ramirez engages the students in dictating a story based on the common experience they just had. The students eagerly participate in dictating their sentences. The students dictated the following story.

### Making and Tasting "Amarillos"

Today, Ms. Ramirez *teached* us to make "amarillos." (Pedro) We *peel* the "amarillos" and we cut them in pieces. (Juana) Then, we fried the "amarillos." (Brian) The "amarillos" are soft after you fry them. (Steven)

After we fried the "amarillos", we ate them. (Janet) I like the "amarillos," Mary said. They are sweet. Ricardo said: *"I no like dem, dey are mushy!* But many like the "amarillos." We *sink* yummy. (Margarita) We *cook* more tomorrow! (Maria).

Ms. Ramirez wrote down exactly what the students dictated. She also wrote the name of the student who dictated the particular sentence. This helps the students in developing positive self-concepts since they are proud to see their names on the chart paper, board, or overhead. In addition, when reading the story out loud, students have no difficulty reading the sentences since they remember what they dictated. This type of reading requires minimal decoding skills because they already know the content.

Ms. Ramirez continues by saying, "Now we are going to read our "slopy copy" and make any necessary revisions. As the students read their sentences, she encourages other students to help decide whether or not some minor changes need to be made. Thus corrections were made. The edited story reads as follows:

Today Ms. Ramirez taught us to make "amarillos". (Pedro) We peeled the "amarillos" and we cut them in pieces. ( Juan) Then, we fried the "amarillos". (Brian) The "amarillos" are soft after you fry them. (Steven) After we fried the "amarillos", we ate them. (Janet) I like "amarillos". Mary said. They are sweet. I don't like them, they are mushy! Ricardo said. But many of us like the "amarillos". We think they are yummy. (Margarita) We will cook more tomorrow! (Maria)

In the upcoming days, Ms. Ramirez will employ the story dictated by the students as the text for reading instruction. This dictated story provides the textual material that will serve as a basis for teaching such skills as capitalization; punctuation, including quotation marks and exclamation marks; relational words; vocabulary development and even aspects of grammar (such as past tense of verbs). In addition, Ms. Ramirez will address some language interferences that her Hispanic children are having (such as the "th" sound which they are substituting for "d" voiced and "s" voiceless and the use of *no* instead of "do not" or contraction "don't" to indicate negation).

The LEA approach is based on the premise that reading is facilitated when it stems from what the students already have as background knowledge.

In the language acquisition sequence of listening, speaking, reading, and writing, students who can "speak" or "dictate" stories are likely to have much more success in trying to read those stories, because the vocabulary is already in their background knowledge. As soon as they see in print what they have dictated, they are able to read it because they already can speak the words. Thus, all the teacher has done is demonstrate the process by which his or her own meanings, expressed orally, are put into print form. When students can read their own stories, they are able to experience the success of independent reading. This is reinforcing and helps to develop an interest in further reading.

To illustrate the point just discussed, try reading the following passage:

> La casita de campo estaba rodeada de muchos arboles frondosos los cuales le deban una sombra *exquisita*. La pareja de enamorados, sentados en el balcon, escuchaban el riachuelo que atraviesa el *terreno*. Pajaros de todos *colores* y tamanos, llenaban la *atmosfera* de canticos placenteros.*

How did it feel to try to read something in a language you do not know? Probably, very frustrating, to say the least. However, if you had dictated the passage, you would know the vocabulary; thus, making it so much easier for you to read.

If you know any Spanish, you may have identified some of the words. You may have been able to attain some meaning of the passage by using the context surrounding the words you knew. However, if you do not know any Spanish at all, the only words you may have been able to "guess" would be the four in italics: "exquisita" (for "exquisite")," terreno" (for "terrain") "colores" (for "colors"), and "atmosfera" (for atmosphere"). These words called "cognates", might have made you think that the paragraph relates to some type of atmosphere that is exquisite and something regarding some type of terrain and colors, but that is about all. These three words did not help you in gaining the meaning of what you read. This is exactly what your second language learners experience.

The beauty of the LEA is that it builds on the linguistic, social, and cultural strengths of the students, because it captures in print a common experience the students have had employing language. It can also be employed for students, individually or in small groups, to dictate their own stories based on their own social/cultural background.

*English translation:

    The small country home was surrounded by many thick trees that gave it a delightful shade. The very-much-in-love couple, sitting on the porch, could hear the sound of the flowing water from the creek that flows through the property. Birds of all sizes and colors filled the atmosphere with pleasant melodies.

## Points to Remember

❑ When integrating language and content, the second language is developed at the same time that subject matter content is being taught.

❑ There are numerous advantages of integrating language and content:
   A. Language is not taught in isolation, it is taught in context.
   B. Second language learners acquire new vocabulary and language structures as they are immersed in interesting academic content.
   C. The language acquisition process is an integral part of the social-cognitive development.
   D. Second language learners acquire language concepts that are tied to the subject content.

❑ There are numerous models of integrated approaches. The following are just a few:
   A. Experiential learning
   B. Content-based language learning
   C. Sheltered English, or specially designed academic instruction in English (SDAIE)
   D. Language Experience Approach (LEA)

❑ In experiential learning, second language learners acquire English by "living" the experience; it is characterized by "adventurous" learning.

❑ In content-based language learning, the emphasis is on developing language while an academic subject area is employed.

❑ In SDAIE, subject matter is taught in the second language by employing sheltering techniques.

❑ In the Language Experience Approach, the teacher employs the dictated story to develop lessons that address students' language deficiencies.

# Chapter 13

## *Curriculum Design and Day-to-Day ESL Instruction*

## KEY ISSUES

❏ Generic principles that promote high academic standards

❏ Steps in planning interdisciplinary content-based thematic units

❏ Bloom's Taxonomy

❏ Gardner's Eight Intelligences

❏ Activities to develop multiple intelligences

"Most teachers realize that today's students comprise a great diversity of individuals, with a full range of cultural, ethnic, and economic heritage and first languages. They realize that America's people are multi-everything — multilingual (features of languages), multiethnic, and multicultural (our features of customs, religion, traditions, history)—and that the students in their classrooms represent the changing demographics of our pluralistic nation" (Roberts & Kellough, 2000).

Careful planning and preparation by a community and a school are the most important preliminary factors in the ultimate success of school language development programs. Developing curriculum and planning for each day's instruction are the most important components of the program once it is in place. Each day's lesson fits into a larger framework of planning that makes it a part of long-range goals and unified, sequenced objectives. A planning process organized around communicative principles will develop activities that enable students to function effectively in situations that require them to seek and provide information, to express ideas and opinions, and to control their environment in a variety of ways. Such a planning process will first attempt to give students control over their immediate environment and then become more outward, enabling them to discuss their interests, needs and concerns in the school beyond their classrooms, in their families, and in their communities. At the same time the English language learners will use the new language in contexts that are planned to be rich with cultural meanings and associations.

Planning in an immersion, content-based classroom will focus on and take its direction from the goals of the subject-content area. In this type of situation, there is an extra dimension of planning, that focuses on language development and on subject-content goals at the same time. While the organizing principle for instruction will be the subject-matter content, the language skills necessary to progress in communication about the subject-matter content must also be intentionally developed through the planning process. This suggests that it will, most of the time, be necessary to do language development activities in preparation for, or as a component of a lesson, directed toward subject-content goals. The teacher of subject content in a second language must always be aware of the language skills demanded by the concepts and the activities involved in the subject-content goals. The teacher must also plan carefully for the concrete experiences and the visual reinforcement that will make the academic language of instruction comprehensible to the students (Curtain & Pesola, 1994). This will help the English language learner develop the linguistic skills necessary for dealing with the subject-content material.

## Five Generic Principles

A review of the literature on innovative programs of school reform for diverse students (Collier, 1995) has uncovered a core list of principles that promote the achievement of high academic standards for English language learners.

## Principle #1

Facilitate learning through joint, productive activity among teachers and students.

Learning takes place best through joint, productive activity. Students must be actively involved in the learning process. Research has shown that teachers talk from 65% to 95% of the time. In order for the English language learner, as well as the native speaker of English, to be actively involved in the daily lessons, teachers must allow students to communicate by giving them opportunities to converse/exchange ideas on a regular basis. Those students who are at the preproduction level must be engaged in interacting nonverbally but in activities in which the teachers are ascertaining comprehension of the concepts and vocabulary.

## Principle #2

Develop students' competence in the language and literacy of instruction throughout all instructional activities.

Language proficiency in listening, speaking, reading, and writing is the road to high academic achievement. Thus, language development must be a part of every lesson; a part of the entire school day. Language and literacy development should be fostered through meaningful use and purposeful conversation between teacher and students, not through drills and decontextualized rules (Berman et al., 1995; Speidel, 1987). Reading and writing must be taught both as specific curricula and within subject matter. The teaching of language expression and comprehension should always be integrated into each content area.

## Principle #3

Contextualize teaching and curriculum in the experiences and skills of home and community.

Lessons need to provide experiences that show how rules, abstractions, and verbal descriptions are drawn from and applied to the everyday world. The use of personal, community-based experiences as the foundation for developing school skills affords students opportunities to apply skills acquired in both home and school contexts.

## Principle #4

Challenge students toward cognitive complexity.

Often, English language learners are excused of certain academic challenges on the assumption that they are of "limited" English proficiency or they are forgiven any genuine assessment of progress because the assessment instruments are not adequate. As a result, both standards and feedback are weakened; thus academic achievement for these students is handicapped. Although the motives for such actions have been benign, the effect is that the English language learner is, thus, denied the challenges for academic progress. The clear concensus among researchers in the field is that English language learners, just like native language speakers, require instruction that is cognitively challenging, instruction that requires thinking and analysis, not only rote, repetitive, detail-level drills. Working with a cognitively challenging curriculum requires careful planning, so students are stretched to reach within their zones of proximal development (Vygotsky, 1962) where they can perform with teacher guidance. It does not mean drill- and-kill exercises, and it does not mean overwhelming challenges that discourage the students. It is very important that teachers keep in mind Krashen's Input Hypothesis ( i+1) when planning for instruction. Small increments of knowledge are crucial to ensure academic success.

## Principle #5

Engage students through dialogue, especially in instructional conversation.

In the United States the instructional conversation is rare. More often, teaching occurs through the recitation of a script in which the teacher assumes the major role; teachers assign a task, students complete the task, and the teacher assesses. True instructional conversation transforms the classroom into a "community of learners". Teaching must become "a warm, interpersonal, collaborative activity" (Dalton, 1989) if students are going to grow academically.

## Planning Interdisciplinary, Content-Based Thematic Units

Thematic teaching provides context for concepts and activities through their relationship to a thematic center. One significant function of the theme is to focus on meaningful and interesting information and experiences as reasons for the students to acquire subject-content knowledge as they develop language proficiency. It also helps to connect ideas and information, making them more comprehensible and easier to remember. Students are immersed in a theme and are exposed to numerous encounters of some of the same content, yet from different perspectives and in meaningful contexts. This intertwining of ideas, concepts, vocabulary, and language structures facilitates the acquisition of knowledge as well as the development of English language competence.

## Figure 13–1
## Sample Theme Words

| | | |
|---|---|---|
| activists | cooperation | innovations |
| addresses (speeches) | crusades | inspirations |
| administrations | cultures | inventions |
| adventures | declarations | issues |
| aeronautics | demonstrations | justice |
| agreements | departures | lodgings |
| ambitions | depths | machines |
| arbitrations | deprivations | migrations |
| aristocracies | determinations | minorities' rights |
| beginnings | dictators | modern society |
| blockades | dignity | nationalism |
| bonanzas | dilemmas | nations |
| boundaries | diplomacy | navigations |
| boycotts | disasters | needs |
| bravery | discoveries | neighborhoods |
| breakthroughs | diversity | nonviolence |
| buildings | dynasties | oppressions |
| business | emancipations | ordeals |
| calamities | emigrations | patterns |
| campaigns | encounters | prejudice |
| celebrations | environments | pollution |
| changes | escapes | resistance |
| clothing | extinctions | resources |
| colonizing/colonies | families | searches |
| companionships | fighters | segregation |
| conversation | freedoms | self-awareness |
| constitutions | getaways | settlements |
| controversies | governments | social groups |
| courage | hardships | survival |
| conflict with climate | heritages | symbols (freedom) |
| conflict with self | heroes | transportation |
| conflict with others | hibernations | others suggested by students |
| | independence | |

Source: Roberts P.L., & Kellough, R.D., (2000). A guide for developing interdisciplinary thematic units, (2nd ed.). Upper Saddle River, NJ: Merrill-Prentice Hall.

## Choice of Theme

The first step in developing a thematic unit is to select a theme. In choosing a theme, teachers should always take into consideration students' interest as well as teacher interest, relationship to the curriculum goals/objectives for the grade level (curriculum frameworks, benchmarks, statewide standards, etc.) or age of the class, and the potential for the application and development of appropriate and useful language functions. Other factors influencing the choice and development of a theme might include school-wide or across-the-curriculum emphases, holidays or special school or community events, and available materials and resources.

The curriculum for a school year might well consist of several themes, each related to the others by systematic reinforcement of the unit just completed, and by careful preparation for and transition to the units that follow. Language functions and basic vocabulary are encountered and reinforced from unit to unit due to the spiral character of the general elementary school curriculum (Curtain & Pesola, 1994). Building upon prior knowledge and scaffolding are indispensable in thematic teaching.

Figures 13-1 and 13-2 provide samples of theme words and theme sentences. These are simply some examples. Themes must stem from the subject content used as the "umbrella" for developing the content-based thematic units.

Once the theme has been determined in a thematic unit, a resourceful teacher finds ways to relate the theme to as many subjects as possible. For example, Figure 13-3 shows a web of a theme such as Immigration to America (from 1890–1924).

This theme could evolve as an interdisciplinary unit in the following fashion:

- Mathematics: Graphing skills (learn how to create a pictograph; develop a pictograph to show the number of immigrants that came to the United States during that period and from what countries, interpret data from a pictograph)
- Science: How people solve problems (study famous immigrant inventors and their contributions)
- Social Studies: Map skills (study where immigrants came from; countries and location; continents; neighboring countries; capitals; bodies of water)
- Art: Create two-dimensional works of art (study and make flags of countries where immigrants came from)

- Music: Recognize and describe romantic and twentieth century music and composers (study famous composers whose music immigrated to United States between 1890 and 1924)
- Language Arts: Writing skills ( recording thoughts; focus on a central idea; study letter writing and compose a letter expressing feelings to someone left behind)

These are examples of how a specific theme can develop into an interdisciplinary content-based unit. The length of the unit will depend on the depth and breath given to it in each subject.

Figure 13–4 provides some grade level themes that could be employed in Social Studies/History as umbrellas for developing content-based interdisciplinary units of instruction in the elementary school.

---

### Figure 13–2
### Sample Theme Sentences

Change can be beneficial.

Cultures can clash.

People can be courageous and clever.

People can be independent and resourceful.

Laws and rules affect our families.

People are interdependent.

People can overcome handicaps.

People are sensitive to nature.

People have conflicts with themselves.

People have conflicts with the climate.

People have conflicts with others.

People remember their loved ones and preserve their memory.

People search for freedom.

War costs humans in different ways.

The weak and strong can help each other.

Others suggested by students.

---

Source: Roberts P.L., & Kellough, R.D., (2000). A guide for developing interdisciplinary thematic units, (2nd ed.). Upper Saddle River, NJ: Merrill-Prentice Hall.

# Figure 13-3
## Sample Web

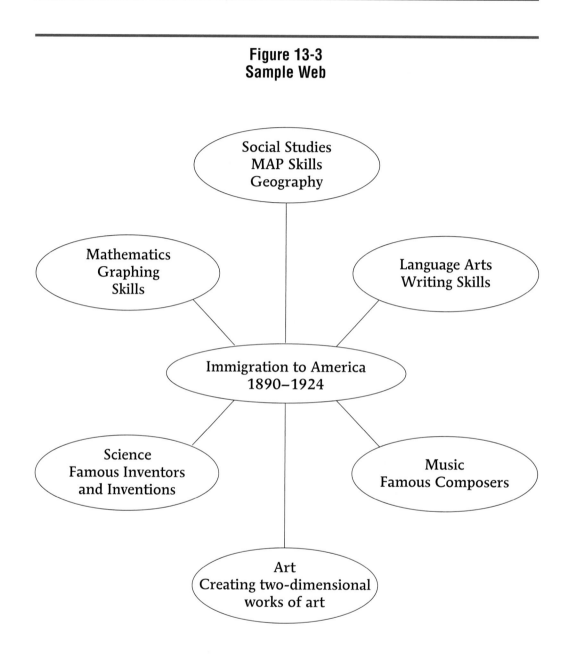

**Figure13–4**
## Sample Sequential Grade Level Themes for Social Studies/ History, Grades K-6

Kindergarten:   Awareness of Self in a Social Setting

1st Grade:      The Individual in Primary Social Groups (e.g., Understanding School and Family Life)

2nd Grade:      Meeting Basic Needs in Nearby Social Groups (e.g., The Neighborhood)

3rd Grade:      Sharing Earth's Resources with Others (e.g., The Community)

4th Grade:      Understanding Human Life in Varied Environments (e.g., The Region)

5th Grade:      Understanding People of the Americas (e.g., The United States and Its Close Neighbors)

6th Grade:      Understanding People and Cultures (e.g., The Eastern Hemisphere)

Adapted from: Roberts, P. L., & Kellough, R. D., (2000). A guide for developing interdisciplinary thematic units (2nd ed.)Upper Sddle River, NJ: Merrill-Prentice Hall.

## Choice of Topics

Once a theme has been identified, subthemes as well as specific topics to be studied can be identified. Topics are areas of study under the theme or subthemes.

A thematic interdisciplinary unit on Living Things in the World could explore many topics; one could be tree frogs. Figure 13–5 illustrates a sample breakdown.

## Formulation of Goals and Instructional Objectives

Formulating goals and instructional objectives for a particular unit allows the teacher to create a clear picture of what the unit is going to be about. As Graves (1996) explains, goals are general statements or the final destination; the level(s) students will need to achieve. Instructional objectives are teachable chunks that, in their accumulation form the essence of the unit. Clear understanding of goals and objectives will help teachers to be sure what material to teach, and when and how it should be taught (Sysoyev, 2000). Instructional objectives must be realistic and attainable within the time frame allocated. Instructional objectives drive the students' performance. Assessment of student achievement in learning

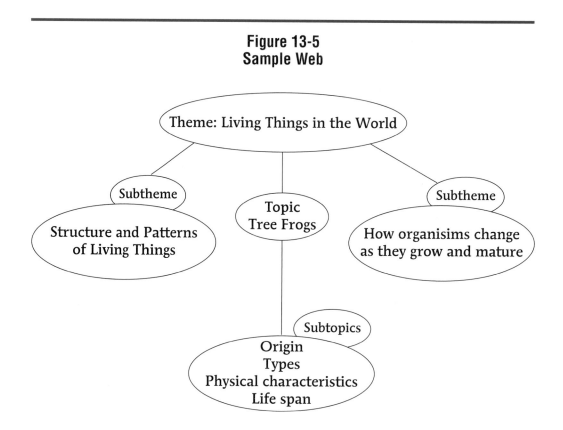

**Figure 13-5**
**Sample Web**

should be an assessment of this performance. When the assessment procedure matches the instructional objectives, the assessment is referred to as *aligned* or *authentic* (more on assessment later in this chapter) (Roberts & Kellough, 2000). In Florida, as in other states, curriculum frameworks have been developed at the State Department level. These can be accessed at www.firn.edu/doe/menu/sss.htm.

## Classifying Instructional Objectives

When planning instructional objectives, it is useful to consider Bloom's Taxonomy and his three domains of learning objectives: the cognitive domain, the affective domain, and the psychomotor domain.

The **cognitive domain** involves mental operations from the lowest level of simple recall of information to complex, high-level evaluative processes. Bloom (1984) identified six levels of mental operations in the cognitive domain: knowledge, comprehension, application, analysis, synthesis, and evaluation. Whereas the intellectual needs are primarily within the cognitive domain and the physical needs are within the psychomotor domain, the other three areas of developmental needs (emotional/psychological, social, and moral/ethical) are mostly within the affective domain.

There are specific verbs that can be employed when writing instructional objectives for each domain. Figure 13–6 provides some appropriate examples for each of the six levels of mental operations identified within the cognitive domain.

## Figure 13–6
### Examples of Verbs for Bloom's Cognitive Domain

1. **Knowledge Action Verbs**

| | | | | | |
|---|---|---|---|---|---|
| choose | complete | define | describe | identify | indicate |
| list | locate | match | name | outline | recall |
| recognize | select | state | | | |

2. **Comprehension Action Verbs**

| | | | | | |
|---|---|---|---|---|---|
| change | classify | convert | defend | estimate | expand |
| explain | generalize | infer | interpret | paraphrase | predict |
| recognize | summarize | translate | | | |

3. **Application Action Verbs**

| | | | | | |
|---|---|---|---|---|---|
| apply | calculate | demonstrate | develop | discover | modify |
| operate | participate | perform | plan | predict | relate |
| show | use | | | | |

4. **Analysis Action Verbs**

| | | | | | |
|---|---|---|---|---|---|
| analyze | break down | categorize | compare | contrast | debate |
| deduce | diagram | differentiate | discriminate | identify | illustrate |
| infer | outline | relate | separate | subdivide | |

5. **Synthesis Action Verbs**

| | | | | | |
|---|---|---|---|---|---|
| arrange | categorize | combine | compile | constitute | create |
| design | develop | devise | document | explain | formulate |
| generate | modify | organize | originate | plan | produce |
| rearrange | reconstruct | revise | rewrite | summarize | synthesize |
| tell | transmit | write | | | |

6. **Evaluation Action Verbs**

| | | | | | |
|---|---|---|---|---|---|
| appraise | argue | assess | compare | conclude | consider |
| contrast | criticize | decide | discriminate | evaluate | explain |
| interpret | judge | justify | rank | rate | relate |
| standardize | support | validate | | | |

Source: Roberts, P.L., & Kellough,R.D., (2000). A guide for developing interdisciplinary thematic units (2nd ed.). Upper Saddle River, NJ: Merrill-Prentice Hall

The **affective domain** involves feelings, attitudes, and values and ranges from the lower levels of acquisition to the highest level of internalization and action. Bloom (1984) identified five levels within this domain: receiving, responding, valuing, organizing, and internalizing. Figure 13–7 provides some appropriate verbs that can be employed when writing objectives to address the affective domain.

The **psychomotor domain** originally dealt with gross-to-fine-motor control. It ranges from simple manipulation of materials to the communication of ideas, and finally to the highest level of creative performance. Bloom (1984) identified four levels within this domain: moving (gross-motor coordination), manipulat-

---

## Figure 13–7
## Examples of Verbs for Bloom's Affective Domain

1. **Receiving Verbs**

| | | | | | |
|---|---|---|---|---|---|
| ask | choose | describe | differentiate | distinguish | hold |
| identify | locate | name | point to | recall | recognize |
| reply | select | use | | | |

2. **Responding Verbs**

| | | | | | |
|---|---|---|---|---|---|
| answer | applaud | approve | assist | command | comply |
| discuss | greet | help | label | perform | play |
| practice | present | read | recite | report | select |
| spend (leisure time in) | | | | | |

3. **Valuing Verbs**

| | | | | | |
|---|---|---|---|---|---|
| argue | complete | describe | explain | follow | form |
| initiate | invite | join | justify | propose | protest |
| read | report | select | share | study | support |

4. **Organizing Verbs**

| | | | | | |
|---|---|---|---|---|---|
| adhere | alter | arrange | balance | combine | compare |
| defend | identify | integrate | modify | order | organize |
| prepare | relate | synthesize | | | |

5. **Internalizing Verbs**

| | | | | | |
|---|---|---|---|---|---|
| act | complete | display | influence | listen | modify |
| perform | practice | propose | qualify | question | revise |
| serve | solve | verify | | | |

Source: Roberts, P.L., & Kellough, R.D., (2000). A guide for developing interdisciplinary thematic units (2nd ed.). Upper Saddle River, NJ: Merrill-Prentice Hall

**Figure 13–8**
**Examples of Verbs for Blooms Psychomotor Domain**

1. Moving (gross motor coordination)

| | | | |
|---|---|---|---|
| adjust | clean | jump | obtain |
| carry | grasp | locate | walk |

2. Manipulating (fine motor coordination)

| | | | |
|---|---|---|---|
| assemble | calibrate | play | turn |
| build | connect | thread | |

3. Communicating (communication of ideas and feelings)

| | | |
|---|---|---|
| analyze | describe | explain |
| ask | draw | write |

4. Creating (students' coordination of thinking, learning, and behaving in all three domains)

| | | |
|---|---|---|
| create | design | invent |

Source: Created from A. J. Horrow's *Taxonomy of the Psychomotor Domain*, 1977.

ing (fine-motor coordination), communicating, and creating. Figure 13–8 provides some appropriate verbs that can be employed when writing objectives to address the psychomotor domain (Roberts & Kellough, 2000).

When developing/selecting the instructional objectives for designing interdisciplinary thematic content-based units, teachers must list subject-content objectives as well as language objectives. The language instructional objectives are those aspects of language that are indispensable for the second language learner to attain the subject-content objectives. The language objectives, thus, stem from the subject matter content to be taught. For example, the development of new vocabulary by having students recognize, identify, and use (if at the speech emergence level) new vocabulary is indispensable to ensure comprehension of the material in which this new vocabulary is embedded. In addition, aspects of language that may cause language interference problems or simply language problems for the English language students involved in the lessons must also be identified.

For example, a teacher has a number of Hispanic students in his/her class. There are some specific language interference problems those students may have. Some of these are: the use of the adjective in front of the noun ( in Spanish it is used after the noun); the use of "not" and the auxiliaries "does/do" to indicate negation (since in Spanish only *no* in front of the verb indicates negation). If this teacher is teaching a unit on living things around the world and the topic is frogs, these may be some aspects of language he/she could address in the social studies portion of the unit. (refer to section that follows on conceptualizing the content).

## Conceptualizing the Content

The content is the body of knowledge/information/concepts to be taught. It is what the teacher expects the students to know at the end of the unit. It is the "what" that is going to be taught. When identifying the content, it is important to use resources available in the school ( i.e., curricular materials, as well as children's literature fiction/nonfiction, and outside resources such as the internet). Because the content is the body of knowledge students will be acquiring, it is important that teachers do research and expand their own knowledge of the particular content they will be teaching. Teachers must be well versed in the theme/topic to be taught, to effectively teach it to students. For example, if a teacher is teaching a unit on living things in the world (Topic: Frogs) and one of the objectives is: "use of simple maps, globes, and other three- dimensional models to identify and locate places" (Sunshine State Standard for Social Studies B1. 1.2), part of the content to be taught is the types of frogs that are found in different parts of the world. In teaching about tree frogs, the following content would be included:

Africa: *red* tree frog

Asia: *flying* tree frog

Australia: *white* tree frog

Madagascar: *tomato* tree frog

North America: tree frog

South America: *red-eyed* tree frog

Southeast Asia: *barking* tree frog

In this lesson, students would be learning map skills: locating places in the world where the different types of tree frogs exist. In addition, the English language learners would have a great opportunity to practice the use of an adjective in front of a noun (which could be a language interference for Hispanic students and even French-speaking students). The teacher could also address the use of "not" with the auxiliary "does/do" and the use of contractions in a yes/no-type question activity. For example:

Teacher: Does the red tree frog exist in Asia?

Student: No, the red tree frog does not exist in Africa or no, it doesn't. (A Hispanic student may reply: "No, no exist".)

Teacher: Do flying tree frogs exist in Africa?

Student: No, flying tree frogs do not exist in Africa or no they don't. (A Hispanic student may respond: "No, no exist.")

Teacher: Do red eyed tree frogs exist in Madagascar?

Student: No, they do not or no they don't.

The use of contractions would provide practice with what could be a language interference for Hispanic students, because contractions are nonexistent in the Spanish language.

## Instructional Procedures

Once the content (what will be taught) has been determined, the next step is to decide "how" the content will be taught. There is a sequential order in which lessons should unfold. The teacher must decide what series of activities are necessary to develop the lesson and in what order to attain the specified objectives. The sequence in which the activities take place is crucial for a successful lesson and, therefore, for the attainment of the objectives. Teachers must always ask themselves what is the best way to sequence the activities to ensure that they are "building upon" and providing the scaffolding so necessary for the students' success in the attainment of the objectives. Teachers must also ask themselves what the students need to know/need to be able to do for each activity. Identifying prerequisite knowledge and skills is crucial when deciding how to sequence the activities in each lesson.

The instructional procedures are the sequence of activities described in the lesson plan. There are numerous ways in which the instructional procedures can be clustered. It is important to note, however, that all lessons are developed in stages: beginning, middle, and end. Lessons usually begin with a warm-up and/or review activities, a way to connect the day's lesson to previous lessons and a way to motivate and interest students for the activities that will follow. Once the warm-up has taken place, the class is ready for the presentation and practice stages of the lesson (Jensen, 2001). These stages have been referred to with a variety of labels such as: engage, study, and activate (Harmer, 1998); lead-in, elicitation, explanation, accurate reproduction, and immediate creativity

(Harmer, 1991); verbalization, automatization, and autonomy (Ur, 1996); initiating activity, core activities including guided practice, and closure activities (Florida Atlantic University adopted lesson plan format, 1997). All of these labels describe stages in which (1) the content and/or language form is introduced and presented; (2) comprehension is checked before a form of guided practice is implemented;(3) there is some type of guided practice; and (4) there is some type of application activity where in students apply independently or in cooperative groups the knowledge/concepts they have just acquired, and some type of closure activity including an end-of-lesson review.

## Materials

It is imperative for the teacher to decide what materials need to be developed to successfully deliver each lesson of the unit. Once this decision is made, materials need to be developed and listed in the section of the unit designated for this purpose. In addition, any other type of materials or resources that will be employed for the lessons must be listed.

In determining the materials to employ, it is imperative that the objectives for the lessons are kept foremost in the teachers' mind because the materials are crucial for the attainment of the objectives.

In addition, in developing the materials, teachers must address the issue of providing comprehensible input for the second language students. The use of visuals, graphs, charts, objects, realia, and materials with which students can be involved physically to make learning as concrete as possible is indispensable. It is important to always remember that input is comprehensible when students can attach meaning to what is being presented. Thus, materials employed for the lessons are key to the success of the lessons.

## Assessment

Why is it important to assess?
Assessment of student achievement is designed to serve in the following ways:

a.  To assist in student learning

   A teacher must determine how well the students are acquiring the knowledge, concepts, and skills being developed through the units. If students are not attaining the objectives, reteaching must take place to assist the students in their attainment of the objectives.

b.  To identify students' strengths and weaknesses

When restructuring lessons for reteaching (if needed), teachers can build upon the students' strengths and address their weaknesses identified through the assessment process.

c.  To determine teaching effectiveness

When analyzing assessment results, competent teachers will determine how well they were able to reach the students and attain the objectives. In reflecting, teachers can determine which strategies were successful and which may need to be restructured, and which materials were effective and which ones need to be revised.

d.  To determine teacher effectiveness in addressing the needs of second language learners

When reviewing the data resulting from students' performance, teachers can determine how well their second language learners are attaining the stated language and content objectives. Teachers could ask themselves: "Are the students progressing academically or are they falling behind? If they are not progressing, what am I doing that needs to be modified? Am I making input comprehensible? Am I involving the students in the lessons, providing activities in which they can participate? Am I scaffolding and building upon what they already know?"

e.  To communicate and involve parents and guardians in their children's learning

Parents/guardians, communities, and school boards all share in the accountability of the children's academic success. Today, more than ever, schools are reaching out to engage parents/guardians and communities at large in their communities at large and their children's education. Teachers employ assessment results to communicate with parents/guardians and communities important collaborate function in the education of their children.

The following eight principles guide an assessment program (Roberts & Kellough, 2000):

1.  Teachers need to know how well they are doing.
2.  Students need to know how well they are doing.
3.  Assessment is a reciprocal process, and includes assessment of teacher performance and student achievement.
4.  Assessment results should aid teaching effectiveness and contribute to student growth.

5. Assessment results should be attained from a variety of sources and different types of data-collecting devices.

6. Assessment is an ongoing process.

7. Reflecting on assessment results is an on-going process.

8. Teachers should be held accountable for facilitating student learning and for assessing student progress.

## How Can Teachers Assess Students' Acquisition of Knowledge?

There are numerous ways in which teachers can assess acquisition of knowledge. Ordinarily, to assess unit objectives, teachers develop their own assessment instruments. The following are some types of items that teachers can develop/ employ: *arrangement type*—students are asked to arrange or place in order of occurrence lists of events, such as historical, mathematical for problem solving, growth patterns of living things, events in a story, etc.; *completion type*—students are asked to complete a sentence given; *correction type*—students are asked to correct certain information given in context that is incorrect; *essay type*—students are asked to compare a response to a question or problem, in the form of sustained prose using their own words, and ideas, based on what they learned in the unit of instruction; *grouping type*—students are asked to select and group several items presented that are related in some way; *identification type*—students are given unknown "specimens" to identify by name or some other criterion known to them; *matching type*—students are asked to connect/match items from two lists that are related in some way; *multiple-choice type*—students are asked to select from a series of responses the response that best fits the statement (stem) presented; *performance type*—students are asked to solve a problem or accomplish a task; *short explanation type*—students are asked to compose a short response to a given question or problem; *true-false type*—students are asked to respond to the accuracy of given statements by indicating if the statement is *true* or *false*. (Roberts & Kellough, 2000).

This list is by no means exhaustive nor represent on a continuum those types that are most affective to least effective. The effectiveness of the type of assessment will depend on what is being measured and for what purpose.

## Providing Alternative Assessment

Well-designed assessment procedures are essential to meeting the needs of second language learners. *Alternative assessment* has become an umbrella term for any type of assessment other than standardized, multiple-choice-type assessments.

Examples include short answer response, extended response, observation, individual or group performance assessment, or portfolios. *Performance assessment,* a currently popular type of alternative assessment, requires the student to perform some type of task, which is then evaluated using some pre-established criteria.

### Purpose and Definitions

*Performance assessment* and *portfolios* are complementary approaches for recording students' academic progress and language development. Both represent authentic assessment and are considered forms of *alternative assessment.* Valdez Pierce and O'Malley (1992) clarify these terms as follows:

**Alternative assessment**
- is any method of finding out what a student knows or can do that is intended to show growth and inform instruction and is not a standardized traditional test;
- is by definition criterion-referenced;
- is authentic because it is based on activities that represent actual progress toward instructional goals and objectives and reflects tasks typical of classroom and real-life settings;
- requires integration of language skills; and
- may include teacher observation, performance assessment, and student self-assessment.

**Performance assessment**
- is a type of alternative assessment;
- is an exercise in which students demonstrate specific skills and competencies in relation to a continuum of agreed-upon standards of proficiency or excellence; and
- reflects student performance on instructional tasks and relies on professional rater judgment in its design and interpretation.

**Portfolio assessment**
- is the use of records of a student's work over time and in a variety of modes to show depth, breadth, and development of the student's abilities;
- is the purposeful and systematic collection of student work that reflects accomplishments relative to specific instructional objectives and goals;
- can be used as an approach for combining the information from both alternative and standardized assessments; and
- has as key elements student reflection and self-monitoring.

## Teacher Reflection

Once a unit is completed and daily lessons have begun, teachers reflect on the individual lessons. Notes should be made and kept for future references and for making necessary modifications to the original plan(s). Teachers must reflect on their delivery of instruction and on students' response to the lesson. The following are some questions that teachers can ask themselves (responses must be logged in the reflective journals):

1.  Did I capture the students' attention with my initiating activity? If no, what would I have done differently?
2.  Were the activities sequenced effectively? If no, how would I sequence them differently the next time I teach this lesson?
3.  Were my materials appropriate for the lesson? If no, how would I modify them? What would I add/delete?
4.  Did I make input comprehensible? How? Were my strategies effective for my second language learners?
5.  Were students actively involved in the lesson?
6.  Did I make learning concrete?
7.  Was my pacing adequate to accomplish my objectives? If no, what changes would I make?
8.  Did I attain my objectives?

## Providing for Multiple Intelligences/Learning Styles When Planning for Instruction

The Theory of Multiple Intelligences (Gardner, 1983) has made an impact in most school curricula today. Gardner defines *intelligences* as "the capacity to solve problems or to fashion products that are values in one or more cultural settings" (Gardner & Hatch, 1989). His theory, based on biological and cultural research, expands the traditional view that there are two types of intelligences (verbal and computational). He includes other types of intelligence such as visual/spatial relations, physical activity/bodily/kinesthetic, musical, interpersonal, intrapersonal, and the newest one, naturalist. His theory states that all eight intelligences are needed to function productively in society and must be considered to be of equal importance (Blaz, 1999).

Teachers must be aware of the fact that students come into their classrooms with different sets of developed intelligences. Thus, teachers need to develop a

## Figure 13–9
## Gardner's Eight Intelligences

- **Linguistic:** Involves the ability to use listening, speaking, reading, and writing to express and appreciate complex meanings; to remember information.
- **Logical-Mathematical:** Involves using deduction, induction, patterning, interpreting graphs, numbers, and sequencing of ideas to express and appreciate complex meaning; to remember information.
- **Visual/Spatial:** Involves using three-dimensional ways to perceive imagery, navigate, produce, and decode information.
- **Kinesthetic:** Involves using the mind to control bodily movements and manipulate objects; to remember information, to give output.
- **Musical:** Involves using rhythm, tone, melody, and pitch to recall information, and give output.
- **Interpersonal:** Involves communicating and collaborating with others in order to recall information and produce output.
- **Intrapersonal:** Involves maintaining self-esteem, setting goals for oneself, and acquiring values in the learning process; looking inward to acquire information and to give output.
- **Naturalist:** Involves sensing patterns in and making connections with elements of nature to acquire knowledge and remember information.

Source: Adapted from Blaz (1999), *Foreign Language Teacher's Guide to Active Learning.*

variety of activities on a regular basis to provide for the differences in students' learning styles . Figure 13–9 provides a list of Gardner's eight intelligences and a brief description of each.

## Planning Activities that Appeal to Multiple Intelligences

### Linguistic Intelligence

Linguistic intelligence encompasses listening, speaking, reading, and writing to acquire knowledge. It is the intelligence that has been addressed mostly in the delivery of instruction and in testing in the western educational system (Lazear, 1992).

According to research, listening is the first activity in which second language learners must be engaged, particularly in the beginning stages of language acquisition. However, listening activities should always be purposeful and meaningful. Thus, when students are engaged in listening they should be actively involved. Other types of listening activities are: the use of audiotapes or videotapes (videotapes are more effective), CD-ROMS, satellite broadcasts, films on video, music on audio/visual tapes, poems on audio tapes, etc. for more advanced learners.

When employing these audio materials, teachers must develop some type of interactive activity so students are listening for specific purposes. For example, if listening to an audio-conversation, students could have a sheet to fill in information as it comes available: Who is/are the speaker(s)?, Where are they?, What is/are the topic(s) of conversation?, Is there a problem?, Was the problem resolved?, Have you ever had that same problem?, How did you resolve it?, What did you learn about the personality/character of the speaker(s)?, and any other appropriate questions. Another way to keep students actively listening is to have students listen for: idiomatic expressions they recognize; known vocabulary; questions asked by the speaker(s). As students listen, they jot these down. Then, they share with a partner what they "heard". In these activities, students are employing at least three aspects of the linguistic intelligence: listening, speaking, and writing.

Other activities for developing the linguistic intelligence would be having students engage in: meaningful conversations-topics of interest; discussions of material studied; sharing descriptions; memorizing speeches; giving oral reports; conducting interviews; games. A fun game for students to play is "Who am I?" For a history/Social Studies class, students are asked to pick a historical character. One student comes to the front and the rest of the students have to "guess" by asking yes/no type questions who is the historical figure this student selected. If students are doing a unit on animals, the same game can be played by asking the students to pick an animal.

To stimulate conversation, teachers can engage students in creating a "Conversation Necklace": the teacher passes around different types of color raw pasta that can be stranded in yarn or twine (ex: penne pasta, rigatoni, etc.). Students select a few pieces. Once they all have their pieces, they have to say a sentence for every piece chosen. As students say a sentence related to the topic/theme being studied, the pasta is stranded in the yarn or twine. At the end of the activity, the necklace is placed on display. A jar of marbles could also be employed. Students pick marbles from a basket. As they say their sentences, the marbles get placed in a jar. When the jar is full, they have a popcorn party. Cooperative groups are also excellent for stimulating listening and speaking.

For developing the reading and writing aspects of the linguistic intelligence there are so many activities that only a few will be mentioned. The sky is the limit! Using the textbook is an obvious activity, however, before the students read the material they should be familiar with the vocabulary they will encounter. Teachers must always employ listening and speaking activities prior to having students read. After they read, they should be engaged in some type of activity where they are reviewing and applying what they read. Newspapers and magazines (censored) are excellent reading materials; role-playing and dramatization, too. Role-playing and dramatization require much practice thus the practice becomes meaningful since the students are preparing for an audience. Students do not necessarily have to be the characters themselves. They can use different types of puppets such as string, finger, and stick puppets. They can draw their characters on transparencies or story rolls/scrolls, and narrate/dramatize using the transparencies or story rolls.

Teaching students how to write poetry and then have "an afternoon of poetry sharing" is an excellent way to motivate students to write; or students can be encouraged to select favorite poems from poetry books, to share.

## Logical-Mathematical Intelligence

The students who have strong logical-mathematical abilities are able to detect patterns, reason deductively, and think logically. This "scientific reasoning" is most often associated with the sciences or mathematics, but it may be quite effectively developed and applied through the teaching of language arts.

Students can read stories that later they can graph (Blaz, 1999). For example, after reading the following story, students can be asked to graph the favorite animals for each child in the story.

*There were 6 children. They all went to the zoo. As they walked, they discovered their favorite animals. Maria thought her favorite animal was the parrot, but when she saw the giraffe, she exclaimed: now I know what my favorite animal is! John and Shantel were most impressed by the roaring lion. That was their favorite. Pedro and Jose, each had a different favorite. Pedro liked the zebra, while Jose preferred the Florida Bobcat. Evelyn was walking along when she saw her most favorite animal of all: the billy goat. They all had a grand time at the zoo.*

### Favorite Animals

| Name | Giraffe | Lion | Zebra | Bobcat | Billy Goat |
|------|---------|------|-------|--------|------------|
| Maria | | | | | |
| John | | | | | |
| Shantel | | | | | |
| Pedro | | | | | |
| Jose | | | | | |
| Evelyn | | | | | |

Students can also develop their own graphs based on topics of interest: their own favorite cars, authors, characters, books, foods, clothing, people, their views on specific issues discussed in lessons, etc. Another way to appeal to the mathematical logical intelligence is by having students compare/contrast what they have learned. An excellent tool to do this is the Venn Diagram. Other recommended activities include, engaging students in finding connections/relationships between objects. The "odd-one-out"(Wright, 1999) is a great game to play to engage students in this type of activity. Students are given a series of pictures. They must decide which one does not belong in the group and state why. Another activity could be to give students a series of pictures and have them connect them (establish a relationship) among them and say or write how they connected the pictures. These activities are very effective in pairs or cooperative groups.

## Visual-Spatial Intelligence

This is the ability to visualize, manipulative, and create mental images in order to solve problems. Students/people with visual-spatial intelligence think in three-dimensional ways, and are able to recreate, transform, or modify these thoughts/perceptions and to navigate, and both produce and decode graphic information (Blaz, 1999).

Creating a "visual rich environment" in the classroom is one way to develop and appeal to the visual-spatial intelligence. Encouraging students to interact with the displays by noticing changes/new displays, students' work displayed and as Blaz (1999) suggests even giving extra credit questions on tests based on displayed material are excellent ways to help develop this intelligence. Changing the seating arrangement on a regular basis will benefit the visual-spatial oriented students since they "see" everything from a different perspective.

The visual-spatial learners have the ability to visualize in their mind, thus, activities such as pantomiming, imitating, and mental imagery are excellent for them.

Having the students close their eyes and imagine themselves in a setting the teacher is describing is another way to reach the visual-spatial learner. Once they have completed the mental imagery activity, they can describe their scene either orally or in writing. Any type of visual arts activities are also recommended, for example, drawing, assembling, building, crafts, and illustrating in three dimensional projects are effective for these students; flow charts and story maps are just as effective.

## Musical Intelligence

This intelligence is defined as the ability to recognize and compose musical pitches, tones, and rhythms. Unfortunately, every time there is need to streamline curricular offerings in the schools, the music program is one of the ones to suffer cuts. Thus, elementary school students in general, are not exposed to a wide variety of musical experiences unless the regular classroom teacher incorporates music into the daily lessons. Regular elementary school teachers do not need to be musicians to bring music into their daily activities. The use of tapes or CD's is an excellent way to incorporate music into units of instruction. Having children listen to songs for specific purposes is an excellent way to acquire new vocabulary. For example, children listen for words they recognize; they tell the teacher the words, the teacher writes the words on the board/word strips. Later, these words are employed to recreate the song, etc. Teachers can also use tunes to traditional children's songs to create songs that relate to the content of a unit of study. Even aspects of grammar if they can be tied in to music, helps the musical student acquire the concepts with more facility. The following very old song illustrates this idea:

> *Found A Peanut*
> *Found* a peanut
> Found a peanut
> Found a peanut, just now
> I just now found a peanut
> Found a peanut, just now.
> *Broke\** it open
> Broke it open
> Broke it open, just now
> I just now broke it open
> Broke it open, just now
> *Found* it rotten...
> *Ate* it anyway...
> *Got* sick...
> *Saw* the doctor...
> *Gave* me medicine...
> *Died* anyway...

\*changed from cracked to broke to use an irregular verb

There are eight (8) irregular verbs in the past tense of this song. There are two more verses that can be added in a Christian religious environment. Those are: went to heaven...; saw an angel... If the teachers are in this type of environment, they would have a total of ten (10) irregular verbs.

Popular music is also an excellent tool to employ. Students not only acquire language but also are exposed to cultural aspects. Students can listen and circle phrases they hear or orally answer questions regarding the theme or some aspect of culture depicted in the song.

There are other ways to bring rhythm activities into the curriculum. Dancing is a great way to teach culture as well as enriching the vocabulary to which your second language learners are exposed. Popular dances as well as folklore are fun as well as educational. Choral reading (prose) and choral poetry are other ways to employ rhythm in classroom activities. For students to read prose or poetry in unison they must learn to read together, pause together, where to accent syllables, and what sounds the vowels make, which are very important aspects of language. Students begin to feel the beat, rhymes, and mood of the piece they are reading in an effort to read well. (Refer to chapter 20, for more ideas on how to incorporate music into the curriculum.)

## Bodily-Kinesthetic Intelligence

Kinesthetically talented people use their mental ability to coordinate their bodily movements and to manipulate objects (Blaz, 2001).

Kinesthetic learners need to have an opportunity to "move". A variety of activities that take children from one area of the room to another provide this opportunity. Employing the exact sitting arrangement for the entire school day is counterproductive for the kinesthetic learner. In addition to providing opportunities to physically move, students also need to be involved in movement activities. Allowing students to respond physically, such as in TPR, also appeals to the kinesthetic intelligence. The use of manipulative games that involve physical movement, cooking, and field trips are excellent activities for the kinesthetic learner. Drama and simulations are additional activities to appeal to the kinesthetic intelligence. (Chapter 20 provides more ideas on how to include drama in the curriculum.)

## Interpersonal Intelligence

The ability to communicate personal feelings to others and to understand others' feelings and intentions are characteristic of this intelligence. Interaction with others will appeal and develop this intelligence, which relies upon all the other intelligences. To strengthen this intelligence students should be taught relational skills. Opportunities to practice listening, encouraging others, and reaching consensus are effective strategies to enhance the interpersonal intelligence. Since communication is both verbal and non-verbal, activities where students focus on the non-verbal language such as gestures, facial expressions and movements are an excellent way to begin teaching how to express emotions and convey meaning. A fun activity would be to survey students, including the second language learners, to find out gestures employed in different cultures and their meanings. Then, have students teach these to each other and engage in using them to convey meaning. Emphasis should be given to gestures/facial expressions employed to convey emotions. For example, in Puerto Rico, a "wink" with the left eye is a sign of approval, while in the United Stated, a "thumb up" is a sign of approval; in Puerto Rico, an upward movement of the nose and holding it in that position for a few seconds, means confusion or lack of understanding. This activity is an excellent way to involve second language learners and make them feel they have something to contribute to the lessons, even if they are still at the pre-production stage or at the early speech emergence stage.

Another way to develop the interpersonal intelligence is by having students share "All about me". Students can share about their hobbies; they can make collages using magazine or computer clip art pictures capturing their likes/dislikes, their favorite activities, people, etc. Once students have shared, engaging the class in a discussion of what was shared is essential. "Show and tell" is also an excellent activity to encourage interpersonal listening. Those students who are listening to the presenter are required to ask questions for clarification as the speaker presents, not interrupting but waiting for pauses from the presenter.

Cooperative groups is another effective teaching strategy to employ to appeal and develop the interpersonal intelligence. Students are required to interact with each other to complete an assignment. In addition, interacting with other adults provides an opportunity for meaningful communication. Teachers should encourage volunteers to come into their classrooms: parents, retirees, college students. This is an excellent way to involve the community and at the same time provide opportunities for the students to interact with adults. Students can read a book to the adults and then discuss feelings about character; or discuss their position/point of view or issues that came up in the story. The adults can share their life experiences with the students and the students can engage in a conversation expressing their feelings, common interests, and any unusual experiences the adult may have had.

## Intrapersonal Intelligence

The seventh intelligence is the ability some people have to understand their own feelings and motivations, and to use this self-perception to plan and direct their own life. In order for students to develop this intelligence, teachers must engage students in activities that help them to get to know themselves. Students need to have an opportunity to explore "deep within" their inner thoughts. Blaz (1999) suggests the following questions as prompts for journal writing:

- Who is your hero/heroine?
- If you had three wishes, what would they be?
- What is one of your fears?
- If you could change anything about yourself, what would it be?
- What is your life motto?
- When I am in school/at a dance/at home, I am...
- Ideal parents are...
- Teachers seldom are...
- Agree or disagree: Sports are very important.

Second language learners who may not be able to respond in English, could use their native language (if teacher can translate it, or has access to a translator) or they could draw/use magazine pictures to respond. Helping students explore human values is another way to develop self-knowledge, so important for intrapersonal intelligence to be strengthened. Children's literature, human interest stories from the newspaper, current events, and videos of movies where human values are evident are excellent resources to employ.

## Naturalist Intelligence

The ability to notice changes in the environment and to express concern about environmental issues are what form naturalist intelligence. Students who have strong naturalist intelligence are those who notice and remember patterns and things from nature. They have keen sensory skills—sight, smell, sound, taste, and touch, These are the students who love animals, camping, hiking, and being outdoors. Units about animals, endangered species, and ornamental/medicinal plants are excellent to develop this naturalist intelligence. Experiential learning (as discussed in chapter 12) would also provide ample opportunities for developing this intelligence. Taking students on walks to notice specific aspects of nature and then having students either discuss/write, or draw what they saw and how it made them feel are also effective activities to appeal to the naturalist intelligence. Today, teachers can use the internet to visit Web sites that show nature and outdoor activities in a way that could not be done a few years ago. Students do not have to be deprived of these activities today, if these are not within physical access to them.

The following multiple intelligence inventory developed by Christison (1996), can be employed by pre-service as well as inservice teachers to determine their strongest intelligences.

## Multiple Intelligence Inventory for Teachers
## Mary Ann Christison

**Directions:** Rank each statement below as 0, 1, or 2. Write 0 in the blank if the statement is not true. Write 2 in the blank if you strongly agree with the statement. A score of 1 places you somewhere in between. Compare your scores in different intelligences. What is your multiple intelligence profile? Where did you score highest? lowest?

### *Linguistic Intelligence*

_____ 1. I like to write articles and have them published.

_____ 2. I read something almost every day that isn't related to my work.

_____ 3. I often listen to the radio, cassette tapes of lectures, and books.

_____ 4. I always read billboards and advertisements.

_____ 5. I enjoy doing crossword puzzles.

_____ 6. I use an overhead projector, posters, quotations, etc., in my teaching.

_____ 7. I am a good letter writer.

_____ 8. If I hear a song a few times, I can usually remember the words.

_____ 9. I ask my students to read and write most of the time in my classes.

_____ 10. I have written something that I like.

## *Musical Intelligence*

_____ 1. I have a very expressive voice in front of my class, varying in intensity, pitch, and emphasis.

_____ 2. I often use music and chants in my lesson plans.

_____ 3. I can tell if someone is singing off-key.

_____ 4. I know the tunes to many different songs.

_____ 5. I play a musical instrument and play it frequently.

_____ 6. If I hear a new song once or twice, I can usually remember the tune.

_____ 7. I often sing in the shower.

_____ 8. Listening to music I like and am in the mood for makes me feel good.

_____ 9. When I hear a piece of music, I can easily harmonize with it.

_____ 10. I have no trouble identifying or following a beat.

## *Logical Mathematical Intelligence*

_____ 1. I feel more comfortable believing an answer is correct if it has been measured or calculated in some way.

_____ 2. I can calculate numbers easily in my head.

_____ 3. I like playing card games such as hearts, gin rummy, and bridge.

_____ 4. I liked math classes in school.

_____ 5. I believe that most things have a logical and rational explanation.

_____ 6. I like brain-teaser games.

_____ 7. I am interested in new developments in science.

_____ 8. When I cook, I measure things exactly.

_____ 9. I use problem-solving activities in my classes.

_____ 10. My classes are consistent; my students know what to expect in terms of rules and routines.

## Spatial Intelligence

_____ 1. I pay attention to the colors I wear and colors other people wear.

_____ 2. I take lots of photographs on trips and vacations.

_____ 3. I like to use video in my lessons.

_____ 4. It is easy for me to find my way around in unfamiliar cities.

_____ 5. I like to draw.

_____ 6. I like to read articles with many pictures.

_____ 7. I am partial to textbooks with illustrations, graphs, charts, and pictures.

_____ 8. I like doing puzzles and mazes.

_____ 9. I was good at geometry in school.

_____ 10. When I enter a classroom, I notice whether the positioning of the students and teacher supports the learning that is to take place.

## Bodily/Kinesthetic Intelligence

_____ 1. I like to go on rides at amusement parks.

_____ 2. I like to dance.

_____ 3. I engage in at least one sport.

_____ 4. I like to do things with my hands, such as knit, weave, sew, carve, or build models.

_____ 5. I find it most helpful to practice a new skill rather than to read about it or to watch a video.

_____ 6. I often get my best ideas when I am jogging, walking, vacuuming, or doing something physical.

_____ 7. I love being in the outdoors.

_____ 8. I find it very hard to sit for long periods of time.

_____ 9. I do activities in my classes that require that my students get out of their seats and move around.

_____ 10. Most of my hobbies involve physical activity of some sort.

## Intrapersonal Intelligence

_____ 1. I regularly spend time meditating.

_____ 2. I consider myself independent.

_____ 3. I keep a journal and record my thoughts.

_____ 4. I would rather adapt lessons or create my own than use lessons directly from a book.

_____ 5. I frequently create new activities and materials for my classes.

_____ 6. When I get hurt or disappointed, I bounce back quickly.

_____ 7. I can articulate the main values that govern my life and describe the activities that I regularly participate in that are consistent with these values.

_____ 8. I have hobbies or interests that I enjoy doing on my own.

_____ 9. I frequently choose activities in the classroom so my students can work alone or independently.

_____ 10. I give my students quiet time, thinking time, time to reflect on what they are doing.

## Interpersonal Intelligence

_____ 1. I would prefer going to a party rather than spending the evening home alone.

_____ 2. When I have problems, I like to discuss them with my friends.

_____ 3. People often come to me with their problems.

_____ 4. I am involved in social activities several night a week.

_____ 5. I like to entertain friends and have parties.

_____ 6. I consider myself a leader and often assume leadership roles.

_____ 7. I have more than one close friend.

_____ 8. I love to teach or show someone how to do something.

_____ 9. I am comfortable in a crowd or at a party with many people I don't know.

_____ 10. My students have input into the choice of content and the learning process in my classrooms.

**Scoring:** Add your total score in each area. The higher your total score, the stronger that intelligence.*

*For permission to use this questionnaire, contact the author by e-mail (see e-mail address in the "Contributors" section of this volume) or at Snow College, International Center/ESL Dept., Ephraim, Utah 84627. E-mail address: maryannchristison@snow.edu.

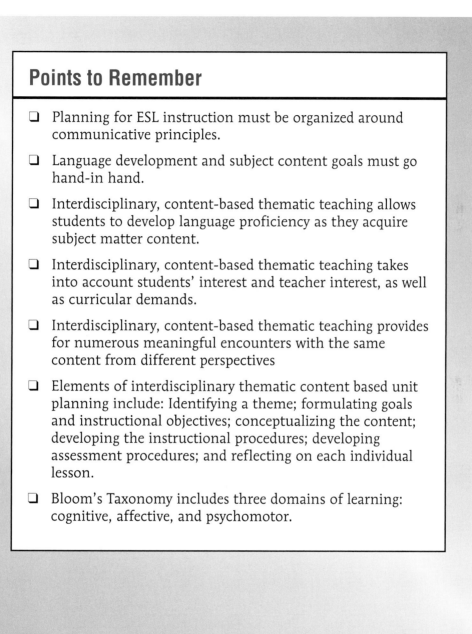

## Points to Remember

❑ Planning for ESL instruction must be organized around communicative principles.

❑ Language development and subject content goals must go hand-in hand.

❑ Interdisciplinary, content-based thematic teaching allows students to develop language proficiency as they acquire subject matter content.

❑ Interdisciplinary, content-based thematic teaching takes into account students' interest and teacher interest, as well as curricular demands.

❑ Interdisciplinary, content-based thematic teaching provides for numerous meaningful encounters with the same content from different perspectives

❑ Elements of interdisciplinary thematic content based unit planning include: Identifying a theme; formulating goals and instructional objectives; conceptualizing the content; developing the instructional procedures; developing assessment procedures; and reflecting on each individual lesson.

❑ Bloom's Taxonomy includes three domains of learning: cognitive, affective, and psychomotor.

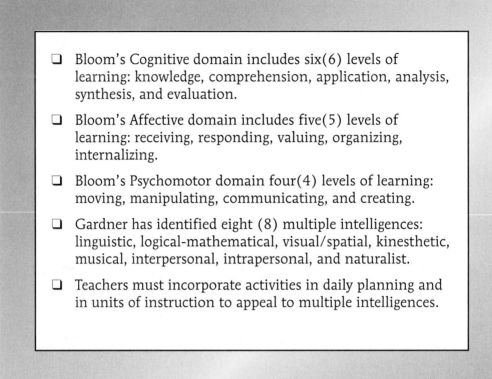

- ❑ Bloom's Cognitive domain includes six(6) levels of learning: knowledge, comprehension, application, analysis, synthesis, and evaluation.

- ❑ Bloom's Affective domain includes five(5) levels of learning: receiving, responding, valuing, organizing, internalizing.

- ❑ Bloom's Psychomotor domain four(4) levels of learning: moving, manipulating, communicating, and creating.

- ❑ Gardner has identified eight (8) multiple intelligences: linguistic, logical-mathematical, visual/spatial, kinesthetic, musical, interpersonal, intrapersonal, and naturalist.

- ❑ Teachers must incorporate activities in daily planning and in units of instruction to appeal to multiple intelligences.

# Part IV

## Development and Instruction of Language Skills for Second Language Learners

# Chapter 14

## Listening Development and Instruction for Second Language Learners

## KEY ISSUES

❏ Research on teaching listening to English language learners

❏ Types of spoken language and listening tasks

❏ Listening difficulties faced by second language learners

❏ Some strategies/skills for effective listening skills

❏ Some techniques for teaching listening skills for multiple levels of language proficiency skills

❏ Alternative assessments for listening comprehension

There are three English language learners (ELLs) in Ms. Santos's class of 15 native English speakers. One student is in the preproduction stage and two are in the speech emergence stage of language acquisition. The theme for today's arts class is "bugs." Ms. Santos reads a poem on bugs and asks students to circle words as they hear them. Instead of words, the English language learners are asked to circle pictures. The words are given in minimal pairs—for instance, the students will hear the phrase "Bugs, bugs on a tree." On their paper, they are given the words *tree* v. *three* and are asked to circle what they heard. The ELLs are given a picture of a tree and a picture of the number 3. They are to circle the words they heard.

Another activity Ms. Santos often uses in her class is a game called "Chinese Whispers". Alma is chosen to think of a short sentence that she whispers into Jose's ear. This continues until everyone in class has heard Alma's sentence. Then Ms. Santos asks the last student to repeat the sentence back to the class. Students check to see if the sentence was the original sentence. This game presents a low-anxiety environment for students, who have a lot of fun with this listening activity.

How will these listening activities help ELL students with listening skills in English?

# Introduction

"Ni hou ma?" "Apa khabar?" "Assalamualaikum." "Hola." "Bonjour."

These are greetings in Chinese, Malay, Arabic, Spanish, and French, respectively. To respond to these greetings, one must first listen to the sounds of the language before deciphering any meanings. It is important to understand that although listening skills are given the least attention among the other skills, they are a crucial element in the language acquisition process. Human beings have to be exposed to the sounds of the language before they can acquire the language. The classic case of a wild child such as Genie, a little girl who was kept in a dark closet by her father from the time she was a baby and was later discovered at the age of 13, reinforces the significance of listening in the language acquisition process. Genie's father barked at her and prevented her mother or brother from talking to her. Because she never heard the human language from the time she was born, Genie's native language was never fully developed, even though she went through speech therapy during her young adult and adult years. The story of Genie reinforces the social interactionist view of language acquisition, which forwards the idea that input from the environment that is usually received through listening is necessary and crucial for language to develop in humans.

David Nunan calls listening comprehension the "Cinderella skill" in second language learning; it is often overlooked by its older sister: speaking. For a long time in the area of language learning, learners' competence in a language was measured by their ability to speak and write. However, for learners to respond in the forms of speech and written notes, they have to use listening or reading skills. Therefore, listening skills are crucial elements in the performance of a second language learner. Through listening, children and adults obtain their learning and understanding about the world and human affairs. In real life, learners use all language skills to communicate, so listening, speaking, reading, and writing skills should be taught as integrated skills. However, to give readers an in-depth look at listening, this chapter focuses exclusively on listening in a second language. It explores research reports on teaching listening skills; types of oracy (spoken and listening) tasks; the use of strategies, skills, and techniques for effective listening skills at multiple language proficiency levels; and the type of assessments for listening comprehension.

Listening is the ability to identify and understand what others are saying. An able listener is capable of understanding a speaker's accent or pronunciation, grammar, and vocabulary; and grasping meaning.

According to researchers Howatt and Dakin, listening is the ability to identify and understand what others are saying. An able listener is capable of simultaneously understanding a speaker's accent or pronunciation, grammar and vocabulary, and grasping meaning. A list of microskills of listening which Willis (1981 p. 134) calls *enabling skills* are:

- Predicting what people are going to talk about
- Guessing at unknown words or phrases without panic
- Using one's own knowledge of the subject to gain understanding
- Identifying relevant points; rejecting irrelevant information
- Retaining relevant points (note-taking, summarizing)
- Recognizing discourse markers (e.g., well; oh, another thing is; now; finally)
- Recognizing cohesive devices (e.g., such as and which)
- Understanding different intonation patterns and uses of stress, etc. that give clues to meaning and social setting
- Understanding inferred information (e.g. speaker's attitude or intentions)

The array of microskills in listening shows that listening is not a passive skill. The microskills are used simultaneously to enable a person to receive and respond to messages. Recapitulate a conversation you had with someone yesterday. What did you hear first? During the conversation, did you have to predict the speaker's message? Was there information in the conversation that you found relevant? Was there any information that you did not focus on? Did you hear intonation patterns that made you understand the speaker's meaning better? Discuss your experience with the class.

Listening is a complex process that involves the listener, the speaker, the content of the message, and any visual support that accompanies the message (Brown & Yule, 1983). Several factors that influence a listener's listening skills are interest in the topic, the listener's background knowledge that facilitates understanding of the topic, and the ability to use negotiation skills such as asking for clarification, repetition, or definition of points not understood, all of which make the incoming message more understandable.

Five major factors affect listening comprehension:

1. Text characteristics (listening passage/text or visual supplements);
2. Interlocutor (speaker's persona; character)
3. Task (purpose and associated)
4. Listener (listener's personal response)
5. Process (listener's cognitive activities and the nature of interaction between speaker and listener)

The research section in this chapter will address these major factors that affect listening. In using the listening skills, listeners have to deal with the speaker. If a speaker uses colloquial language and reduced forms, listening comprehension is more difficult. The rate at which speakers deliver their speech—whether it is too fast or too slow—also influences the listener's understanding of the message. The more the listener is exposed to the speaker's speech habits, the easier it is for the listener because he or she will use these speech habits as clues to decipher meaning. Another factor that influences listening is the content of the message. Content that is familiar to a listener is easier to understand than content for which a listener has no background knowledge. In addition, visual support such as pictures, graphs, diagrams, gestures, and facial expressions can increase listening comprehension if employed appropriately and the listener is able to interpret them correctly.

## What Happens When We Listen?

Contrary to some people's belief that listening is a passive skill, it is an active skill that is gaining researchers' attention. Like the other skills, most of what is known about listening comes from research in native language development; however, there's a greater focus on inquiry into second language listening as the importance of teaching listening increases (Rubin, 1995).

Listeners are not usually conscious of the steps they take in the listening process. These steps can occur simultaneously, sequentially, in rapid succession, or move backward and forward as needed. The listener:

- Determines a reason for listening (e.g., getting direction to the Cravis Center)
- Takes the raw speech and deposits an image of it in the short-term memory (remembering the right and left turns to the Cravis Center)
- Attempts to organize the information by identifying the type of speech event (conversation, lecture, radio ad) and the function of the message (persuade, inform, request)
- Predicts information expected to be included in the message
- Recalls background information (schemata) to help interpret the message
- Assigns a meaning to the message
- Checks that the message has been understood
- Determines the information to be held in long-term memory

■ Deletes the original form of the message that had been received into short-term memory (Brown, 1994; Dunkel, 1986)

Other processes at work are the two types of cognitive processing: bottom-up and top-down processing.

## Top-down Processing

Top-down processing refers to listener's understanding the big picture of the message. Here, listeners utilize the schemata or background knowledge they have of the subject in interpreting the message. For instance, students listen to the teacher's lecture on the many uses of lemons. The teacher shows students a map of India and explains that lemons probably come to us from India and were first planted in the United States during the California gold rush as a means to fight scurvy. The teacher proceeds to show how lemon juice can remove rust or mildew stains. She also demonstrates another use of lemon by squeezing lemon juice into a container, dipping a swab into the juice, using it to write a message on a white paper. When the paper dries, the message appears on the page. She then says that lemon juice contains a compound that is colorless when dissolved in water. When heated, the compound breaks down and produces carbon, which is black. Students process the teacher's lecture by looking at the map and observing the experiment, primarily focusing on the uses of lemon that they can relate to. In this activity, students use *top-down* processing in listening to the lecture. Because students are already familiar with the subject matter, they raise questions only on issues that they would like to be clarified.

## Bottom-up Processing

In *bottom-up* processing, the meaning of the message is interpreted based on the incoming data—from sounds, to words, to grammatical relationships, to meaning. Stress, rhythm, and intonation also play a role in bottom-up processing. Anderson and Lynch (1988) call this the "listener as a tape-recorder" view of listening because it assumes that the listener takes in and stores messages sequentially, similar to a tape-recorder- one sound, one phrase, and one utterance at a time. Beginners of Spanish would focus on sounds of individual words and the intonation pattern to help them understand a statement or a question. They can repeat these words several times in an attempt to understand the meaning of the sentence or question.

All of the steps and processes mentioned influence the techniques and activities teachers choose to incorporate into their lessons to assist learners in learning to listen as well as listening to learn.

## Why Is Listening Difficult for Second Language Learners?

Part of successful listening is the ability to concentrate on the message and maintain attention in listening to the message. One of the difficulties that second language learners face is the lack of attention they give to the speaker due to their limited understanding of the message. When students do not comprehend instruction or can only understand bits and pieces of the message, it is inevitable that they will have a shorter attention span. Another difficulty results in the continuous flow of speech in "real time" that may not be "played back" for the second language learners. Second language learners also have to distinguish all the sounds, intonation patterns, and voice qualities in the second language and to discriminate between them and similar sounds in their native tongue.

## What Does Research Say About Listening?

Nunan traces the comings and goings of the attention given to listening comprehension skills. In the 1960s, the emphasis on oral language skills gave the teaching of listening skills a boost. Teaching listening became fashionable again in the 1980s, when Krashen's (1982) ideas about comprehensible input gained prominence. Then, James Asher's work on Total Physical Response (TPR) reinforced the notion that second language is learned most effectively in the beginning stages if the pressure to produce utterances is taken away from the learners. In the 1980s, work in the first language field also encouraged proponents of listening in a second language. The works of scholars such as Gillian Brown (1984, 1990) made a breakthrough in emphasizing the importance of developing oracy (the ability to listen and speak) as well as literacy in school. Prior to this, reading and writing were the only skills considered important and warranted instruction, while listening and speaking skills were taken for granted because native speakers were considered to be born with these skills.

Current research and theory once again point to the benefit of allowing beginners in a second language to go through a silent, or prespeaking period (Dunkel, 1991). An experimental group was deliberately kept from oral production in a study that involved beginning students of Russian at the Defense Language Institute (Rubin 1996). The group was required instead to respond only in writing. They were then merged with students in the regular Russian program. After 12 weeks of instruction, it was found that the experimental group performed significantly better in listening comprehension than the control group. In addition, the experimental group outperformed the control group on the other three skills(speaking, reading and writing).

Learners are given the opportunity to store information in their memories when they are not expected to produce speech immediately. This will also spare them the trauma of task overload and speaking before they are ready. The silent period can be long or short depending on each individual learner's readiness for speech production. The silent period may be comprised of several class periods of listening activities that foster vocabulary and build comprehension, such as Total Physical Response (TPR). In TPR, the teacher gives a series of commands and students demonstrate their understanding of the message by acting out the commands. For instance, the teacher says, " Walk to the door," and the student walks to the door. When the learner feels comfortable enough to speak, he or she will begin to give the commands. A listening period containing productive tasks enhances rather than inhibits language acquisition for both beginners and advanced-level learners.

Griffiths (1995) suggests that different languages have different "normal" rates and the rates defined in studies using English cannot be applied exactly to students of other languages. Tauroza and Allison (1997) also note that normal rates vary among text types and that the range of what is considered normal may vary from language to language. However, there are conflicting findings about speech rate on comprehension. Griffiths found that speech faster than 200 w.p.m. is hard for lower-intermediate learners to understand. He found that this level of student performed best at 127 w.p.m. Working with intermediate-level students, Kelch (1987) found significant comprehension effects for slowed speech (124 w.p.m). On the other hand, Blau (1990) found that speech ranging from 145 to 185 w.p.m. did not significantly affect comprehension of intermediate- and advanced-level students.

Another measuring impact of the rate is the kind of listening required. King and Behnke (1989) studied the interaction of the task with listening type for native speakers. They found that comprehensive listening performance deteriorated significantly as speech comprehension levels increased (i.e., faster speech), while interpretive and short-term listening comprehension remained stable until a high degree of time compression (60%) was reached. Voss (1980) studied repeats, false starts, filled pauses, and unfilled pauses in spontaneous speech. He found that all types of hesitation phenomena cause perceptual problems and, thus, comprehension errors for nonnative speakers (NNs). NNs get stuck in bottom-up processing of phonetic utterances that do not affect comprehension, while native speakers (NSs) discard these utterances in favor of top-down processing. Fishman (1989) compared NSs of English with NNs who were at a fairly high level of ESL competence. He identified 10 categories of error (largely phonological) and found that although native speakers made 2.5 times fewer errors than nonnatives, the same error categories turned up in L1 and L2 listeners. He concluded that in principle, the perception strategies used in the L1 and L2 follow similar lines. Markham (1990), in his study on the interlocutor characteristics, stated "Gender bias is a pervasive factor that exerts an influence on ESL students' recall of orally presented material." For example, he found that both groups recalled more from the non-expert female speakers than from the female experts. Shohamy and Inbar (1988) considered how different types of questions influence success in L2 listening tasks. They found that subjects performed better on questions referring to local cues in the text than on those referring to global cues. Low-level test takers can respond to the local cues in the text. Students who respond to global cues can also respond to local cues, but not vice-versa.

### Types of Spoken Language

Second language learners should be exposed to as many types of spoken language as possible. Types of spoken language include:

- Formal lectures
- Casual chats
- Face-to-face interactions
- Telephone messages
- Radio and TV presentations
- Native speakers' speech in all kinds of situations

## Listening Difficulties Faced by Second Language Learners

Part of successful listening is the ability to concentrate on the message and maintain attention in listening to the message. One of the difficulties that second language learners face is the lack of attention they give to the speaker due to their limited understanding of the message. When students do not comprehend instruction or can only understand bits and pieces of the message, it is inevitable that they will have a shorter attention span. Another difficulty results in the continuous flow of speech in "real time" that may not be "played back" for the second language learners. Second language learners also have to distinguish all the sounds, intonation patterns, and voice qualities in the second language and to discriminate between them and similar sounds in their native tongue.

### What Constitutes Successful Listening?

Nunan (1989) listed the following characteristics of what successful listening:

- Meaningful words and phrases derived from segmenting the stream of speech

- Recognition of word classes
- Use of one's own background knowledge to relate to the incoming message
- Utterances and parts of the aural text are identified for their rhetorical and functional intent
- Identification of information focus and emotional attitudinal tone through rhythm, stress, and intonation
- Ability to extract gist from a longer aural text without having understood every word

## Tips on Selecting Listening Techniques and Activities

When selecting materials and activities for second language learners, teachers should have these considerations:

- Listening should be purposeful and interesting. Tasks such as following instructions to classroom routines provide purposeful listening, and listening to taped stories is an interesting listening activity.
- Materials should be authentic. Examples include children programs such as Magic School Bus, Sesame Street, and Blues Clues. Opportunities to develop both top-down and bottom-up processing skills should be offered. A top-down approach would involve students giving the title of a taped story that they listen to and bottom-up approach would be to involve students in answering specific questions on the taped story that they listened to such as, "Who is Andy talking to on the phone?"
- The development of listening strategies should be encouraged. Playing video with the sound off will elicit students' prediction of the script of the video; and playing it with the sound on will confirm or modify students' predictions.
- Activities should teach, not test. Students should not only provide a one word answer to listening tasks, but they should also be able to provide main ideas and details of what they have heard. The prelistening activity can involve students in using language to predict. Postlistening activities can help students assess their accuracy in their prediction. This task will help them develop listening skills that are beneficial beyond the classroom.

# Some Strategies/Skills for Effective Listening Skills Using the TESOL Standards

In preparing a lesson that focuses on listening skills, TESOL standards for K–12 students should be included.

## TESOL ESL Standards for Pre-K–12 students

### Goal 1: To use English to communicate in social settings

Standard 1:   Students will use English to participate in social interaction.

Standard 2:   Students will interact in, through, and with spoken and written English for personal expression and enjoyment.

Standard 3:   Students will use learning strategies to extend their communicative competence.

### Goal 2: To use English to achieve academically in all content areas.

Standard 1:   Students will use English to interact in the classroom.

Standard 2:   Students will use English to obtain, process, construct, and provide subject matter information in spoken and written form.

Standard 3:   Students will use appropriate learning strategies to construct and apply academic knowledge.

### Goal 3: To use English in socially and culturally appropriate ways

Standard 1:   Students will use the appropriate language variety, register, and genre according to audience, purpose, and setting.

Standard 2:   Students will use nonverbal communication appropriate to audience, purpose, and setting.

Standard 3:   Students will use appropriate learning strategies to extend their sociolinguistic and sociocultural competence.

## A Listening Lesson

The teacher can facilitate the development of a listening activity by creating listening lessons that guide the learner through three stages: pre-listening, the listening task, and the post-listening task. In an activity that involves a student listening to a telephone conversation, students are asked to predict the content of discussion between the speakers. In the actual listening task, students can fill out answers to specific questions while identifying the pictures of words they heard in the conversation. In the post-listening activity, students are asked to verbally recall the information they heard or write a brief summary of the information they gathered after listening to the taped conversation.

### *Using Goal 1, Standard 1 in Grades Pre-K–3*

To use English to communicate in social settings, students will use English to participate in social interactions. Some descriptors for listening lessons are engaging in conversations, using nonverbal communication in social interactions, and sharing and requesting information. Some of the sample progress indicators include using the telephone, engaging listener's attention verbally or nonverbally, or describing feelings and emotions after watching a movie or listening to a recorded radio programs.

### *Listening Activities for Students at Multiple Levels of Language Proficiency*

Lund (1990) offers teachers numerous activities for developing second language learners' listening skills and ways to check their comprehension:

- Taking action: Listeners respond through TPR.
- Making choices: Listeners select from alternatives such as pictures, objects, texts, or actions.
- Transferring: Listeners transform the message they heard in the form of drawing pictures filling a chart.
- Answering: Listeners answer questions about the text.
- Condensing: Listeners take notes or make outlines of text heard.
- Extending: Listeners go beyond the text by continuing the story or solving a problem.
- Modeling: Listeners perform a similar task.
- Duplicating: Listeners simply repeat or translate the message.
- Conversing: Listeners are active participants in face-to- face conversations.

## Listening Activities Using TESOL Standards

Teachers' daily class routine—(calendar activity, the class lining up, or a restroom break) can be a useful resource for listening task. The expressions used daily by teachers to accomplish the morning work or class work act as a source of repeated, patterned expressions that English learners will hear and understand. The actions performed as a result of these expressions will help students to participate in social settings. The language they hear in the classroom from the teacher or from other students will assist them in learning how and when to use the appropriate expressions to fulfill their needs in the social setting. For instance, when English learners hear others in class asking the teacher, "May I go to the restroom?" they will be able to utter those words themselves when they need to go to the restroom. Other examples include asking to borrow items from others in class—"May I borrow your eraser, please?"

Listening to messages that are comprehensible to nonnative speakers of English is crucial. For learners in preproduction stage, actions, gestures, and visuals are important accompaniments to the messages they hear. Key words and phrases need to be emphasized and repeated. Daily routines in class, such as the expression "Hand in your work" should be acted out so that English language learners can match what they hear to what needs to be done. While giving instructions, teachers should be specific in their directions—students at this stage need a lot of guidance to understand directions. For instance, if the task requires that students circle the correct answer, teachers should demonstrate what "circle" means. Also at this stage, giving action related commands (TPR) will help learners with their language. A game such as "Simon Says" will help students learn common verbs like sit, stand, walk, and run. In game called "Detecting Mistakes", students have a picture in front of them and they listen to a description of that picture. When the teacher mentions items that are not in the picture, students are to call out, "That's a mistake." Frequent activities at the listening center where students listen to taped story books will help them immensely in getting used to the sounds of the new language.

Students at the early production and speech emergence levels of language acquisition can be challenged with listening activities that expect them to produce short verbal responses. One such activity is the guessing game in which students listen to a short description of an item and then have to guess what it is. Teachers can use tasks and texts that are at different levels of difficulty. For the intermediate fluency students, teachers can provide a taped story for them to listen to and later ask to retell the story briefly.

Listening skills should be an integral part of all lessons in the class. Using some listening strategies such as focusing on key items and carrying out tasks requested after listening to important information are crucial in preparing students to function in their new language. Teachers should not force beginning students to respond. They should also understand that students need this silent stage to mull over what they hear and make sense of what they hear. That is why it is hard to measure comprehension without any proof of performance from students. Nevertheless, the preproduction stage, or the silent period, is a crucial period in which students listen attentively to the new language around them.

What listening skills should students be taught at this stage? What listening tasks are they expected to do? How can teachers incorporate these basic listening skills and tasks in their daily classroom instructions?

Imagine you are teaching a new student from Mexico who does not know one word of English. What is the first thing you will do to help him with his 'listening' of the English language?

| Language proficiency stages | Tasks |
| --- | --- |
| Preproduction | • Students listens to commands and acts out commands.<br>• Students selects a picture that shows the word he hears. |
| Early production | • Student listens to a dialog and provides one- or two-word responses. Listener uses duplicating strategy; he repeats or translates the message.<br>• Students check off items—this usually involves a list of words that the learners listen to and check off or categorize as they hear them (e.g., picture bingo).<br>• Picture dictation—student draws picture from verbal dictation. |
| Speech emergence | • Student highlights key points of the lecture he listens to.<br>• Listener models a similar task, (e.g, he reproduces what he heard). |
| Intermediate fluency | • Conversing—student is asked to be an active participant in a face-to-face conversations. |

In designing tasks, teachers should provide learners with opportunities to employ a flexible range of listening strategies. Teachers can have students listen to the same text several times, but each time students are asked to perform different tasks. For instance, in using the weather forecast, the first task may be to ask students to give the gist of the weather report. The second task may be to ask students to match the places that experience heavy rainfall. Finally, students might be required to listen for details, for example, the temperature in certain places and the expected percentage of possible rain in the certain areas. Students should also be expected to be involved in reciprocal listening. This means that listeners are asked to take part in the interaction. Examples of such tasks may be to ask students to role play a situation that will involve listening skills in the real world—answering the telephone, getting directions, or listening to classroom instructions.

Many books and articles address the techniques of teaching listening. An example is *New Ways of Teaching Listening,* a book edited by David Nunan and Lindsay Miller, published by TESOL publishers. This text contains a series of classroom techniques that have been tried by teachers. Another good source for listening activities is the Internet Journal, which lists examples of activities and lesson plans.

## Listening Comprehension Assessment

Besides formal tests, teachers can get a broad picture of their students' listening abilities by collecting data from other sources: self-assessment and student portfolios. Students can assess their own listening skills by responding to a self-assessment sheet that teachers create according to certain criteria. The table below is an example of a self-assessment sheet:

|  | ☺ | 😐 | ☹ |
|---|---|---|---|
| 1.  I understand most of what I hear. |  |  |  |
| 2.  I understand some of what I hear. |  |  |  |
| 3.  I understand very little of what I hear. |  |  |  |

Teachers can develop a portfolio system in which students' work based on listening tasks can be included. Over a period of nine weeks in which students have completed many listening tasks, teachers can request students to put their best work in their portfolio. An example of a listening task can be as simple as an activity called Blind Drawing. Teachers can describe a simple picture to the students while they draw what they hear. Students can also be paired up to do this activity, each taking turns to give the description. A little more complex activity is "What's this film about?" After deciding on certain language obejctives such as the use of adjectives or nouns, teachers show the first three minutes of a movie, television commercial, cartoons, without any visuals, just the sound (cover the monitor screen with a cloth). Then students are asked to define or list the items they heard. They play the film again, this time with sound and image. Ask students to compare their answers to the items they saw in the film.

Douglas (1988) called for listening tests that are integrative and integrated, conceptualized, and that challenge learners to deal with a variety of listening tasks and conditions. Some forms of listening comprehension assessment are checklists that teachers can create to assess specific listening skills. For instance, students are assessed for their comprehension of phoneme change in minimal pairs such as /pin/ and /bin/; rising and falling intonation (He's gone out); or stress on words that signal a change in meaning of the same statement (She scolded him). Another form of listening comprehension is through the use of anecdotal reports in which teachers observe students' behaviors when they have a face-to-face conversation. By observing students' facial expressions, gestures, and one or two-word responses, teachers are able to assess their listening skills.

Considerations in selecting suitable passages for listening comprehension tests are just as important as the task. Teachers should evaluate the level of the materials to the desired difficulty, interest, and relevance. Difficulty also resides in text, interaction of text variables with tasks, background knowledge, memory and inferencing ability. When using authentic, unedited passages for lower-ability examinees, teachers should look for passages that are more "listener friendly"—those closer to the spoken language than to the written language.

## Points to Remember

❑ Listening is the ability to identify and understand what others are saying.

❑ An able listener is capable of understanding a speaker's accent or pronunciation, his grammar and his vocabulary and meaning.

❑ Factors that influence listener's listening skills are interest in topic, listener's background knowledge of topic, and the ability to use negotiation skills.

❑ Listening skills involve two types of cognitive processing: top-down and bottom up. Top-down processing refers to listener's global understanding of the message while bottom-up processing involves the interpretation of the message through analysis of the smaller components of the language such as sounds and words.

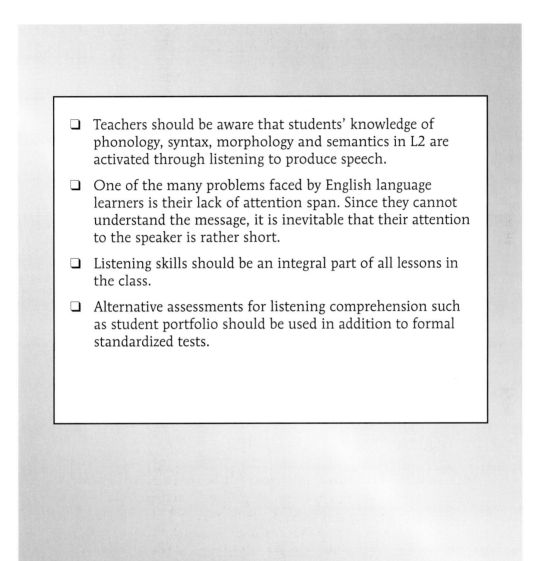

❏ Teachers should be aware that students' knowledge of phonology, syntax, morphology and semantics in L2 are activated through listening to produce speech.

❏ One of the many problems faced by English language learners is their lack of attention span. Since they cannot understand the message, it is inevitable that their attention to the speaker is rather short.

❏ Listening skills should be an integral part of all lessons in the class.

❏ Alternative assessments for listening comprehension such as student portfolio should be used in addition to formal standardized tests.

# Chapter 15

## *Second Language Oral Development and Instruction*

### KEY ISSUES

❏ Research on oral communication skills

❏ English language learners' difficulties in speaking

❏ Strategies/skills for speaking

❏ Techniques for teaching speaking at multiple levels

❏ Techniques for correcting errors

Ms. Santos likes to use games as a culminating activity in her lesson. Today she uses a game called "passing a parcel" for a lesson on adjectives. Ms. Santos puts her students in a circle and asks them to describe a picture that she shows them. The first student who starts the game describes what she sees in the picture and then passes the picture to the student sitting next to her. The next student repeats the earlier student's statement and adds her or his own statement to it. So, Cathy looks at the picture in front of her and says, " I see a red ball on the beach," and passes the picture to Tim who then says, "Cathy sees a red ball on the beach and I see the blue ocean." Kim Huh continues with "Cathy sees a red ball on the beach, Tim sees the blue ocean, and I see the golden sand." This activity is completed when every student has a chance to come up with a statement that describes the given picture and also repeats the prior statements made by the other students.

**H**ow does this activity promote English language learners' oral language development?

This activity is a great oral development activity for English learners at various language proficiency levels because it not only gives them the opportunity to use spoken English at their ability level in producing their own oral description of the pictures but it also gives them the opportunity to listen to and repeat statements made by their peers. This is a fun way to reinforce their oral development and correct usage of adjective placement in English sentence structure where an adjective precedes a noun.

> *Ms. Santos begins her class every morning by reading poetry to her third-grade students. Several of her students are English language learners. She introduces the poem, reads it once, and then her students echo-read with her. After they have read the poem, Ms. Santos discusses the meaning of the poem with her students. She then arranges the poem into some kind of choral reading wherein students notice contractions, rhyming words, word patterns, and "words in words." Students then talk about ideas for illustrating the poem. At the end of the week, students take a poem of their choice home to share with their families.*

How does this activity promote oral language development for English language learners?

English L2 learners may come from homes that have provided them with a rich oral language environment, and certainly a firm background in the home language is a strong indicator of eventual success in learning another language (Cummins,1980,1981). However, at times students do not bring a well-developed language background from their first or second language; therefore, teachers should provide students with classrooms that are rich in meaningful oral language. Students' presence within the classroom for more than 8 hours a day should enable them to be exposed to opportunities that develop their oral language. How, then, should a classroom that promotes oral language development look? To answer this question, teachers first have to understand what speaking is. Speaking is an interactive process of constructing meaning that involves producing, receiving and processing information (Brown, 1994; Burns & Joyce, 1997). Speaking requires that learners not only know how to produce specific points of language such as grammar, pronunciation, or vocabulary (linguistic competence), but also that they understand when, why, and in what ways to produce language (sociolinguistic competence). Speech has its own skills, structures, and conventions that are different from written languauge (Burn & Joyce, 1997; Carter & McCarthy, 1995; Cohen, 1996). To succeed in a given speech, a speaker synthesizes this array of skills.

# Research on Oral Communication Skills

Rivers (1981) reported that outside the classroom, listening is used twice as often as speaking, which is used twice as much as reading and writing. Inside the classroom, speaking and listening are the most often-used skills (Brown, 1994). Although they are recognized both by teachers and students as critical for functioning in an English language context, the teaching of speaking and listening has often been described as "the Cinderella of language teaching" (i.e. she never got to the ball). The teaching of speaking and listening has always taken a back seat in the teaching of the four language skills (listening, speaking, reading, and writing).

Spoken language has two main functions: transactional and interactional. The primary goal of transactional function of oral language is transference of information and it is message oriented (Brown & Yule, 1993). The speaker's purpose of the speaker is to convey his message. Primarily, transactional spoken language is used to get work done in the real world: for instance, an employer giving instructions to employee, a teacher explaining math concepts to students, a patient discussing her symptoms with a doctor, a child telling Santa Claus what she wants for Christmas. In all of these situations, the speakers' purpose in communicating to listeners is to make their message clear so that they will not be misunderstood, which will cause both speakers and listeners to be frustrated. When the message is the reason for speaking, the message must be understood. So, speakers usually (painstakingly) make themselves understood through repetition or rephrasing of their message.

The primary goal of interactional spoken language is to maintain social relationships and, therefore, it is listener oriented. Many social interactions seem to contain interactional content where the purpose of communication is to be nice to the listener. Most people spend a great deal of time chatting and interactional chats are frequently characterized by shifting topics and a great deal of agreement on them. Two speakers conducting interactional speech should end up feeling comfortable with each other and friendly. We find speakers in these exchanges do not usually disagree with each other and do not argue, so the exchange does not require repetition of what was said. The listener might nod his head even if he does not hear what the speaker is saying. Interactional spoken language usually contains more generalized vocabulary and sparse information-packing. Most interactional chats contain greetings and farewells and a great deal of expression of opinion. Participants take turns in leading the conversation.

Within spoken language it is also important to understand "short turns" and "long turns" (Brown and Yule, 1993). A short turn consists of one or two utterances; a long turn consists of a string of utterances that may be as long as an hour's lecture. Short turns obviously demand much less of a speaker in the way of producing structures.

Consider the following conversation as an example of short turn:

D:  oregano and basil + did you +

J:  oregano + tarragon

D:  do you like—

C:  it was all right

D:  my mother's favorite is Five Brothers + but I like the Del Monte's + it's delicious!

C:  and Alfredo sauce I love as well—it's yummy

D:  what's that

C:  it's the creamy sauce that has a bunch of spices in them

The primary interactional conversation among the three female friends consists of swapping turns. The longest of these short turns consists only of statements that contain additional information: *it's the creamy sauce that has a bunch of spices in them.* Compare this to what is needed to summarize the content of a book or your medical history to your doctor—it is obvious that what is needed in long turns is considerably more demanding than what is required of a speaker in a short turn. When a speaker takes the floor for a long turn, she or he takes responsibility for constructing a structured sequence of utterances to help listeners construct a coherent mental representation of what she or he is trying to say (Brown & Yule, 1983). What the speaker says must be structured coherently. She or he must speak clearly and specify any relevant properties, before moving on to saying what happened. If the speaker is retelling a story, he or she must specify the main characters in the story and clearly recount the sequence of events in the correct order.

Consider the following long turn in the retelling of a story:

Theresa: No, it wasn't escary. But well,... First it was scary but then the other one no. Because there was... First a little girl... There was a television and the father was sleeping in the ... in a ... sillion? In like a chair. And then the little girl pass the television and she said, "Right here!" Then...then a hand get out of the television and she said, "ouch!" And then a little boy was sleeping and the little girl sleep here and the boy here and then he see all the time a tree and it look like a face... And then he was escary. Then he tell his father and his father said o.k. Just count 1,2,3 to not escare. Then... then... the...he... the little girl and the little... the

two brothers go in with the mother and her father because they're still escare.
(Excerpt from Peregoy & Boyle, 2001)

## Models of Spoken Language

It is obviously easier to provide models of good written language than to do so with spoken language. Even though we oftentimes see teachers who expect students to provide complete sentences, we find that native spoken language obviously reflects the "performance" end of the competence-performance distinction. It reveals so many slips of tongue, errors, incomplete utterances, speaking in the here-and-now under pressure of time, and comparing what the speaker is saying now to what he just said to what he is trying to say later. Therefore, students should not be overly corrected when they produce partial sentences, or incomplete phrases of the sort produced by native speakers. When nonnative speakers listen to native speakers, they hear language that is produced spontaneously and they then realize that the speakers in this foreign language talk like human beings, and it is similar to talk in their native language. Native speakers do not produce ideal strings of complete, perfectly formed sentences; they use language manipulatively, exploratorily, to communicate with and make up what they say as they go along. Native speakers of English are perceived to speak perfect English when they address a public audience. Although nonnative speakers often simulate this type of perfect English it is not appropriate when conducting a conversation.

Examine the following scenario in which an English learner communicates:

Tan can walk into a shop that sells jeans, asks for a pair of jeans in excruciating English, and get rewarded; he walks out of the store with the jeans he wants. His same performance in his English class results in some sort of punishment—a low grade, a frown from his teacher and peers, and sometimes even a reprimand. It is of no surprise that some English language learners remain silent! Students realize that their teacher is not interested in what they have to say, but in how they say it.

By age 3 or 4, a child can communicate most of what he wants to say. However, it is not until age 8 that the majority of children achieve the ability to produce all of the sounds of adult speech. Furthermore, it is not until around age 10 that the speech of the majority of children reaches the syntactical level of adult speech. It is almost certain that second language learners will not reach the native level in their second language, at least not in class. A more realistic goal is to expect a functional ability to make themselves understood.

## Why Is Speaking Difficult for Second Language Learners?

Speech is somewhat like an iceberg: Most of the act of speaking is not directly observable. What we hear is the culmination of a series of five internal processes: (1) People's thoughts are an outgrowth of their feelings, desires, and needs. They have something to say and are motivated to communicate their thoughts to others. (2) Speech involves the conversion of thoughts to language. (3) The sounds, words, and forms used are stored in internal cognitive networks. (4) The speakers' competence is brought into play as they begin the conversion of thought to speech. (5) The listeners can hear the result, the performance skill, in action. In short, the speaker's cognitive networks contain the motivating force behind the thoughts, the content of speech, and the knowledge of the language system by means of which thoughts are converted into speech. All except the overt oral message itself are internal processes.

Learning to speak is obviously more difficult than learning to understand the spoken language. More effort is required on the part of the student. The entire process covers a greater period of time to develop than does listening comprehension and is more taxing on the students' energies. For second language learners, the act of speaking is a display of their competence of the second language, and not all of their competence can be seen through their performance. One of the difficulties that second language learners face is the actual pronunciation of the sounds of the language. Lenneberg (1962) in his statement on the critical period hypothesis, forwarded the idea that at puberty the wiring of the brain is complete and the muscles surrounding the vocal cord harden, both of which result in nonnative speakers' difficulty in pronouncing sounds with a native-like accent. Second language learners who started learning a second language after puberty may not be able to produce native-like pronunciation. A newborn has the ability to recognize all of the universal sounds in any language, but the wiring of the brain for native language sounds occurs in the language environment in which he grows up. When sounds from other languages are not reinforced, they will wilt away. This explains why some English language learners experience difficulty in producing sounds that are not present in their native language: examples are the /th/ and /sh/ sounds for Spanish speakers learning English, and the rolling r sound in Spanish that English speakers may find difficult to produce.

Even though pronunciation is one of the many problems faced by English language learners, it is by far the least significant because as long as speakers can communicate their meanings, some flaws in pronunciation will not prevent them from being understood. In fact, some speakers choose to retain their L1 accent when speaking English because of solidarity and identity issues. Perhaps the real difficulty faced by nonnative speakers of English is in the application of the grammatical rules they have learned. This is more apparent in adult learners of English, as they typically have the procedural knowledge of the target language (i.e. the "what" of the language but a limited opportunity to apply the knowledge in the actual performance of communicating in the language—the "how" of the language).

Many foreign students who come to the United States to further their studies perform better in the reading and writing skills than they do in speaking and listening because they learned to read and write in English in their home countries, but lack oral communication skills due to limited opportunities to communicate in English. This lends to the discussion of accuracy versus fluency in oral communication. English language learners may attain a high level of accuracy in the production of the English language in situations in which they have enough time and knowledge to apply the rules they have learned. However, they may lack the natural flow to communicate in English because they have not attained the automaticity to communicate spontaneously in English, thereby disabling them from attaining fluency.

Krashen (1981) believes that when a learner acquires a language, he will attain fluency in the language, whereas a learner who learns a language may not attain the same level of fluency. Bialystok and MacLaughlin (1982) look at fluency from the point of both a novice and an expert learner. The expert learner who knows how to juggle the constraints of a new language will be more fluent than the novice learner who is struggling to bring his new knowledge to bear. Of concern to teachers in this issue of accuracy versus fluency is which is the more significant criteria to expect of learners. Teachers have to be aware of several factors that may influence students' fluency or accuracy in oral production. Some factors are students' personality and motivation. Extrovert learners will display fluency over accuracy because they are not inhibited about speaking even though their oral production may not be accurate. Introvert learners may take their time about speaking in English for fear of being embarrassed by their nongrammatical English or mispronunciation of English words.

They are those who will overuse the language editor that Krashen (1981) describes in his Monitor Model. Learners who are instrumentally motivated to learn English may only practice the use of the language in limited environments, perhaps only in the workplace or school, whereas learners who are integratively motivated to learn the language will practice using the target language more frequently and in wider dimensions—they want to learn English in order to integrate and feel like they belong in the English-speaking community. Teachers should not sacrifice students' attainment of fluency over accuracy; rather, they should allow students to develop both accuracy and fluency over time. They can help students to achieve the fluency goal by not overly correcting students' mistakes and, more importantly, they have to be mindful of the way they correct errors. Modeling correct language structures and rephrasing students' utterances in grammatically correct English will enable students to learn their mistakes in a less threatening manner. By the same token, teachers can help students achieve the accuracy goal by not allowing students to continuously speak English with mistakes uncorrected; errors that are not corrected can be fossilized and become a part of learners' spoken and written English. In the next section, we will look at tools for developing oral language skills, but first let us examine the characteristics of learners at various levels of oral language proficiency.

English language learners progress in their acquisition of the target language in stages. As soon as they are in the target environment, they will be subjected to the forms and function of the language. Although at the beginning, or preproduction, level they are silent, they are still interacting with the target language. They are making sense of the new language by comprehending and internalizing what they see and hear around them. At this stage, they should not be forced to speak; however, they should be included in classroom instruction by doing tasks that are manageable and easily accomplished.

Teachers should be aware that newcomers vary in the duration of the silent period stage—some stay in this stage for about a week while others may take a few months. Teachers can make this transition into the new language less frustrating for learners by pairing them up with more proficient learners who can help them get around the class and school and also be successful in accomplishing their school work. Teachers should choose materials and design activities that meet students' language proficiency level. In the preproduction stage, teachers can put students in computer stations to utilize computer software that allows them to see and hear English spoken in a meaningful way.

By listening to English sounds and repeating them, students will move along in their acquisition stage—from the preproduction to the early production stage. At this stage, students begin to produce one or more words in English. Teachers should also paraphrase and use gestures, repetition, visuals, and acting out as means of communicating with students in a comprehensible way. Students can be included in class instruction and be made to feel that they belong by doing tasks such as drawing murals or by being a class helper, or by helping teachers with chores around the class: distributing papers, cleaning the board, compiling papers, etc. When teachers engage students in these tasks, students will feel they are a part of the classroom and become motivated to interact and communicate in a meaningful way. Also, teachers should be mindful of the questioning techniques they use. Students at preproduction stage can be asked to point at an object, nod their head, clap their hands—to do something to show their comprehension. They also can answer to a yes/no question or questions for which they can provide a one- or two-word answer.

Students who have exited the silent stage and the early production stage will be able to produce multiple words in a more coherent structure. They are able to understand and speak English in face-to-face interactions and they are less hesitant to speak. These students are at another stage of language proficiency: the speech emergence and the intermediate levels. At these levels, students are still developing their English language and, thereby, teachers will find students making grammatical errors such as the third-person singular verb, *he like* instead of *he likes,* and the nonuse of possessive form such as *Mary bag* instead of *Mary's bag.* At this stage, teachers are cautioned not to jump on students' mistakes. Instead, they should celebrate students' accomplishments at producing the sounds of a new language and experimenting with the new language rules they are still juggling. Sometimes teachers' good intentions and over-zealous manner in correcting students' mistakes may cause more harm than good. Students should not be corrected in mid-conversation because they will not be able to internalize the correction—these spoken mistakes are not concrete in nature. Rephrasing or modeling and repeating students' utterances with correct grammar will peripherally expose students to the correct form of the spoken language and this is a better way of addressing students' developmental errors. Consequently, teachers should focus on correcting errors in a more concrete manner (i.e., through the written form). For example, students can be alerted to their errors of verb conjugation through their readings of stories that contain verb conjugations or they can be asked to write sentences using verb conjugations.

At the speech emergence and intermediate stages, English language learners can produce phrases and short sentences. Students at the speech emergence stage will produce utterances that are telegraphic, whereas intermediate students will be able to engage in conversations more fluently and they begin to develop more academic language. At both of these stages, teachers can present English language learners with more linguistically demanding tasks. They can be put in collaborative groups to solve problems, assume a speaking role in a class play, retell a story, and verbally share their native culture with the rest of the class. They can also be assigned to more challenging responsibilities such as being a buddy to a newly arrived student or run simple errands for teachers such as handing in papers to the office. Teachers may find students developing their English skills rather rapidly at this stage. Although students are displaying near native language abilities, teachers should continue using sheltering techniques and provide instructions that are comprehensible. Even though intermediate-level students are capable of understanding streams of verbal language, teachers should use graphic organizers, such as charts, visuals, diagrams, and realia to make learning more meaningful to students. Teaching strategies that match student learning styles by providing multiple representations of delivering content are helpful to learners. Teachers can engage learners in concrete experiences—learning by doing. Visual and kinesthetic learners will benefit by experiencing instructions that use pictures and diagrams, by role-play, and by creating a product. At this stage, teachers should also be aware of the different questioning techniques that they can use: Students can be asked to read their journal entries that give their opinions about certain issues in a story; students can be asked to tell a different ending to a story, students can be asked to share their reasons for liking or disliking certain characters within a story, etc.

In presenting the abilities of these English language learners who are in varying levels of language proficiency, the activity and task guidelines are by no means carved in stone or set in a rigid mould. Teachers should exercise their discretion on tasks and materials selection through their observation of their students' abilities. Some teachers may want to give students who are at the early production stage more challenging tasks than those prescribed as what they can do at their level of proficiency. For instance, instead of merely asking students to respond with yes or no, teachers ask them to respond with a simple sentence structure such as "Yes, it is a dog." This is an acceptable initiative, as it puts into practice Krashen's input hypothesis—providing students with instruction that is I + 1— input that is a bit beyond their current level of proficiency.

## Tools for Promoting Oral Language Development

Although oral language development is treated as a self-contained chapter in this book, it is important to note that all language skills—listening, speaking, reading and writing—should be incorporated into English language learners' experience in the process of learning the new language. Although there are criticisms made about Krashen's (1981) acquisition versus learning hypothesis, in which he posits that learners who acquire the language will master the language better than the learners who learn the language, the practical application of his hypothesis is valuable. Teachers are encouraged to provide a natural environment in the classroom where English will be acquired. Teachers can achieve this goal by focusing on the most important elements in oral language development: comprehensible input and social interaction. By maintaining a routine classroom schedule, teachers are adding to the natural environment by providing a simulation of a real-world workplace. Designating certain activities at a certain time, such as snack, lunch, journal response, DEAR (drop everything and read), students are taught how to tell and manage time. In addition, by designing problem-solving tasks that involve students working in collaboration, teachers provide real opportunities for English language learners to communicate and to practice using their newly learned language. Teachers who avoid using collaborative groups in their class because they have a low tolerance for noise may not realize that they have deprived English language learners of their only chance to communicate in English—many of these students go home to a non English speaking-environment.

English language learners will have a better chance of learning English more rapidly when teachers incorporate new and innovative techniques that use English as a vehicle of communication. All learners, especially English language learners, will benefit from instruction that is fun and exciting and in a non-threatening atmosphere. The next section discusses several ways to promote English language learners' oral language development.

## Peer Tutoring

Peer tutoring, or a buddy system, is an effective tool that teachers can use. How is peer tutoring effective in teaching English to English language learners? In a peer tutoring set-up, students receive individual attention. They also receive undivided attention as they read, spell, ask questions and provide answers. Students are given sustained time to read and share their viewpoints. English language learners can practice conversational English while discussing academic English. They may find the buddy system structure less inhibiting and thus, become more comfortable speaking up as compared to speaking up in front of the whole class.

## Poetry

Poetry is yet another tool to help English language learners in developing their oral language skills. The benefits of poetry are obvious. Poetry is less intimidating because the short stanzas are easier and more manageable to memorize. The nature of reading poetry, which begs for reading and rereading, provides English language learners with ample opportunity to practice enunciating the words, and repetition promotes fluency. The rhythm, repetition, and rhyme of poetry facilitate students' comprehension of the meanings. The very nature of reciting poetry, first collectively and later individually, builds students' confidence in experimenting with their new language. Teachers can employ several strategies in using poetry in class. Teachers can model reading the poems aloud and then ask students to read the poem in unison. Some students who are at the early production stage can participate by repeating only certain stanzas. Teachers can divide the class up into two groups for "call and response method." In "Sh, sh baby's sleeping" poem, one group can recite the first two lines while the other group can follow suit with the other lines. Singing poems that use music makes the words more memorable. Poems can also be acted out in a form of a play. Many poems are easy to act out and they do not require extensive preparation.

This affords learners who have a kinesthetic learning style to maximize learning through acting out the poem. English language learners at the preproduction and early production stages can participate in this class activity because they can act out the poem.

## Games

Games can be incorporated as a tool to help English language learners develop their oral language skills. Games, too, have obvious benefits for English language learners. They allow learners to practice what is taught in a fun way. Games allow learners to experiment with the English language in a nonthreatening way. Students learn what is taught in a hands-on way and games will motivate learners with varying levels of proficiency to learn the new language without the burden of having been forced to learn language structures. Examples of games are card games, board games, simulation, and party-type games. An example of card games, "Happy families," is inexpensive and is comprised of sets of four cards depicting various families. When all of the cards are distributed, each student has to guess who has a member of the family he or she wants. Students then take turns asking for the particular family member they want. This game can be adapted to address any language feature, such as the reinforcement of question forms like "do, does, did" or it can be used for practicing telephone skills. Students are asked to role-play the act of answering the telephone. A student will ask for a particular member of the family by asking, "Is Phil home?" and the person answering the phone will have to say, "Sorry, Phil is not home" or " Hold on, please."

For intermediate learners, simulation games such as "Who Wants to be a Millionaire?" or "Jeopardy" can be adapted for collaborative participation. Students can be put in groups to make up questions and the teacher chooses and picks the questions to be used in the game. Students can take turns being the game host. Points are awarded to groups that answer the questions correctly. Small tokens can be given to the winning team. A very important point to note in using games is that they should be linked to syllabus concepts to be learned and must have a definite and purposeful place in lesson plans. Games that are effectively used in lessons reinforce students' learning of linguistic features and content area learning and are not just fillers of classroom time.

## Songs

Songs are not meant for kindergartners and first-graders only; songs should be used in higher grade levels, too. Teachers should make a point to allow students to sing at least one song a day. Songs should be used every day because songs make everyone alive and happy and they usually bring laughter to learners. The repetitive and rhythmic nature of songs will reinforce learning of grammatical structures that may be difficult for learners. Teachers should choose songs that relate to students' interest. Today's younger students like hiphop music—teachers can use the beat but should modify the lyrics to the linguistic or content features they are teaching. For example, learners have proven to be able to learn the names of the 50 states and their capitals by rapping them out.

## Show-and-Tell

Children at all grade levels perform show-and-tell in different forms. Show-and-tell has been used by teachers for a long time to recognize students' individuality in the classroom. Students are asked to bring in their favorite toy or their favorite personal item to share with the class. Students welcome the notion of talking, sharing, and describing what they know best, therefore motivation for oral language skills is high. This is an excellent way to open up pathways for newcomers to feel secured in their new environment as their identity and culture are being recognized. Younger English language learners and those at the preproduction and early production levels can be asked to give a one-or two-word description of the objects they bring in to share with the class. The adaptation of show-and-tell for these learners can be in the form of a game of 20 questions wherein the learners answer questions raised by their peers. All they have to say is "yes" or "no" or provide a one-word answer. If students forget to bring items from home or may not have items to share, teachers can have them draw a picture to share with the class. The objective of show-and-tell is realized when students stand in front of the class communicating verbally with their peers. The oral language development in this form of communication is meaningful because learners receive immediate feedback verbally and nonverbally from their audience. The negotiation of meaning that takes place in such an activity presents real experience for English language learners to learn and develop their social, academic, and linguistic skills.

For intermediate learners, a variation of show-and-tell can be in the form of a poster display. Students can describe their posters on "how to save manatees," for instance. Students can work in pairs or groups to come up with slogans on how to save the manatees. Their posters can include artwork as well. Each team member is given time to explain the team's ideas to the class. Oral language development in such a task is seen at two levels: occurring when students work in their own group, brainstorming ideas and conversing with each other about an academic topic and then taking it to another level in which they have to perform individually for a wider audience—the whole class. Therefore, show-and-tell is indeed a tool that works for students at various language proficiency levels because it draws on students' motivation to share with others what they know best—themselves, their possessions, or their creations. One of the most effective ways to promote oral language development, it scaffolds learners' early speaking skills that start from their own comfort zone—their own world.

## Recording Studio

Teachers can designate a small area in their class as a center for a recording studio where students take turns working on their oral language skills as they record their own voices. English language learners at preproduction or early production levels can be paired with learners at intermediate levels. Teachers can assign specific tasks for them to work on; for example, learners can recreate their own stories from looking at wordless books or cartoon scripts. More advanced learners can work on retelling of stories from their favorite book and providing a different plot or ending to the stories. Here, the purpose of the activity is clear: Learners are expected to complete a task that piques their interest and motivation. As the pair works on meeting a common resolution to put on tape, both students are communicating with each other meaningfully as they examine the task at hand. The bonus point of this activity is when teachers can take the audiotape home to hear and evaluate their students' oral language skills. They can also use it in class for a listening comprehension activity. Children welcome and enjoy different ways of learning that involve anything other than filling in worksheets, so this activity can also serve as a reward for good behavior.

## Riddles and Jokes

Riddles and jokes can be a lot of fun for learners. Riddles can be used in a closure activity within a lesson in which students are asked to find answers for riddles that involve their new knowledge on the subject they have just learned. Florida Alantic University student teachers were observed using a book that exclusively contains riddles about spiders. It was a wonderful culminating activity of their thematic unit in which riddles were used as a form of assessment. Children were encouraged to discuss in their groups the answers to the riddles.

Similarly, jokes give students and teachers a break from the monotony of a routine day's work. Teachers must consider their students' age and cultural backgrounds when sharing jokes. More proficient learners can be asked to share their own jokes with the class. Riddles and jokes help promote English language learners' oral language development in a fun and nonthreatening way, enhancing learners' use of the spoken English language at varying functional levels.

## Choral Reading

Just as the term suggests, choral reading involves participation from everybody. Remember when you were asked to sing the chorus of a song? Wasn't it fun to hear the booming sound of everyone's voices? Of course, the best part of choral reading is even if you do not know the words of the song or the passage, you can fake it by following the words a split second after the other people have spoken them out loud. Choral reading is a valuable tool for oral language development, especially for beginning English language learners. They are placed in a nonthreatening situation where they are not forced to perform before they are ready for an individual performance. This activity allows them to hear the pronunciation and intonation of the English language spoken by their peers as they repeat after them. Research indicates that choral reading helps children learn the intonation of English stories and improves their diction and fluency (Bradley & Thalgott, 1987). Choral reading also raises the enthusiasm and builds confidence of early readers (Stewig, 1981) and helps expand their vocabulary (Samson, Allen, & Sampson, 1990). Choral reading can be made more interesting by having students act out certain parts of the reading. Teachers can divide the class into different groups; each group assumes different responsibilities. Some groups can narrate the story by choral reading while others pantomime parts of the narrated story. This activity can be suitable for themes such as "Thanksgiving." Levels and complexity of the activity can be increased by using props and costumes in the dramatization of the choral-read story.

## Television, Videotape and CD-ROMs

The use of technology such as television, videotape recorders and computers in most classrooms is no longer a luxury but a necessity. With the advent of technology, television and videotape recorders and computers are easily accessible to teachers in classrooms. From time to time, teachers show students a movie as a means of a reward for good behaviors. Teachers can incorporate oral language development activities into their lesson objective by showing students snippets of the movie without the sound. Students work in pairs or groups to create the dialog of the scenes they have just seen. This activity enables students to interact with what they see in addition to watching the movie. Low-proficiency level learners can be paired up with more-proficient learners or they can be asked to identify the characters or story line by circling pictures and words. Learners can take part in choosing the movies they want to watch. An extension of this activity would be a script-writing task and dramatization of scenes of a home-made class movie; teachers can videotape their own class staging a play. Adaptations of using television and videotape or CD-ROMs are numerous. Teachers can explore current affairs by letting students watch news or documentary programs and engaging students in discussions of current happenings around the world. Activities using this technology provides English language learners with ample opportunities to develop and enhance their oral language skills. Picture a class busy at work. Students are talking and doing meaningful tasks that interest them. They are involved in a fun activity without even realizing that they are actually learning! Teachers have accomplished motivating their students to learn!

## Oral Language Development in Content Area Instruction

Content area teachers in middle and high schools and elementary school teachers should include language skill objectives in their content area lessons. These teachers should teach to two objectives: content and language. Let us examine the development of English learners' oral language development in the following content area instructions: math, science and social studies.

### Math

Although math is considered a universal language, English language learners can experience difficulties in learning mathematical language in English which includes unique vocabulary, sentence structure, semantic properties, and text structures, both oral and written. For instance, English language learners who are familiar with the concepts of addition, subtraction, and multiplication will be able to do the numerical problems but may not understand the different terminology used to describe the addition and subtraction operations. Even though learners who have developed these math concepts in their native language transfer their academic skills from L1 to English, they must still re-label these concepts using English words. For example, several words can be used for the addition operation, such as add, plus, increase by, the sum of, more than, etc., which English language learners may not realize are synonyms. Therefore, content area teachers should help learners expand their vocabulary and understand the English language structure to enable them to solve word problems. In achieving this objective, the language objective teachers can engage students in collaborative groups to solve word problems—teachers can put students in pairs and use a cooperative learning structure of think-pair-share to solve word problems. Students can create their own word problems by discussing their ideas and writing them down so other students can solve the word problems they have created. Competitive games can be played in teams, create word problems and students compete to solve them. Teachers can model think-aloud protocol by showing students how to think through math problems by verbalizing their thoughts while solving their math problems. There are many activities (some of which were mentioned earlier) that teachers can incorporate into their math lessons, including concrete objects, the use of manipulatives, diagrams, charts, and tables, and also activities that involve students in the act of speaking out and using their spoken English to communicate with peers and solve the math problems.

## Science

Science is another content area that contains cognitively demanding oral language uses. As in teaching math, teachers should have two lesson objectives for teaching science: content objectives and language objectives. The process-oriented inquiry approach (Kessler & Quinn, 1987) is one of the teaching strategies that teachers can use to teach science. In this approach, students work in pairs or groups to define a problem, state a hypothesis, gather data, record observations, draw conclusions relating data to hypothesis, and explain and summarize findings. Academic language is used to convey the thinking involved in observing, classifying, comparing, measuring and inferring, predicting, and synthesizing and summarizing. English learners' motivation to learn science is high as they investigate real science problems that engage their natural curiosity. They are involved in hands-on activities in solving their science problems and most importantly for oral language development, they talk to other students when carrying out the investigation. Look into this class where Ms. Evans is teaching a science lesson on the basic needs of all living things, using the scientific inquiry:

Ms. Evan teaches the concept of the eating habits of two types of whales: baleen and toothed. Students use combs and chopsticks to simulate the eating habits of these two types of whales. Students also make their own whale and act out a poem using their whale. Students listen to a story called "The Whale Song" and engage in class discussion on whales' basic needs. Ms. Evan's science lesson, which is rich in oral language activities, is conducive to oral language development.

## Social Studies

Opportunities for oral language development in social science studies are abundant. Usually the main mode of information delivery is aural-oral—teachers lecture and students listen and take notes from the lecture. This is perhaps the most difficult way of comprehending instruction for English language learners because understanding academic lectures, according to Cummins (1981), is a cognitively demanding task in which context is highly reduced. Visual aids such as pictures, graphs, timelines, flow charts, and gestures are crucial in the presentation of highly academic discourse to English language learners. There are ample oral language development activities that teachers can utilize when presenting social studies subjects such as historical or political events. Reenactments or simulations and debates can be incorporated easily into social science lessons. Students can roleplay important historic and political leaders and discuss issues pertaining to the topics they are studying. Social science inquiry should be encouraged; students can survey, interview, and observe their own communities and families when researching key concepts such as racism and prejudice in the 1950s.

Teachers need to find ways to present the content through the use of visuals, dramatizations, and other multimedia. They also should use some innovative ways of increasing students' oral language performance using the academic language.

Look into Ms. Wagner's first-grade class which is studying how individuals, ideas, and events can influence history:

The class is learning about a space program (NASA) and the people who have influenced it. Students learn what a space shuttle is and describe what happens when it is launched. They will be able to explain the notable figures in the space program. Students work at computer stations in pairs doing research on notable astronauts using pre-selected sites. Students discuss their findings with each other. They are then asked to compile a fact sheet about these astronauts to use in a game of "20 questions" played at the end of this activity. The class will ask each team about its own astronaut.

This lesson is lively and interesting, with plenty of speaking opportunities for English language learners.


## Oral Language Assessment

There are several ways to assess English language learners' oral language in the classroom. Teachers can use the Student Oral Language Observation Matrix (SOLOM) (Peregoy & Boyle, 2001), observation checklists, and anecdotal observations. The five focused language traits within SOLOM are comprehension, fluency, vocabulary, grammar, and pronunciation. In using observation checklists, teachers can develop their own lists of oral language behaviors to focus on such as conversational interactions, presentational skills, vocabulary, and particular grammatical structures. Anecdotal observations contain on-the-spot assessment of students' oral language performance during classroom activities. These assessment techniques allow teachers to evaluate English language learners' use of spoken English in the social contexts of the classroom. The next section explores each of the three assessments in greater detail.

## Student Oral Language Observation Matrix (SOLOM)

The use of SOLOM is more personal than using standardized and commercialized tests such as the Language Assessment Scales (LAS) in assessing students' progress. SOLOM can be used intermittently over a period of time to chart students' progress in their oral language. It gives teachers a much closer look at their students' improvements in specific areas of the spoken language. Although the evaluation made by teachers using SOLOM is subjective, its frequent use sensitizes teachers to analytical linguistic dimensions, making evaluations of students' progress accurate and meaningful. The beauty of using SOLOM lies in its function. SOLOM allows teachers to observe students communicating in real-life contexts. Teachers should use SOLOM to observe students' participation in classroom presentations, students' discussions of ideas with peers in collaborative groups, students' conferences with teachers, and students' performance of routine classroom activities. As a result, teachers are able to truly evaluate their English language learners' oral language progress in authentic contexts within the classroom which makes oral language assessment more meaningful.

Refer to Figure 15-1 for an explanation of how to use SOLOM. Each trait (i.e., comprehension, fluency, vocabulary, pronunciation, grammar) receives a rating from 1 to 5, according to the descriptors. After placing a check on the appropriate descriptors, the scorer tallies the ratings of all five traits. Once the numeric score is obtained, it is matched to the phases of English language proficiency: Phase I, 5–11, non-English proficient; Phase II, 12–18, limited English proficient; Phase III,19–24, limited English proficient; and Phase IV, 25, fully English proficient. Teachers should tape-record their conversation with an English language learner, and then listen and analyze the taped conversation using SOLOM to evaluate and comment on the student's oral language skill.

## Anecdotal Observations and Checklists

Anecdotal observations and checklists are more open-ended forms of evaluating students' oral language performance. Refer to Figure 15-2 for an example of a checklist and Figure 15-3 for an example of an anecdotal observation. Teachers can include their own specific evaluation needs in these assessment tools. They can adapt and modify the checklist and anecdotal models to suit their own goals and objectives of their programs. These two assessment tools present teachers with a blank page that will take practice and training to fill. Nevertheless, teachers have the advantage of expounding on their observations of students' on-the-spot oral language skills without being constrained to other peoples' criteria. Both of these forms focus on the participant structures or interaction patterns; therefore, these forms are best used during group work or observations of students' daily classroom routine of getting their work done. Each form contains language

# Figure 15-1. SOLOM: Student Oral Language Observation Matrix

| | 1 | 2 | 3 | 4 | 5 |
|---|---|---|---|---|---|
| **A Comprehension** | Cannot be said to understand even simple conversation. | Has great difficulty following what is said. Can comprehend only "social conversation" spoken slowly and with frequent repetitions. | Understands most of what is said at slower-than-normal speed with repetitions. | Understands nearly everything at normal speed, although occasional repetition may be necessary. | Understands everyday conversation and normal classroom discussions without difficulty. |
| **B Fluency** | Speech is so halting and fragmentary as to make conversation virtually impossible. | Usually hesitant; often forced into silence by language limitations. | Speech in everyday conversation and classroom discussion frequently disrupted by the student's search for the correct manner of expression. | Speech in everyday conversation and classroom discussions generally fluent, with occasional lapses while the student searches for the correct manner of expression. | Speech in everyday conversation and classroom discussions fluent and effortless, approximating that of a native speaker |
| **C Vocabulary** | Vocabulary limitations so extreme as to make conversation virtually impossible | Misuse of words and very limited vocabulary; comprehension quite difficult. | Student frequently uses the wrong words; conversation somewhat limited because of inadequate vocabulary. | Student occasionally uses inappropriate terms and/or must rephrase ideas because of lexical inadequacies. | Use of vocabulary and idioms approximates that of a native speaker. |
| **D Pronunciation** | Pronunciation problems so severe as to make speech virtually unintelligible. | Very hard to understand because of pronunciation problems. Must frequently repeat in order to make himself or herself understood. | Pronunciation problems necessitate concentration on the part of the listener and occasionally lead to misunderstanding. | Always intelligible though one is conscious of a definite accent and occasional inappropriate intonation patterns. | Pronunciation and intonation approximate that of a native speaker. |
| **E Grammar** | Errors in grammar and word order so severe as to make speech virtually unintelligible. | Grammar and word-order errors make comprehension difficult. Must often rephrase and/or restrict himself or herself to basic patterns. | Makes frequent errors of grammar and word order that occasionally obscure meaning. | Occasionally makes grammatical and/or word-order errors that do not obscure meaning. | Grammatical usage and word order approximate that of a native speaker. |

SOLOM PHASES: Phase I: Score 5–11 = non-English proficient; Phase II: Score 12–18 = limited English proficient; Phase III: Score 19–24 = limited English proficient; Phase IV: Score 25 = fully English proficient.
Based on your observation of the student, indicate with an "X" across the block in each category that best describes the student's abilities. The SOLOM should only be administered by persons who themselves score at level "4" or above in all categories in the language being assessed. Students scoring at level "1" in all categories can be said to have no proficiency in the language.
SOURCE: Courtesy of California State Department of Education.

## Figure 15-2
## Informal Chart to Follow the Oral Language Development of Your Students

| Classroom Involvement | Beginning Level | Intermediate Level | Advanced Level |
|---|---|---|---|
| Functions:<br>　Informal talk<br>　Reporting<br>　Discussing<br>　Describing<br>　Explaining<br>　Questioning<br>　Debating<br>　Evaluating<br>　Persuading | | | |
| Interaction patterns:<br>　Partners<br>　Small groups<br>　Large groups | | | |
| Linguistic elements:<br>　Vocabulary<br>　Syntax<br>　Organization<br>　Ideas<br>　Audience sensitivity | | | |

Other comments:

Student Name _____ Date _____

Source: Based on *Oral Language Guidelines,* by M. H. Buckley, 1981. Unpublished.

functions such as informal talk, reporting, discussing, debating, reflecting, which allow teachers to look for appropriate use of language. They also contain linguistic elements that display English language learners' progress in English phonology, morphology, syntax and semantics. The checklist form is used in a slightly different way. Teachers jot down their observations of students who are at these levels of language proficiency: beginning, intermediate, and advanced. The anecdotal form is more of a running record of the entire interaction.

## Figure 15-3. Oral Language Observation Chart

| | |
|---|---|
| Participation structure:<br>Formal presentation — individual / group<br>Structured cooperative group work<br>Informal group work<br>Pair work | |
| Language functions:<br>　Heuristic<br>　　Hypothesizes<br>　　Predicts<br>　　Infers<br>　　Considers<br>　　Asks<br>　　Reports<br>　Informative<br>　　Describes<br>　　Explains<br>　　Synthesizes<br>　　Summarizes<br>　　Clarifies<br>　　Responds<br>　　Retells<br>　Instrumental<br>　　Requests<br>　　Asks for<br>　Regulatory<br>　　Directs<br>　　Commands<br>　　Convinces<br>　　Persuades<br>Personal and interactional<br>Divertive and imaginative | |
| Language forms:<br>　Vocabulary: particular to domain<br>　　　　　and general vocabulary<br>　Sentence structures:<br>　　declarative<br>　　question<br>　　command<br>　　exclamation<br>　　grammatical correctness<br>Morphology:<br>Phonology:<br>Discourse: | Overall Evaluation: |

Source: Based on *Learning How to Mean: Exploration in the Development of Language*, by M. A. K. Halliday, 1975, London: Arnold.

In all of the oral language assessment mentioned, the key point for teachers to note is that the use of a task-based approach should possess some constancy of elicitation input. Every student is assessed on the same learned concepts. Teachers can use the following task types to elicit spoken English:

1. Static relationships
   a. Describing an object or photograph
   b. Instructing someone to draw a diagram
   c. Instructing someone how to assemble a piece of equipment
   d. Describing/instructing how a number of objects are to be arranged
   e. Giving route directions
2. Dynamic relationships
   a. Story telling
   b. Giving an eye-witness account
3. Abstract relationships
   a. Opinion-expressing
   b. Justifying a course of action

Examples of these task-based approaches can be incorporated easily in simulation and games used by teachers in their classroom. The show-and-tell activity allows students to use the spoken language to describe objects or photographs they bring to the class. Teachers can use the game "One Sees and One Doesn't" to assess students' spoken language in following instructions in drawing a diagram. Students take turns describing a picture or an object for their partner to draw. The person who is drawing the picture can ask clarifying questions to help draw the described object/picture. In this activity, a lot of spoken language can be generated to enable teachers to assess their English language learners' oral language development.

Hands-on activities such as the use of clay, Lego pieces, or even match sticks for students to make objects can be used to elicit spoken language. Students are instructed to assemble objects like a toy car, a miniature bridge, or a dinosaur. This enables teachers to listen in on students' spoken language and make the necessary assessment.

The dynamic relationship tasks, such as story-telling and giving an eye-witness account, can be accomplished easily within lesson instructions. Students can retell stories they have read to the whole class or to their partner. Learners can perform a short skit on events that range from witnessing an accident to witnessing a bank robbery, bringing forth spoken language that meets the function of an eye-witness account.

Activities involving abstract relations such as an expressing opinion and justifying a course of action are more cognitively demanding—specific language structures are needed to do the job of convincing the audience. For older learners, teachers can present a controversial issue that students can debate. A more authentic task in the classroom can be election of a class president. Teachers ask students to give a speech to express their opinion on who is the best candidate for the position. These tasks are enjoyable and motivating and, at the same time, enable teachers to assess students' oral language development.

## Techniques for Correcting Speech Errors

Research has shown that correcting speech errors has very limited benefit to students. Many experienced teachers can testify that correcting students' errors is a frustrating and futile task. Plann (1977) conducted a study in which he examined grammatical and morphological errors in the speech of children learning Spanish in an immersion program in the United States. He reported the following:

> The third grade teacher has tried to call the children's attention to these errors by correcting them and having them repeat the correction; the fourth grade teacher has attempted to teach these grammar points more formally, giving the class explanations at the blackboard and then having children do oral drills and written follow-up exercises. However, although the students seem to grasp the concepts, both teachers admit there has been little improvement in the children's speech. (Plan, 1977, p. 222).

Although it has been reported that correcting errors has very little impact on learners, teachers do have the responsibility to correct them. To prevent fossilization of learner errors, error correction does assume a small place in language learning. A more important discussion on error correction involves the manner or techniques that teachers need to know about. Before teachers examine the "how" of speech error correction, it is important to be aware of the priority they attach to the errors they correct. Errors made by L1 and L2 children are called *developmental errors,* which will gradually disappear when the children become more proficient in the language. In choosing the errors to correct teachers should also be aware of global and local errors. *Global errors* affect overall sentence organization and significantly hinder communication (Dulay, Burt & Krashen, 1982). Global errors include wrong order of major constituents (e.g., Chinese language use many people; missing, wrong, or misplaced sentence connectors; e.g. not take this train; we late for work or she will be rich until she marry; missing cues to signal obligatory exceptions to pervasive syntactic rules—the employee's work looked into the boss; and regularization of pervasive syntactic rules to exception—we amused that play very much).

*Local errors* are errors that affect single elements (constituents) in a sentence and do not usually hinder communication significantly. Local errors include errors in noun and verb inflections, articles, auxiliaries and the formation of quantifiers. The distinction of global/local error can be seen in these examples:

> Why love we each other? vs. why we love each other?

The first is more "un-English" than the second. The first violates the SVO word order in English and therefore is a global error. The second does not; the auxiliary "do" is missing in the second, making it a local error.

Teachers, if compelled to correct, should focus on correcting more global errors than local. There are several techniques in speech error correction that may have some impact on learner errors. Here are some dos and don'ts of speech error correction:

## Dos

1. Model or rephrase students' utterances using the correct form. Speech is learned through listening to speakers, so modeling speech give the students a chance to listen to correct speech.

2. Make note of students' speech errors and incorporate the correct form in instruction.

3. Use a nonthreatening form of correcting errors by using a nonintrusive signal code such as "thumbs down" when students make errors. This will give them a chance to self-correct.

4. Ask students to tape record their own oral language and listen to these tapes on your own time. Discuss the errors during student teacher conferences.

5. Have students compare their own taped oral reading to a model tape or a tape produced by a more proficient peer. English language learners can imitate the correct pronunciation.

6. Make speech error corrections in written form to enable students to grasp and concretize the corrections.

7. Errors should always be corrected in context and not in isolation.

8. Create a learning environment that consists of a community of learners who will help each other in correcting their mistakes.

9.  Engage students in a speech-rich environment. This enables them to listen to speech and practice their own speech. Meaningful speech experiences can help reduce speech errors.

10. If fluency is the goal of oral language development, design meaningful tasks that allow students to speak freely and keep correction of grammatical errors to a minimum.

## Don'ts

1.  Do not correct errors made in conversations because the likelihood of learners' remembering these corrections is almost nonexistent.

2.  Do not overly correct students' speech errors. This will result in students' reluctance to participate in class.

3.  Do not correction in the form of oral drills. This may not impact students' learning of the correct form.

4.  Do not overwhelm students by correcting the different forms of errors that they make all at once.

5.  Do not let students continue making the same error without some form of intervention.

6.  Do not correct form over meaning, especially in speech errors made by beginners.

7.  Try not to correct students' speech errors in front of the whole class. This may embarrass them and hinder them from speaking up.

8.  Do not correct accent if learners' speech is intelligible. This can be an identity issue.

Speaking is the key to communication. Teachers can help learners improve their speaking and overall oral language competency by examining what good speakers do, by examining the kinds of speaking tasks used in the class, and by recognizing learners' specific needs in learning spoken English.

## Points to Remember

❏ Teachers should provide English language learners with classrooms that are rich in oral language.

❏ Speaking, an interactive process of constructing meaning, involves producing, receiving and processing information and requires learners not only to know how to produce specific points of language such as grammar, pronunciation, or vocabulary (linguistic competence), but also to understand when, why, and in what ways to produce language (sociolinguistic competence).

❏ Spoken language has two main functions: transactional and interactional. The primary goal of transactional function of oral language is transference of information and it is message oriented. The primary goal of interactional spoken language is to maintain social relationships and, therefore, is listener oriented.

❏ Second language learners display their competence of the second language through speaking. Unfortunately, not all of their competence can be seen through their performance. One of the difficulties that second language learners face is the actual pronunciation of the sounds of the language.

❑ Spoken language has "short turns" and "long turns." A short turn consists of one or two utterances, while long turn consists of a string of utterances that may be as long as an hour's lecture. Short turns demand much less of a speaker in the way of producing structures.

❑ Comprehensible input and social interaction are important elements in a classroom that provide a natural environment for oral language development.

❑ Strategies for oral language development include use of games, songs, poetry, and a recording studio; technologies such as television, VCR, audiotape recorder, and computers; and show-and-tell and choral reading.

❑ Oral language assessment includes SOLOM, observation checklists and anecdotal records.

❑ Oral language development should be an important part of teaching content area lessons such as math, science and social studies.

❑ There are two types of error: global and local. Teachers should spend more time correcting global errors because they impede meaning. Local errors do not hinder communication.

# Chapter 16

## Second Language Vocabulary Development and Instruction

### KEY ISSUES

❏ Research on teaching vocabulary to English language learners (ELLs)

❏ Difficulties faced by English language learners (ELLs) in learning vocabulary

❏ Some strategies/skills of teaching/learning vocabulary for ELLs

❏ Techniques of teaching vocabulary for multiple levels of language proficiency

❏ Alternative assessments for vocabulary learning

*"The mind remembers what the mind does."*

**—Rivers, 1981**

Mr. Olson is a first-grade teacher. He uses thematic units in his class. This week, his class is learning about ocean life. He incorporates content area centers such as social studies, science and math into his lessons. All of these centers consist of tasks that contain literacy skills. As Mr. Olson teaches the math, social studies, and science concepts, he also teaches to the language objectives. Today, his class is learning new words such as *hermit crab, symbiosis, camouflage,* and *schools of fish* and they are introduced through total physical response and the use of realia. Mr. Olson shows his students a real hermit crab. For the phrase, *schools of fish,* he asks students to act out the movement of schools of fish by moving as a group. He then asks students to write sentences using these new words in their discovery journal. Mr. Olson always ends his lesson by reviewing the vocabulary words as a means of assessing his students' level of comprehension of the concepts.

## Introduction

Many second language learners can attest that when they are faced with an unfamiliar text in a nonnative language, their first challenge seems to be its vocabulary. When texts have many new words, students quickly despair and are discouraged. Therefore, there is no doubt that there is a close connection between vocabulary knowledge and success in reading comprehension tests, as shown in many studies.

## What Is Vocabulary Learning?

Vocabulary learning is more than the study of individual words. Nattinger and DeCarrico (1992) observed that a significant amount of English language is made up of lexical phrasal verbs (two or three words) to longer institutionalized expressions (Lewis, 1993, 1997). Lexical phrases can often be learned as single units, so the principles of learning them are similar to those for learning individual words.

### Why Is Vocabulary Difficult for Second Language Learners?

Second language learners experience difficulties in learning L2 vocabularies because they have to relabel familiar concepts with foreign terminologies. These new vocabulary items have to be learned and stored in their long-term memory and their retrieval may not be easy initially. With learning strategies and practice, second language learners will be able to acquire the new vocabulary.

### Research on Vocabulary Teaching

Hunt and Beglar (1998) propose a systematic framework for instruction of vocabulary development through the use of three approaches: incidental learning, explicit instruction, and independent strategy. *Incidental learning* of vocabulary is defined as an approach that requires teachers to provide opportunities for extensive reading and listening. *Explicit instruction* involves diagnosing the words learners need to know, presenting words for the first time, elaborating word knowledge, and developing fluency with known words. Hunt and Beglar (1998) define *independent strategy* as an approach that involves practicing guessing from context and training learners to use dictionaries. They also caution teachers that students' level of language proficiency has to be considered when choosing each approach. They propose that, in general, explicit instruction is best used with students who are at the beginning and intermediate levels because at these levels, students' vocabularies are limited. For intermediate and advanced learners, vocabulary learning is suggested through the use of extensive reading and listening and it is best to train students to use the dictionary earlier on in the curriculum.

### Incidental Learning

Nagy, Herman, and Anderson (1985) state that most words in first and second languages are probably learned incidentally through extensive reading and listening. In their study, they found that for native speakers of English, learning vocabulary from context is a gradual process. They estimated that, given a single exposure to an unfamiliar word, there was about a 10% chance of learning its meaning from context. Likewise, L2 learners can be expected to require many exposures to a word in context before understanding its meaning. Several recent studies have corroborated their statement confirming that incidental L2 vocabulary learning through reading does occur (Chun & Plass, 1996; Day, Omura, & Hiramatsu, 1991; Hulstijn, Hollander, & Greidanus, 1996; Zimmerman, 1997). Extensive listening is also found to increase vocabulary learning (Elley, 1989).

### Explicit Instruction

For second language learners entering a university, Laufer (1992) found that knowing a minimum of about 3,000 words was required for effective reading at the university level, whereas knowing 5,000 words indicated likely academic success. Coady (1997) proposes that beginners should supplement their extensive reading with study of the 3,000 most frequently used words until the words' form and meaning become automatically recognized (i.e., "sight vocabulary").

### Independent Strategy Development

One of the principles of Independent Strategy Development is guessing from context. Studies have shown that guessing from context is a complex and often difficult strategy to carry out successfully. To guess successfully from context, learners need to know about 19 out of 20 words (95%) of a text, which requires knowing the 3,000 most common words. In addition, learners need to know the same part of speech as the unknown word. They should also break down the unknown word into parts ("rewrite" becomes "re + write") and determine if the meaning of the parts matches the meaning of the unknown word. Another principle within the Independent Strategy Development is to teach students how to use dictionaries. Use of bilingual dictionaries has been found to result in vocabulary learning (Knight, 1994; Luppescu & Day, 1993). Hulstijn, Hollander, and Greidanus (1996) showed that compared to incidental learning, repeated exposure to words combined with marginal glosses or bilingual dictionary use led to increased learning for advanced learners. Luppescu and Day's (1993) study on

Japanese students reports that use of bilingual dictionaries resulted in vocabulary learning unless the unfamiliar word had numerous entries, in which case the dictionaries may have confused learners. Knight (1994) found that use of a bilingual dictionary may be much more likely to help lower-proficiency learners in reading comprehension because their lack of vocabulary can be a significant factor in their ability to read. Laufer and Hader (1997) found that students who use bilingualized dictionaries that contain L2 definitions, L2 sentence examples, as well as L1 synonyms had better comprehension of new words than students who used either bilingual or monolingual dictionaries.

## Strategies and Skills in Vocabulary Learning

Robb (1999) developed a basic vocabulary strategy that can be used with any grade level. There are three steps to this strategy:

1. Identify the vocabulary words that students will need to comprehend the reading.
2. Pre-teach only three to five words. More than five words will confuse or bore students.
3. Connect the new words to concepts that students already know. For example, to help students grasp the meaning of the word "perplexed," link it to the word "confused."

In using this approach, the teacher can first identify the key concepts in the unit on simple machines: tools such as levers, pulleys, and wedges. The teacher then pre-teaches a few new words (e.g. lever, fulcrum, and effort or load). The teacher can also draw pictures on chart paper of such simple machines such as a shovel, a wheelbarrow, and a bottle opener and label them with the different elements of a lever. Then the teacher connects the new words to ones that were familiar to the students. The result is the following:

Lever—A crowbar used to loosen a large stone or tree stump from the ground; a bottle opener used to pry off a cap

Fulcrum—A seesaw and a balance scale and the point at which they balance

Effort or load—The resistance of a bottle cap or the weight of children on a seesaw, of dirt in a wheelbarrow, and of a stone or tree stump

Teachers can use many methods to teach vocabulary or to encourage vocabulary self-learning by their students. Hulstijn (1992) and Hulstijn, Hollander, and Greidanus (1996) distinguish between incidental and intentional vocabulary learning. They claim that both approaches are present in foreign language learning— students learn vocabulary intentionally as part of course requirements but also gain knowledge of words incidentally through reading. Their study shows that intentional vocabulary learning is more effective for retention. In other words, words learned intentionally through reading are better retained than words learned incidentally. They suggested that learning words through incidental learning is inefficient because of these reasons:

   a.   The readers' false belief that they know the words
   b.   The readers' decision to ignore the words
   c.   The readers' ignorance of the connection between the form of a new word and the meaning contained in the context
   d.   The readers' inability to infer a word from context
   e.   The nonrecurrence of new words (i.e., a single encounter of words)

Paribakht and Wesche (1997) claim that systematic vocabulary instruction, in addition to learning through reading, is a more successful approach. Koren (1998) claims that even a new and exciting computer program that enables incidental learning will not make students retain vocabulary efficiently without further off-line effort by the learners. Her study supports the literature that incidental vocabulary learning is not particularly efficient, therefore intentional learning should be encouraged.

One way to promote vocabulary development is through Sustained Silent Reading (SSR) that teachers can use in class. Once students develop the ability to read in a sustained fashion, then most of the reading should be done outside of class. Another strategy for vocabulary development is through the learning of word-pair translation; vocabulary cards should be used because learners can control the order in which they study the words. Moreover, additional information can be added to the cards. When teaching unfamiliar vocabulary, teachers need to consider the following:

   1.   Students need to hear the pronunciation and practice saying the word aloud in addition to just seeing the form because the stress patterns of the words are important. Words are stored in the memory in both ways.

   2.   Students should start learning vocabulary by learning semantically unrelated words. They should avoid learning words with similar forms and closely related meanings at the same time. For example, "affect" and "effect" have similar forms and are likely to cause confusion. Likewise, words with similar, opposite, or closely associated meanings may interfere with one another if studied at the same time.

3.  Students should be encouraged to study words regularly over several short sessions instead of studying them for one or two longer sessions. Repetition and review should take place almost immediately after studying a word for the first time.

4.  Students should study five to seven words at a time, dividing larger numbers of words into smaller groups. As learners review these five to seven vocabulary cards, they will more quickly get repeated exposure to the words than when larger number of words (20–30) are studied.

5.  To promote deeper mental processing and better retention, teachers can use activities like the keyword technique. Learners remember words better when a word is associated with a visual image.

6.  Teachers can add various L2 information to the cards for further elaboration. Learners can consciously associate newly met words with other L2 words that they know, and add these words to the card. In addition, they can add sentence examples, parts of speech, definition, and key word images.

In teaching vocabulary, teachers should also be aware of receptive and the productive knowledge. *Receptive knowledge* means being able to recognize one of the aspects of knowledge through reading and listening, and productive knowledge means being able to use it in speaking and writing. Therefore, teachers should be selective when deciding which words deserve deeper receptive and/or productive practice as well as which types of knowledge will be most useful for their students.

Students can be taught to elaborate word knowledge through expanding the connections between learners' knowledge and new information. Students can choose L2 words from the surrounding context and then explain the connections to the recently learned word (Prince, 1996). Nation (1994) suggests that teachers should create opportunities to meet these useful, recently learned words in new contexts that provide new collocations and associations. Exercises that can deepen students' knowledge of words include sorting lists of words and deciding upon the categories; making semantic maps with lists either provided by the teacher or generated by the learners; generating derivatives, inflections, synonyms and antonyms of a word; making the trees that show the relationships among superordinates, coordinates, and specific examples; identifying or generating associated words; combining phrases from several columns; matching parts of collocations using two columns; completing collocations as a cloze activity; and playing collocation crossword puzzles or bingo.

Teachers should provide students with opportunities that build fluency. An activity that promotes fluency includes the recycling of already known words in familiar grammatical and organizational patterns so that students can focus on recognizing or using words without hesitation. Other activities that promote fluency include the development of sight vocabulary through extensive reading and studying high-frequency vocabulary. Fluency exercises include timed and paced readings. In timed reading, learners can increase their speed by sliding a 3 by 5 inch piece of paper down the page while attempting to understand 80% of a passage. Learners' practice should be looking up groups of words rather than individual words when reading. Students can practice timed reading on passages that have already been read. In paced readings, the teacher determines the time and pushes the learners to read faster. One type of paced reading is "reading sprint," in which learners read their pleasure reading book for 5 minutes and count the number of pages they have read. Then they try to read the same number of pages as the time decreases from 5 minutes, to 4, to 3, to 2 for each sprint. Finally, they read for 5 minutes again at a relaxed pace and count the number of pages they have finished.

Students should be trained to use dictionaries. Unfortunately, in most classrooms, very little time is provided for training in dictionary use. Students may need extra practice to locate words with many entries. Furthermore, learners need to be taught to use all the information in an entry before making conclusions about the meaning of a word. Learners should be alerted to the value of good sentence examples that provide collocational, grammatical, and pragmatic information about words. Teachers should also emphasize the importance of checking a word's original context carefully and comparing this to the entry chosen because context determines which sense of a word is being used. Teachers should also explore electronic dictionaries with multimedia annotations, which offer a further option for teachers and learners. Teachers may want to investigate the CD-ROM dictionaries published by Collins COBUILD, Longman, and Oxford. However, these CD-ROM dictionaries do not link most of their entries to a visual image. The one exception is *The New Oxford Picture Dictionary* CD-ROM (1997), which includes 2,400 illustrated words (mainly concrete nouns) and is available in a bilingual version.

## Techniques of Teaching Vocabulary for Multiple Levels

### Beginning Level

English language learners who are at the beginning level stage of English proficiency may either have no word recognition at all or may possess a very limited amount of word recognition, spoken or written. Students at this level may frequently misuse words, making communicating with others difficult because of limited vocabulary. Teachers can use several strategies to help these learners develop word recognition at this level. Word families help these learners to handle learning new words in a manageable way because students can be taught to separate onset and rimes in a word. For instance, the teacher can introduce the rime -en, and students and teachers can collectively brainstrom for words that they can form using this rime with different onsets, such as p, h, d, t, m. "Word family flaps" is an activity that uses word families. Each student will have a specific word family to work with. Each student will get a pre-made flap card—a piece of paper folded in half, lengthwise, and then cut so that there is one empty space and three flaps. On the empty space, the child will write the word family (e.g., -ake). On the underside of each flap, the child will draw a picture of a word made from that word family (cake, lake, rake). On the top of the flap "cake," the child will write the letter "C" to indicate what letter was added to the word family to make the word. All of the children's flaps will be bound together and posted in the classroom for practice saying words.

Another enjoyable activity for these students is the creation of a word wheel, wherein the rimes match with the onsets to form words as they turn the wheel. Another strategy that teachers can use is to provide these learners with words that have root words that originate from their native language. For instance, Spanish learners may recognize the word denture from the Spanish word dentadura. Teachers can then explain that diente means teeth in English. This will not only help students to bridge new knowledge to old, but helps them later in searching and recognizing words with root meaning (e.g. dentist, dental, orthodontist, etc.). For other languages that may not have the same root words as English, such as the Asian languages, teachers can teach students to look up etymologies of words in the dictionary. Likewise, students can learn about cognates.

Teachers should also adapt vocabulary lists for students by choosing between five to eight words that have root meanings that come from their native language.

At this level, teachers can utilize fun activities to reinforce the already taught vocabulary by having the students play a word grab-with-song activity. This is a simple activity that does not require a lot of preparation. For this activity, the teacher needs a song that students know most of the words from and a stack of word cards. The word cards are placed on the board using putty (blue tack) or magnetic strips. The teacher lines students up in two rows and she plays the song. As the song is playing, each student in each row will walk up and grab the word he or she heard in the song. This is a great word recognition activity for beginning learners.

A game-like activity that teachers can use to teach word association is called "What's the Word?" On an index card, the teacher writes a word, for example, school and writes four or five key words that cannot be used to describe that particular word (e.g., *teachers, blackboards, students, desks, tests*). Any other words can be used except for the words written on the index card. Students then guess the word on the index card. Another recognition activity that is suitable for beginning students is the "Chime-In" poster. Students are invited to repeat a word and write its beginning letter on an index card. For instance, when a student sees the word man, the student says the word and then says the first letter of the word, which is /mmm/.

## Using Mnemonic Associations

Learners can learn and remember words through mnemonic links. Cohen (1990) suggested eight types of mnemonic associations:

1. Linking the word to the sound of an L1 word, to the sound of an L2 word or to a sound of a word in another language
2. Attending to the meaning of a part or several parts of a word
3. Noting the structure of part or all of the word
4. Placing the word in the topic group to which it belongs
5. Visualizing the word in isolation or in a written context
6. Linking the word to the situation in which it appeared
7. Creating a mental image of the word
8. Associating some physical sensation to the word
9. Associating the word to a key word

In applying this list and assuming that the native language is English and we are learning Malay as our second language, the following would be appropriate:

1. **Linking the word to the sound of an L1 word, sound of an L2 word or a sound of a word in another language** Suppose a student wants to learn the Malay word *bendara* ("flag") for example. In remembering the word *bendara*, he/she could think of the English word *banner* because it has a similar sound.
2. **Attending to the meaning of a part or several parts of a word** To remember the Malay word *perjalanan* ("journey"), a student may associate with part of the word *jalan* ("road").
3. **Noting the structure of part or all of the word** Learning the Malay word *terbang* ("fly") from the already learned word *kapal terbang* ("airplane").
4. **Placing the word in the topic group to which it belongs** These Malay words can be categorized in the category for greetings: *Selamat pagi*

("Good morning"), *Selamat tengahari* ("Good afternoon"), *Selamat malam* ("Good night").

5. **Visualizing the word in isolation or in a written context**  Visualizing the word in isolation involves remembering of the configuration of the word; for instance, the student can memorize the Malay word *makan* ("eat") by remembering that it has two a's or it has a k in the middle of the word.

6. **Linking the word to the situation in which it appeared**  A student first heard the Malay word *tidur* ("sleep") when someone said that Alan sleeps in class. He/she could remember it by remembering the situation in which it was heard and, in this case, the situation of Alan sleeping in class.

7. **Creating a mental image**  A student can learn the Malay word *senyum* ("smile") by picturing the image of his/her mom smiling at him/her.

8. **Associating some physical sensation to the word**  Remembering how faces scrunch up when people eat a sour mango, which then reminds the learner of the Malay word *masam* ("sour").

9. **Associating the word to a keyword**  The Malay word *hujan* can be learned by first thinking of the English word *hurricane* as the key word and then have the mental image of the downpour. To retrieve the meaning *hujan*, evoke the word *hurricane*, which in turn will reevoke the image of the downpour. This strategy combines strategies 1 and 7.

# Flashcards

## Picture Flashcards

Beginning learners can prepare words on small flashcards. Individual words are written on the front of the flash cards and students can draw pictures on the back of the flashcards. Flashcards should be made small so that learners can transport them easily from one place to another so that they can study the words.

## Native Language Flashcards

Learners can also make flash cards that contain native language meanings of words on the back of the cards or native language mnemonics that will remind them of the target language words that they are learning.

Teachers can monitor students' learning of new vocabularies by giving bonus points to students who create their own flashcards and an inventory of flash cards. Students can exchange an inventory of flash cards with their peers in the classroom.

## Beep It, Write It and Frame It

This strategy is best used with new English language learners. Students are asked to sound the words out, write them out in the air, and use imagery to frame them in their mind. Students tend to learn the vocabulary words better when they learn and remember the words in many different ways: pronouncing them out, kinesthetically writing the words out in the air, and then visualizing the words in their head.

## Enrichment Packets

Along with teaching vocabulary items using pictures, teachers can—on their own or with the help of students—create vocabulary packages by using department store catalogues. Using these catalogues offers teachers and students a natural categorization of vocabulary words, especially nouns. The categories range from furniture to sports to clothing. For instance, under the category of clothing, teachers can cut and mount the pictures of different types of clothing on index cards. Words that describe the items are listed on the back of the cards. Students can work individually using these enrichment packages or they can work in groups to sort the picture cards out and learn the new vocabulary items. Students can create their own dictionary based on the words that they want to learn.

## Semantic Maps or Word Webs

Semantic maps or word webs can work both ways: convergent or divergent. In the convergent approach, teachers draw a circle with arrows pointing inwards. Each arrow is linked to another smaller circle. For instance, the teacher fills in six smaller circles with words/pictures such as *glove, bat, ball, bases, umpire,* and *players.* Students then guess the word in the larger circle that is in the middle—baseball. For the divergent approach, the teacher draws a circle with arrows pointing outwards. At the tip of each arrow is a word that contains similar meanings to the word in the big circle. For instance, the teacher writes the word *happy* in the big circle. Students can fill in the smaller circles surrounding the big circle with *pleased, glad, joyful, delighted,* or *thrilled.*

## Songs

Teachers who use songs in the classroom allow their beginning English language learners to "hide behind the music" (McDonald, 1984). McDonald states:

> ...avoids the heat of an spotlight landing on a timid student. It also warps the students' perceptions of how difficult it is to use the new language.

The result is ... a loss of certain inhibitions, a new respect for one's own voice and the learning of whatever vocabulary, grammar and punctuation the song has to offer.

The repetitive nature of words in the chorus part of songs makes learning words for beginning learners easier as well as enjoyable. These students can chime in only on the chorus parts of the songs and that will make learning the words manageable. Because they will be singing the song alongside the other students, they will be less intimidated by the task of producing the sounds of the target language. A catchy tune rings in these learners' ears and makes them want to repeat the words of the song over and over. This repetition reinforces their learning of new words and grammatical structure. The use of songs offers a variety to the classroom structure and takes away the monotony of a classroom routine in which students only read and write. Singing will lower students' affective filter and make them want to learn because of the gaiety and fun-filled atmosphere.

Activities that utilize songs can offer practice with similes, metaphors, and vocabulary learning. The words and combination of words in similes and metaphors are some of the more difficult features of the language for nonnative speakers. Certain songs contain a lot of similes or metaphors. Songs such as the "Traveler" have phrases such as "riding like the wind" and "like a crazy fool." The song "The Green, Green Grass of Home" contains expressions such as "lips like cherries." Bette Midler's song "Wind Beneath My Wings" is rich with similes and metaphors that English language learners can learn from in a fun way. Many songs contain words that deal with a particular theme or emotion. Students can be asked to identify various words and then they can form clusters of words. The teaching of vocabulary using the song "Bridge Over Troubled Waters," for instance, can have the clusters:

darkness          down and out

friends just can't be found          loneliness          weary

feeling small          tears (are in your eyes)

dry them

I'll comfort you          comfort          on your side

lay me down

# Games

Teachers can use commercially made games such as Pictionary, Scrabble, Password, Hangman, and Jeopardy, or students can create their own games while learning new words. The famous game show "Who Wants To Be a Millionaire?" can be adapted to search for meanings of words students have learned from literature reading or content area. In the more competitive and kinesthetic game "Fly Swatter," teachers write words on the board or a poster board and put students in two teams. Each team has a fly swatter. When the teacher reads the definitions of the words, one student from each team walks up to the board and swats the word that fits the definition. The student who swats the correct word first gets a point for his or her team. This game is a lot of fun and students learn vocabulary words without realizing that they are learning.

A crossword puzzle is a common game that students enjoy as they are challenged to link meanings with vocabulary terms. Software programs are available that allow teachers to construct their own crossword puzzles or games that they can use to teach different sets of words to students. When students encounter words, new and old, and discuss these words in terms of meanings, origin, and analysis, they will incorporate them into their daily use in speech as well as writing.

# Teaching Vocabulary through TPR

Asher (1972) first reported the field testing of teaching language using commands. He called the method Total Physical Response (TPR). Teachers can teach beginning learners using commands or mime—children like to imitate and love to role-play. Action words like *cry, laugh, tremble, eat, run, hop* can all be acted out easily by newcomers to the target language without having to produce the sounds of these words. The beginners may find this strategy of learning vocabulary less intimidating and fun to do. Teachers can easily use short poems from Silverstein's collection of poems for students to act out. Jazz chants are other examples of materials that students can use in a TPR activity when learning new vocabulary.

# Intermediate Learners

English language learners who are at the intermediate level frequently use wrong words and their vocabularies are inadequate for a smooth conversation. Terms may be used inappropriately due to constraints in lexical usage. They may be able to use some idiomatic expressions that approximate those of the native speakers. Vocabulary teaching strategies that teachers can use with these learners include structural analysis, semantic feature analysis, categorization, and dictionary use.

## Structural Analysis

In structural analysis, students are taught a simple technique of using word parts to determine meaning. Because there are many affixes in the English language, teachers can teach students to locate word meanings by showing them prefixes and suffixes in words that can determine part of the meaning of the words. For instance, the words *bimonthly, rephrase,* and *semi-circle* are words that can be taught using the structural analysis—parts of the words such as *bi* ("two"), *re* ("again") and *semi* ("half") give students clues to the meanings of the words.

Intermediate learners possess a little more of the language and are able to learn new vocabulary through a semantic feature analysis technique in which they have to categorize and recognize the relationship of interrelated terms. This technique is best used at the end of a unit of study. Teachers create a matrix of columns and rows. For instance, in teaching vocabulary words from a literature book *Red Riding Hood,* teachers can set up the following table:

### Figure 16-1
### Semantic Feature Analysis for Red Riding Hood

|  | Human | Animal | Small, Vulnerable | Big, Uses Deceit |
|---|---|---|---|---|
| Wolf |  |  |  |  |
| Red Riding Hood |  |  |  |  |
| Hunter |  |  |  |  |

First, a grid of rows and columns is created. The topic or concept is placed above the grid as a title (characteristics of characters in *Red Riding Hood*). Down the first column on the left, members of the topic or concept or word (wolf) are listed. Across the top row, place the features or attributes of the members of the topic or concept or word (e.g. human, animal, uses deceit) are placed. Spaces can be added to enable students to add their own attributes of the word or concept. Students then determine which characteristics belong to each member of the concepts under study, and place Xs in those boxes. A follow-up discussion of these words or concepts will help students have a better comprehension of the usage of these words or concepts in context.

## Dictionary Use

Dictionaries are usually used to find out the meaning of unknown word. However, a lot of information is contained in dictionaries that learners can access to use vocabulary productively.

The following activities are examples of how teachers can teach vocabulary through the a use of dictionary. Teachers can write an unfamiliar word on the board and tell the learners to form groups. Then learners are asked to follow these steps to gather information about the word that will help them write an original sentence containing the word (Nation, 1994):

1. Find the meaning of the word.
2. Use the grammar notes and an example in the dictionary to find out about the grammar of the word.
   - What part of speech is it?
   - If it is a noun, is it countable or uncountable?
   - If it is a verb, does it take an object?
   - Look at the example and note the similarity in their sentence patterns.
   - Copy these patterns to write a new sentence.
   - Have each group write its sentence on the board and discuss the results.

Another activity that teachers can use is the following (Rutledge, 1994): Introduce students to a dictionary of synonyms. Give students a short passage in which several words are identified as key words. Have the students supply synonyms for the key words by looking them up from the dictionary of synonyms. Students can also attempt to write sentences using the words they found in the dictionary that are synonymous to the key words the teachers identified.

Of course in addition to these strategies, songs, games, and TPR can also be used to teach vocabulary to intermediate learners. The level of difficulty for these learners will have to be varied from that of the beginners.

## Vocabulary Teaching in Content Areas

Content areas teachers must teach to two objectives: language and content. Besides teaching concepts within math, science, and social studies, teachers must make a point to teach key content vocabulary as well as elements of language structure and functional language use. Language objectives should be identified in lesson plans, introduced to students at the beginning of the lesson, and reviewed throughout the lesson (Echevarria, Vogt, & Short, 2000). Analogy, the process of linking newly learned words to other words with the same structure or pattern, can help learners develop key vocabulary. Teachers can teach and review vocabulary items using analogy. For instance, in a seventh grade world culture class, students learn that Muslims are monotheistic (i.e., they believe in one God). The word "mono" (meaning one) in this lesson is emphasized. Students then are referred to other words with the same morpheme (e.g., monopoly, monogyny, monologue). Teachers can review and recycle words drawing students' attention to tense, parts of speech, and sentence structure. Students become familiar with the newly learned words and English structure as teachers repeat and reinforce language patterns. Let us examine a teaching scenario of a social studies unit on Egypt in which students' second language acquisition, especially the learning of vocabulary, is supported. In this unit, students are to: (a) describe how archeologists learned about the building of pyramids, (b) describe five discoveries made by archeologists during the exploration of the pyramids, and (c) define and correctly use the following vocabulary: *pyramids, evidence, excavation, architecture,* and *sepulchral chambers.* In the first lesson plan on this unit, teachers can include the following activities:

1. Brainstorm words about pyramids that students already know.
2. Create an interactive "Word Wall" using the brainstormed words.
3. Group the reading of the first five pages of the chapter.
4. Invite students to select words from their reading to add to the Word Wall.
5. Complete the first section of the graphic organizer listing initial steps used by the archeologists.
6. Include in the graphic organizer words from the Word Wall (*pyramid, evidence, excavation, architecture,* and *sepulchral chambers*).

The subsequent lesson plans in this unit will contain the review of key words taught in the first unit. Students will continue to extend the Word Wall to include other words they learn throughout the unit and they will be challenged to articulate the key vocabulary orally and in writing. During this unit of study on pyramids, many terms and phrases related to pyramids are introduced, discussed in the text, and included on the Word Wall, graphic organizer, and worksheet. However, teachers can still limit the number of words students are expected to master to five or six. This is one way in which teachers use scaffolding techniques in helping English language learners learn English vocabulary through content area study. A note on using a Word Wall: Words should be organized around a theme and placed in categories to facilitate and speed up the learning of new words. For real beginners, however, some of these vocabulary words can be explained through the use of picture files or a bilingual dictionary. The multiple modalities of introducing vocabularies will facilitate learners in learning the new vocabulary items.

Students then can incorporate the ongoing vocabulary study in this unit in their individual word study books (Bear et al., 2000). A student-made personal notebook that includes frequently used words and concepts is an individual word study book. Bear et al. (1996) recommend that vocabulary in word study books be organized by English language structure, such as listing together all the words studied so far that end in *-ion, -sion,* and *-tation*. This may prove to be a useful framework. Another way to use the word study book is to group words according to topic (e.g., pollution-related words).

## Assessment

How do teachers assess their English language learners' competence and production of vocabulary? There are many standardized tests that focus on vocabulary testing; however, classroom teachers can use nonverbal assessments to gauge their students' proficiency of the English vocabulary. Teachers can observe students' acquisition of vocabulary through their performance in a TPR lesson. When teachers give commands using action words, students' response through doing the action words—such as walk to the door, jump up and down—will inform the teacher that the students understand the vocabulary. This assessment can take the form of a game of "Simon Says." Another alternative assessment is by using recognition tasks. Beginning students, especially, can be given pictures of vocabulary items to identify and categorize. Another type of assessment that tests students' vocabulary knowledge is through the cloze test. To construct the cloze test, teachers can choose an unfamiliar passage of 250 to 300 words and delete every fifth word in the passage, leaving the first sentence intact. Students' ability to fill these blanks will indicate that they can handle materials independently, or need some assistance. Another observation teachers can make is when students work on the list-group-label method. Students, in groups or individually, engage in a brainstorming session of putting words in their correct category. Teachers list a topic such as *mammals* and students brainstorm for words that are associated with the topic (warm-blooded, give birth to their young). Students then label these words as belonging to a certain category (physical attributes). Students can discuss why these words belong to one category and not the other. In moving away from the traditional assessment, teachers can also use games to assess students' comprehension of vocabulary. For instance, a game called "One Looks, One Doesn't" tests students' ability to produce final products based on their understanding of key vocabularies. Students are given a picture or an object to describe for their partner. The partner's ability to reproduce the object demonstrates that he or she recognized these key terms. Teachers then can use these products as evidence of students' comprehension of learned vocabulary or concepts. Riddles can also be used to assess students' comprehension of vocabulary items within a unit of study. For instance, after studying a unit on insects, teachers can put students in two teams. The teams compete in solving the riddles that are either made by the teacher or by their own peers. Through observation, teachers can find out which students need assistance and which students have mastered the vocabulary items within the unit. Of course, the true measure of vocabulary acquisition is through its use. Teachers can ask students to write sentences using the given vocabulary words. Students' appropriate usage of the vocabulary words in their writing is another means of assessing their mastery of new vocabulary. A more common way of assessing students' acquisition of vocabulary is guessing meaning from a context clue. Students are given a passage that contains words that they have to find definitions or synonyms for through the other words in the passage. They are given multiple-choice questions from which they can choose the correct answer.

In summary, there are many creative ways for teachers to assess their students' proficiency skills in vocabulary. Teachers can observe beginning students' comprehension of word meanings through nonverbal gestures such as TPR and picture drawings. For intermediate learners, teachers can use semantic feature analysis, the list-group-label method, multiple choice questions, riddles, cloze tests, and sentence making to test students' recognition of word meanings. Teachers measure students' mastery of vocabulary through observation, anecdotal records, and charts.

## Points to Remember

❑ Vocabulary learning involves more than learning individual words in a word list.

❑ Second language learners experience difficulties in learning L2 vocabularies because the re-labeling of concepts they have acquired in the native language with foreign terminologies makes it difficult for them to retrieve the newly learned words in the target language.

❑ The three approaches to vocabulary development are incidental, explicit, and independent strategies.

❑ Incidental learning of vocabulary is an approach that requires extensive reading and listening. Explicit instruction involves diagnosing the words learners need to know, presenting words for the first time, elaborating word knowledge, and developing fluency with known words. Independent strategy is an approach that involves practicing guessing from context and training learners to use dictionaries. There are three steps to this strategy:

1. Identify the vocabulary words that students will need to comprehend the reading;

2. Pre-teach only three to five words (more than five words will confuse or bore students); and

3. Connect the new words to concepts that students already know.

❑ Explicit instruction is best for beginning and low-intermediate students, while high-intermediate and advanced students can learn vocabulary through the use of extensive reading and listening. Training students to use the dictionary earlier on in the curriculum is highly encouraged.

❑ Vocabulary development is promoted through Sustained Silent Reading (SSR) and word-pair translation.

❑ Teachers should also consider receptive and productive knowledge when teaching vocabulary. Students with receptive knowledge recognize new vocabularies through reading and listening, and students with productive knowledge can use the vocabulary words through speaking and writing.

❑ Students can be taught to elaborate word knowledge by expanding the connections between learners' knowledge and new information. Exercises that can deepen students' knowledge of words include sorting lists of words and deciding upon the categories; making semantic maps; and generating derivatives, inflections, synonyms, and antonyms of a word, etc.

❑ Beginning level students may either have no recognition or a very limited amount of word recognition, spoken or written; they also often misuse words making communicating with others difficult. To promote word recognition at this level, teachers can use word families, cognates, and words that have root meaning from students' L1, and adapt the amount of words students learn at a time.

❑ Teachers can be creative in teaching students to use the mnemonic associations to develop their vocabulary.

❑ Techniques that teachers can use to teach vocabulary include picture flash cards; "beep it, write it, and frame it"; enrichment packets, semantic maps or webs; and songs, games, and teaching vocabulary through TPR.

❑ Intermediate learners frequently use wrong words and their vocabularies are inadequate for a smooth conversation. Strategies to be used with this group include structural analysis, semantic feature analysis, categorization, and dictionary use.

❑ Content area teachers should teach to two objectives: language and content.

❑ Teachers should use both standardized and alternative assessments to evaluate students' vocabulary development.

# Chapter 17

## *Second Language Reading Development and Instruction*

### KEY ISSUES

- ❑ What research tells us about the nature of the reading process

- ❑ Critical reading and thinking in literacy instruction in content areas

- ❑ Difficulties in second language reading

- ❑ Characteristics of beginning and intermediate readers

- ❑ Strategies to assist beginning and intermediate readers

- ❑ Selecting appropriate literature for ESL readers

- ❑ Alternative assessments of reading

The following vignettes describe a regular third-grade class in an urban school district. ESOL and non-ESL students make up the class, which is taught by a monolingual English teacher. The students' English proficiency levels vary. The first vignette describes a science lesson and the second vignette describes a language arts lesson in class.

## Science Lesson

The class has been studying concepts about planets and the solar system. Today, students will be discussing how day and night are created. The teacher, Ms. Lopez, starts the discussion by asking the students to respond to her questions by raising their hand. She asks, *"How many have seen the sun rising in the morning?"* and waits for a response. She then asks another question, *"How many of you have seen the sun set?"* and mentally notes their responses. She then proceeds by asking the class, *"Now, can anyone tell me in which direction the sun rises and the sun sets?"* After listening to their answers, Ms. Lopez then asks, *"Do you think the sun is moving?"* Students volunteer their predictions individually.

Then Ms. Lopez tells the students that they are going to visualize what really happens when the sun rises in the morning. She tells the students that she needs a knitting needle, an orange, and an unshaded lamp for this experiment and shows them each item as she lists it on the board. She then begins to demonstrate the concept by pushing the knitting needle through the center of the orange, which represents the earth. Next. Ms. Lopez places the unshaded lamp near the center of the room. She then dims the light in the room and announces to the class that the lamp represents the sun. Then she turns on the lamp. She asks a student to volunteer to hold the orange by the needle and turn it counter-clockwise like a top and walk around the room. Ms. Lopez then asks a few beginning students of English to share their observations by asking yes/no questions such as the following: *Is this part (pointing to the ball) darker/lighter?"* and then simple questions such as, *"Which part of the orange is bright? Which part is dark? Was the sun (lamp) moving?"* She poses the same type of questions to the whole class and the students share their observations. Ms. Lopez then introduces other concepts such as the earth's rotation, revolution, and axis into the discussion by asking the students to spin and walk around the lamp in a circle. After the demonstration, she draws a diagram to explain the concept and labels the diagram using the words she introduced earlier. They then read a text on the topic, and highlight the vocabulary they previously learned through their science experiment. Ms. Lopez creates mixed-ability groups so that the more-proficient students can write the instructions for the experiment, whereas the less-proficient students will have to listen to the instructions read to them and carry out the experiment.

### Language Arts Lesson

Mrs. Connor's class has been discussing planets and the solar system for several weeks now. Today, students are going to read a story book entitled *"Richie's Rocket."* Truang, who is just beginning to feel comfortable using English words and phrases, is listening attentively to his teacher and classmates and tries to participate in the class discussion. Before reading the story, Ms. Connor tells the class that they are going to read a story about a boy named Richie. Then, she points to the picture of a rocket on the cover of the book and asks the class, *"What do you think this object is?"* Huang tentatively raises his hand and volunteers, *"It's a rocket."* Ms. Connor responds, *"Yes, it is!"* and then points to the back cover of the book and asks the class, *"Now where do you think this rocket is going?"* Many students raise their hands and offer predictions while Ms. Connor writes down each prediction on the board. Next, she points to specific pictures in the book that reflect the various settings, characters, and plot development in the story. For every picture, she asks several types of questions: *"Who are the characters in the story?" "What are they doing?" "Where is Richie?" "Where is he now?" " Who is with him?" "How does he feel?"*

After this initial discussion, Ms. Connor draws a graphic organizer and asks students to complete the story map as they read the story. As she reads the story, she points to pictures of items that are mentioned in the story, and highlights and repeats selected words to help some students recognize sounds and words. She reviews the story with the class by having the students go over their map and asks follow-up questions with the aid of pictures in the story. Ms. Connor rereads the story and identifies words, phrases, and literary language that may be difficult for the students. For example, she explains the meaning of "something was up" by rephrasing it as "Richie was doing something." Sometimes she demonstrates meanings of words like *climbed* or *pushed* by acting them out or opening her eyes as wide as possible to explain the expression *"eyes grew wide."* Ms. Connor then asks the class different types of questions: *"How do you think Richie feels about his journey to the moon?" "Point to me pictures that describe his feeling." "Do you think Richie really went to the moon?" "Why do you think that?" "Point to me a picture that tells you that."* She uses the students' responses to introduce the element of fantasy.

After a lengthy discussion of the book, Ms. Connor describes the follow-up project. The students are going to perform a play of the book they have just read. She asks the students to select lines from the story to create a new dialogue for their play. Then, she asks the more-proficient students to read and write the lines and the less-proficient students to act out the actions that accompany the dialogue. The students also discuss which lines are appropriate for their play and consult their teacher when they need assistance. Students in this class will create props needed for their play.

After examining the vignettes, what can you say about how the lessons were organized and delivered? What did the teacher do to initiate a discussion with the students on the lesson's topic? What techniques did the teacher use to enhance content learning and language and literacy development of English learners of different levels of linguistic abilities?

# What Does Research Tell Us About Reading?

## Reading as an Interactive Process

Most of the current views of second language reading stem from first language research. Literature and research on first language reading have helped us understand what fluent readers do which has direct implications for second language reading and instruction. This body of research has provided us with a description of the reading process: fluent reading is rapid, purposeful, interactive, comprehensive, flexible, and develops gradually. In essence, reading is a process consisting of six general component skills (Grabe, 1991):

- Automatic recognition skills
- Vocabulary and structural knowledge
- Formal discourse structure and knowledge
- Content/world background knowledge
- Synthesis and evaluation skills
- Metacognitive knowledge and skill monitoring

Fluent readers typically read every word, but do so at a rapid rate because they have automatic recognition skills in word identification to make connection and inferences vital to comprehension. Fluent readers also have a sound knowledge of language structure (grammar), vocabulary, and discourse structure (knowing how a text is organized) which are vital to comprehension. Fluent readers can process information rapidly, so they are able to focus on more conceptual details using textual information and background knowledge as needed for confirming and predicting information they expect to read. Fluent readers are more effective in using strategies than less proficient readers; they self-monitor, plan ahead, check comprehension, test the effectiveness of their strategies, and revise strategies to achieve expected goals.

The following sections discuss the interactive reading approach, which draws heavily on cognitive, psycholinguistic, and sociolinguistic models of reading. This research is extremely important because it views reading as an active and constructive process instead of a passive one (Anderson & Pearson, 1988; Carrell &

Eisterhold, 1988; Eskey, 1973; Harste, Woodward & Burke, 1984; Goodman, 1988; Rosenblatt; 1994; Samuels & Kamil, 1984; Saville Troike, 1973; Smith, 1988; Widdowson, 1983). The research also takes into account the critical contributions of both automatic processing skills and high comprehension and reasoning skills to reading. In the remaining discussion, several perspectives on reading as an interactive process and their influences on reading instruction are discussed.

## Psycholinguistic Perspective

During the early 1960s and 1970s, Goodman developed a model of reading, known as the **psycholinguistic perspective.** This model sets the stage for viewing reading as an interactive and active process. In this model, readers do not just extract meaning from written texts. Instead, they construct meaning from written texts by using three cueing systems: syntactic, semantic, and graphophonic. We use syntactic knowledge by relying on what we know about the way language works to process what we read or hear. We use semantic cues by drawing on our past experiences and background knowledge to a story or an expository text. We use graphophonic cues by sounding out words and to recognize words holistically. Goodman's model also highlights that reading operates within a sociolinguistic context that includes readers and writers. Because language is social, people have used it to convey meaning. Likewise, efficient readers are not only efficient, but are effective in using strategies that will help them to assimilate and accommodate the writers' thoughts rather than rely solely on the printed message.

Goodman (1994) states that "readers use their selection strategies to choose only the most useful information from all that is available" (p.1125). For instance, when a reader reads the sentence, *"Jupiter is the fifth planet from the sun,"* he or she may use real-world knowledge of Jupiter and the sun, and other context clues or sound out the words *fifth* and *planet* to construct meaning. In other words, readers will select from any of these three cueing systems and confirm their predictions by relating to past experiences and knowledge about language to construct and minimize uncertainty in making meaning. According to Goodman, a reader does not have to process all or most of the letters in the words *fifth* and *planet* to arrive at the meaning unless these words occur in isolation. In his model, little emphasis is placed on teaching phonics or subskills which could fragment the process of reading or make reading more abstract and difficult. While this model may not be able to capture the more detailed processes of reading, it has certainly initiated a holistic perspective of reading as being meaning driven rather than being fragmented subskills.

Other reading experts (Anderson, 1978, Stanovich, 1980) have characterized Goodman's model as concept driven, in which top-down procedures (holistic approach) interact with bottom-up procedures (subskills approach). **Top-down procedures** include using appropriate background knowledge, text mapping strategies, text previewing, and introduction and discussion of key vocabulary to obtain overall comprehension of text. The emphasis on deriving meaning is not far from what early readers do when they begin to read or are read to. Early readers often memorize the whole story before they focus on individual words in the story. In contrast, **bottom-up procedures** include identifying letters and words, matching sounds and letters, phrase identification, or "reading in meaningful groups of words or sense groups" (Nutall, 1982). Bottom-up procedures make learning easier by breaking the complex task of reading into smaller component skills. Hence, instruction proceeds from the simple to the more complex tasks. While readers must be able to process letters and words to comprehend what they read, Samuel (1994) asserts that more experienced readers tend to process words holistically or break them down into components whereas novice readers may focus on processing every letter or word.

Similar findings have also been found in second language reading. Researchers in second language reading have found that the process of reading in the first language is similar to reading in the second language (Carrell, Devine & Eskey, 1988; Eskey & Grabe, 1993; Grabe, 1991). Second language readers must use all their knowledge of print, sound, discourse, semantics, and grammar to construct meaning from text. In addition, the reading process is affected by readers' background knowledge on text topics and text types or structures, and their use of appropriate strategies such as inferencing, skimming, guessing the meaning of words in context, and interpreting what they read to achieve their reading purpose. Because readers are expected to put their personal response and interpretation at the center of the reading process, it is no longer important that readers stick close to the author's message.

## Schema Theory of Reading

Influenced by Goodman's earlier model of reading as a "psycholinguistic guessing game," **schema research theory** revealed the importance of background knowledge, which is often neglected in earlier psycholinguistic model of reading. Anderson, Reynolds, Schallets, and Goetz (1977, p.369) eloquently expressed:

*"Every act of comprehension involves one's knowledge of the world as well."*

Schema theory is a reader-centered model of second language reading that explains that oral and written texts can only provide directions for interpretation but meaning is constructed by the background knowledge that the reader brings into the process of reading (Carrell & Eisterhold, 1983). These previously acquired background knowledge structures are called **schemata.** To understand how background knowledge affects comprehension, it is useful to distinguish between formal and content schemata. "Formal schemata" refers to background knowledge of text structures and genres whereas "content schemata" refers to knowledge of the content of a text. For example, we can recognize that there are different types of writing, each serving a different purpose. Our schema of writing genres may include stories, scientific reports, newspaper articles, recipes, poetry, drama, advertisements, and so on. We also recognize that ideas can be organized differently, commonly referred to as text structures. Emergent readers who have had stories read to them almost invariably begin with "once upon a time" when asked to tell a story. Early on, children have demonstrated their knowledge of story grammars. Story grammar refers to the principal components of a story: main character, problem, action, and outcome.

Research has also supported the view that awareness of text structures can assist readers to form expectations about the text that will enable them to locate, summarize, store and recall information easily (McNeil, 1992; Meyer, Brandt, & Bluth, 1988; Pearson & Campbell, 1994; Taylor, 1980). Knowledge of text structures facilitates comprehension by serving as templates from which readers can make predictions of ideas that might be expected in text. Generally speaking, students may find narrative text much easier to comprehend than expository texts. There are two reasons for this: First, the content of the narrative text is usually more familiar than the factual information found in an expository text. Second, expository texts tend to include more complex and varied structures which require students to master several different text structures. In some expository texts, ideas follow an attributive or enumerative pattern, in which the main idea is stated first, followed by supporting details. This pattern is signaled by the use of cohesive ties such as *first, second, in addition, moreover,* and so on. These cohesive ties serve as signposts that indicate how ideas are related within and across paragraphs and, thus, enable readers to read and remember information more efficiently. Table 17-1 groups cohesive ties in various categories according to their functions.

Other types of text structures found commonly in expository texts include comparison-contrast, cause-effect, problem-solution (Peregoy & Boyle, 2001), and pro-con. Sometimes more than one structure can be found in a single text, making it difficult for less-proficient readers to find and comprehend information efficiently. Finally, expository writing often includes complicated verb structures and embedded clauses which are not often heard or are used infrequently in social, informal discourses, for examples *"can be misused if not implemented properly"* and *"need no longer fear."*

**Table 17-1**
**Cohesive Ties**

| Relationship | Words |
| --- | --- |
| Addition | also, in addition, too, moreover, besides, then |
| Example | for example, thus, for instance, namely, specifically |
| Contrast | but, yet, however, on the other hand, in contrast, conversely |
| Comparison | similarly, likewise, in the same way |
| Concession | of course, to be sure, certainly, granted |
| Summary | hence, in short, in brief, in summary, in conclusion, finally |
| Time sequence | first, second, third, next, finally, before, soon, later, meanwhile |
| Place | in the front, in the back, at the side, adjacent, nearby, in the distance, here, there |

Awareness of text structure can facilitate comprehension, so it is important that teachers are aware of how to teach these strategies to students in a flexible, opportunistic manner that will lead to student reading achievement. Teachers can use concept maps to graphically illustrate the relationship between key ideas in a text. Perkins (1992) suggests these visual diagrams enable students to simplify complex ideas that can be "downloaded" onto paper using as few complex words and syntax as possible, and thereby reducing cognitive overload and freeing them to focus on the content. Figure 17-1a–h demonstrates different types of graphic organizers that could be used to teach text structures. Another aspect of text structure that students can use to facilitate comprehension and memory is the use of headings and subheadings in text. Students can use subheadings and headings to preview and make predictions about the content. This strategy enables readers to establish a purpose/goal for reading and monitor how well they have achieved their goals in reading.

# Figure 17-1
## Graphic Organizers

### Figure 17-1a  Attribute Wheel

### Figure 17-1b  Decision-Making Model

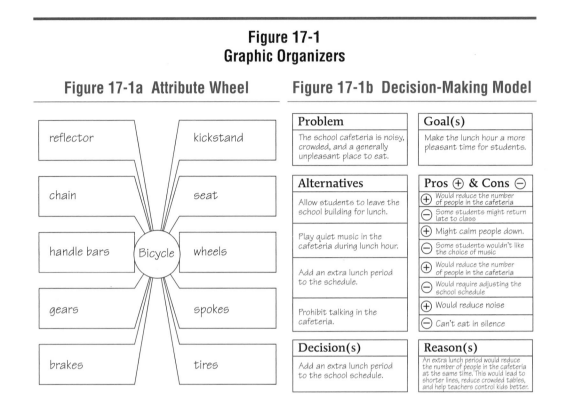

### Figure 17-1c  Character Map

### Figure 17-1d  Venn Diagram

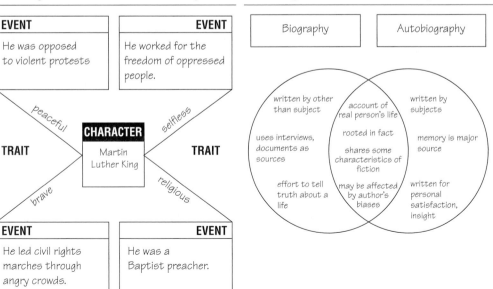

# Figure 17-1
## Graphic Organizers *(continued)*

### Figure 17-1e  Web

### Figure 17-1f  Sequence Chain

### Figure 17-1g  Story Map

### Figure 17-1h  Main Idea Table

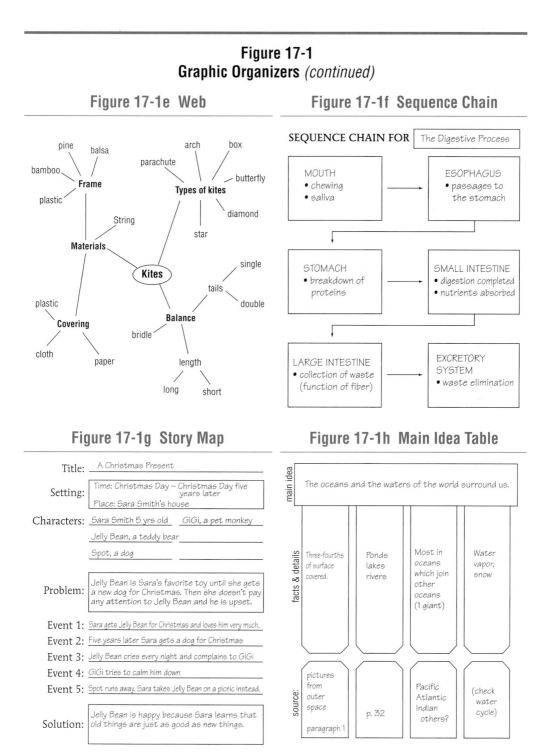

# Rosenblatt's Transactional Theory of Reading

Rosenblatt's (1994) transactional theory defined reading transaction as an event in which the text is conditioned by the reader and the reader is conditioned by the text. In other words, "meaning does not reside ready-made 'in' the text or 'in' the reader but happens or comes into being during the transaction between reader and text" (p. 1063). This reading transaction can be affected by two different approaches or attitudes that readers take, which are referred to as the *efferent* or the *aesthetic* stance. "Efferent" is taken from Latin to mean "carry away." When solving a math or science problem or reading instructions, readers may take the efferent stance, as the focus is on obtaining information. When readers take an aesthetic stance, they focus on how words can evoke feelings, attitudes, associations, and ideas. In other words, readers focus on "experiencing the piece" (Rosenblatt, 1978, p.10). This is particularly useful when reading and experiencing literature. Because literature often makes greater demands on the reader's careful reading and reflection, Rosenblatt (1991) explained that aesthetic reading should then result in a deeper level of involvement for students. For instance, in reading Kenzo's, *A mother for Choco,* a young reader may feel sad for Choco who is desperately looking for a mother figure, and might be able to relate the feelings of sadness to a similar experience. To promote aesthetic reading, teachers should find ways to encourage readers to focus on the personal experience by using pictures and having students imagine while reading or viewing, identifying themselves with the characters in the story, making connections with other stories and their personal experiences (Cox & Many, 1992), and encouraging reflection and discussion of personal feelings, attitudes, and values that relate to the story (Rosenblatt, 1991).

To foster children's imaginative and creative responses, teachers should allow children to choose their preferred form of responses which may include writing a poem, a letter, a journal log, or an oral response, dramatizing, drawing, and so on. Teachers should also give ample wait time for students to respond, share, discuss, and reflect on their ideas. Typically, ESL students need more than 1 second wait-time to respond to teacher questions; this wait-time could be even longer depending on the student's English proficiency. If the questions being asked call for simple recall of information, elaboration, or explanation, English learners should be given more than 3-second wait time to construct a response to teacher's questions; sometimes it is helpful to pose the questions before calling on students to answer so that they have time to reflect and compose their answers.

It is important to remember that readers may not take an either/or stance to reading literature. In fact, readers may take both stances or move closer to a particular stance depending on their expectations and focus (Dias, 1990). For instance, when a young reader reads the story, *The Magic School Bus: Lost in the*

*Solar System,* and responds to the exhilaration, surprise, and fear felt by the children in the bus when their bus blast off into space, the reader's stance becomes aesthetic. At the same time, the reader may also take away information about the moon, the sun, and the various planets and, thus, the stance becomes efferent.

## The Reading-Writing Connection

Skills for reading can also be acquired through multiple engagements in the process of writing. Research examining the link between reading and writing has echoed similar patterns in reading and writing processes. Both reading and writing activate schemata about the language, content, and form of the topic in making meaning (Carrell, 1988; Horowitz, 1988). Research on native speakers and English language learners has also shown a reciprocal relationship between reading and writing (Carrell, 1987; Flower & Hayes, 1980; Johns, 1991; Krashen, 1984; Tierney & Gee, 1990). Children who write continually apply a range of skills that require them to apply phonics, syntax, text genres, and conventions. Readers are often called upon to do so when they create "drafts" in their minds. Good readers also discover ideas and form opinions about what they read, which can become the basis for what they write. Contrastive rhetorical studies have also demonstrated that the patterns that English learners choose to write vary from culture to culture and can be quite distinct from the English rhetorical pattern (Anderson, 1991; Kaplan, 1990). The implications of schema theory research (Carrell, 1988) and contrastive rhetoric research demonstrate that English language writers can benefit from studying rhetorical organization and cues in English texts to communicate successfully.

## The Importance of the Interactive Perspective

There are several reasons why ESL researchers and classroom practitioners should be interested in the interactive models of reading. First, these models tries to account for an array of processing that distinguishes good and poor readers. It is consistently found that good readers recognize letters and words rapidly, which frees their cognitive space for thinking about the meaning of what they read. In other words, good readers automatically recognize words and do not rely heavily on context-guessing to arrive at an interpretation of the text. Not only can experienced readers process words rapidly, they also have a large reservoir of vocabulary that is a prerequisite to fluent reading skills. Second, the interactive models assume that bottom-up and top-down skills are used for text comprehension and interpretation. Good readers can read fast because their eyes can quickly process good-sized chunks of text in building up the overall meaning for the text. In contrast, many beginning English readers try to read word-by-word, placing an intolerable amount of strain on their memory system and, ultimately, lessening their chances of comprehending the text (Carrell, 1988; Cohen, Glasman, Rosenbaum-Cohen, Ferrara, & Fine, 1979; Hosenfeld, 1984; McLaughlin, 1987). They may spend more time processing word meaning or are afraid to use context even though they have used this skill effectively in reading texts in their primary language. These models imply that many lower-level processing skills, as well as higher-level skills, are basic to good reading. Although vocabulary knowledge is vital to good reading, it is only a part of the reading process. Inexperienced second language readers who rely heavily on this single strategy may have difficulty comprehending text accurately and fluently. In other words, a beginning reading approach that encourages the use of multiple strategies for identifying words and understanding meaning would be beneficial to beginning readers. Low-level readers can benefit from "phonics" instruction and basic recognition exercises to improve their speed and accuracy of reading, and at the same time, learn to use their background knowledge of text structures or stories and relevant experiences to compensate for their lack of syntactic knowledge to comprehend text. Students can still benefit from a reading program that adopts an "as-needed approach," in which a teacher identifies whatever skills the students require and teaches these skills within meaningful reading activities that emphasize communication and meaning. Finally, these interactive models highlight that the reading process is not simply a linguistic analysis; rather, it requires readers' skillful use of appropriate comprehension strategies. As students are increasingly expected to read and write longer and more complex texts in higher grades, it is important that they learn how to use effective strategies employed by good readers and writers.

## Social-Interactionist Perspective of Reading

Children learn to read not only by actively engaging in the act of reading itself, but are often facilitated by the quantity and quality of interactions in which adults discuss matters that are of interest to them. In short, children learn language and progress from one stage to another by interacting with others. L. S. Vygostsky (1978), a Russian psychologist and a leading developmental theorist, stressed the social nature of language and learning and how adults play an important role in both. In his theory, Vygostsky explained that through interaction, children will move from their zone of **actual development** to their zone of **potential development** through adults' expert guidance. This progression is known as the **zone of proximal development.** Actual development refers to the current level of the student whereas potential development refers to what the child might be capable of achieving with assistance. For example, if a student cannot comprehend an unfamiliar word in a passage, the teacher or parent might prompt the student by asking, *"Are there other words that you know that look like this word?" "What do you think it means?" "Can you guess its meaning by looking at other words in the sentence?"* Through constant guidance and stimulation, children's knowledge and skills will be fostered. In a longitudinal study of children, Wells (1986) found that children who are actively involved in conversations with their parents tend to remember more words and achieve a higher level of development. What exactly, then, is the role that parents play in the language development of children? Parents and other adults help children by extending their children's responses and providing relevant and pertinent knowledge of the world and vocabulary that will raise children's thinking to higher levels (Raines & Isbell, 1994).

## Critical Reading and Thinking in Literacy Instruction in Content Areas

The link between critical thinking and literacy instruction in content areas is especially important when dealing with second language learners who are still developing their English language proficiency. Some teachers may feel that second language learners cannot handle challenging content and tasks because they do not have adequate English proficiency to express and understand complex concepts in the new language. While success in academic learning hinges upon a threshold of linguistic proficiency, it is important for teachers to prepare English language learners for the type of cognitively demanding academic work required beyond the primary levels so that they can achieve academic parity with their fully proficient, English-speaking peers. This means that complex academic information to be learned must be broken down into simple components using simplified language and a variety of scaffolding strategies that make content understandable to the new language learner, as seen in the vignettes at the beginning of the chapter. Scaffolding strategies are used as a metaphor to reflect the instructional supporting structures that are employed on a temporary basis until the student has mastered the content. For example, to assist learners in understanding bird migration and the effects of urban development on wildlife in the wetlands, teachers can set up a simulated activity in which students can "experience" the effect of destroying wetlands. This activity requires squares of vinyl that represent rest and feeding areas in wetlands. The squares are set up around the classroom or in an outdoor, open space. Students can "fly" (jump) south, stopping at their favorite wetlands. As they travel, these wetlands will be replaced with a mall, a gas station, or other structures and students will have to stop at other rest and feeding areas. Teachers can prompt the discussion by asking how students feel about urban development and its effect on the wildlife (Dobson, 2001). By using a variety of scaffolding strategies, beginning learners of English can participate in the experience and obtain access to content that has depth and breadth in scope that more proficient students are often privileged to and interesting instruction that deemphasizes rote memorization.

To achieve academic success, new English learners must learn the academic language, which differs in many ways from the social language (Cummins, Chamot & O' Malley, Kessler & Fillmore, 2001). Academic language requires sophisticated knowledge of complex language structures and vocabulary, has fewer context cues, and expresses content that is more cognitively demanding. It is also used for very specific purposes that are particular to academic learning; these purposes include ability to explain, inform, justify, compare and contrast, describe, prove, debate, and persuade and to evaluate facts, concepts, ideas and opinions. English learners must learn how to use both lower and higher thinking processes to fully understand difficult, unfamiliar, and new ideas. This calls for greater use of content area reading as a vehicle for developing academic language functions and skills (Chamot & O'Malley, 1994; Crandall, 1987; Hudelsohn, 1989; O'Malley and Chamot, 1990).

As discussed in chapter 13, Table 17-2 illustrates a hierarchy of cognitive levels of thinking based on Bloom's (1956) taxonomy, their corresponding learning process and products. These cognitive skills can be divided into two levels: lower- and higher-order thinking. Lower-order thinking skills are cognitive operations that require recall, comprehension, and application of information to tasks that are similar to the learning. Tasks that call upon these levels of thinking include memorizing, listing, recording, describing, restating, showing/demonstrating, dramatizing, applying, and other such skills. Higher-order thinking requires breaking down information into its components, composing, inventing, predicting, synthesizing, and evaluating information.

While it is important to sequence instruction that begins with lower-level skills, it is also important to include a substantial portion of higher-order thinking skills in each lesson. Many statewide and national performance assessments, such as the Florida Comprehensive Assessment (FCAT) of Reading, Writing, and Math, measure high levels of cognitive thinking at higher grade levels. FCAT fifth-grade reading and writing assessments consist of equal numbers of items that assess lower- and higher-order thinking. The proportion of higher-order thinking questions increases by 10% at eighth grade and 20% at tenth grade (Region V Academic Center for Educational Excellence, 2000). This demonstrates the importance of maintaining a rigorous curriculum for English language learners

**Table 17-2**
**Bloom's Taxonomy of Cognitive Levels**

| Level | Cue Words | | Products | |
|---|---|---|---|---|
| **Knowledge**<br>Recall: Remembering<br>previously learned<br>material | observe<br>repeat<br>label/name<br>cluster<br>list<br>record<br>match | memorize<br>recall<br>recount<br>sort<br>outline<br>define<br>read | labels<br>list<br>fact<br>recitation | names<br>definition<br>test<br>knowledge |
| **Comprehension**<br>Translate: Grasping<br>the meaning of the<br>material | recognize<br>express<br>locate<br>identify<br>restate<br>paraphrase<br>tell<br>describe | report<br>explain<br>review<br>cite<br>support<br>summarize<br>reproduce | reproduction<br>summary<br>description | retelling<br>report |
| **Application**<br>Generalize: Using<br>learned material in<br>a new and concrete<br>situation | select<br>manipulate<br>organize<br>show<br>how to<br>dramatize<br>test out | use<br>sequence<br>imitate<br>frame<br>apply<br>illustrate<br>imagine | illustration<br>diagram<br>collection<br>puzzle<br>report | lesson<br>diorama<br>map<br>diary |
| **Analysis**<br>Break down material<br>into its component<br>part so that it may be<br>more easily understood | examine<br>distinguish<br>map<br>characterize<br>compare-contrast | classify<br>outline<br>relate to | questionnaire<br>report<br>chart<br>diagram<br>list<br>summary | survey<br>graph<br>outline<br>conclusion<br>plan<br>category |
| **Synthesis**<br>Compose or put new<br>material together to<br>form a new whole | propose<br>compose<br>design<br>emulate<br>speculate<br>invent | plan<br>formulate<br>construct<br>imagine<br>create | formula<br>firm<br>new game<br>poem<br>art products<br>media projects<br>advertisement | invention<br>prediction<br>story<br>solution<br>project<br>machine |

*continued*

**Table 17-2**
**Bloom's Taxonomy of Cognitive Levels** *(continued)*

| Level | Cue Words | | Products | |
|---|---|---|---|---|
| **Evaluation** Judging the value of material for a given purpose | compare: pro/con prioritize/rank judge rate criticize justify persuade value | decide evaluate argue convince assess predict | judgment opinion scale value evaluation investigation editorial recommendation | panel verdict conclusion report survey |

while they are developing their English language proficiency. Teachers must prepare all learners to function in an increasingly complex technological world where the demand for literacy is high. This means that readers must be challenged to be critical of what they read, be selective and efficient in choosing information that is important, and evaluate what they read or hear and use insights from varying perspectives to make a judgment. To read critically, readers must be able to suspend their judgment and consider viewpoints other than their own or the more popular views. They must also feel free to offer divergent viewpoints and support controversial opinions. In short, teachers who value these principles view teaching and learning as an inquiry process in which students formulate and reformulate their own thoughts as well as those of others, through experimentation, testing, and evaluation. Critical thinking and problem-solving abilities are important skills for students to learn. Teachers can utilize scaffolding strategies such as graphic organizers and cooperative learning structures to stimulate critical thinking.

## The Role of Questions in Comprehension and Critical Thinking

Teachers frequently use questions in the classroom for several reasons: to probe into what learners already know; to help students develop concepts; to build students' background knowledge; to expand students' thinking by analyzing, synthesizing, and evaluating; and to increase students' retention of information. The questions asked by teachers also shape students' comprehension and how they understand a concept or its significance in a text. Because of their importance, teachers must take great care in planning their questions. Essentially, there are two basic types of questions: low-level and high-level. Low-level questions such as the following tap students' knowledge to recall information that has been previously learned or memorized by asking them to recall facts, names, and events.

> *This book tells a true story about how a river changes. What is the river like*
> *    at first?*
> *Who lives by it?*
> *What are the events that happen next?*
> *What is the river like then?*

High-level questions lead students to higher levels of thinking and typically begin with *"what, why and how."* Examples of this type of question are as follows:

> *Why do we have to fight wars?*
> *What is the best way for us to protect endangered species from becoming*
> *    extinct?*
> *What is friendship?*
> *What would be a good title of this poem?*
> *Who do you consider to be the greatest hero that ever lived?*

Several factors must be considered when developing questions for new English language learners: (a) Ask questions that suit the ability levels of the students. Students with more literacy experience may be able to handle complex concepts although their English skills may be lagging behind, whereas some students may have difficulty in both areas. Teachers must be able to strike a balance in the amount of low-level and high-level questions they ask students and, at the same time, be able to adjust the levels of linguistic demand placed on how students' should respond to their questions. In other words, students can respond to a high-level question such as, *"What similarities do you see between the two planets or characters?"* in several ways depending on their English proficiency. They can draw a Venn diagram to highlight similarities and differences using limited phrases and words or compose an extended response orally or in writing; (b) focus on important concepts and not trivial facts. (c) Ask clear questions using simple and clear language that students can understand and use scaffolding strategies to facilitate comprehension. (d) Sequence questions starting from the least demanding to those that require higher mental analysis. Start with a simple yes/no question and recall questions requiring a one-word response such as, *"What is this?"* or *"Who is this person?"* before asking open-ended questions requiring longer utterances such as, *"What did the character do?"* or *"What is solar energy?"*

(e) Ask factual questions that require knowledge recall and application as well as productive and evaluative questions that invite a range of plausible responses to stimulate thinking.

## Why Is Reading Difficult For Second Language Learners?

Although research has demonstrated that readers use the same processes in both first and second language reading, some second language readers still find reading in the second language to be more difficult. There are a few reasons for this apparent difficulty. First, second language readers do not have second language proficiency and relevant background knowledge or experience that may be pertinent to the text. Read the following expository passage and try to consider how second language readers may process this passage:

> By voting against mass transportation, voters have chosen to continue on the road to ruin. Our interstate highways, those much praised golden avenues built to whisk suburban travelers in and out of downtown, have turned into the world's most expensive parking lots. That expense is not only economic—it is social. These highways have created great walls separating neighborhood from neighborhood, disrupting the complex social connections that help make a city livable (Bandouin, Bober, Clarke, Dobson, & Silberstein, 1977, p.159).

What lexical items might not be familiar to an ESL reader? First and foremost, words like *interstate highways, suburban,* and *mass transportation* may be difficult for ESL learners who do not have a cultural background of life in the big cities found in many developed countries in North America, Europe, and Asia. Some ESL learners may come from countries that have less-developed infrastructure and road systems as well as limited mass transportation systems. In addition, the concepts of suburban life and suburban commuters might be foreign to some ESL readers. Lack of such cultural knowledge can inhibit ESL readers in identifying the main ideas in the text. For instance, ESL readers may fail to see the important connection between the overabundance of highways and a reduced need for mass transportation and thereby conclude that this passage does not make much sense. This conclusion may stem from their background knowledge or an experience that led them to believe that highways are made for mass transportation. However, in the United States, where many people own cars, the massive number of cars affects the overabundance of highways and the reduced need for massive transportation. This lack of relevant social-cultural knowledge on the part of the readers can translate into comprehension difficulties when they are asked if they understand the author's position on mass transportation. In addition, ESL readers may not interpret the opposition between cars and mass transportation because they do not have any conception of interstate highways and how this word is associated with crowding, congestion, and rush hour traffic in urban areas. It is obvious that much of this background knowledge cannot be found anywhere in the passage. However, to fully understand the author's argument, the reader has to draw on prior knowledge to "fill in the gap" necessary for comprehension.

In addition, second language readers may lack a sound foundation of grammar and vocabulary in the language, unlike first language learners, before they begin formal reading instruction in school. Transfer effects from the home language may also cause difficulties for the second language learner. For example, the transfer of L1 syntactic knowledge and false cognates into the second language can cause interference in vocabulary recognition and comprehension for beginning readers.

False cognates are words that look similar but are, in fact, very different. These words can only sometimes be translated by the similar word in the other language. Examples of false cognates in English and Spanish are as follows:

- *Absoluto* vs. *absolutely*
  (alone *absoluto* means "absolute/complete." When preceded by *en* as in *absolutamente,* it means 'not at all/by no means.")

- *Exito* vs. *exit*
  (*Exito* means "It's a hit or a success. If you're looking for the way out, look for *una salida*).

- *Nombre* vs. *number*
  (*Nombre* means *"name or noun." Number* is *un número*).

Despite these limitations, second language students may have certain advantages. The more academically oriented ESL learners typically have a large vocabulary in their first language and, thus, learning vocabulary in English is just a matter of finding a label for a concept that is already well-understood. They also tend to be quite motivated to learn English for instrumental (desire to learn English to get a good education, job, salary, social recognition, etc.) or integrative reasons (desire to integrate into the new country), which can greatly improve their academic learning. Teachers can assist students' comprehension by providing the necessary background knowledge associated with the words they must know. It is also important for teachers to make texts readable by ensuring that they do not contain too many difficult structures and unfamiliar vocabulary and concepts for students to understand. This strategy can offset some difficulties that ESL readers may have because of their lack of second language proficiency.

Another difficulty that ESL readers may have in L2 reading lies in the differences between orthographic systems. Writing systems differ greatly in terms of the symbols they utilize. Chinese language uses a logographic system (derived from the Greek word "logos," meaning *word*) in which each character represents a word. Although any student of Chinese language must be able to recognize an enormous number of symbols (at least 5,000 characters to read a newspaper article written in Chinese), it is not necessary for Chinese speakers to pronounce the word in order to read the written language (Language Files, 1994). Contrarily, English readers rely on graphophonic cues, in addition to context, to distinguish between nouns and verbs, compound words and adjective-noun phrases, and homonyms. For example, English speakers use stress placement in words like *conduct* and *permit* to distinguish between a noun and a verb and in words like *blackboard* and *greenhouse* to distinguish between a compound noun or an adjective-noun phrase. Although these words appear to be the same or similar in spelling, their distinct pronunciations result in different meaning. ESL readers may have difficulties with English homonyms because these words have the same spelling and pronunciation but different meanings. For example, the word *pool* can be used to refer to a *pool table* or a *swimming pool,* each with different meaning entirely. Unless ESL students have some vocabulary, knowledge of language structures, and background knowledge of topics, they may not be able to interpret these types of expressions and structures easily.

In syllabic languages like Japanese, each symbol represents a syllable used in composing words, whereas English uses letters to compose mono- or polysyllabic words. Unlike English words, a Japanese word may constitute more than one syllable. English, Hebrew, Arabic, and Russian use alphabetic writing systems; however, they differ in terms of letter symbols and directionality for reading. Arabic reads from right to left, whereas English and Russian read from left to right. In addition, Hebrew writing requires that only consonants be written down and, in order to read Hebrew, readers must "fill in" the vowels by inferring the overall context of the sentence. This is contrary to Russian and English, in which both consonants and vowels are available. These writing differences may have some effect on word recognition and comprehension, especially for beginning readers of English. Table 17-3 provides some examples of logographic, syllabic, and alphabetic writing systems.

To be fluent readers of English, readers must be able to recognize letters and words and must possess the eye-motor coordination necessary for rapid reading. It is no surprise, then, that new English language learners with different writing

## Table 17-3
## Logographic, Syllabic, and Alphabetic Writing Systems

| Basic Types of Writing | Symbols |
|---|---|
| Logographic | Chinese<br>他是中國人<br>He be center country person |
| Syllabic | Japanese<br>これは本です。<br>Ko re wa hon de su |
| Alphabetic | Some examples of Russian Cyrillic Alphabet |

| | | |
|---|---|---|
| Б | б | b |
| В | в | v |
| Г | г | g |
| З | з | z |
| С | с | s |

Hebrew:

פסח     "psx" (Passover)

שמש     "sms" (sun)

systems in their primary language may not be able to do rapid reading as well as their fully proficient peers. However, teachers should not see this as a sign that warrants a "phonics instruction" and/or basic writing skills approach. These basic skills must be embedded in meaning-focused activities to help ESL readers achieve comprehension and communication.

Another significant difficulty that English language learners may have with reading is attributed to the "social contexts of literacy use in students' first language" (Grabe, 1991, 388). In some cultures, written texts represent "truth" and, as such, students from such cultures are not encouraged to "challenge" or "reinterpret" the text in light of other texts (Grabe, 1991, p.389). This factor can be compounded further by limited access to libraries and print information available in more literate societies. In such a situation, students may prefer rote memorization of knowledge to challenging or reinterpreting texts. Their differences in expectations about literacy use may lead them to see little value in doing extensive reading; consequently, this can have a profound impact on their academic reading skills in English.

## Characteristics of Beginning Readers

As discussed earlier, beginning English readers are unfamiliar with the English alphabet and thus, must be reminded that English texts must be read from left to right. They must also learn the correspondence between sound and symbol in English before they can read text independently. They also recognize a few sight words, and may not be able to process beyond sentence level text. At this stage, they are beginning to comprehend short, simple texts with predictable text structure and language patterns; but they still need to develop a larger sight vocabulary. Some may not have read in their first language and consequently, will need extensive reading and writing opportunities in and beyond the classroom. They must also become familiar with the various purposes we use reading and writing for, such as communication and personal enjoyment. Because of these reasons, these students need more contextualized lessons that are supported by a variety of visuals and scaffolds.

## Characteristics of Intermediate Readers

Intermediate readers can read with greater fluency than their beginner counterparts because they have a larger sight vocabulary and are more familiar with reading a variety of different texts such as stories, news articles, and letters. However, they still have difficulty reading texts containing new vocabulary and unfamiliar topics independently and can benefit from instruction that employs a variety of scaffolding techniques. They can generally speak with some degree of fluency and thus, are able to participate in discussion with peers in literature circles. The following section describes some effective language arts strategies that can be applied to content area teaching for beginning and intermediate readers of English.

# Strategies for Teaching Beginning Readers

## Language Experience approach

The Language Experience Approach, as discussed in chapter 18, has been noted to present fewer difficulties for beginning readers who are developing their English language proficiency (Tinajero & Calderon, 1988; Walter, 1995). This approach allows children to dictate their stories based on their personal experience. The teacher/teacher aide, and /or parents write the story and use it as reading material to instruct the students. This approach integrates listening, speaking, reading, writing, and thinking through teacher-led discussion that helps students organize and reflect on their experiences. There are two different approaches to recording students' oral dictated stories. One approach entails recording of students' exact words, with minimal rephrasing of the student's language to show acceptance of the student's language and to prevent any difficulty in reading materials that do not contain language that is familiar to the reader (McMillan, 1995). However, in the second approach, the teacher corrects any words that are mispronounced to reinforce graphophonic awareness. This approach also draws on students' culture and, thus, they read texts containing familiar and high-interest content that serve as a foundation for developing second literacy. This approach is not confined to narratives only; in fact, it can be used for content-area learning in which group experience stories can be used to summarize key topics, concepts, or events.

The following steps are recommended for implementing this approach successfully: (1) The teacher starts with a group story by having the class share and discuss experiences related to a field trip, a literature selection, or other personal experiences. (2) The teacher encourages students to dictate how the story is written by asking them to contribute words, phrases, or sentences. (3) The students read and discuss their story. Teachers can model how to make revisions to their story and then involve students through the thinking process of revising their story. For example, if a student reads, *my brother* and *me goed to the park,* the teacher can model the standard form and ask students how their ideas should be written. (4) The teacher encourages students to read their story through choral reading, followed by echo reading where every student gets a chance to read different portions of the text. (5) The teacher uses the story to help students discover different aspects of print by doing different types of activities such as creating a big book version of their story, illustrating their story, matching words from the story to another set of words written on cards, and identifying letters, words and punctuation (Walter, 1996). This group activity can help learners build a sense of community among students with varied backgrounds. Another advantage is that this approach is simple enough for parents or caregivers to adopt as one of many home literacy activities.

## Reading Aloud

Many students of all ages and abilities can benefit from a reading-aloud activity. When teachers read aloud to students, they make reading fun and, at the same time, assist students in developing print concepts, phonics knowledge, sight vocabulary, and comprehension. Books selected for reading aloud should be age-appropriate in terms of language, length, and plot complexity. For beginning readers, choose a text that has a predictable structure and supporting illustrations. This text could be connected to a theme study in which students have learned key concepts and vocabulary.

It is important to remember that listening to a story is not an easy task for beginning readers. Teachers can make this listening task easier by doing a few things. Teachers can ask several prereading questions such as, *"What do you think is this story about?" "What picture tells the story?" "Can you point to the title?" " Who wrote the book?"* or *"What is the author/s name?"* while holding the book for students to see the cover. At the same time, some children with little or no experience with books can learn how to hold a book. As teachers read the book, they can point to the text so that students can see the direction of the print. To facilitate comprehension, teachers can stop at certain places in the text and ask students to predict what they think will happen next, how they think the story will end, and what they like about the story so far. Teachers can discuss different parts of the story by asking *"What is happening here?" "What is the character doing?"* and so forth. Taped recordings of books can also be used in learning centers to reinforce language patterns. As students listen, they can also look at the illustrations in the book to understand concepts.

Another way to reinforce comprehension and listening during oral reading is to have learners spot the mistake made by the teacher during oral reading. To do this, teachers must select several words in the text that can be substituted with other words that carry different meanings. For example, the sentence, *"He bought a fish at the store"* could become *"He sold a fish at the store."* Students are given a copy of the text and underline the words that are different from what is read. Higher-level readers, can try to catch or write the exact words spoken by the teacher (Hegelsen, 1993). Once students understand the procedure, they can be divided into pairs. Each student can make a change in different paragraphs or parts of a text and read his or her part to the other students and catch each other's mistakes. This strategy can also be applied to content reading by having students read aloud certain passages containing key concepts they have learned, listen to their peers' or teacher's oral reading, and spot any difference between the text and the oral reading.

## Choral Speaking

This strategy encourages learners to participate in dramatic activities as they enjoy reading literature selections such as poems, songs, and pattern books. They can create props and add sound effects, gestures, and movements to make a story come alive. This is a fun and interesting way to introduce oral language patterns, vocabulary words, and sentence patterns. It also helps build students' confidence by making them feel that learning English is easy and fun. For example, teachers can select a poem such as the following:

**When the day is cloudy**
When the day is cloudy
The thunder makes a low rumble
And the rain patters against the lodge
Then it's fine and nice to sleep.
(Ada, Violet, & Hopkins,1993)

First, the teacher recites the poem and the children make sound effects such as rubbing their hands together in a circular motion to evoke the rustling leaves before the storm; snapping their fingers one at a time, lightly at first followed by faster and harder rhythms to suggest the patter of the first tiny raindrops; and clapping their hands to indicate the rain is pouring and slapping their hands on a desk as the rain pounds on the roof. These movements can be reversed to indicate the end of the storm. Teachers can then recite individual lines and have the students repeat in unison; this strategy is referred to as *echo reading*. Teachers can also have students fill in any missing word when they read a portion of the sentence. This encourages students to listen and works best with brief selections. If students do not want to participate in the choral-speaking activities at the beginning, they can be encouraged to do the body movements instead.

Another way to make students become involved in their reading is to have them read a selection aloud together; this is *choral reading*. Choral reading works best if the stories, poems, and songs have repeated structures; for example, selections such as Brown bear, brown bear what do you see? (Eric Carle), The Napping house (Audrey Wood), and Bear's walk: A Never-ending story (Alma Flor Ada). After students have read such a book and heard the story many times, they can easily predict what the story will say and become familiar with predictable structures or refrains from the book such as, *"Ooh! What's that I see?" It's just a cat/ a fox/ some bunnies."* When selecting books with predictable structures,

Peterson (1992) recommends books containing language patterns that relate to the content, are supported by illustrations found in the text, and relate to the background experiences of the learners. Texts that introduce nonsense refrains such as those that are found in the familiar story of The Three Little Pigs (Ziefert, 1995) may actually interfere with the beginning reader's comprehension.

Similar strategies could also be used to facilitate comprehension. When reading content contains difficult words and concepts, teachers can model and/or invite students to use nonverbal means such as gestures, body movement, and sounds that they can understand. Teachers can also use visual forms of input such as maps and diagrams to provide additional means for comprehending difficult content.

## Literature Circles

Literature circle is a type of discussion group that incorporates cooperative learning principles and provides students with materials based on student choices. This type of discussion group allows students to discuss their responses and engage in the same type of talk used when discussing literature or content area books with peers. This approach is well-suited for ESL readers who are still struggling with reading and works better in cooperative learning groups. Essentially, five to six students read the same book from a selection of texts with varying difficulty levels and interests.

Groups of five to six students are formed based on their choices of book selections. Teachers can try to match the book with the ability level of the students. Then each student is assigned a role by the teacher, or the group can decide who will fulfill each role. The roles reflect the things that students should be doing when they read. A discussion leader develops questions and leads group discussion. The summarizer summarizes the text; the literacy reporter finds passages/lines that stand out because they contain memorable language patterns or key ideas, and describes events that are funny, sad, mysterious. When reading content books, the reporter can locate passages that use different and interesting language patterns to mean the same concept or different concepts. The reporter reads passages out loud and directs the group to read the selection silently or dramatizes them. The illustrator illustrates the main idea of the text by using a graphic organizer or drawing. The word chief searches and defines difficult words or expressions found in the text with the aid of a dictionary. The connector finds links between books that the group has read or links the book(s) with other real events or situations. By playing these roles, readers become aware of the importance of questioning, making connections, summarizing, visualizing, and coping with difficult words that underlie the reading process. Each of the roles can be modeled, discussed, and practiced by the students. Job sheets can be handed out to assist students in carrying out the assigned role (Gunning, 2000). Figure 17-2 shows a sample job sheet for the literacy reporter.

## Shared Reading with Big Books

Shared reading is a process in which students read a big book along with a teacher. Big books are oversize versions with colorful and supportive illustrations and have one to three sentences per page. They present predictable story structures and language patterns that students can follow very easily. Big books can be produced commercially; students can also select a familiar text and make their own big book. They can copy the exact story into their personal big book, write

---

## Fig. 17-2
## Literacy Reporter Sheet

The literacy reporter's job is to locate and discuss passages that contain colorful language, figures of speech, or special techniques the author has used to tell the story. Write the page and paragraph number of these passages. Explain why you think they stand out.

Book Title: _____A River Ran Wild_____

| **Quotes** | **My Reasons** |
|---|---|
| **P. 5** | |
| *Long ago a wild river ran wild through a land of towering forests. Bears, moose, and herds of deer, hawks, and owls all made their homes in the peaceful river…* *One day a group of native people …came upon the river valley. From atop the mountain… they saw the river nestled in its valley, a silver sliver in the sun.* | *I like the way the writer describes the beauty of the place. The river was beautiful. It is home to many animals in the forests* |

Groups are given about a week or two to complete a selection and schedules for how much and when reading can be done in school or at home. Then each group shares its book with the whole class.

---

the author's name on the cover and after drawing their own illustrations, add their name to the cover as the illustrator (Peregoy & Boyle, 2001). They can also dictate and write their own versions of the story. Big books help students develop new vocabulary, and a sense of the rhythm and syntax in the language while learning about the reading and writing process in an enjoyable and enriching way.

## Thematic Units

A thematic unit is a way of organizing instruction around a central idea or topic. This central idea can be a theme such as "endangered animals" and can explore other unifying ideas such as "What does 'endangered' mean?" "What animals are considered endangered species and where are they located?" "Why are some animals in danger?" "What efforts is the world making to combat this problem?" "Is there a better solution to combat this problem? If so, what is it and why is it better than the existing solution?" A thematic unit has several advantages: (1) It integrates content from different areas of learning and, thus, helps students to make connections between areas of knowledge and stimulate deeper level thinking. (2) It helps students to make connections among listening, speaking, reading, and writing as they listen, talk, and write about what they have read or heard. (3) It helps teachers to integrate language arts and content lessons in a flexible way, thereby reinforcing both language and content which are vital to students' academic success. The following suggestions are ways to create and implement a thematic unit instruction. (1) Students can collaborate with the teacher in identifying a topic or theme they wish to explore; teachers match themes or topics to students' age level (i.e., their interest) and a variety of content and skills from language arts, social science, art, and math. (2) The teacher helps students to identify inquiry questions they wish to explore and decides on materials and activities that will help students to find answers to their inquiries. Before students can explore the topic or theme related to endangered species, they are asked to imagine how they might feel if someone destroyed their homes to build another building or parking lot. (3) The teacher conducts a holistic evaluation that must include a variety of information that reflects students' understanding of major concepts, skills, and strategies. Students' written notes, journal logs, diagrams, tests, oral retelling or summaries, essays, and illustrations are examples of authentic assessment that can be collected.

# Strategies For Intermediate Learners

Intermediate readers generally have a larger sight vocabulary and demonstrate more automatic processing skills that help them to read more fluently than their beginning counterparts. They generally have little problem understanding texts such as stories, letters, and simple magazine and news articles. However, they may find expository texts and some stories difficult to read because of unfamiliar vocabulary, complicated syntax, and text structures that do not permit them to focus on conceptual aspects of the text. These students need further assistance in processing texts for comprehension and higher- level thinking. The following section describes various strategies that are effective in fostering comprehension and higher-level thinking of intermediate learners of English. Bear in mind that all of the strategies that were recommended for beginning readers could also be used effectively with intermediate learners by using texts with higher difficulty with respect to language and concepts.

## Directed Reading-Thinking Activity (DR-TA)

Directed reading-thinking activity is an approach that coaches students to make explicit connections between print and meaning by responding to questions as they read segments of the text. This strategy replicates how the mind works and helps students to develop strategies that facilitate comprehension. This strategy can be used with narrative as well as expository texts. The process can be modeled by reading segments of the text or having students read independently or with a partner. The procedures for directed reading-thinking activity are as follows:

- Divide the text into segments that will promote deep-level reflection.
- Build students' background knowledge of the text prior to reading by pointing to the book cover and the title, headings and subheadings and asking predicting questions such as, "What kinds of information do you expect to read from the text?" "Why do you think this?"
- Have students read the first segment of the text and then compare it to the original text. They must verify their predictions or identify which predictions were inaccurate or still unknown.
- Have students continue to read the next segment and respond to more predicting and verifying questions based on their reading.
- After reading the whole text, have students discuss their predictions and overall reactions and reread the whole text again.

## Graphic Organizers

Intermediate readers can use graphic organizers to help them to understand stories as well as difficult content and vocabulary they are likely to encounter in expository texts. They can be used in pre- , during, and post-reading activities.

These visual maps allow students to "see" the interrelationship between ideas by organizing major and subordinate concepts in a text and discovering the underlying text structure. They are also effective in assisting learners to elaborate on their ideas, and relate new information to old knowledge. In other words, graphic organizers are effective tools for enhancing thinking and learning. Some types of graphic organizers are shown in Figure 17-1a–h (McTighe, 1992). Students can also use these graphic organizers as a prewriting strategy for generating a plan for their writing or as a focal point for group discussions that becomes the final tangible product. In a cooperative learning group, graphic organizers can become a means for expanding students' own thinking as they consider facts, details, abstract ideas, and different points of view.

### Learning Logs/Journals

Learning logs, commonly known as journals, are excellent tools for getting students to discover their thoughts and write about what they read. Students can use journal logs to react to the text they have read, discuss specific elements or techniques that writers use to convey their points, identify difficulties in their reading that need further clarification, discuss real-world issues that are addressed in the text, and/or propose or evaluate a solution to a problem-solving task that is related to the book. There are several ways in which teachers can use journals to further their students' learning. Students can use logs in literature response groups in which they read and discuss each other's informal comments and reactions about the book or use them as means to reflect and discuss difficult concepts related to a body of knowledge. Teachers can allow students to write whatever they wish in their journal or they can provide some structure by posing several questions that allow students to discuss key points and concepts covered in a content lesson.

The following book provides a plethora of instructional reading activities that aim at teaching pronunciation, vocabulary, and concept development in diverse and creative ways:

Schinke-Llano, Linda & Rauff, R. (Eds.). (1996). *New ways in teaching children.* Bloomington, IL: Pantagraph Printing.

## Selecting Appropriate Literature For ESL Readers

Few students, whether they are native speakers of English or learners of English, are fully proficient in academic language before entering school. This gap is even bigger if the students lack literacy experiences such as having books read to them in any language or even having books in their homes to read. To facilitate this learning, teachers must provide instructional support that will make input to be learned understandable and use authentic materials that draw attention to how language is used for academic purposes so that learners stay motivated to learn. Using authentic children's literature is one source of input for academic language. Fillmore (2001) and Allen (1994) suggest these criteria when selecting texts for beginning and intermediate learners:

- Introduce vocabulary, grammar, and discourse conventions in the language they are learning.
- Introduce stories with a predictable structure, repetitive language, and discourse patterns that support children's understanding.
- Use multicultural texts that present topics that are interesting and relevant to students. These books typically reflect the multicultural groups in the students' communities.
- Use international texts and books written by authors outside of the students' country and reflect daily concerns, history, social life, art, and customs of various cultures outside of the student's country. These texts can provide students a window to the world and may be published in multiple languages. Some folktales or fables from around the world have been translated into English from different languages.
- Introduce materials that contain simple language and concepts before moving to books with more complex language and words that are conceptually abstract.
- Offer a variety of writing genres.
- Use multilevel books to make provision for individual learner differences.
- Encourage children to choose their own book to read.
- Take into account children's background knowledge.
- Use "real-world" materials/print to help students discover the values and functions of written language.
- Use content area textbooks to support curricular areas like science, math, and social studies.
- Use materials with plenty of illustrations.

The following section provides a sample of materials that are suitable for all levels because they provide the necessary literacy scaffolds that ESL learners need to make learning meaningful and use language in a communicative manner. However, teachers must remember that texts do not often reveal how language works or provide clues to how words are used and the meanings they carry. These materials will become usable input if teachers: (1) provide support and discuss difficult words and structures to help learners understand, (2) direct learner's attention to how a particular language or word is used in a text as well as in other texts, and (3) explain how grammatical cues indicate relationships between ideas such as cause-effect, consequence, comparison-contrast, sequential order, and so on (Fillmore, 2001).

## Materials that Support Language Acquisition

### *"Real-World" Materials*

Emergent literacy studies have shown that children's early literacy experiences begin with their ability to read environmental print that is readily available to them. Through their experiences with environmental print, children learn about the function and features of written language. Second language learners also exhibit similar literacy experiences. As such, it is important that instruction provides a rich input of written language from newspapers, food cartons, menus, letters, catalogs, brochures, book jackets, and so on. Children can look at the editorial section of a newspaper or magazine and compose a letter to the editor raising an issue of concern. They can also look at menus and compare prices of different foods, categorize different types of foods, discuss the nutritional value of particular foods, or suggest a different menu that is more nutritional and reasonably priced.

To get a deeper level of understanding from a literature text, students can use "real-world" materials such as reproductions of historical letters, dramatic photographs, and excerpts from movies or critical reviews to engage readers emotionally and intellectually. These materials can also be used to develop genuine writing activities with interdisciplinary connections. For example, when students are asked to read the war novel, *The red badge of courage,* they can research and read reproductions of Civil War letters, and newspaper articles. They can view dramatic photographs or paintings of notable people, troops, ships, artillery, and battles, and then write responses to the letters. Students can also write a response to a critical review of a book in which they have to use various sources to locate incidents or moments that affirm the authenticity of the author's work. Other authentic writing activities could include a composition comparing how a movie based on a novel effectively "echoes" the sentiments of the characters in a book or a reflective paper in which students write the lessons about war they could use today (Paulenich, 1992). After discussing the book, students can also examine the illustration on the book jacket and recreate a new book jacket complete with illustrations and a synopsis of the story. "Real-world" materials provide an excellent opportunity for students to become more active in reading by responding to whatever is pertinent to them rather than merely pursuing the writer's meaning. These materials also provide an excellent opportunity for exploring critical reading and thinking, as readers actively examine and analyze facts and opinions. They search for evidence and logical fallacies by having a "dialogue" with the text or writing to the text and reading each other's writing. In this way, the interactive process takes on a transactional nature of reading, as students develop their personal voice and purpose which influence what and how they read and write.

## Concept Books

One of the tasks that English language learners encounter in acquiring a new language is the development of new vocabulary to express knowledge and experiences that they have acquired in their primary language. Concept books can help new English learners to acquire vocabulary by describing different dimensions of an object, a class of objects, or an abstract idea. Some concept books have texts that come in varying lengths that are appropriate for different levels of English learners. For example, Byron Barton's *"Machines at Work"* offers clear and simple pictures of what machines can do, such as bulldoze a tree, knock down a building, dig up a road, load a truck, and so on. This book introduces a simple, imperative structure (used typically in giving instructions or commands) to describe each picture and, thus, is appropriate for beginning English language learners. Other concept books like John Malam's *Highest, Longest, and Deepest* introduces the concept of dimensions by illustrating and comparing various geological elements of the earth such as mountains, glaciers, lakes, deserts, rivers, coral reefs, volcanoes, caves, oceans, and waterfalls. Each illustration is labeled and accompanied by a short description of several sentences or paragraphs. This concept book is suitable for older ESL learners who have more experience and knowledge about language.

Concept books can also help students learn ways to organize new information. Christopher Maynard's colorful book, *"Incredible Mini-Beasts"* helps students learn about different types of small insects, their habitat, anatomy, diet, and self-defense mechanisms. Concept books can also help learners to link old and new experiences. Marc Brown and Stephen Krensky's *"Dinosaurs, Beware! A Safety Guide"* teaches children about safety rules using colorful pictures that illustrate many safety tips and actions of dinosaurs undergoing the consequences of their actions as understood by people around the world. For example, the book describes and illustrates some safety tips for traveling, such as using bicycle reflectors, warning others of your approach with a bell or horn, or obeying road signs and traffic lights. These illustrations and explanations invite students to share experiences that are similar or different in their cultures and country of origin. Concept books can also teach word recognition and grammar. For example, Betsy Maestro's *"Taxi: A Book of City Words"* is an excellent book for teaching word concepts and prepositions. Each picture in this book is large and colorful, and has one or two sentences such as *"A busy yellow taxi takes passengers to a railroad station/ zoo/ office building."* The text highlights one- or two-word concepts like *taxi* and *railroad station,* respectively, as well as prepositions such as, *"...drives over a bridge and through a tunnel."*

The following books are excellent resources that provide annotated bibliographies of books suitable for different age and grade levels. Brown categorizes books by text types or genres such as picture books, legends, fables, folktales, fiction, and nonfiction for primary and secondary grades. It also provides a cross-reference list of these books based on topic and ethnicity/culture. Gunnings book provides a list categorized by author, title, theme, subject, skills, and language structures.

Brown, Dorothy (1994). *Books for a small planet.* Bloomington, IL: Pantagraph Printing.
Gunning, T. (2000). *Best books for building literacy for elementary school children.* Boston, MA: Allyn & Bacon.

### Pattern Books and Poems

Pattern books and poems are texts that have predictable story and/or language structures and frequently contain pictures that help students to understand the text. For example, *"Birds Can't Fly"* makes use of repeated phrases such as *"birds can fly but they can't swim"* and *"birds have feathers but they don't have hard shells"* to compare and contrast birds with other animals. This book introduces students to characteristics of birds and such as ostriches and other animals including alligators, turtles, and fishes. Students can elaborate by using their newly acquired vocabulary in a familiar pattern such as *"Birds can ___ but they can't ___."* Beginning readers can create their own phrases by using this predictable language pattern to create their own versions of big books, complete with illustrations. The following patterns books and poems can be used with old and young English language learners:

Brown, M. W. (1947). *Goodnight moon.* New York: HarperCollins.
Ginsburg, Mirra. (1992). *Asleep, asleep.* New York: Greenwillow.
Bryan, Ashley. (1985). *Turtle know your name.* New York: Macmillan.

### Text Sets

Text sets are related books that allow students to make connections between texts, which consequently enhances involvement in and thinking about what they read. Sets may cover the same theme or topic, such as chili pepper festivals, their history, and growth cycle. They may also be from the same genre; for example, bibliographies, fiction, and collections of poems, fairy tales, and so forth. A text set can also have collections of books written by the same author. Text sets can offer different versions of the same tale or present cultural versions of the same tale or story such as the traditional *Cinderella* tale and Louie's (1982) *Yeh-Shen: A Cinderella Story from China*. Text sets should represent a range of interests and difficulty levels that are appropriate for mixed-ability groups. Harste, Short, and Burke (1988) recommend text sets be used to promote oral discussion. Students can read all the books or select some in the text sets and discuss them in a literature circle group. They can compare and contrast the books they have read. If they have not read the same books, they can share the contents of the books they have read, and then compare and contrast them. The following are examples of text sets that have been divided into several categories:

**Theme:** (in these texts, the theme is "sharing")
Rocklin, J. (1998). *Not enough room.* New York: Scholastic,
Hoberman, M. A. (1997). *One of each.* Boston: Little Brown.
Galbraith, K. O. (1991). *Roommates and Rachel.* New York: Macmillan.
Pfister, M. (1992). *The rainbow fish.* New York: North-South Books, Inc.

**Topic:** (the following texts are about animals in hibernation)
Bancroft, H. & Van Gelder, R.G. (1997). *Animals in winter.* New York: HarperCollins.
Preller, J. (1994). *Wake me up in spring.* New York: Scholastic.

**Text types:** (the following texts are "how," "what," and "why" stories)
Zoehfield, K. (1994). *What lives in a shell?* New York: HarperCollins.
Kipling, R. (1973). *How the rhinoceros got his skin.* New York: Walker.
Ripley, Catherine. (1997). *Why does popcorn pop? And other Kitchen Questions.* Toronto: Greey de Pencier Books, Inc.
Zoehfeld, K .W .(1995). *How mountains are made.* New York: HarperCollins.

Other text types include the "if" books such as:
Mansell, Dom. (1991). *If dinosaurs came to town.* Boston: Little Brown.
London, J. (1997). *If I had a horse.* San Francisco: Chronicle.

**Text structures:** (basic organizational plot structure)
In the following texts, the plot shows a cause-effect link.)
Aardema, V. (1975). *Why mosquitoes buzz in people's ears: A West African folk tale.* New York: Dial.
Wood, Audrey. (1984). *The napping house.* New York: Harcourt Brace Jovanovich.

In the following texts, the characters are sequenced according to size:
Carle, E. (1977). *The grouchy ladybug.* New York: Crowell.
Ets, M. (1972). *The elephant in the wall.* New York: Viking.
Tolstoy, A. (1968). *The great big enormous turnip.* New York: Franklin Watts.

**Different versions of the same tale:**
Ziefart, H. (1995). *The three little pigs.* New York: Penguin.
Scieszka, J. (1989). *The true story of the three little pigs.* New York: Viking.

**Cultural versions of the same tale:**
Clark, A. (1979). *In the land of small dragon.* New York: Viking. (Vietnamese)
Climo, Shirley. (1989). *The Egyptian Cinderella.* New York: HarperCollins.
Climo, Shirley. (1993). *The Korean Cinderella.* New York: HarperCollins.
Louie, A .L . (1981). *Yeh Shen: A Cinderella story from China.* New York: Philomel.
Martin, R. & Shannon, D. (1992). *The rough-face girl.* New York: Putnam (Algonquin).
Mbane, P.(1972). *Nomi and the magic fish: A story from Africa.* New York: Doubleday.
Whitney, T .P. (1970). *Vasilisa the beautiful: A Russian folktale.* New York: Macmillan.
Steel, F. (1976). *Tattercoats.* New York: Bradbury.

**Same author/illustrator:**
De Paola, Tomie. (1988). *The legend of the Indian paintbrush.* New York: Putnam.
———(1983). *The legend of the bluebonnet: An old tale of Texas.* New York: Putnam.
———(1980). *Tony's bread: An Italian folktale.* New York: Putnam.

**Culture**

This set of books depicts a particular culture and comes from a variety of genres:

Breckler, R. (1992). *Hoang breaks the magic teapot.* Boston: Houghton Mifflin. (Vietnamese in the United States)

Brown, T. (1991). *Lee Ann: The story of a Vietnamese American girl.* New York: Putnam.

Kent, Z. (1991). *The story of Saigon airlift.* Chicago: Children's Press.

Nhuong, H. Q. (1982). *The land I lost: Adventures of a boy in Vietnam.* San Francisco: Harper and Row.

Other categories of text sets include books:

- of the same story or content with different illustrators
- about the same set of characters such as *Amelia Bedelia* and *Frog and Toad*

## Reading Assessments

Current views on reading research reveal that reading is a developmental process consisting of holistic reading and writing processes as well as integration of language arts. Keeping this in mind, a single, norm-referenced test simply cannot capture all the complexities involved in reading. Instead, schools must strive to develop alternative forms of assessment by collecting a variety of information to learn about students' ability as well as their attitudes toward reading and knowledge about reading. Alternative forms of assessment are also known as *authentic assessments* to reflect the actual learning and instructional activities that can measure what students know and can do. Assessment information can also help teachers to evaluate the effectiveness of current instruction and plan future instructional activities to address students' needs. Authentic assessment can take various forms.

## Anecdotal Records of Classroom Observation

Teachers can systematically document their students' literacy development by using anecdotal records or checklists with clearly defined sets of traits or behaviors. Teachers can organize anecdotal records by jotting down any spontaneous observations about the student behavior on index cards, post-it notes, or address labels. For example, a teacher may note that Latifa was able to capture the gist of a passage by recognizing familiar root words, even though she skipped several unfamiliar words; or Ravi had difficulty understanding the text on tornados because he does not know what a tornado is. The teacher can follow these initial notes by recording additional, related events such as the students' work habits and strategy use on specific tasks. With anecdotal records, teachers can record useful information that may not show up on a test, in retelling, or in students' written work. Teachers can observe the quality of their students' comprehension and the strategies they seem to be using, find out what difficulties they have that hinders comprehension, or observe what they do when they read different types of texts.

A checklist is a useful tool to document students' literacy development because it can be tailored to teachers' specific evaluation needs. Teachers can also minimize their time recording by simply checking off the observed behaviors. The list of behaviors can be modified or added to accurately reflect the progress the student is making throughout the year. Figure 17-3 provides an example of a story retelling checklist and Fig. 17-4 provides an example of a think-aloud checklist that can be used when a reader explains his or her thought processes while reading a text.

## Informal Reading Inventory

An informal reading inventory (IRI) is an assessment tool that records errors in oral reading and comprehension in order to determine students' reading levels. It is generally given at the beginning of a school year to obtain placement information for new students. To determine placement levels, students are asked to read books at the easiest level first and continue at the next level until the reading becomes obviously difficult for them. Like a directed reading activity, the students are told that they are going to read some stories and answer some questions about their reading. Before reading, students are asked to read the title and predict what the story will be about. This helps to set a purpose for the reader and determine his or her background knowledge. Typically, as students read the story orally, their reading errors, such as omissions, insertions, substitutions, and mispronunciations, are recorded. Any hesitations, repetitions, and self-corrections are not considered errors. However, developing English learners are bound to mispronounce unfamiliar words, especially those that contain sounds that are difficult for them to produce. Hence, they may substitute a new word to replace the difficult word. While it is easier to count all mispronunciations or substitutions as errors, it is important to interpret these errors in light of what students comprehend. After the students have read aloud, they are asked to answer comprehension questions about the text or construct an oral retelling. The same procedure is repeated for the silent reading portion. Using texts of the same level,

# Figure 17-3
## Story Retelling Checklist

Name _____ Date _____

Title _____ Author _____

Quarter:        1st      2nd      3rd      4th

Text Difficulty:    High predictability    Moderate predictability    Advanced

Response:        Drawing/pictures      Oral response        Written response

| Performance Tasks | Initiates | Responds to Prompt | Comments |
|---|---|---|---|
| Names main characters | | | |
| Describes setting | | | |
| Starts retelling at the beginning | | | |
| Identifies problem or issues | | | |
| Identifies major events | | | |
| Reports events in chronological order | | | |
| Describes resolution | | | |

Adapted from a format developed by ESL teacher K. Harrison (1994), Fairfax County Public Schools, and based on National Education Association (1993)

## Figure 17-4
## Think-Aloud Checklist

Student _____ Date _____

Story/Text _____ Grade/Teacher _____

Place a check (✔) or write examples in the spaces.

| Reading Strategy | Frequently | Sometimes | Rarely |
|---|---|---|---|
| 1.  Uses prior knowledge | | | |
| 2.  Self-corrects words and sentences | | | |
| 3.  Rereads | | | |
| 4.  Makes predictions | | | |
| 5.  Forms opinions | | | |
| 6.  Paraphrases | | | |
| 7.  Summarizes | | | |
| 8.  Adds ideas | | | |
| 9.  Other: | | | |

Adapted from Glazer and Brown (1993).

students are asked to read a selection silently and then answer comprehension questions. The percentage score for word recognition is computed by dividing the total number of correct words by the number of words in the selection. Comprehension is calculated by averaging the scores for the oral and the silent sections. Table 17-4 shows placement levels of IRI.

## Table 17-4
## Placement Levels for IRI

| Level | Word Recognition in Context (%) | Average Comprehension (%) |
|---|---|---|
| Independent | 99 | 90–100 |
| Instructional | 95–98 | 75–89 |
| Frustration | 90 | 50 |
| Listening capacity | | 75 |

Gunning, 2001, p.490

## Miscue Analysis

Miscue analysis is another assessment device to determine oral reading errors that reflect deviations from the print (Goodman & Burke, 1972). Miscues provide information about readers' attempts at making sense of the text. The following are procedures for doing a miscue analysis (Gunning, 2001; Peregoy & Boyle, 2001):

1. Ask students to read a text that they have not read previously. Choose a selection that is grade-level appropriate. If the selection is short, take a running record of the whole piece. If the selection is lengthy, take a sample of 100 to 200 words from the text.

2. Make one copy of the reading selection for the student and another copy for the teacher to write on. A sample of the coding system is shown in figure 17-5. Get a tape recorder and a blank tape to record the oral reading.

3. Prepare the student by giving the following instruction: "This is a passage that I want you to read aloud. If you come across a word that you don't know, try to figure it out on your own and then continue to read. After you have finished reading, I will ask you to tell me what you remember about the passage." After the student has finished reading, ask probing questions to find out what the student remembers about the text and ask additional questions to assess comprehension level.

4. The student can listen to the taped oral reading for fun.

5. Teachers can analyze the tape recording for any miscues.

## Figure 17-5
## Marking Miscues

1. **Insertion:** the child inserts a word not in the text; place a caret where the insertion is made and write the inserted word above it.

   *also*

   Example: The cat was ^ in the kitchen.

2. **Omission:** the child leaves a word out; circle the word the child omits.

   Example: Many people find it ⬭difficult⬭ to concentrate.

3. **Substitution:** the child replaces one word with another; place the child's substitution over the replaced word.

   *dog*

   Example: The doll was in the little girl's room.

4. **Word Supplied by Tester:** child can't get word and tester supplies it; put supplied word in parentheses.

   *(school)*

   Example: Joe ran to school.

5. **Word Missed then Corrected by Reader:** child says word wrong then immediately corrects it; place missed word above word and place a check by it.

   *rat* ✓

   Example: The cat is sleeping.

## Interpreting Miscues

Miscues can tell us about students' reading competencies and help us make decisions about how to assist them. Figure 17-6 provides an example of a reader's reading miscue (Peregoy & Boyle, 2001, p. 296). These miscues reveal the reader's reading competencies in the following areas:

1. The reader shows a persistent difficulty with –ed endings of words and diagraphs, such as *th-* in *thousand* and *sh-* in *shining* (a sound made up of two letters), and blends (a blended sound made up of two letters) such as *bl-* in *blanket, sp-* in *spoke,* and *st-* in *stopped.*

2. The reader has difficulty with sight words such as *from.*

3. The reader chooses to use *John* instead of *Juan* at first but then switches back to Juan the second time the name appears and uses the Spanish cognate *mision* for *mission.* These miscues, however, do not affect the reader's comprehension.

## Figure 17-6
## Candy's Miscues on the Guadalupe Passage

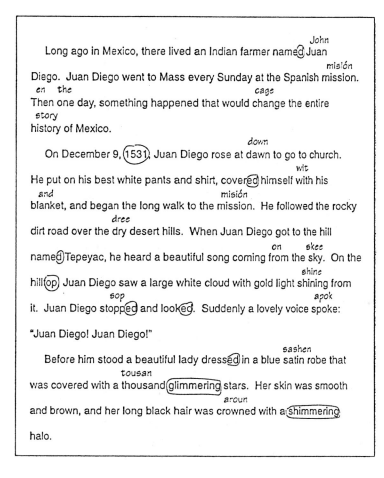

These miscues are then analyzed and interpreted in light of the student's responses to comprehension questions to determine if they affect comprehension. Although the reader made digraph errors and mispronounced *Juan* and *mission,* these errors do not seem to interfere with the student's comprehension. Moreover, these errors may reflect the learner's developmental level in oral English. Because meaning is unimpeded, these errors were ignored. However, the reader's difficulty with blends could result in confusion and, thus, additional instruction in this area may be appropriate.

## Self-assessment

Although current views in reading have stressed the importance of metacognitive knowledge and self-monitoring skills in fluent reading, these components have largely been neglected in classroom assessment. Research has indicated that students who are actively involved in self-assessment become more responsible for their own learning (Rief, 1990; Tierney, Carter, & Desai, 1991). Students who are new to self-assessment need teachers to show them how to evaluate their own progress and, thus, will be learning a new skill. Teachers can help students remember their goals for each task by having them jot their goals on an index card. Students can refer to these cards from time to time or they can discuss their goals in small groups or individual conferences. Some questions that might be asked to help students self-assess their reading are as follows (O'Malley, & Pierce, 1996, p.100):

- What have you learned about reading in this class?
- How do you feel about reading?
- What three things do good readers do?
- What do you need to improve in reading?
- What do you do when you come to words you don't know?

Students' self-assessment can also take other forms: checklists, scoring rubrics, sentence completion, and learning and reflection logs. Figure 17-7 shows a sample of self-assessment that contains short sentences and pictorial responses that are appropriate for young learners and those who have low literacy skills. When dealing with pre-readers, teachers can read the questions aloud and jot down student responses. Figures 17-8 and 17-9 are examples of assessment in which students check off items on the list that apply to them. Figure 17-10 is an example of a developmental reading rubric developed by elementary and secondary school teachers that assesses reading behaviors at different levels. Figure 17-11 is an example of a reading log that can be used to assess the number and types of books students have read and their reaction to each selection. This log can help students discover the types of books and content that have high appeal to them and may explain their ability to read various texts in the classroom.

## Running Records

A running record is an informal reading assessment that records student oral reading errors to determine students' word recognition skill, the strategies readers use when they read, and whether the material is at the appropriate level. To get a better sense of students' reading ability, teachers can assess students' comprehension by asking them to retell a story orally. Teachers typically use passages of about 100 to 200 words at different grade levels to determine students' strengths and weaknesses. Teachers can select passages from books currently used in their program or students can make their personal selection. Unlike the IRI, teachers do not have a copy of the text to mark and, hence, they must write notes quickly. Despite this limitation, many teachers use this assessment because it can be used informally in classroom instruction to evaluate students' reading competencies. Figure 17-12 shows an example of a running record (Clay, 1979 in Peregoy, 2000).

**Figure 17-7**
**Self-assessment of Emergent Reading**

Name _____ Date _____

How do you read? Circle one of the faces.

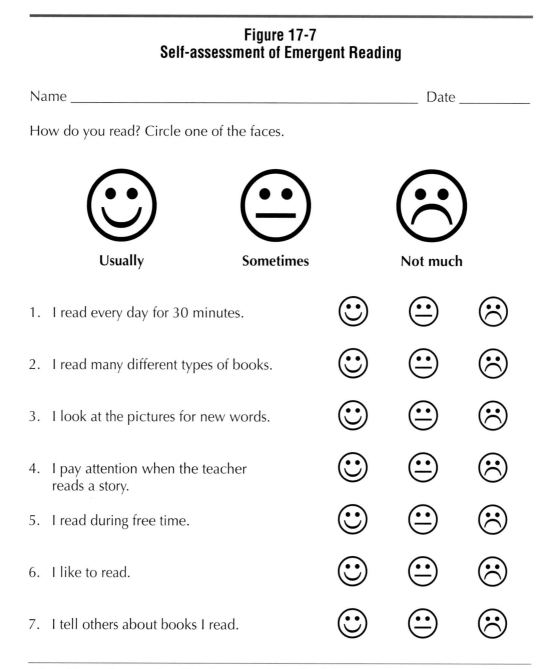

1. I read every day for 30 minutes.

2. I read many different types of books.

3. I look at the pictures for new words.

4. I pay attention when the teacher
   reads a story.

5. I read during free time.

6. I like to read.

7. I tell others about books I read.

Adapted from a form developed by elementary ESL teacher J. Eury (1994), Fairfax County Public Schools, Virginia

## Figure 17-8
## Self-assessment of Reading Strategies

Name _____ Date _____

Check (✓) the box that indicates how you read.

| Reading Strategies | Often | Sometimes | Almost Never |
|---|---|---|---|
| 1.  I think about what I already know on the topic. | | | |
| 2.  I make predictions and read to find out if I was right. | | | |
| 3.  I reread the sentences before and after a word I do not know. | | | |
| 4.  I ask another student for help. | | | |
| 5.  I look for the main idea. | | | |
| 6.  I take notes. | | | |
| 7.  I discuss what I read with others. | | | |
| 8.  I stop and summarize. | | | |
| 9.  I choose books from the library on my own. | | | |
| 10.  I make outlines of what I read. | | | |

Adapted from Applebee, Langer, and Jullis (1988) and Rhodes (1993)

**Figure 17-9**
**Self-assessment of Reading Activities**

Name _____ Date _____

Read each statement. Put a check (✔) in the box that is most true for you.

| Statement | Most of the Time | Sometimes | Not Very Often |
|---|---|---|---|
| 1.  I like to read. | | | |
| 2.  I read at home. | | | |
| 3.  I read different kinds of books. | | | |
| 4.  I read easy books. | | | |
| 5.  I read difficult books. | | | |
| 6.  I read books that are just right. | | | |
| 7.  I talk with my friends about books I have read. | | | |
| 8.  I write about books I have read (literature response log). | | | |

Adapted from a self-assessment developed by ESL teacher K. Harrison (1994) and based on Sharp (1989) and Fairfax County Public Schools, Virginia (1989).

**Figure 17-10**
**ESL Reading Rubric**

Pre-Reader
- Listens to read-alouds
- Repeats words and phrases
- Uses pictures to comprehend text
- May recognize some sound/symbol relationships

Emerging Reader
- Participates in choral reading
- Begins to retell familiar, predictable text
- Uses visuals to facilitate meaning
- Uses phonics and word structure to decode

Developing Reader
- Begins to make predictions
- Retells beginning, middle, and end of story
- Recognizes plot, characters, and events
- Begins to rely more on print than illustrations
- May need assistance in choosing appropriate texts

Expanding Reader
- Begins to read independently
- Responds to literature
- Begins to use a variety of reading strategies
- Usually chooses appropriate texts

Proficient Reader
- Reads independently
- Relates reading to personal experience
- Uses a wide variety of reading strategies
- Recognizes literary elements and genres
- Usually chooses appropriate texts

Independent Reader
- Reads for enjoyment
- Reads and completes a wide variety of texts
- Responds personally and critically to texts
- Matches a wide variety of reading strategies to purpose
- Chooses appropriate or challenging texts

Adapted from a draft compiled by the ESL Portfolio Teachers Group, Fairfac County Public Schools, Virginia (1995).

## Figure 17-11
## Reading Logs: Books I Have Read

My Name _____   Grade _____   Date _____

| Title | Author | Date I Began Reading: | Date I Finished Reading: | How I Feel About It: |
|-------|--------|-----------------------|--------------------------|----------------------|
| Gorilla | | 4/16/95 | 4/18/95 | this book is abat a litto gile that wats to se a rel garela then her Fader bot her a toy garila That he gu and gu and gu an to a ril gorila o wel I lob the store |
| Matthews Dream | Leo Leone | 6/8/95 | 6/9/95 | I likd the part wen Matthews was in hes drean I lik ol of the ameizen pekchers and Matthews paiten in to. thes book is abat a moos tha waders what he wat to be and he does no want he wats to be. a paiter |

Adapted from a reading log developed by elementary ESL teacher J. Eury (1994) and a sample from first/second grade ESL teacher L. Morse (1995), Fairfax County Public Schools, Virginia.

**Figure 17-12**
**Some Guidelines Used for Recording Running Records**

1. Check each word that is read correctly.  In the example below there are five checks because all words were read correctly.

   Joe went to the store.    ✓ ✓ ✓ ✓ ✓

2. When a student gives an incorrect response, place the original text under it.

   Student:    sale

   Text:       store

3. If a student tries to read a word several times, record all the attempts.

   Student:    stare │ st- │ story

   Text:       store

4. If a student makes an error and then successfully corrects it, write **SC**.

   Student:    stare │ st- │ story │ ("store") SC

   Text:       store

5. When the student gives no response to a word, use a dash to record it.  If a student inserts a word, the word is recorded over a dash. If a student can't proceed unless you give a word use a **T** to record that you **told** the word to the student.

   a. doesn't give response:    Student:   –
   b. inserts a word:           Student:   star
   c. student told word:        Student:   T

Source: Based on the Early Detection of Reading Difficulties, 1979, by M. Clay, New Zealand: Heinemann.

## Points to Remember

❑ Reading is an interactive process consisting of various subskills: automatic recognition skills, vocabulary and structural knowledge, formal discourse structure, and content/world knowledge, synthesis and evaluation skills, and metacognitive knowledge and skill monitoring.

❑ Research has identified some characteristics of fluent readers: they have greater automatic skills in word recognition and knowledge of text structures that allow them to read at a rapid rate, freeing them to focus on conceptual ideas at the deeper level. On the contrary, less fluent readers do not have a sound foundation of automatic skills and tend to focus on word level, which limit their ability to use their content or previous knowledge to facilitate comprehension.

❑ ESL students may have different expectations of text structures in their primary language that would influence what they do in reading and what they understand. As such, these students could benefit from instruction that highlights and enhances their awareness of text features such as cohesive ties and text organization. Awareness of text structures can help readers to develop a purpose for reading and match their strategies to their purpose. Consequently, readers become actively involved in their reading.

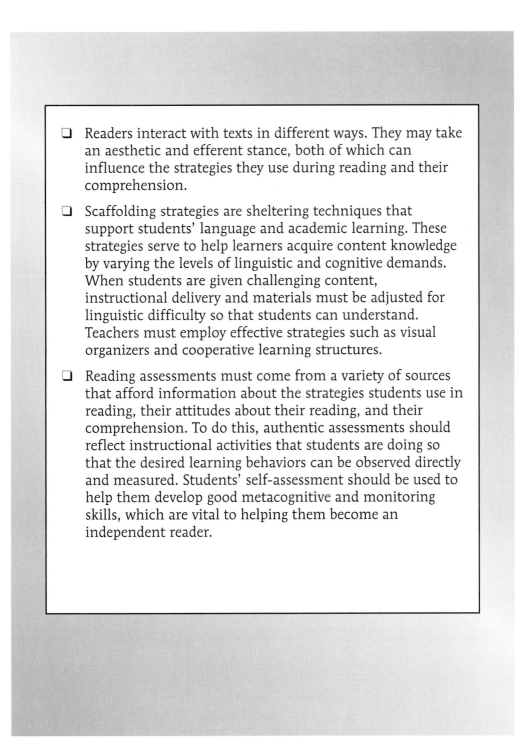

❑ Readers interact with texts in different ways. They may take an aesthetic and efferent stance, both of which can influence the strategies they use during reading and their comprehension.

❑ Scaffolding strategies are sheltering techniques that support students' language and academic learning. These strategies serve to help learners acquire content knowledge by varying the levels of linguistic and cognitive demands. When students are given challenging content, instructional delivery and materials must be adjusted for linguistic difficulty so that students can understand. Teachers must employ effective strategies such as visual organizers and cooperative learning structures.

❑ Reading assessments must come from a variety of sources that afford information about the strategies students use in reading, their attitudes about their reading, and their comprehension. To do this, authentic assessments should reflect instructional activities that students are doing so that the desired learning behaviors can be observed directly and measured. Students' self-assessment should be used to help them develop good metacognitive and monitoring skills, which are vital to helping them become an independent reader.

# Chapter 18

## *Second Language Writing Development and Instruction*

## KEY ISSUES

❑ First and second language writing research and practices

❑ Difficulties in second language writing

❑ Characteristics of beginning and intermediate writers

❑ Strategies to promote early literacy development and academic writing

❑ Recommendations for developing appropriate writing tasks

❑ Alternative assessments of writing

Mr. Tyler's mainstream, third-grade classroom has ESL learners who are beginning, intermediate, and fully proficient writers of English. The class has been studying living things and everything connected with living things, such as cells, how cells grow, and what living things need. Near the end of the unit, the students brainstorm all the facts they have learned and work together to publish a class book.

First, Mr. Tyler records the information shared by the students onto large sheets of paper. This list becomes the "draft copy" of their writing project. When all ideas are written down, the students cut their sheets into separate sentence strips. Mr. Tyler instructs the students to sequence the sentences by putting them in the order that they believe best describes their thoughts about living things. Then, the students paste, tape, and rewrite each sentence onto another sheet of paper. These sheets become their first writing draft.

Mr. Tyler then carefully divides the students into groups based on his knowledge of the students' strengths. For example, specific groups are responsible for editing different aspects of the writing such as checking for spelling errors; correct use of prepositions, and transitional phrases to make ideas between sentences and paragraphs flow; verb tenses; and pronouns. In this way (Mr. Tyler believes), students of any level can become "experts" in something and make meaningful contributions to their own learning. Each group is then assigned a page of its final paper to illustrate. Once all the pages are illustrated, the students brainstorm some possible titles for their book and then vote on the title. Mr. Tyler asks the students if they would like to include anything else in the book. Some students ask how they should write the authors' names on the cover of the book because all students in the class are authors. Mr. Tyler suggests that they could create a separate page called the "Authors Page" in which all students could sign their names. He also asks the students to include a page for "readers' comments" so that anyone who reads the book can write comments on the page. They then laminate their book and bind it using plastic rings.

When the book is ready, Mr. Tyler assigns students to take it home on different nights so that they can read it together with their parents. A note attached to the book asks parents for their encouraging feedback and compliments about the book.

Now that the students have published their class book, they are working on creating their own individual books. Students allow other classmates to take their book home to share and read with their parents and, thus, get positive feedback from their fellow classmates and their parents.

In what way do the writing activities in Mr. Tyler's classroom help students to develop writing skills?

What do you consider to be important components of writing instruction for all learners?

# Second Language Writing Research

The following sections will describe various perspectives of first and second language writing research, beginning with earlier paradigms to more current research trends. These sections will discuss the paradigm shifts in writing research and how they affect classroom writing.

## Traditional Perspective of Writing

Research on second language writing has been influenced and shaped by research in first language writing. Traditionally, L1 composition teachers emphasized the written product in terms of grammatical accuracy and stylistic quality. Similarly, ESL writing classrooms also emphasized grammatical correctness. Influenced by the behaviorist work of psychologist B. F. Skinner, teachers believed that the best way for students to learn a language was to teach them a series of incremental steps and give positive reinforcements in the form of a reward or praise. To ensure students' success in language learning, they must first practice simple structures and gradually move to learning complex structures. Teachers must also correct student errors to develop fluency in the language. Focus on grammar and controlled writing continued to dominate most ESL writing classes until the 1970s.

## Process—Writing Movement

The traditional view of writing was challenged when researchers such as Emig (1977) and Elbow (1973) began to look at what writers do when they write. In their seminal work, they found that writers not only focus on grammar, but they actively engage in thinking as they write and discover ideas through free-writing and brainstorming. This research initiated the process writing movement which is a major influence in how teachers approach writing in their classrooms today. The focus of most writing instruction today moved away from the final product and correction of errors to thinking and discovering ideas by using free-writing techniques such as keeping a notebook or dialogue journals, as well as other pre-writing techniques like outlining and clustering in the initial stages of composing. The composition classroom now concentrates on helping student writers develop their authentic voice and perception of their subject. Teachers work with students in the phases of the writing process, resulting in a final product.

## Social Nature of Writing

In the 1980s, research in writing examined the social nature of writing. In this perspective, writing knowledge and behaviors are conditioned by social and historic situations in which writing processes are performed. In other words, individuals' conceptions of writing are always developed relative to their previous situations and experiences with writing, as well as previous encounters with texts and contexts of writing. For example, a writer who has just returned from a cultural exchange program abroad would describe his or her experiences differently for different writing situations: (a) in a letter to his or her family or (b) in an essay for a social studies or composition teacher. The writer has to make different rhetorical choices for the two groups because these two groups may construct meaning differently. Hence, to communicate successfully, the writer must have an awareness of the cultural, social, and rhetorical expectations of the discourse communities. *Discourse community* refers to a group of people with similar values, aims, aspirations, and expectations (Reid, 1993). Bartholomae (1985) expressed this notion eloquently in his article *"Inventing the University:* "The student [i.e., the university student] has to learn how to speak our [i.e., academic community] language, to speak as we do, to try on the peculiar ways of knowing, selecting, evaluating, reporting, concluding, and arguing that define the discourse of our community" (p. 34). While the ability to write grammatical sentences is a prerequisite to proficiency in writing, it alone cannot be a sufficient condition for generating text. Many composition teachers have encountered students who can write perfectly accurate sentences but cannot generate written text. This apparent difficulty may stem from unfamiliarity with the multiple rhetorical conventions for different discourse communities.

Teachers can help student writers develop this awareness by guiding students to write beyond their own, limited present experience and knowledge. Dialogue journals, peer journals, and personal journals are effective tools for helping students develop an awareness of audience expectations and themselves as writers. Teachers can also provide good sources of literature and essays written by a variety of writers and on a variety of topics for students to read, respond to, and recast their interpretation to increase awareness of the dialectal activity among the reader, the writer, and the text. L1 composition studies (Flower, 1979; Kirsch, 1990; Kroll, 1985; Piche and Roen,1987; Rubin, 1984, 1985) underscore that writing processes are also influenced by the circumstances in which writers write and the writers' attempt to balance their purpose as authors of their own text with the readers' purpose. These studies strongly suggest that increased audience awareness and knowledge of textual conventions are characteristics of mature or proficient writers. This "to-and fro" interplay between the reader and the text (Rosenblatt, 1988) is also echoed in L2 writing research (Mangelsdorf, Roen, & Taylor, 1990).

Research in contrastive rhetoric has underscored the influences of oral culture and social values on how individuals from different cultures choose to write (Anderson, 1991; Connor, 1987; Kaplan, 1988;). These different cultural thought patterns reveal writers' preferences for organizing written texts in different languages, their views, and values about writing. Rhetorically, English is considered to have a linear structure exemplified by the introduction of a general idea or topic followed by supporting statements or ideas. Writers of Thai and Arabic language exhibit different organizational patterns that allow for higher degrees of digressions, repetitions, and use of narrative structures that are deemed less suitable to academic writing. In addition, writers may have different views about what is important in a subject or the appropriate way of communicating with someone who is older or an authority figure. These views will affect the way a writer writes. Because writing is a very complex skill that most students will find difficult to master without formal instruction, it is sometimes necessary to highlight these differences explicitly to second language writers by providing many good models of writing in English and opportunities to use writing extensively in learning other skill areas so that students can see the various forms, uses, and value of learning to write.

## Emergent Literacy Perspective

The concept of emergent literacy is rooted in research on reading and writing behaviors that evolve from children's earliest experiences. This research reveals that children develop literacy long before they enter school (Clay, 1982; Ferreiro & Teberosky, 1982; Harste, Woodward, and Burke, 1984; Read, 1971). This perspective is contrary to the early reading readiness perspective in several ways. The reading readiness perspective held that children would experience failure or difficulty if they were rushed into reading before they were ready. Some experts view that the maturational process is based on motor development whereas others believe that students can learn to read if they are given carefully planned, step-by-step instruction. This type of instruction tends to emphasize skill-based approaches in which students progress from a sequence of simple to more complex skills in reading for comprehension. Table 18-1 highlights the various reading readiness subskills and corresponding learning objectives for kindergarteners (Morrow, 1983, 1993 in Peregoy & Boyle, 2001).

Many experts in reading found the readiness perspective would severely limit the reading and writing levels that students will ultimately achieve if they do not receive literacy experiences until they start school.

Many researchers of first and second language writing have found similarities between L1 and L2 writers. Harste, Woodward, and Burke (1984), in their study of preschool literacy learning, revealed that children have already had some experience with language and opportunities to use language in a wide variety of settings before they start school. By observing and analyzing individual 3-, 4-, 5- and 6-year-olds, they challenged earlier readiness assumptions about children's reading and writing as a product of maturational processes by showing how children's knowledge about the reading and writing process reflects the kinds of lit-

## Table 18-1
## Reading Readiness Subskills and Sample Objectives

| Subskills | Sample Objectives |
| --- | --- |
| Auditory discrimination | Identify and differentiate familiar sounds (car, horn, dog barking, siren)<br>Identify rhyming words<br>Identify sounds of letters |
| Visual discrimination | Recognize colors<br>Recognize shapes<br>Identify letters by name |
| Visual motor skills | Cut on a straight line with scissors<br>Color inside the lines of a picture<br>Hop on one foot |
| Large-motor skills | Skip<br>Walk on a straight line |

eracy opportunities they have encountered and experienced before coming to school. Children at very early ages have shown their understanding about the concept of print and print conventions in English. These concepts of print include the following:

- Printed words represent spoken words.
- Letters are strung together to form words and sentences are made up of words. This is the alphabetic principle.
- Writing has an organized structure, moving from left-to-right or right-to-left.
- Conventions for writing are different for oral and written language. Written conventions such as periods, questions marks, exclamations marks, capital and small letters, and text features signify different functions. The context of children's written language parallels what adults do with written texts. Identifiable surface text features reflect knowledge of different genres such as notes, stories, letters, grocery or birthday lists, maps, and so on.
- There are many exceptions of sound-letter correspondences in English.

Figure 18-1 shows samples of writing produced by English-speaking children (Harste, Woodward, & Burke, 1984).

## Figure 18-1
## Writing Samples of English-Speaking Children

Michelle Morrison

where is this ? IT is in the

ITis. In heren   Where IS The

Transcription:

Where is the (flower)?
It is in the (grass).
Where is the (grass)
It is here

Michelle Morrison

O ΛE with hr       (

₤hth₤chctₒₒ   com with

KdL   And   StLL

And OΛL ₫ΛKₙ  SLLₚₙ

ΛF†        BΛB₉†
₉ΛoK LLΛL Love  PΛEⁿE
And PKLₙ₉Λ†

Transcription:

Dolly with her treasure chest. Come with cradle and stroller and doll rocker, sleeper outfit, baby seat, little love panties, and powder set.

Research in ESL writing (Hudelson, 1991, 1984,1989) has also demonstrated how young second language writers begin to experiment using written symbols and drawing as a means of supporting their written texts, just like first language writers (Clay, 1975; Harste, Woodward, & Burke, 1984). Figures 18-2 shows written samples produced by beginning writers of English. Notice that the writing has no meaning without the accompanying picture. It is clear that the writer did not yet grasp the specific relationship among print, meaning, and language. However, the writer does understand that writing should convey a message and uses letters and visual cues to represent the spoken message.

To understand the complex processes involved in understanding written language, teachers must ask this question: What must beginning writers of English know to reconstruct the alphabetic principle that they see being used around them? If we consider that speech streams are made up of individual sounds

### Figure 18-2
### Writing Samples of Beginning Writers

strung together to form words, and a combination of words forms sentences, we will know that sounds can be represented by a letter or a combination of letters. For example, when saying the word *cake,* we do not say /k/ /ey/ /k/, but rather produce a blend of sounds. Further, we do not coarticulate the final letter *e.* However, young children may find it difficult to discern individual words because what they hear is simply one continuous sound. This task is further compounded by their effort to pay attention to the meaning conveyed by spoken language. They also have difficulty in detecting sounds because the skill requires learners to reflect on language on an abstract level. Despite this apparent difficulty, young children display a remarkable ability in understanding the concept of rhyming words like *bat, cat, sat, pat.* This demonstrates that children understand the concept of speech sounds by replacing the initial consonant sound to create a new word. This concept of speech sounds, or phonemic awareness, has been shown to be an important skill in early reading development and spelling and is a strong predictor of success in reading (Adams, 1990).

Research on emergent literacy in English as a nonnative language has demonstrated that English language learners follow a pattern similar to that exhibited by native speakers of English (Heald-Taylor, 1991; Hudelson, 1984, 1986). However, second language learners may come from different L1 backgrounds and vary considerably in their English proficiency and literacy experiences. Because of these reasons, second language writers may benefit from instruction that emphasizes skill building at the word and sentence levels as well as comprehension by engaging in meaningful activities such as reading and talking about predictable stories, poems, public signs, advertisement clips, and songs. These activities will help them explore the purpose and nature of reading, use writing as a means to express what they have learned, and use appropriate strategies to meet their purpose for writing.

The early reading and writing behaviors of children reflect not only cognitive processes but also their culture. Figure 16.3 shows written artifacts produced by children of various cultures (Harste, Woodward & Burke, 1984, p.82).

## Development of Alphabetic Writing

Several studies revealed an understanding of how children attempt to connect symbols and sounds in creating their own texts (Peregoy & Boyle, 1990; Sulzby, 1985). Using students' journal entries, Peregoy and Boyle identified similar categories between Mexican American children's writing strategies in Spanish and those of English-speaking kindergarteners' studied in Sulzby's research. Figure 18-4 presents seven developmental scripting strategies from Peregoy and Boyle's (1990) emergent writing research.

## Figure 18-3
## Written Artifacts by Children of Various Cultures

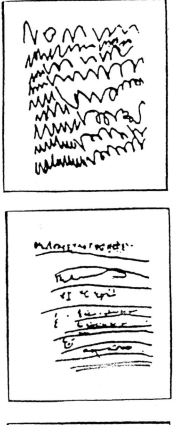

Dawn, a 4-year-old from the United States, writes in unconventional script using a series of wavy lines. Each line is written from left-to-right. Dawn creates a page of such lines starting at the top of her paper and finishing at the bottom.

Najeeba, a 4-year-old from Saudi Arabia, writes in unconventional script using a series of very intricate, curlicue formations with lots of "dots" over the script. When she completes her story, she says, "Here, but you can't read it, cause I wrote it in Arabic and in Arabic we use a lot more dots than you do in English."

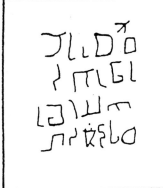

Ofer, a 4-year-old from Israel, prints from right-to-left, then left-to-right, using a series of rectangular and triangular shapes to create his story. His grandmother says his writing, "…looks like Hebrew, but it's not." She is concerned because Ofer sometimes writes "backwards." This sounds like the concerns of many parents and teachers in the United States, with the difference being that left-to-right is "backwards" in Hebrew, and right-to-left is "backwards" in English.

## Figure 18-4
## A Continuum of Developmental Scripting Strategies

| Writing Type | Definition | Example |
|---|---|---|
| Scribble writing | wavy lines or forms that don't look like letters, but look a little like writing | |
| Pseudo letters | forms that look like letters, but aren't | |
| Letters | recognizable letters from the alphabet: often seen in long rows | edmch |
| Pseudo words | letter or pseudo letters that are spaced so they appear to be words | eracmh a ora |
| Copied words | words that have been copied from displays in the classroom | JOSE Verde |
| Self-generated words | words students created that are close enough to conventional spelling to be recognized | mesa sol |
| Self-generated sentences | conventional or nearly conventional sentences that communicate ideas | lo tengo 6 años |

Peregoy & Boyle, 1990, p. 12.

The categories shown in Figure 18-4 represent developmental sequences from the least to the most advanced. They are not discrete developmental sequences but rather are distributed along a continuum. In other words, some children in these studies used several scripting strategies in a single written text. Initially, young children use drawing to help develop their ideas for writing; they use wavy lines and forms that look like writing to represent ideas and write on topics that are familiar to them. As children begin to use print in the classroom, they develop early signs of letter formation that eventually become recognizable letters and words strung together to form sentences. In experimenting with written language, children gradually reconstruct the spelling system to convey their meaning. Accuracy in conventional spelling does not develop until much exposure and opportunities to use written language in formal instruction.

Children's writing samples reveal their spelling/scripting strategies. Figure 18-5 illustrates some interesting spelling strategies used by Linh, who was born in Vietnam and did not attend kindergarten when she first arrived in Canada. When she wrote the first sample, she was a first grader and was able to speak only a few words and simple phrases in English.

In Figure 18-5a, we see evidence of Linh's use of scribbling to symbolically represent the stories she wrote. Upon close examination, it appears that her scribbles have a strong resemblance to Chinese characters. A month later (in Figure 18-5b), she began using horizontal scribble that moved from left to right, indicating her awareness of the direction of English print. After 2 months (in Figure 18-5c), Linh used both conventional alphabet letters and scribble to symbolically represent her story about Halloween. In Figure 18-5d, she used scribble to rep-

### Figure 18-5
### Linh's Writing Samples

Linh: Sept. 12, 1983. Age 5.9

(a)

I walking with my friend
to play with her.
I play the teacher.
It fun to play.
and my friend, I'm
the teacher. my friend
is a kid.

Linh  Oct. 6, 1983. Age 5.10

(b)

**Figure 18-5** *(continued)*
**Linh's Writing Samples**

Obc de fghUKLMno p q r
$tUV WX YZ–ABC DE

My friend went out
trick or treating. She give
me candy. Her name is
Binh. I give her a candy.
Then I go home and give my
sister one candy or two. My
mom came home and said
I can't go out.

Linh Nov.1,1983. Age:5.11

(c)

rain~day

I went outside with my
cousin. My cousin's name
Kien. My and my friend
is coming and we go inside
and we had hot water.

Linh Nov. 15, 1983. Age: 5.11

(d)

my mom m
a c r e 2
a c my mom
I am m f
m c

My mom make me a cookie.

Linh: Dec. 1983. Age: 6.0

(e)

**Figure 18-5** *(continued)*
**Linh's Writing Samples**

I wecnd to The frnn
hnn and my fnn gnnn
Me a big pnnn and \Snn
to my fnn fnnn fnn
a Pnnn and I wechd
hnn and I eat snnn I hn
fnn gnn to my mnn

I went to the friends
house and my friend gave
me a big present. And I
said thank you
to my friend for
a present. and I went
home and I eat supper. I had
fun. Showed to my mom.
    Linh: Jan. 23, 1984. Age: 6.2

(f)

I am a rain drop.
and I'm droping
down. And I'm.
geting cold.
        The End.
    Linh    May 8, 1984    Age: 6.8

(g)

resent her text except for the word *rain-day*, which she copied from a group chart. By December, she was well aware of the sound-symbol relationships as revealed by her use of initial consonant spellings in words like *made* and *cookie*, as shown in Figure 18-5e. Although her subsequent texts contained decipherable words, complete thoughts about a single topic, and some correct spellings, she still relied on scribble as placeholders for parts of words she cannot spell. Gradually, she could spell words by sounding out the word (*wechd* as shown in Figure 18-5f and *droping, geting* as shown in Figure 18-5g) and use grammar and punctuation appropriately. These samples clearly demonstrate the nonlinear sequence of an emergent writer's scripting strategies. These texts also reveal an emerging writer's understanding that writing has meaning and purpose. It is also apparent that as Linh learned how to spell and included familiar sight vocabulary, she was gradually learning other aspects of literacy development like punctuation and writing sentences that convey complete, topically related thoughts. As Linh became more confident in her writing, her texts became longer and reflected her ability to integrate all conventions of writing: the symbolic representation, spelling, and composition.

## How Do Home Environments Promote Early Literacy?

Children in many literate societies develop literacy skills well before they enter school. This evidence strongly suggests that children are exposed to language and literacy functions they see and use around them through environmental print in the form of magazines, billboards, food labels, road signs, television ads, and different uses of literacy at home. Literate children also come from homes where printed texts are readily available. One prevailing misconception commonly held by teachers to explain differential school achievement of language minority students and those from low-income families is to attribute it to their deficient home environments, undeveloped language and values, and low self-esteem. However, a body of research refutes this commonly held assumption by demonstrating that children learn different functions of literacy that are used in their homes regardless of their poverty and educational levels (Harste, Woodward, and Burke, 1984; Taylor & Dorsey-Gaines, 1988). Moreover, low self-esteem can also be a function of the educational structures, beliefs and practices encountered by the students.

One barrier to school success is attributed to how teachers' expectations of students from non-English cultures can influence their behaviors toward students and student achievement. Teachers who have high expectations for their students tend to spend more time interacting with students, give them more praise, and teach them valued and challenging curricula, all of which can increase student learning. However, teachers who unconsciously form lower expectations for students may not spend as much time interacting with students, and assign less-challenging content and work in and outside the classroom, which will reduce learning opportunities and result in a wider gap between mainstream and English language learners. While differences in cultural and social class differences may affect the speed at which students learn certain things, it is important for teachers to recognize and understand ways to use children's home language and literacy experiences as a means of facilitating their language and literacy in development in English.

Families can become more involved in their children's education and literacy development in several ways. For a start, parents can model the value of literacy to their children through literate behaviors such as reading newspapers, stories, or any available print material in their homes. Parents can also offer literacy opportunities in their everyday activities by making up a grocery list, reading and writing messages, looking for coupon ads in the newspapers, or reading public signs at the stores and on the road. These activities expose children to the value, function, and structures of written language that are instrumental to early literacy development.

Too often, we hear arguments that poor and linguistically diverse parents are apathetic about their children's education or are unable to contribute to the improvement of their children's school success. This popular view can be proven wrong if schools arrest the problem by responding in ways that are socially and academically promising for parents and their children to succeed. Schools can provide many ways in which parents can become involved in their children's literacy development. The vignette at the beginning of the chapter describes how teachers can encourage parents to read their children's publications and provide feedback to their children. Not only will children feel a sense of pride for their work and experience purposeful writing for a real audience from whom they will get feedback, they are also able to see the growth that their children are making in school. Parents who do not speak, read, or write in English can provide feedback in their home language or illustrate their reactions through drawings that can be translated. Even parents who lack high educational levels and English proficiency can appreciate the value of literacy in their everyday life and "know" when their children are making learning gains. In addition, some ESL students may come from families with a strong oral tradition of sharing family stories and experiences. These families can be an excellent source of information for their respective cultures. Parents can share personal stories and pictures with their children, be invited to share books and cultural items, or demonstrate how to create something in their culture that could culminate in a writing activity for the whole class. These kinds of writing activities are usually fun and engage learners in deeper levels of thinking processes.

## Differences between Oral and Written Language

The emergent literacy perspective has provided ample evidence that children use their oral language as a foundation for developing early literacy. Although written language is an extension of oral language, they are not exactly reflections of each other. One difference between oral and written language lies in their conventions. Some ESL students need explicit instruction in making sentences and paragraphs connect to each other; in spelling words, especially those with irregular patterns; or in introducing and organizing ideas in writing for an imagined or a real audience. Unlike writing, oral language provides more opportunities for the listener to ask questions for clarification, to use both verbal and nonverbal context cues, and to learn about the speaker to interpret the speaker's message. However, writers must learn to organize and express their thoughts clearly using precise and accurate language, without the benefit of elaboration to the prospective reader. This is often a major struggle for many ESL writers in their early development of writing in English. Some ESL students who have a strong oral language tradition in their primary language may benefit from explicit instruction in writing. These students need models of good writing behaviors and exposure to different types of texts and functions of literacy uses. Table 18-2 lists various types of classroom writing and their functions (Peregoy & Boyle, 2001, p. 83).

### Table 18-2
### Types of Classroom Writing and their Functions

| Forms of Print Used in Class | Sample Functions of Print Used in the Classroom |
| --- | --- |
| Lists | For organizing and remembering information |
| Order forms | For purchasing items for classroom activities |
| Checks | To pay for classroom book orders |
| Ledgers | To keep account of classroom responsibilities |
| Labels and captions | To explain pictures on bulletin boards or other displays |
| Personal journals | To generate ideas on a project, etc. |
| Buddy journals | To develop or promote a personal relationship |
| Record-keeping journal | To keep track of a project or experiment |
| Interactive journal | To converse in writing; to promote a personal friendship |
| Notes | To take information down so it will be remembered |
| Personal letters | To share news with a companion or friend |
| Business letters | To apply for a job; to complain about a product; to recommend a procedure |
| Narratives | To relate stories to others; to share tales about other persons or to illustrate themes or ideas |
| Scripts (e.g., reader's theater) | To entertain the class by acting out stories |
| Essay forms: | |
| Enumeration | To list information either by numbering or chronologically |
| Comparison/contrast | To show how two or more things are different or alike |
| Problem/solution | To discuss a problem and suggest solutions |
| Cause/effect | To show cause/effect relationships |
| Thesis/proof | To present an idea and persuade readers of its validity |

Teachers need to be familiar with what writing is all about: why people write, what kinds of things they write and for what purposes, and what writers of different kinds of writing need to write successfully. At the elementary levels, students should get ample opportunities to read and write different types of narrative and descriptive texts that emphasize telling, retelling, and descriptions. Students in secondary schools must, however, get more training and practice to compose texts beyond telling and retelling. Once students enter middle and secondary schools, they are expected to learn to compose with the ability to transform information (Grabe & Kaplan, 1996). This type of ability is often demanded in creative writing, and expository and argumentative texts that emphasize high levels of reasoning and thinking. These types of writing often require a number of critical thinking skills such as collecting and organizing information; analyzing and presenting evidence to support a claim or a position; synthesizing information; and evaluating evidence from different and sometimes opposing positions. Collaborative writing projects, in which students conduct research on their topic of choice within a cooperative structure, can help them develop both thinking and language proficiency. (Specific strategies such as structured controversies and case studies that emphasize higher-order thinking will be discussed later in this chapter.) Teachers must also be cognizant of the various stages of writing development to evaluate whether students are making normal progress in their writing development and plan reinforcement activities based on the students' needs. In addition, teachers must provide opportunities for learners to read good literature and opportunities to respond to them through social and intellectual exchanges with others. This process will help learners view writing and reading as a thinking activity, wherein students have to apply their knowledge of combining sentences into a coherent discourse to solve a problem for both the author and the intended audience.

## Why Is Writing Difficult For Second Language Writers?

Although there are similarities between first and second language writers, specific factors are unique to second language learners that may make writing in English quite difficult. One difficulty is that written language requires a greater degree of formality and lexical (vocabulary) range, and longer and complex sentences that are not often used in oral language. For example, new English language learners may recognize and understand expressions like *"cool it"* (to become calm), *"he lost a cool million"* (entire or full amount), or *"cool one's heels"* (to be kept waiting for a long time) easily because of their frequent use in everyday oral conversations but they may not realize that these informal forms are less acceptable in written discourse. Students' early development of writing reflects, to some extent, the oral language they have acquired, so it is not surprising to see occurrences of informal vocabulary use in their academic papers that could affect writing quality. Moreover, the same word can carry multiple meanings in different contexts and this may be confusing to new language learners. In other words, having a wide vocabulary is not always a sufficient condition to good writing; writers must have knowledge of different levels of formality and context-based meanings with respect to vocabulary use.

Similarly, knowledge of grammar is essential to good writing and teachers know that they must give some attention to grammar when responding to students' work. However, second language learners may not realize that there are levels of formal and informal grammar used by native speakers of English. For example, we often hear native English speakers utter statements such as, *"Kim and me went to the store"* and *"Who do you give the book to?"* Second language learners may pick up these forms and use them in academic writing when, in fact, the standard form is *"Kim and I went to the store"* and *"To whom do you give the book?"* In addition, there is a mismatch between form and function in learning English grammar that many new English learners will find confusing and complicated. For example, the English present progressive tense *–ing* is used to describe actions in progress, as in *"She is reading a book."* However, the same *–ing* form can be used to describe action in the future (*"You are throwing a party this Friday"*) or to describe a habitual action (*"The earth's temperature is always rising"*). In fact, future action can be expressed using any of the following forms: *"I will study tomorrow; I am going to study tomorrow; I will be studying tomorrow."* In other words, students must learn a variety of forms that express a similar function that they will hear and are expected to use in real-life communication.

In addition to structural difficulties, ESL writers must also learn the conventions of written English. They have to learn how to initiate a discussion in written language, explain, elaborate, and present opposing views and refute them, all of which require some attention to audience and purpose for writing. These highly complex skills can be an enormously daunting task for new English learners who are unfamiliar with the expectations of a new discourse community because they have to confront changes in thinking and behavior that they ordinarily are not summoned to do. Teachers can help students to develop necessary skills for successful communication by focusing students' attention on audience expectations and explaining how rhetorical conventions of academic prose fulfill the expectations of the academic audience.

Another difficulty is evident in the way culture affects communication patterns. Studies in writing across cultures reveal cultural patterns of prose structure that are quite distinct from English prose. To communicate effectively within another culture, second language learners must learn the social processes and conventions for that culture. In addition, differences in attitudes and values about what constitutes cheating and plagiarism in academic writing may vary from culture to culture. Students who come from traditional cultures that emphasize respect for authority and those with expert knowledge may find copying is the best way to preserve the integrity of the author's work, whereas this behavior is interpreted as plagiarism in U.S. classrooms. Moreover, in many Latin and Arabic cultures, cooperation rather than competition is emphasized; hence, students sometimes expect cooperation from their peers in writing assignments that they may be required to do independently. Teachers can help ESL students become linguistically and culturally proficient of the expectations of the English-speaking academic community by encouraging them to discuss linguistic and cultural reasons for their writing errors in English. In this respect, students' self-assessment of writing can become a valuable tool for raising such awareness. It is also necessary for teachers to demonstrate that these errors are not necessarily "incorrect forms," but rather a set of unique conventions that fulfill the expectations of the target audience.

## Characteristics of the Beginning Writer

Beginning writers demonstrate minimal writing skills because they lack familiarity with the language and the writing process. They generally lack a wide knowledge of vocabulary and sentence patterns and, thus, must first become acquainted with the English alphabet and simple sentence structures. They also need to acquaint themselves with English spelling and the sound-symbol relationships in written language. As such, beginning writers may write using phonetic spelling, a common strategy in which they write out the words based on how they sound them out. Although these phonetic spellings are incorrect, they can offer valuable information to teachers about what learners already know about letters and the sounds they represent. This information can then be used to design appropriate phonics lessons for students based on their need. Teachers must also bear in mind that much of the language produced by the beginning writer will closely mirror oral language. As such, the Language Experience Approach described in the chapter on reading and in the following section on shared writing is effective because they encourage students to practice writing early on by getting them to read, copy, and transcribe their own familiar texts. Writing development is further honed by inviting students to talk, brainstorm, and map their ideas and to use repeated language structures to expand their vocabulary and language use. Figure 18-6 demonstrates an example of beginning-level writing.

## Figure 18-6
### Beginning-level Sample Writing

Source: Broward County Public School K–3 Literacy Folder

Although the writer wrote a fairly short text and used relatively few words to describe his little brother, he was able to convey his feelings about his younger brother quite clearly. It is evident that the writer already knows contracted forms (*don't* and *can't*). The writer also demonstrated early attempts at combining sentences using conjunctions such as *and* and *but* that seemed to mirror how the writer would speak orally. The text also used invented spellings that reflect sounding-out strategy (*"youst"* for *used; "hier"* for *here*) and a visual strategy that indicates that the writer has seen the word but did not get the sequence correct (*"abuot"* for *about*). Although the writer did not use many invented spellings in this text, it is important to note that he wrote a considerably short text. It is also obvious that the writer may need further practice in capitalization and punctuation as well as guidance in developing ideas.

# Characteristics of the Intermediate Writer

Although intermediate writers have a more developed knowledge of simple sentences, mechanics, and conventional spellings than their beginner counterparts, they still need to master a variety of simple and complex sentence structures and develop organizational strategies for paragraphing and ordering their ideas in written composition. In higher grade levels, students may be introduced to more advanced vocabulary in their academic content which can make their spelling skills appear less conventional initially. Thus, they need constant, repeated exposure and multiple passes to difficult content and need to become familiar with the spellings of complex words. Intermediate writers may still rely heavily on using a few sentence patterns while developing their English language skills as a conservative strategy to avoid errors. Because of this, teachers must encourage student writers to view error making as an active part of learning by responding to students' writing and providing opportunities for students to focus on different aspects of composing such as accuracy, quality of ideas, and organization of ideas. While intermediate writers may write longer texts than those written by beginners, they may still make frequent and obvious errors in punctuation, grammar, and usage as they juggle other composing constraints. The essay shown in figure 18-7 demonstrates an example of intermediate second language writing.

---

**Figure 18-7**
**Intermediate-level Sample Writing**

My Mom came from Cyoba and my dad came from Racha. My Daddy is going to take me to Racha this summr. My Mom is going to take me to Cyoba when she feels safe. Racha is clod so my daddy likes cold. Cyoba is hot so my mommy likes hot. My mom shows me lots of magasens about Cyoba.

My dad tels me about racha. My Dad's Dad was ararond in the time Anastasha was alive. My mom was varey rich intil the Bad Prasadint in Cyoba tock thar money away. Now thay are powr but Daddy givs Mommy Money.

Source: Broward County Public School K–3 Literacy Folder

From this example, it is clear that the writer had quite a good vocabulary to express different ideas about his parents. The writer also wrote a longer text than that written by the beginner shown in figure 18-6. He has a good grasp of sentence structures in English and knowledge of present forms for expressing future (*"My daddy is going to take me to Racha this summr"*) and frequent and habitual action (*"Cyoba is so hot so my mommy likes hot"*) as well as past forms (*"My mom came from Cyoba…"*). The writer also attempted, quite successfully, to use subordinate clauses in complex sentences such as *"My mom is going to take me to Cyoba when she feels safe,"* *"My mom was varey rich intil the Bad prasadint in Cyoba tock thar money away,"* and *"Now thay are powr but daddy gives Mommy money."* The writer also shows the ability to develop a topic using relevant supporting details. However, he used invented spellings and tended to use a few simple structures consistently throughout the paper (for examples: clauses beginning with *so* as in "Racha is clod so my daddy likes cold" and "Cyoba is hot so my mommy likes hot") to express cause-effect relationships. The writer also used capitalization correctly most of the time except for some words. This can be reinforced through a series of reading and writing activities. This writer also needs further practice in developing different types of sentences and organizing ideas to improve his writing.

## Strategies for Assisting All Second Language Writers

### Process Writing

Process writing is a teaching approach that breaks down writing into manageable chunks or stages. It is a way of getting students to experience what most writers think and do when they write. These stages are not intended to be sequentially linear; rather, they are evolving processes that cause the writer to move back and forth between stages. These stages are broken down into five components: pre-writing/brainstorming, drafting, revising, editing, and publishing.

### *Stage 1: Pre-writing*

In the first stage, writers are expected to think and plan for what they will write. A few techniques can be used to assist students in generating ideas. They are as follows:

- **Brainstorm:** Students call out ideas, words, or phrases. The teacher accepts all ideas from students and writes them down on the board. This activity helps students to generate many ideas that they may not be able to produce alone.

- **List:** Students list every idea that they can link with the topic without using complete sentences. This will help students to focus on the important and interesting ideas they have instead of struggling to find the correct form for those ideas.
- **Freewrite:** Students write very quickly in 2 to 3 minutes, any ideas they have that are associated with the topic. They have to write continuously until the time is up. If they run out of ideas, they will write "*what shall I write next*" until the next idea comes along.
- **Visual map:** The teacher constructs a visual map, starting with a central idea in the middle circle and asks students to generate as many ideas as they can. This map can be used to help students organize or classify ideas into categories or subcategories and to help them decide which ideas are important enough to include and which should be excluded. Figure 18-8 shows an example of a visual map commonly referred to as clustering (see examples of graphic organizers in the chapter on reading). Essentially, this is the initial plan of their writing.

**Figure 18-8**
**Visual Map**

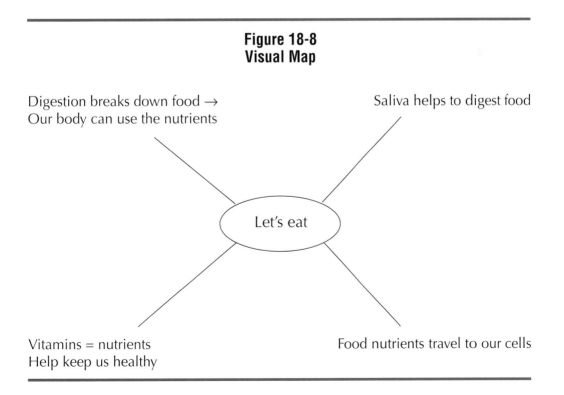

Digestion breaks down food →
Our body can use the nutrients

Saliva helps to digest food

Let's eat

Vitamins = nutrients
Help keep us healthy

Food nutrients travel to our cells

## Figure 18-9
## Question Dial

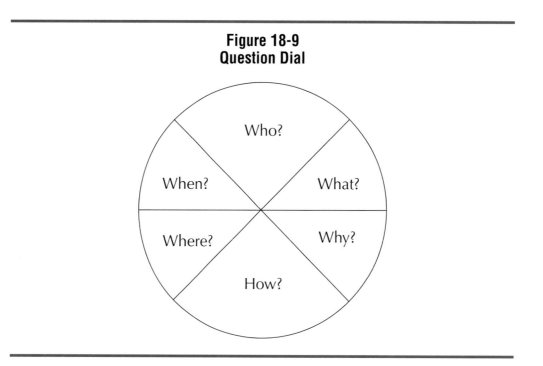

■ **Question dial:** Students generate many ideas using questions that journalists routinely ask themselves when gathering material for a story: Who? What? Where? When? Why? How? Figure 18-9 shows an example of this technique.

### Stage 2: Drafting

Based on the plan students have created, they write their first draft, paying attention to their purpose and audience as they write. The significant part of this stage is to get students to focus on selecting words, sentence structures, and style that make sense to the author and convey meaning to the reader. Teachers can provide feedback to developing writers through conferencing to help students focus on content and meaning. Some questions that can be asked during conferencing may include, but are not limited, to the following:

■ What is the essay about?
■ Why are you writing it?
■ Whom are you writing for?
■ What is your favorite part? Why?
■ What ideas did you leave out? Why?

These questions encourage students to elaborate and think about their topic at a deeper level of meaning, which makes a difference in students' thought processes and development of mature writing skills.

## Stage 3: Revising

Students exchange their texts with their classmates to get new insights from their peers about what they have written. In this stage, students are encouraged to think as they rewrite and incorporate feedback to make writing clearer and more interesting. Because some students may not be accustomed to reading their peers' writing, much less give feedback to their peers about the writing pieces, these students may need additional help on how to give constructive feedback. Figures 18-10, 18-11, and 18-12 illustrate structured worksheets that teachers can give students for peer review (Reid, 1993, p. 211–212). These questions can help students learn how to provide feedback to one another. Teachers can also model the use of these questions when discussing a shared writing piece produced by the class.

## Figure 18-10
## Worksheet: Reader-Writer Response

1. Writer: What one question would you like your reader to answer or what one problem did you need a second opinion about?

2. Reader: Answer the question. Be specific. Then complete the following statements:

   a. The best part of this paper was _____.

   b. When I finished the essay I thought/felt _____.

   c. One place I disagreed was where you said _____.

   d. One experience or idea I had that was similar to this was _____.

   e. When you said _____, I thought about _____.

   f. One suggestion I want to make to improve the paper is _____.

## Figure 18-11
## Worksheet: Group Response

Instructions: The writer provides draft copies for the readers.

1. Readers: Ask the writer: "How can we help you?"

2. Writer (who comes to class with notes that anticipate the question): Indicate specific areas in which you need help.

3. Readers: Listen and take notes, then offer verbal and written feedback and suggestions.

4. Writer: Listen and take notes. (Writer retains full authority to evaluate the advice and make the final decisions.)

## Figure 18-12
## Worksheet: Audience Analysis

1. What do you think influenced the writer to write this essay or paragraph? In other words, why did the writer choose this topic?

2. Who is the audience the writer is trying to change or influence?

3. What does the writer know about the audience? What doesn't the writer know about the audience?

4. What do you think is the writer's purpose in writing this paper?

5. What change or action does the writer think the audience will make?

6. What does the writer use to influence the readers?

7. Does the essay work? Does it answer questions that the readers will need?

## *Stage 4: Editing*

In this stage, students proofread their papers for accuracy in grammar, sentence structures, spelling, and organization. Many students find this a challenging task because error correction requires tacit knowledge of language that many beginning writers do not yet possess. Hence, these writers may not be able to edit their own texts effectively to result in improved quality of writing. At the same time, some teachers are reluctant to correct student errors in writing because such an approach prevents students from learning to analyze their texts for accuracy and becoming aware of errors as a natural process of developing their writing skills. To help learners understand errors as part of the learning process, teachers must develop a means of providing error correction feedback that would lead students to correct independently. One suggestion to facilitate student's self-correction is to provide them with a marking code that lists different symbols to represent different types of writing errors. For example, Sp for spelling, T for tense, and so forth. Table 18-3 shows sample marking code (Chitravelu, Sithamparam, and The, 1995:p.194).

Another way to facilitate students' self-correction is to utilize students as experts in some areas of language. For example, in the vignette at the beginning of this chapter, the classroom teacher, Mr. Tyler, assigned specific tasks to different individuals based on what he believed to be the students' areas of strength. This

### Table 18-3
### Sample Marking Code

| Symbol | Type of error |
|--------|---------------|
| SP | Spelling |
| T | Tense |
| P | Punctuation |
| WC | Word choice |
| WO | Word order |
| WF | Word form |
| SV | Subject-verb agreement |
| C | Capitalization |
| ? | Unclear |
| ^ | Add a word |
| X | Omit this |
| // | New paragraph needed |

strategy helps students to build their self-esteem as they are recognized to be "experts" in a specific area and build a sense of community. It also reverts the responsibility on the learners to become editors of their own texts.

### Stage 5: Publishing

Publishing students' works that are produced collaboratively or individually is important because it supports and celebrates the writing success of English language learners. Students can publish their favorite poems or stories, their own alphabet or rhyming books, or a class newspaper in which different students are assigned to write different sections such as the editorial, feature articles, advertisements, and news stories. Newspapers can also be an excellent outlet for students to better inform their parents of class announcements and other upcoming projects and provide information about students' writing. This type of newsletter can be published and sent out to parents on a monthly basis to keep parents informed about the classroom. Illustrations can also be published with a foreword written by the students. In addition to publishing stories and poems, students can write essays to gain additional practice in writing that is related to the content information they have learned. To expose students to a variety of writing purposes and tasks, they can publish a book containing letters that were used as a means for carrying out "written conversations" on a topic or issue related to a specific content information. This publication invites students to articulate, examine, compare, synthesize, and evaluate their thoughts in light of the input they receive from other peers in the expressive form of writing that is most familiar to them. Other publishing activities include case studies that discuss a dilemma about an issue they have researched. Students can then read individual or group case studies and offer two written responses to the dilemma, each from a different point of view. These responses do not necessarily have to convey opposing viewpoints. This activity will help students develop a sense of the value and function of their own writing.

## Shared Writing

Shared writing, also known as interactive writing, is often utilized in the Language Experience Approach. In shared writing, students and teachers are involved in the process of composing a text. Through discussion, teachers guide students in selecting topics and building ideas; provide a model for vocabulary, language structures, and text organization; introduce basic concepts of print; and emphasize reading and writing for meaning. The following is a sample dialogue that illustrates how shared writing works to teach phonemic awareness and mechanics:

| | |
|---|---|
| Teacher: | What are some of the things that the click beetle does? |
| Cheng: | It go for a walk in the morning. |
| Teacher: | How shall we write this in our story? |
| Ravi: | The click beetle go for a walk. |
| Teacher: | How many words are there in the sentence? |
| Ravi: | Six. |
| Teacher: | To begin our sentence, do we use a small or capital T? |
| Jack: | Capital t. |
| Teacher: | How do we spell "the"? |
| Felipe: | T-h-e. |
| Teacher: | You're right. What words did you learn from the story that have the /th/ sound? |
| Jason: | *Three.* |
| Maria: | *Then.* The beetle say *"thank you"* to the old beetle. |
| Teacher: | Yes, *then* and *thank* has the /th/ sound. Are there other words? |
| Katya: | Earthworm. |
| Teacher: | How many sounds does *earthworm* have? |
| Cheng: | Six. |
| Teacher : | What comes after the /th/ sound? |
| Maria: | Weh-weh...worm. |
| Teacher: | What is the first sound in *click*? |
| Patrice: | kl-kl. |
| Teacher: | How many letters are there for the /kl/ sound? |
| Patrice: | Two...*k* and *l* |

Another sample dialogue illustrates how shared writing can be used to highlight other aspects of composition:

Teacher:    The teacher reads the following short passage the class had initially written:

*One day a girl was walking on the road. There were a lot of people and cars on the road. She dropped her book on the road. A woman tapped her shoulder. The woman gave her the book. The girl thanked the woman.*

What can we add to make the story more interesting?

Cheng:    We can say it is a busy road in downtown Delray Beach. Can we give her a name too?

Teacher:    I like that, Cheng. What shall we call her?

Teresa:    We can call her "Jenny," like my grandmother.

Teacher:    That is a beautiful name. Okay we shall call her "Jenny." What else can we add so that the reader can see what the day was like?

Thomas:    The day was hot. And so people are wearing hats. They are walking very fast.

Teacher:    Can anyone say the first sentence in our story?

Gloria:    It was a very hot day. There were a lot of people walking on the road.

Tina:    Many people are wearing hats because it was very hot. There are many cars on the road too.

Teacher:    Great. Now what else can we add to make us understand Jenny's feelings?

Krista:    She dropped the book which was a gift from her grandmother. It is her favorite book.

Teacher:    (She writes the students' dictated sentences.) Can we combine these two sentences? How should we write it?

Leo:    She dropped her favorite book which was a gift from her grandmother.

Teacher:    Great sentence, Leo. Now, do you think Jenny knows that her book was missing?

The students in the class unanimously agreed that Jenny did not know she dropped the book until the woman tapped on her shoulder. The teacher continued to write the students' sentences on the board until they completed a new story. The students were then asked to compare any differences in the way the events were told in the two versions.

Because students' shared-writing products are written collaboratively, the final product is written in standard spelling. These products can be placed on the wall so that the class can read the pieces over and over again. Students can use these stories to help them write other stories independently. Teachers can also ask students to point to the words as they read to ensure that they are not reading solely from memory.

## Pattern Writing

Pattern writing, sometimes known as parallel writing, provides opportunities for students to experiment with new words and grammatical structures within a sentence frame that is already familiar to the student. At the simplest level, students are required to substitute words or phrases; this task can be more challenging by requiring students to use more complex vocabulary and sentence level structures. An example of a simple parallel writing task would require students to replace a noun found in a pattern structure such as "I paint my _____ (smile/hair/eyes) just like this" with new words encountered in other story readings and discussions. This is particularly helpful for beginning writers because it allows students to review previously learned structures while using newly acquired words or phrases. This type of scaffolding allows learners to link new and old information and get additional practice in using new structures and words.

## Journal Writing

Writing is essentially a thinking, social activity. Students can benefit from using various forms of journal writing to engage in "conversations" with themselves and with others. Different types of journal writing that are commonly adopted in classroom instruction include personal journals, dialogue journals, and buddy journals. In personal journals, students are encouraged to assess their own writing practices and the effectiveness of their language use and strategies for communicating meaning and understanding about themselves as writers. Students can keep a diary to record their concerns or issues related to their writing three or four times a week in class. Dialogue and buddy journals provide a platform for students to hold "written conversations" about a writing piece with teachers and fellow students who have varied interests and knowledge of a topic. Dialogue journals encourage writers to use free-writing as a way to discover their thoughts, and anticipate how their audience might react to their ideas, and match strategy use to meet the purpose of the audience and the author.

## Strategies For Assisting Intermediate Writers

Because intermediate learners need further training in developing and organizing ideas, and in mastering a variety of sentence structures and styles, several strategies are recommended: pattern writing, structured controversies, case studies, and paragraph organization.

### Pattern Writing

Pattern writing is an effective way to help intermediate writers expand their language proficiency beyond sentence levels. Different types of pattern poems known as diamante and tanka provide opportunities for students to use creative expressions and a variety of grammatical structures, and organize sentences into coherent discourse within a specific pattern. Figure 18-13 illustrates an example of a diamante, which is contributed by Rashid Moore, an instructor in the Teacher Education department at Florida Atlantic University. Figure 18-14 illustrates an example of a tanka.

A diamante is a five-line poem whose subject gradually changes into its opposite. Students can use the following pattern to write a diamante poem on topics that relate to their curriculum units:

**Line 1:** A person, animal, place, or thing

**Line 2:** Two adjectives (or a phrase) that describe line 1

**Line 3:** A total of four verbs: two describe the action in line 1; two describe the action in line 5

**Line 4:** Two adjectives (or a phrase) that describe line 5

**Line 5:** The opposite of line 1

---

**Figure 18-13**
**An Example of Diamante**

Jupiter
Gigantic   Gaseous
Crushing   Freezing   Burning   Floating
Tiny   Rocky
Mercury

---

**Figure 18-14**
**An Example of Tanka**

Drifting in the sky
Clouds come and go in patterns
I look to the sun
The darkness hovers around
Slowly rain begins to fall.

In terms of content, the diamante example in figure 18-13 compares and contrasts features of Jupiter and Mercury. In a few well-chosen words, the writer has touched upon the gravity levels on each planet (*crushing, floating*), their relative temperatures (*freezing, burning*), their surface structures (*gaseous, rocky*), and their sizes (*gigantic, tiny*).

Tanka (figure 18-14) is a traditional Japanese poem that is arranged in 31 syllables with a structure of 5,7,5,7 and 7 syllable lines. This form is considered to best naturally suit the breathing rhythms of the Japanese people. This pattern poem encourages students to explore the delicate shades of meaning conveyed by words and sentence rhythms and "experience" the feelings invoked by words. Its structure is as follows:

1st line: 5 syllables
2nd line: 7 syllables
3rd line: 5 syllables
4th line: 7 syllables
5th line: 7 syllables

## Structured Controversies

In structured controversies, students are expected to research and prepare a position in which they advocate a position, analyze and critically evaluate information, synthesize and integrate information, take the perspective of others, and use logical reasoning to reach the highest quality decision possible based on both perspectives of the controversy. While its analytical and turn-taking perspective is similar to a debate format, it is quite different in terms of how the controversy is resolved. In debates, two opposing sides maintain the position they advocated originally, whereas in structured controversy participants achieve resolutions by arriving at conclusions that take multiple perspectives into consideration. In debates, a judge determines the winner of the best argument. Conversely, in structured controversy, participants are encouraged to create an original response to the controversy by introducing perspectives and facts that have not been originally introduced. This activity deepens students' understanding of their positions and helps them discover higher-level reasoning strategies. An example of a structured controversy on environmental education and regulation pertaining to hazardous waste management could require students to advocate one of the opposing positions: "more regulations needed" or "fewer regulations needed." Other topics that are controversial include the following: Should nuclear energy be used? What caused the dinosaurs' extinction? Should the Florida panthers be a protected species (Johnson & Johnson, 1992)?

Organizing a structured controversy involves the following procedures:

1. Structure the academic controversy by selecting a topic that presents pro and con positions.

2. Assign students to groups of four. Then assign each pair of students to a pro or con position. Preferably, each pair should consist of high-proficient and lower-proficient students.

3. Provide necessary materials and references to help students gather information.

4. Have students share and master their information on both positions and then write a report in which they argue for a position that they feel is the most compelling based on the facts and perspectives they have learned.

## Case Studies

Utilizing the format of a structured controversy, students research different positions on a topic and write a case study. To simplify linguistic demands, the case study can be modified to take the form of a dialogue in which two perspectives are expressed in the everyday language familiar to the students. Teachers can assign students in heterogeneous groups, with high and low readers/writers. Students can be given supporting materials to read and study and a bibliography of further sources of information to research at the library. Teachers can assign two students to investigate the pro and con positions. Each pair must share and master all relevant information for both positions and write a case study that is then read by other groups. Each group then writes a response in the form of a resolution after having read and discussed various perspectives. Following is an example of a case study that intermediate- and secondary-level students can generate.

### "To download or not to download, that is the question…" (by Rashid Moore)

Many teenagers have been downloading songs for free from the Internet instead of paying for the music from stores for a number of years. Many rationalize this illegal activity as a crime only against wealthy record companies. Let's listen in on a conversation between two teenagers on this issue:

*Carlos:*    I just downloaded an MP3 file of "What Does It Take To Be a Fly" by my favorite rapper, Melly. You ought to hear the quality of the file!

*Lay Ping:*    How much did you pay for it?

*Carlos:*    Pay? Are you kidding? I downloaded it for free off the 'net. Why pay money when you can get it for free?

*Lay Ping:*    Don't you think that the musicians like Melly should get paid for their work?

*Carlos:*    Melly? He's a millionaire already! Didn't you see his latest music video? Don't you remember his diamond bracelets and watches?

*Lay Ping:*    Yes, I remember what he was wearing. But doesn't he deserve to wear those things with the money he has earned? After all, he wrote the music and had to pay for the costs of recording it.

*Carlos:*    His music company picked up the costs for recording his music, and the costs of promoting the music. Anyway, musicians like Melly probably only get a few pennies for every CD the record companies sell. So, I'm only taking money away from greedy record companies!

*Lay Ping:*    I know the record companies are rich, but don't they deserve the money they make, too? After all, the record companies take a big risk in signing musicians to contracts and paying for the costs of recording and promoting the musicians. Not every singer sells as well as Melly, you know, and sometimes the record companies take big losses when they back unpopular musicians….

Carlos:     Well, I'm not going to lose any sleep over a billion-dollar company losing a few dollars here and there because some of us want to download some music for free. Don't the record companies realize that we aren't all rich like they are? We can't afford to pay $20 for a CD when we only like a few songs off of it.

Lay Ping:   You say Melly is already rich from selling his music to people who do pay for his CDs. What about new musicians who have not made it big yet? What if every fan of theirs was like you and downloaded their music for free instead of paying them and their record companies for it? Why would they want to record music anymore?

Carlos:     Not everybody downloads music, you know. Some fans will still buy their CDs. Some download a few of their favorite songs just to see if they really like them before buying the CD.

Lay Ping:   What about you personally, Carlos? You play the guitar so well. What if you join a band that gets signed to a record deal? Wouldn't you want to receive all the money you deserve from your CD sales?

Carlos: That would be different.....

Carefully consider the arguments of both Carlos and Lay Ping. Construct an argument that reflects your position on the issue while taking both opinions into consideration.

## Paragraph Organization

As discussed earlier, the organization of written discourse in English is culturally determined and, thus, may not be familiar to English learners who have limited exposure to English writing. Students of English not only have to learn about how sentences are formed, but also how paragraphs and longer compositions are constructed. Outlining is one way to help students learn about the organization of English texts. Outlines can be used for two purposes: as a pre-writing tool and as a tool for revision. An outline that is created before writing helps writers to organize their thoughts. When students make an outline after they have written a text, they will be able to see clearly what they have done and what they could do to make their writing clearer. (Refer to graphic organizers in the reading chapter for different outlines of text structures.)

# Writing Assessment

## Integrated Language Assessment

In process writing, teachers have the opportunity to observe and assess integrated language skills such as reading, writing, listening, and speaking. The vignette at the beginning of this chapter illustrates how teachers can get different assessment information such as the following:

- Students' comprehension of the material they have read and learned
- Students' oral language ability, participation, and thinking skills in discussing information related to the topic
- Students' use of effective strategies for revising and editing their work.
- Students' developmental writing skills through teacher observation

The instruction described in the vignette offers teachers a way of combining assessment and instruction. By giving a variety of instructional opportunities for students to use language in different settings, teachers are able to assess all four language skills without giving students a test that takes away valuable instructional time. In addition, process writing also gives students a chance to edit and revise their papers; this is particularly helpful to the new second language writers.

## Creating Suitable Writing Tasks

Writing performance is influenced by the writing tasks and the conditions in which students write, so teachers must take special care in developing appropriate writing tasks for ESL learners. Writing tasks used for assessment purposes should have the following criteria (O'Malley & Pierce, 1994):

- Reflect the content, language functions, and genre types that students have learned and must know. This type of assessment will reinforce students' learning of knowledge and enable teachers to estimate the effectiveness of their instruction in achieving instructional goals. In other words, students' writing assessment should include writing different types of genre such as letter writing, writing a report of a class experiment or writing instructions for conducting an experiment, or writing a class newsletter on issues of concern to the students.

- Engage students in thinking and composing processes. In other words, students in the upper primary and secondary levels would not benefit from tasks such as *"Write about your favorite toy"* that call upon a narration and/or description alone. Their tasks should closely reflect the kinds of thinking and skills in writing that they are expected to learn and know at their respective grade. To improve on the earlier task prompt, students may be asked to write about how today's toys reflect the tastes and interests of today's youth. For this task, students are required to use prior knowledge and experience about toys as a basis for analyzing the topic from different points, such as their technological capabilities, and visual, interactive, and imaginative appeal to a younger audience.

- Allow writers to choose their own topic. Typically, students write better if they can choose a topic that interests them and on which they have background knowledge. When students choose their own topics, they are likely to produce more interesting compositions. Writing topics should also invite students to demonstrate knowledge that they have already learned in their subject areas.

- Provide a context that defines the writers' purpose and audience for writing. Instead of asking students to write about someone they consider a hero, the writing task could be worded in the following manner: "Many people in this class have someone whom they respect and admire for different reasons. Explain and describe the qualities you admire in a person you consider to be a hero to your fellow classmates and teacher."

## Types of Scoring

There are three different ways of scoring students' writing products: holistic, primary, and analytical.

### *Holistic Scoring*

Holistic scoring assesses the overall quality of a written product based on a set of criteria or dimensions. Figure 18-15 shows an example of a holistic scoring rubric to assess developmental writing levels of ELL students (O'Malley & Pierce, 1994). The rubric has six levels. Appropriate criteria such as idea development, fluency/structure, word choice, and mechanics are assigned to each level, reflecting the developmental nature of writing. For example, students at level 1 exhibit early literacy skills characterized by drawing, copying, and using limited phrases. Students at level 6 demonstrate the ability to use clear language and grammar and convey ideas in a coherent and organized fashion. When using holistic scoring, the student's paper may not meet all criteria in each level. Instead, it shows evidence that a paper has met overall conditions at each level.

## Figure 18-15
## Holistic Scoring Rubric for Writing Assessment with ELL Students

### Level 6
- Conveys meaning clearly and effectively
- Presents multi-paragraph organization, with clear introductions, development of ideas, and conclusion
- Show evidence of smooth transitions
- Uses varied, vivid, precise vocabulary consistently
- Writes with few grammatical/mechanical errors

### Level 5
- Conveys meaning clearly
- Presents multi-paragraph organization logically, though some parts may not be fully developed
- Shows some evidence of effective transitions
- Uses varied and vivid vocabulary appropriate for audience and purpose
- Writes with some grammatical/mechanical errors without affecting meaning

### Level 4
- Expresses ideas coherently most of the time
- Develops a logical paragraph
- Writes with a variety of sentence structures with a limited use of transitions
- Chooses vocabulary that is (often) adequate to purpose
- Writes with grammatical/mechanical errors that seldom diminish communication

### Level 3
- Attempts to express ideas coherently
- Begins to write a paragraph by organizing ideas
- Writes primarily simple sentences
- Uses high frequency vocabulary
- Writes with grammatical/mechanical errors that sometimes diminish communication

### Level 2
- Begins to convey meaning
- Writes simple sentences/phrases
- Uses limited or repetitious vocabulary
- Spells inventively
- Uses little or no mechanics, which often diminishes meaning

### Level 1
- Draws pictures to convey meaning
- Uses single words, phrases
- Copies from a model

### Primary Trait Scoring

Primary trait scoring focuses on specific traits of writing that are being emphasized in instruction at the time the writing assignment is given. These traits can be any one or a combination of some listed in the holistic scoring rubric. Teachers may find primary trait scoring helpful when they want students to focus and demonstrate their ability on specific aspects of writing that need further improvement or are emphasized in the instruction. For example, in a writing task that asks students to write how machines simplify our lives, a teacher can evaluate students' papers on selected criteria such as:

(a) if a paper shows accurate and sufficient content on machines used in daily work, and

(b) if a paper shows coherent presentation of ideas supported by evidence.

Primary trait scoring evaluates students' writing on selected criteria and ignores other traits related to composing.

### Analytical Scoring

In analytical scoring, each component or writing trait is separated and assigned different weights. For example, students can be scored from 1 to 4 on each component. This type of scoring reflects the degree of control the student demonstrates on each component. This type of feedback is useful to students because they know in which areas they are doing well and which areas need further work. A score on each component is computed to get a total score. One limitation of analytical scoring is that it is more time-consuming than holistic scoring. An example of analytical scoring is shown in Figure 18-16. Teachers can also assign different weights to various components based on what is emphasized in the instruction. For example, more weight could be assigned to composing, style, and sentence formation instead of usage and mechanics. Teachers can create an analytical scoring that fits with their program objectives.

## Self-Assessment

To begin self-assessment, students must be able to see samples of exemplary and nonexemplary work (work based on benchmarks) and understand the standards by which the work is judged. Students can be required to keep samples of their work from a certain grading period and be asked to identify the characteristics of exemplary work. If students did not identify important characteristics initially, teachers can ask probing questions that will guide students to look at other aspects of performance. By doing this, students will get a clear idea of how their work will be evaluated. Students can also apply their assessment skill by

# Figure 18-16. Analytical Scoring Rubric for Writing

| Domain Score* | Composing | Style | Sentence Formation | Usage | Mechanics |
|---|---|---|---|---|---|
| 4 | Focuses on central ideas with an organized and elaborated text | Purposefully chosen vocabulary, sentence variety, information, and voice to affect reader | Standard word order, no enjambment (run-on sentences), completeness (no sentence fragments), standard modifiers and coordinators, and effective transitions | Standard inflections (e.g., plurals, possessives, -ed, -ing with verbs, and -ly with adverbs), subject-verb agreement (*we were* vs. *we was*), standard word meaning | Effective use of capitalization, punctuation, spelling, and formatting (paragraphs noted by indenting) |
| 3 | Central idea, but not as evenly elaborated and some digressions | Vocabulary less precise and information chosen less purposefully | Mostly standard word order, some enjambment or sentence fragments | Mostly standard inflections, agreement, and word meaning | Mostly effective use of mechanics; errors do not detract from meaning |
| 2 | Not a focused idea or more than one idea, sketchy elaboration, and many digressions | Vocabulary basic and not purposefully selected; tone flat or inconsistent | Some nonstandard word order, enjambment, and word omissions (e.g., verbs) | Some errors with inflections, agreement, and word meaning | Some errors with spelling and punctuation that detract from meaning |
| 1 | No clear idea, little or no elaboration, many digressions | Not controlled, tone flat, sentences halted or choppy | Frequent nonstandard word order, enjambment, and word omissions | Shifts from one tense to another; errors in conventions (*them/those, good/well*, double negatives, etc.) | Misspells even simple words; little formatting evident |

*4 = Consistent control
 3 = Reasonable control
 2 = Inconsistent control
 1 = Little or no control

evaluating their peers' work samples; this training will eventually help students to begin identifying their strengths and weaknesses and learn to set personal improvement goals based on their weaknesses. Figures 18-17, 18-18, and 18-19 show different types of self-assessments that students can use to monitor their progress and strategy use for effective writing (O'Malley & Pierce, 1996).

## Figure 18-17
## Self-assessment Example #1

Author's Name _____ Date _____

Title of Work: _____

**Genre:**     **Fiction**     **Non-Fiction**     **Biography**     **Autobiography**

| **Purpose and Organization** | **Yes** | **No** |
|---|:---:|:---:|
| 1. I stated my purpose clearly. | ❑ | ❑ |
| 2. I organized my thoughts. | ❑ | ❑ |
| 3. My work has a beginning, middle, and end. | ❑ | ❑ |
| 4. I chose words that helped me make my point. | ❑ | ❑ |
| **Word/Sentence Use** | | |
| 5. I used some new vocabulary. | ❑ | ❑ |
| 6. I wrote complete sentences. | ❑ | ❑ |
| 7. I used correct subject-verb agreement. | ❑ | ❑ |
| 8. I used the past tense correctly. | ❑ | ❑ |
| **Mechanics/Format** | | |
| 9. I spelled words correctly. | ❑ | ❑ |
| 10. I used capitals to start sentences. | ❑ | ❑ |
| 11. I used periods and question marks correctly. | ❑ | ❑ |
| 12. I indented paragraphs. | ❑ | ❑ |
| **Editing** | | |
| 13. I read my paper aloud to a partner. | ❑ | ❑ |
| 14. I asked a partner to read my paper. | ❑ | ❑ |

**Genre: Poetry**

| | | |
|---|:---:|:---:|
| 1. I used descriptive language in the poem. | ❑ | ❑ |
| 2. I used the required format (e.g., quatrain). | ❑ | ❑ |
| 3. I illustrated the poem. | ❑ | ❑ |
| 4. I used nouns, verbs, and adjectives. | ❑ | ❑ |
| 5. I presented the poem to the class. | ❑ | ❑ |

Adapted from Claire Waller, ESL Middle School Teacher, Fairfax County Public Schools, Virginia.

## Figure 18-18
## Self-assessment Example #2

Name _____ Date _____

**Check one box for each statement.**

|  | A Lot | Some | A Little | Not at All |
|---|:---:|:---:|:---:|:---:|
| 1. I like to write stories. | ❏ | ❏ | ❏ | ❏ |
| 2. I am a good writer. | ❏ | ❏ | ❏ | ❏ |
| 3. Writing stories is easy for me. | ❏ | ❏ | ❏ | ❏ |
| 4. Writing to friends is fun. | ❏ | ❏ | ❏ | ❏ |
| 5. Writing helps me in school. | ❏ | ❏ | ❏ | ❏ |
| 6. I like to share my writing with others. | ❏ | ❏ | ❏ | ❏ |
| 7. I write at home. | ❏ | ❏ | ❏ | ❏ |

8. What kinds of things do you like to write about? _____

_____

_____

_____

9. How have you improved as a writer? What can you do well? _____

_____

_____

_____

10. What else do you want to improve in your writing? _____

_____

_____

_____

Adapted from materials developed by the Georgetown University Evaluation Assistance Center (EAC) East (1990), Washington, D.C.

## Figure 18-19
## Self-assessment Example #3

Name _____ Date _____

---

**Check one box for each statement.**

| | Yes | No |
|---|---|---|
| **Before writing:** | | |
| 1. I talked to a friend or partner about the topic. | ❏ | ❏ |
| 2. I made a list of ideas on the topic. | ❏ | ❏ |
| 3. I made an outline or semantic map. | ❏ | ❏ |
| **During writing:** | | |
| 4. I skipped words I don't know and went back to them later. | ❏ | ❏ |
| 5. I substituted a word from my own language. | ❏ | ❏ |
| 6. I used drawings or pictures in my writing. | ❏ | ❏ |
| **After writing:** | | |
| 7. I checked to see if the writing met my purpose. | ❏ | ❏ |
| 8. I reread to see if it made sense. | ❏ | ❏ |
| 9. I added information or took out information. | ❏ | ❏ |
| 10. I edited for spelling, punctuation, capitals, and grammar. | ❏ | ❏ |

**Other strategies I used:**

---

Adapted from materials developed by the Georgetown University Evaluation Assistance Center (EAC) East (1990), Washington, D.C.

# Points to Remember

- ❏ Second language writing research has largely been influenced by L1 writing research. Research in both L1 and L2 writing suggests a shift in the development of writing from an expressive activity in which the product is emphasized to a more balanced writing approach that encompasses both the product and the process.

- ❏ Writing research in L1 and L2 has identified similar findings about writing:

  A. Writing is a recursive and not a linear process; the stages of pre-writing, drafting, revising, and editing overlap and intertwine.

  B. Writing is viewed as a social activity; in other words, writers' approach to writing is influenced by their previous situations and the experiences in which writing is performed.

  C. Writing is seen as an invention and discovery process; teachers must assist learners in generating and discovering content and purpose for writing and attending to audience.

  D. Beginning second language writers exhibit characteristics similar to those of English-speaking children who are first learning to write. They generally do not have a wide knowledge of vocabulary and sentence patterns; they also use invented spellings and demonstrate developmental scripting strategies similar to those of first language writers. Their written language also resembles their oral language.

E.  Intermediate second language writers have a more developed knowledge of simple sentences and mechanics and use more conventional spellings. They may still make errors in grammar, spelling, and vocabulary when expressing difficult content. They do need further practice in using complex sentences, and organizing and developing ideas when writing in English.

F.  Process writing is an effective approach for teaching writing to all learners because it breaks down the process into small, manageable components. These components, or stages, allow developing writers to focus on specific aspects of composing, one at a time and, thus, make it easier for writers to juggle with the constraints of writing in a new language.

❏ Because text organization is culturally determined, second language writers must learn the organizational scheme of English rhetoric. Students can learn about English rhetorical organization by reading and analyzing models of English texts and outlining their texts before and after they write.

❏ Children develop literacy in first and second language writing before they enter school. Their early literacy products show their understanding about the concept of print and print conventions which are similar in both first and second language writing. Children with a strong literacy experience in their first language are more likely to become successful at reading and writing in the second language than their counterparts with limited first language literacy experience.

❑ Second language writing is difficult for second language writers because:

A. They have not grasped the formality levels of structures and vocabulary expected in academic writing

B. They find a mismatch between form and function in learning English grammar, making English writing quite difficult and confusing

C. They have to learn the conventions of English rhetoric, which may be different from those in their first language. These conventions include the structural forms as well as the social attitudes, values, and roles of writing in English and other cultures.

# Part V

# Teaching TESOL Through the Content Areas

# Chapter 19

# *Effective Strategies for Teaching Mathematics to English Speakers of Other Languages*

## KEY ISSUES

❏ State and national standards and guidelines for teaching mathematics to ESOL populations

❏ Math manipulatives and other concrete and visual representations of math concepts

❏ Strategies that specifically address ESOL needs

❏ Strategies/teaching methods for reaching more students like cooperative learning, use of math manipualtives, children's literature, a problem solving approach, technology, and active learning can be effective means

❏ Special accommodations for assessing ESOL students in mathematics

❏ Build on prior knowledge and cultural experiences to make mathematics meaningful

❏ The relationship between limited English proficiency and low mathematics ability

❏ Providing equal opportunities for all students to learn mathematics

Jung Lee is a new student in sixth grade. He and his family just moved from his native homeland of Korea. Jung is good at math and always excelled in school in Korea. Things are changing for him now because he has little grasp of the English language. Jung has become frustrated that he is not able to do many of his in-class and take-home word problems. Reading and speaking in English are difficult for Jung. Jung is quick to do any math that is a basic computational-type problem, but when any words are involved or the instructions are detailed, his confidence and ability to do math are hindered. Jung has always succeeded at math and now his frustration with learning English while doing math in English has really devastated him. Jung has started copying his classmates' work off their worksheets and homework. The students think he is cheating and complain to the teacher. Jung only wants to succeed.

As a fourth-grade teacher, "frustrated" is one word to describe how I feel about the diversity of my student population and how it relates to my successfully reaching all students in my classroom. It is a challenge each day to teach to a classroom of students where as many as 10 students' first language is not English. Nowadays, teachers not only need to know how to teach, but must speak a myriad of languages. In South Florida, kids speak many languages: Spanish, English, Creole, and Samoan to name a few. Along with the difficulties in successfully teaching all subjects to all students in my classroom are other concerns like large class size and difficulties in communicating with the parents of these children. This all definitely makes for a challenging job. What are teachers to do in this day and age with the diverse cultural backgrounds and language barrier issues that stand in our way of teaching and being able to reach all kids equally?

The opening vignettes demonstrate that the language issue is critical in many schools across the country where there are large populations of predominantly non-English-speaking people. Teachers are frustrated and concerned with not being able to reach the students whose first language is not English. One math teachers says, "They speak little or no English. I would like to learn effective strategies that will help me as a teacher to instruct these children." Math is difficult for second language learners. Not only are ESOL students learning in a new language, but they are learning mathematics which is often times very abstract. This chapter focuses on strategies that teachers can use to address the teaching of mathematics to all students, but more specifically, the ESOL students they may have in their classrooms.

Educators are striving to meet the increasingly diverse needs of students in the United States. Teachers of English to Speakers of Other Languages, Inc., and many states have responded to the challenge by developing standards of performance for both teachers and students (Florida Department of Education, 1996; TESOL, 1991). These standards promote strategies which build upon and extend students' cultural background knowledge and experiences. Effectively teaching mathematics to all students, and particularly those with limited English proficiency (LEP), means making interdisciplinary and cultural connections. The National Council of Teachers of Mathematics (2000) says that too often teachers have low expectations for native speakers of English and that expectations must be raised, "mathematics can and must be learned by all students" (p. 13). Mathematical notations may not share cultural uniformity and, for children from diverse backgrounds, these differences can present obstacles to learning (Crandall, 1987; Dale & Cuevas, 1987; Diaz-Rico & Weed, 1995; Moore, 1994). Standards for teaching mathematics developed by NCTM (1989, 2000) and best practices suggested by Zemelman, Daniels, and Hyde (1998) are congruent with strategies that relate mathematics to prior knowledge, background, and real-life situations.

The National Council of Teachers of Mathematics (NCTM) has led the country in a standards-based movement to improve mathematics instructions for all students. In 1989, NCTM published its first standards document, paving the way by setting standards and guidelines. NCTM (2000) recently published its updated version of the mathematics standards. This education association contends such standards are needed to:

- Ensure quality
- Indicate goals; and
- Promote change.

NCTM identified goals and stated that they are both a reflection of the needs of society and the needs of the students in our "Information Age." NCTM's new social goals for education are to promote:

1. Mathematically literate workers
2. Lifelong learners (who are flexible, adjustable, and problem solvers)
3. Opportunities for all
4. An informed electorate in a Democratic country

The updated *Principles and Standards for School Mathematics* (NCTM, 2000 outlined the following principles and content standards as we begin a new millennium:

## *Principles*

- Equity—High expectations for ALL students
- Curriculum—Coherent and articulated N–12
- Teaching—What students know and what they need to learn; effective pedagogy
- Learning—For understanding and prior knowledge
- Assessment—Support learning and give information to teacher and learner
- Technology—What is taught and enhances learning

## *Standards for Pre K–12 in grade-level clusters (K–2, 3–5, 6–8, and 9–12)*

*Content Standards*

- Numbers and Operations
- Algebra
- Geometry
- Measurement
- Data Analysis and Probability

*Process Standards*

- Problem Solving
- Reasoning and Proof
- Communication
- Connections
- Representations

These process standards highlight ways of acquiring and using content knowledge.

The NCTM believes that equity requires accommodating differences to help everyone learn mathematics (p. 13). Some students may need further assistance to meet high expectations. Students who are not native speakers of English may need special attention to allow them to participate fully in class discussions. Some of them may also need assessment accommodations. If understanding is assessed only in English, their mathematical proficiency may not be evaluated accurately (NCTM, 2000, p.13).

Teachers must use a varied approach to assessment in mathematics to get a better understanding of the learners' understanding. Teachers can assess mathematical understanding by using:

- Observation
- Questioning/interviews
- Performance tasks
- Portfolios
- Writings and work samples
- Written/achievement/standardized tests
- Self-assessments

Considering math test accommodations for students with limited English proficiency is important. Teachers need to consider things like the following when assessing mathematical understanding using written tests:

1. Using modified (simplified) English on tests;
2. Providing a glossary with definitions with difficult nonmathematical terms; and
3. Allocating extra testing time for ESOL students.

Providing such accommodations has shown significant increases in the performance levels of LEP students in mathematics (Abedi, 1999).

It is common for teachers to have ESOL students in their classrooms who are very advanced mathematically. Often times, students from other countries have been taught mathematics at a higher level in their homeland and excel compared to their U.S. counterparts. These students may seem advanced when doing most mathematical computations, but when confronted with word problems or complicated directions they may not understand the language. It is frustrating for these students, who obviously know mathematics well, but the new language interferes with their mathematics success and often can wound their confidence. Again, here it is important that the teacher provides special accommodations for these students. Many teachers may say or use the excuse that because their ESOL students cannot read English, they do not have the students do any problem solving. This, however, is unfair to the student who really needs experience with problem solving to learn how to read and understand English. When teaching mathematics, teachers are not only teaching about math, numbers, geometry; etc., they are also teaching communication skills like reading, writing, and speaking/discussion.

In a book entitled *Best Practice: New Standards for Teaching and Learning in America's Schools,* Zemelman, Daniels, and Hyde (1998) outline the best practices for teaching mathematics, which include:

- Use of math manipulatives (concrete math)
- Cooperative group work
- Discussion of math
- Questioning and making conjectures
- Justification of thinking
- Writing in math: thinking, feelings, and problem solving
- Problem-solving approach to instruction is the central theme to teaching mathematics
- Content integration
- Use of calculators, computers, and all technology
- Being a facilitator of learning
- Assessing learning as a part of instruction

This chapter includes a list of ESOL strategies teachers can use when teaching mathematics. It is critical that educators align their mathematics teaching approaches with NCTM's new social goals for education. Teachers of LEP students may find the ESOL strategies useful in their successes for mastering mathematics. Informed educators know that all students, whether LEP or not, must receive an equal education. Teachers must strive to prepare all students for a technologically advancing society. Educators are striving to meet the increasingly diverse needs of students in the United States. Teachers of English to Speakers of Other Language (TESOL, 1991), Inc. and many state officials are responding to the challenges by developing standards of performance for both teachers and students. These standards promote strategies (Crandall, 1987; Dale & Cuevas, 1992; FDOE, 1996; Moore, 1994) that build upon and extend students' cultural background knowledge and experiences. Teachers can make learning comprehensible for the ESOL child by incorporating the following strategies into their teaching. These strategies do not need to be limited only to the teaching of math or to the teaching of ESOL students; all students can benefit from such strategies.

Teachers are increasingly frustrated by the demands of teaching students from diverse backgrounds. Therefore, it is important for teachers to realize these strategies are really "best practice" for not only the LEP students, but for all students and for the teaching of all subjects. The Mathematics Education Leadership Training (MELT) Project at San Diego State University-Imperial Valley Campus works with bilingual teachers to provide sound math instruction for the emergent English speakers, especially the Latino population. MELT has incorporated the first four NCTM's *Process Standards* to help students reach English language proficiency. The ESOL Endorsement Program at Florida Atlantic University in South Florida provides ESOL endorsement for Elementary Education majors going through the program by weaving ESOL theory and practice into each of the methods courses that a student must take as a preservice teacher. The following list provides mathematics teaching strategies along with examples and discussion for English speakers of other languages. Both are reflected in the two ESOL programs just mentioned.

## ESOL Math Strategies

### Teach Vocabulary Using Realia and Demonstration

Teachers can use real objects such as fruit, pattern blocks, beans, Popsicle sticks, marbles, buttons, and M&Ms as manipulatives in demonstrating math concepts. This can reinforce the number sentences visually. LEP students can also learn English and mathematics vocabularies. It is important to utilize concrete objects so students can be engaged in a hands-on activities that not only make the comprehension of abstract math concepts easier, but also enjoyable.

### Relate Math Problems and Vocabulary to Prior Knowledge and Background

Teachers can do research or ask students about the ways they learn math, specially for the teaching of students from diverse backgrounds. For example, Chinese students may be familiar with the use of an abacus to do their calculations. Teachers can perhaps ask these students to show their classmates how an abacus is used and can make cultural connections that make learning more meaningful for all students. Word problems about which ESOL students have no prior knowledge only serve to frustrate the students. Often this will be a barrier to their success in mathematics.

Honoring and recognizing students' ways of learning and experiences will boost their self-esteem by making them feel that they, too, have something to contribute to the learning process, despite their limited English abilities. In addition, teachers can prompt students to talk about their experience in learning some of the math concepts in their country of origin. By capitalizing on students' prior knowledge, teachers who are empathetic to their LEP students' situations bridge the new knowledge to the old, making learning new math concepts more manageable.

## Apply the Math Problems to Daily Life Situations

Creative teachers can use a variety of methods to coach students in applying problems to daily life situations. For example, teachers can use restaurant take-out menus to teach students multiplication and division. Not only do such activities involve students with real-life situations, but they create a fun learning environment. Such an environment will also promote English language acquisition for nonnative English students. Krashen's (1985) metaphoric use of affective filter reinforces the idea that teachers can lower the "affective filter" by fostering a spirit of mutual respect, high expectations, and cooperative learning. Moskowitz (1978) suggested that classrooms that offer techniques designed to relax students, increase the enjoyment of learning, raise self-esteem, and blend self-awareness will increase LEP students' proficiency in the target language.

Topics should not be limited to worksheets for 3 weeks and then forgotten. For example, in a unit on learning how to tell time, teachers can encourage students to tell time throughout the day as they participate in their daily schedule of school activities. As students progress in this skill, the activity can develop into a determination of the amount of time passed or time before a certain event occurs. Not only does this activity directly apply to students' own lives, but it also gives them a sense of control and understanding of their day. No longer do they ask, "When is lunch?" This competence is an important quality to develop in ESOL students.

## Use Manipulatives to Make Problems Concrete Instead of Abstract

Teachers can obtain commercial manipulatives, make their own, or help the students make their own. Examples of manipulatives are paper money, buttons, blocks, cuisenaire rods, tangrams, geo-boards, pattern blocks, algebra tiles, and base-ten blocks. The use of manipulatives provides teachers with a great potential to use their creativity to do further work on the math concepts instead of merely relying on worksheets. Consequently, students learn math in an enjoyable way, making connections between the concrete and the abstract.

To understand the concept of money, teachers can have students "buy" items tagged for sale in the classroom. Students are given an opportunity to describe purchases they or an adult have made. Students select the proper combinations of coins to purchase the item. As each student participates, the class helps by showing the coins on the overhead. By handling the coins, students can correct mistakes and verify counting amounts of money.

Many studies over the years have demonstrated the benefits of using multiple modalities. ESL students, however, are disadvantaged in the one modality teachers seem to use the most, auditory. Claire and Haynes (1994) state, "Of the three learning modes—auditory, visual, and kinesthetic—ESL students will be weakest in auditory learning. It is unrealistic to expect them to listen to incomprehensible language for more than a few minutes before tuning out. But if you provide illustrations, dramatic gestures, actions, emotions, voice variety, blackboard sketches, photos, demonstrations, or hands-on materials, that same newcomer can direct his or her attention continuously" (p. 22).

## Encourage Drawings to Translate and Visualize Word Problems

The Natural Approach (Krashen, 1985; Terrell, 1981) is used extensively in ESOL. One of the four principles of this approach is that the teacher understands that the student will need to have a silent period before being expected to speak English. One of the subsequent strategies of the Natural Approach is to allow students, especially those at the beginning level of their English language developmental stage, to use drawings and symbols in solving some of the math problems. In fact as a comprehension check strategy, teachers can use students' drawings as testimony of their understanding of math concepts. This approach can alleviate frustrations for both teachers and students.

## Use Wait Time to Encourage Understanding

There are two types of wait time: the time the teacher waits after asking a question before asking a student to respond and the time the teacher waits after the student has responded. During these two times, a teacher needs to preserve the wait time; this means that neither the teacher nor any of the students will speak. Allowing sufficient wait time permits the ESOL student the opportunity to process and, perhaps, translate the question before encountering interruptions or distractions from others attempting to answer the question. The wait time after the response allows the student time to monitor the response and do some "self-repair" if he or she feels the answer was incorrect. Both wait times are important because the student must not only listen to the teacher, but to the other students as well. Ignoring sufficient wait time can result in a student losing interest because the class continues at a pace at which the student is unable to maintain. Thus, the student ceases to try.

## Encourage Students to Follow the Four-step Problem Solving Process

Students should be encouraged to use Polya's four-step method when doing problem solving in mathematics. Students should be encouraged to write their thought processes as they go about solving problems. This is in alignment with NCTM's (1989) *Standards*. As students solve math problems they should:

1. Read and understand the problem. They write the problem in simpler terms.
2. Develop a strategy for solving the problem and discuss how they arrived at this strategy.
3. Carry out their plan and show all work justifying their answer.
4. Look back and check to see that their solution appears to be reasonable.

Teaching problem-solving strategies to students will provide them multiple methods to attack problems. Examples of strategies include: working backward, drawing a picture, making a simpler problem, looking for a pattern, trial and error, acting out, and using a table, etc. These strategies can enrich and empower students mathematically as they problem solve.

## Rewrite Word Problems in Simple Terms

Minority language students, especially those who are literate in their first language, often learn many mathematical concepts in their first language. The problems they have are language problems. Mathematics vocabulary can include words of a technical nature such as *denominator, quotient,* and *coefficient,* or words defined by the content such as *rational, column,* and *table.* Teachers can help students better understand math concepts in English by demonstrating to them what these terms mean through the use of visuals and hands-on activities. For example, in teaching fractions, teachers can use paper plates for imaginary pizzas and have students divide them into eight sections. The teacher can later demonstrate a lesson by introducing terms such as *fraction, coefficient* and *denominator* using the student's manipulative. By having second language learners and mainstream students work collaboratively to write math problems, teachers perhaps will be able to see how technical terms might be used or even avoided when students express problems in their own words. Teachers can paraphrase and modify some of the more challenging questions by highlighting key terms. For example, in the problem "five times a number is two more than 10 times the number," students must recognize that "a number" and "the number" refer to the same quantity. However, in the problem "the sum of two numbers is 77; if the first number is 10 times the other, find the number," students need to know they are dealing with two numbers (Dale & Cuevas, 1992). Teachers can use pictures and symbols to illustrate the problem and they can also emphasize that different articles such as "a" and "the" can add to the semantics of a problem.

## Encourage Children to Think Aloud when Solving Word Problems and Have Students Give Oral Explanations of their Thinking, Leading to Solutions

The think-aloud protocol was a research tool originally used by psychologists. This research instrument is now popular with researchers in the language and reading fields. According to Chamot and O'Malley (1989), metacognitive knowledge includes awareness of task demands, of one's own approach to learning and experiences with similar tasks, and of appropriate strategies for the task. Encouraging children to think aloud when solving problems helps teachers to pinpoint students' difficulties in solving math problems. In addition, it can also help teachers instill in their students the metacognitive knowledge and strategies to learn math concepts. When students verbalize step by step how a math problem is solved, they often self-correct their mistakes. Similarly, this process allows peer corrections to occur.

Teachers should encourage higher-level thinking skills in math by having students express their line of reasoning orally. Questions such as, "Why did you add in this problem?" help students to analyze and evaluate procedures undertaken in math. Higher-level thinking is encouraged in many subject areas, but is often neglected in math. Understanding the reasons for certain procedures in math will build competence and deeper understanding.

## Have Students Write Original Word Problems to be Exchanged with Classmates

Having students write original word problems can be turned into competitive games among cooperative groups. Teachers can divide students into groups of three or four and have them write word problems collaboratively. For example, after the group has identified its math problems, the group members take turns in writing and adding to the word problems. The group that comes up with the most difficult word problem that is clear and well-written wins. This activity can reinforce students' writing and reading skills. The use of journal writing has also been shown to reinforce students' mathematics vocabulary and understanding. Writing allows students to elaborate on their thinking and problem-solving processes and strategies (Garrison, 1997).

## Explain Directions Clearly and Repeat Key Terms

Diaz-Rico and Weed (1995) assert that "the difficulties that language minority students have with the language of mathematics lie in four major areas: vocabulary skills, syntax, semantics, and discourse features" (p. 137). Teachers who are sensitive to these students' language difficulties explain directions clearly and repeat key terms. There are several ways that teachers can do this. Common classroom directions such as "hand in your work" or "work quietly" should be written in bold letters and/or illustrated by drawings and diagrams and posted on the classroom wall. Teachers should repeat this direction every day or have students take turns repeating this direction daily so the language learners understand what they need to do. When teaching math formulae and symbols, teachers can assign group projects that elicit students' help to illustrate math concepts.

## Realize that Not All Math Notations Are Necessarily Universal

Although math is considered by many as a universal language, students from South America and many European countries write a period instead of a comma in four-digit or larger numbers. Their decimal mark is a comma; ours is a period. For example, our number 4.547 is interpreted by these students as 4,547 or vice versa. Also, most of the world uses the metric system; therefore, math concepts based on feet, inches, miles, pounds, ounces, cups, pints, quarts, etc., have to be converted. Math concepts that are based on money and time are not universal. American coins often confuse newcomers; one reason is that a relatively large nickel outweighs a coin of twice the value and coin values are not written on the coins. Students from South America and the Caribbean display their work for division problems quite differently from the U.S. style:

Example:   25,000 divided by 5

U.S.:       5 )25,000

Haiti:      25,000 ( 5

Educators often mistakenly assume that the use of math symbols is culture-free and ideal for facilitating the transition of immigrant students into English instruction (California Department of Education 1990, p. 30–31). This is not true, and it is especially not true in the context-based math curriculum that stresses more communication and understanding (Lang, 1995).

## Create Word Bank Charts and Display Them in the Classroom to Be Viewed

Teaching vocabulary in mathematics instruction is important. Teachers can create a literate environment by filling the classroom with word-list charts. Teachers can keep word lists for each unit of study and add new words as they show up throughout a unit. Mathematics vocabulary can be represented graphically. Students can use the new vocabulary to do math journaling; for example, they can write about their reactions to mathematics or describe a math process like adding fractions with like denominators.

## Pair Up ESOL Students with Non-ESOL Students for Computer Activities

According to Krashen, language is acquired in an "amazingly simple way-when we understand messages" (Krashen, 1985, p. vii). He termed this understandable language as "comprehensible input." Peer interaction between native and nonnative speakers of English is one means of promoting "comprehensible input" or understandable language. Research by Diaz-Rico & Weed (1995) showed that in peer interaction, students use four communication strategies that contribute to the occurrence of comprehensible input: (a) embedding language within a meaningful context; (b) modifying language presented to nonnative peers; (c) using paraphrase and repetition judiciously; and (d) negotiating meaning consistently. When teachers pair ESOL and non-ESOL students to accomplish content or language tasks' goals through the use of computers, collaborative work between the pair will promote ESOL students' acquisition of the English language through the learning of content areas such as math, science, and social studies. Students can be encouraged to take group "Internet field trips" together or work on a piece of software in a cooperative fashion.

Computers are patient and never tire of correcting mistakes. They are nonjudgmental in their efforts to teach. By offering a nonthreatening environment, computers can encourage and motivate learning. It is important that teachers explain the computer program before allowing students access to the computer. Students get frustrated if they are uncertain about the procedures and are often unwilling to ask for assistance.

# Group Students Heterogeneously during Cooperative Learning

Cooperative learning has positive results in the education of minority students (Cohen & Tellez, 1994; Kagan, 1989). According to Cazden (1988), classrooms may be "culturally incongruent'" with the backgrounds of many groups if teachers emphasize individual performance, if the teacher is the controlling authority, and if there is little or no student control of participation. Cooperative learning not only restores a sense of comfort in a school setting where there are students from many cultural backgrounds, it also offers students psychological support for each other as they learn the content areas in English. This support provides all parties, teachers and students, a workable sociocultural compromise between the home culture and the culture of the school. By grouping heterogeneously, students from diverse cultures can offer and enrich the mainstream students' learning process with their cultural experience and knowledge.

Cooperative learning encourages students of different backgrounds to work together. This type of learning integrates students socially and helps them to overcome biases against each other. Of significant importance for ESL students, cooperative learning develops communication skills and makes available a range of thinking, experiences, and help from others to increase comprehension of the content and other necessary skills. It is not uncommon to see a gifted ESOL math student who is reluctant to work in a cooperative group setting. Although these students may prefer to work alone, cooperative learning is valuable for developing both social and language skills and these students should be encouraged to work cooperatively.

Kagan (1994) believes that the structural bias hypothesis can explain why ESL students fall behind in achievement compared to non-ESL students. Traditional classroom structures rely heavily on competitive tasks and rewards. He states, "Minority students, especially Hispanic students, are more cooperative in their social orientation than are majority students and cooperative students achieve better and feel better about themselves and school in less competitive classrooms" (p. 2:7). He continues, "Whatever the reasons, the dramatic gains of low achievement students in cooperative learning is our best hope to respond successfully to the challenge provided by the progressive school achievement gap and the achievement crisis in general" (p. 2:8). Diaz (1989) confirms this with research on the cognitive styles of Hispanics. He states, "Hispanic students tend to be more field dependent (sensitive) than field independent. Field sensitive students tend to prefer cooperative learning activities which emphasize human interaction along with the transmission of academic content" (p. 1). Extensive research supports cooperative learning as a valuable learning tool for ESL students.

Think-pair-share activity only takes minutes. It helps students develop their own ideas as well as build on ideas that originated from co-learners. For example, the teacher poses a problem and students think alone about it for a certain amount of time. Students form pairs to discuss and revise their ideas, then share their answers with the class. This helps ESL students filter information and draw conclusions from the material before they are asked to speak.

## Make Interdisciplinary Connections to What Students Are Learning in Math

By using themes in math lessons, teachers can draw interdisciplinary connections that will reinforce learning skills in different disciplines. For example, to teach students the difference between the metric system, which they are usually familiar with, and the U.S. customary system, teachers can utilize map skills from social studies class. Students can role-play as tourists who have just arrived in the United States. Given a map of the United States, they measure the distance between the airport and their destination using the scales provided. They then calculate the distance in miles and convert it to metric.

Themes or integrated curriculum can help ESL students by providing a link to connect knowledge in all content areas. Topics can be selected with the ESL students' backgrounds, interests, and strengths in mind. Themes motivate and involve students in the learning as they use their new language to read, write, and share ideas. Diaz (1989) states, "The ability of a teacher to relate curriculum to elements of daily life with which students are familiar is a critical skill" (p. 3).

This can be accomplished in such simple terms as using connections in the daily oral math problem. By tying math to another subject, students become more proficient in both areas. Lara-Alecio (1996), IDRA (1995), and McCloskey (1992) all advocate the use of interdisciplinary connections, especially teaching English in the content areas of mathematics, science, and computers when teaching to ESL students.

## Make Cultural Connections for ESOL Students When Teaching Mathematics

Teachers can capitalize on the diverse cultural backgrounds of their students when teaching mathematics. For instance, world-study math center can be set up in the classroom in which students from multicultural backgrounds display the origins of math concepts from their cultures (e.g. algebra [Arabic], geometry [Greek], tangram [Chinese], etc.). Math and art teachers can find common themes in which they can team-teach individual subject matter concepts in their classes. Buchanan and Helman (1993) advocate the importance of a math curriculum that is relevant to students' experiences.

## Concretize Math Concepts with Total Physical Response (TPR)

TPR is an approach to second language acquisition that is based on the model of how children learn their first language (Asher, 1982). In the TPR approach, instructors issue commands while modeling actions. Math, teachers can use TPR to illustrate problem-solving math questions. For example, in demonstrating the math concepts of equal to, more than, and less than (=, >, <), teachers can divide the class into two groups with equal numbers of students; for more than and less than, teachers can divide students into two groups with one group containing more students than the other. A more complex TPR activity would be to have students role-play a skit to demonstrate the concept of expansion: Students line up in a row as molecules in a rod; one student role-plays fire heating the rod. More students are added to the original row to signify expansion of the rod. Spectators measure the length of rod and record the difference. Many other creative activities can be made up using TPR. Students will have a lot of fun learning math using this approach because teachers involve students in math concepts instead of solely talking about math concepts.

Total physical response involves students responding physically to commands or directions with their entire body. Physical response also involves manipulating objects or pictures. Student learn by doing and become more involved in the lesson. Students are not required to respond orally—only to follow the direction given by the teacher. To make a speech-print connection, the teacher should write the series of commands on the board for students to read. The teacher models while giving the commands; student volunteers model with the teacher; then other students act out as the teacher gives the command.

To demonstrate the commutative property for addition, students are selected in boy-girl combinations. The teacher creates a ticket booth and then sets the stage for a physical response by beginning a story about buying tickets. By lining up three boys followed by two girls, the students act out the number sentence: 3 + 2 = 5. As the teacher continues the story, the girls buy the tickets first, students switching the order to show 2 + 3 = 5. Students become very excited about "acting" and are more likely to recall concepts taught in this manner.

# Example Lessons With Various Grades/Math Topics

## Number Sense Concepts and Operations

### *Identical Sets (Grades Pre-K–2)*

Items needed: Identical items such as 36 green counting bears, lima beans, or other counters; toothpicks

1. Identical matching: Make a row of eight green bears and have eight more available. Ask the child to "give a bear a friend."
2. Matching many items: Try this task again with a longer row of 18 green bears.
3. Uneven sets: Put out 10 bears and give the child six lima beans or counters. Ask the child to "give every bear a bean (counter)." Listen to the child's response when he or she notices that there are not enough beans.
4. Joined sets: Put out eight bears and show how to connect each bear with a toothpick and a bean. Ask the child to complete the task, starting from the child's left.

### *Algebraic Thinking (Grades 3–5)*

**Cuisenaire Rods.** Give each child a set of cuisenaire rods. Model the problem while the students work with their own materials.

1. What is $2 + 3$? Answer: $2 + 3 = 5$.
2. Which rods stand for 2 and 3? Answer: The red and green. So, $r + g = 5$, which is yellow. So, $r + g = y$
3. Continue to pose other problems to the students, gradually increasing in difficulty until $2y + 3 = 13$.
4. Students can create problems of their own to challenge their friends.

### *Geometry (Grades 6–8)*

**Geoboards.** Each student needs a geoboard and bands or geopaper.
　　Construct the figures on your geoboard or explain why you think it is impossible to do so.

1. a. Make a figure with just one right angle.
   b. Make a figure with two right angles.
   c. Make a figure with at least one right angle but no sides parallel to the edges of the geoboard.
   d. Make a figure with six right angles.

2. Make a figure with exactly two congruent, adjacent sides.

3. Make two figures with different shapes but the same area.

4. a.  Find all possible squares that can be made on a 25-peg geoboard.

   b.  Make a quadrilateral with no parallel sides.

   c.  Make a parallelogram with no sides parallel to the edge of the geoboard.

   d.  Make two shapes that have the same shape but are different sizes.

4. a.  Make a pentagon.

   b.  Make three other pentagons that have at least one more characteristic in common beyond having five sides.

## Measurement

### *Food Labels and the Way We Eat (Grades K–2)*

Items needed: A variety of products such as bottles of ketchup, BBQ sauce, salsa, salad dressing; jars of peanut butter, mayonnaise, mustard; a container of sour cream; soup spoons; a tablespoon for measuring; styrofoam paper plates.

Students measure out various ingredients in two ways. On one plate they put the amount of the product they think they usually eat as a serving. On another plate they carefully measure out 1 or 2 tablespoons of the ingredient. The class discusses whether the standard serving size is appropriate (i.e., "Are 2 tablespoons of peanut butter enough for your average sandwich?")

## Data Analysis and Probability

### *Die Toss (Grades 3–5)*

1. Take one die and roll it 100 times. Keep a record of the number of times each number appears.

2. Divide the number of times you threw the die into the number of times a particular number appeared. This ratio tells you the chances of this number appearing in a certain number of trials.

3. Compare your results in the die activity to the theoretical probabilities.

4. From your record, what was the probability of a number less than 3 showing? What is the theoretical probability of this event occurring?

5. What is the theoretical probability of an odd number (1, 3, 5) showing?

6. What is the theoretical probability of a prime number (2, 3, 5) showing? A multiple of 3 (3, 6) showing? A multiple of 2 (2, 4, 6) showing?

# Summary

The ESOL strategies for teaching mathematics for English speakers of other languages in this chapter are supported by several researchers (Crandall, 1987; Dale & Cuevas, 1992; FDOE, 1996; Garrison, 1997; Moore, 1994; O'Malley, J., Chamot, A., Stewner-Manzanares, G., Kupper., & Russo, R., 1985). Interestingly enough, the strategies appear to be in alignment with NCTM (1989, 2000) *Standards* for teaching mathematics as well as with Zemelman, Daniels, and Hyde (1998) *Best Practices* for teaching mathematics. Likewise, the Florida Department of Education has developed 25 performance standards for Teachers of English for Speakers of Other Languages, Inc. (TESOL, 1991). Four of these standards are more aligned to those of NCTM and reflect the ESOL strategies:

1. Select and develop appropriate ESOL content according to student levels of proficiency in listening, speaking, reading, and writing, taking into account: (a) basic interpersonal communicative skills (BICS), and (b) cognitive academic language proficiency skills (CALPS) as they apply to the ESOL curriculum.

2. Apply content-based ESOL approaches to instruction.

3. Evaluate, adapt, and employ appropriate instructional materials, media, and technology for ESOL in the content areas at elementary, middle, and high school levels. and

4. Create a positive classroom environment to accommodate the various learning styles and cultural backgrounds of students.

Many preservice and in-service public school teachers have become anxious about the teaching of content areas to students from diverse backgrounds. They should be appeased with the notion that the ESOL mathematics strategies truly are "best practice" for all students, not only English speakers of other languages. Therefore, teachers are not short-changing the education of the others in class by using ESOL strategies to meet the needs of only the LEP students. There are many teachers like the teacher in the opening vignette who feel frustrated by not knowing what to do to reach the students whose first language is not English. Teachers in today's classrooms are confronted with the challenge of meeting the needs of students with diverse needs and backgrounds. If math teachers do something about helping their students to develop their confidence and ability to do math, they can impact these students' lives in a positive way forever. Students' careers, and ultimately, many of the decisions they will make in life could rest upon how mathematics is taught to them. Teachers can make a difference in the future of their students in an ever-growing, competitive global world that depends so heavily on mathematics. The NCTM Standards and the literature on diverse learners suggest an active and constructivist, hands-on approach that encourages all students to communicate mathematically. Teachers need to employ a variety of resources and innovative teaching strategies to make learning more meaningful. Students will become more interested in mathematics and will be able to communicate because they all speak the same languages (mathematics and English).

## Resources For Teachers

### Books

National Council of Teachers of Mathematics. (2000). *Principles and Standards for School Mathematics.* Reston, VA: Author.

National Council of Teachers of Mathematics. (1997). *Multicultural and gender equity in the mathematics classroom: The gift of diversity.* Reston, VA: Author.

National Council of Teachers of Mathematics. (NCTM) (1996). *Communication in mathematics: K–12 and beyond.* Reston, VA: Author.

### Web Sites

- National Council of Teachers of Mathematics, http://www.nctm.org
- Multicultural Math Fair, http://mathforum.com/alejandre/mathfair/
- Funbrain Web site for teachers and students, http://funbrain.com
- Funschool Web site for teachers and students, http://www.funschool.com
- Get Smart Web site for Students K–12, http://www.getsmarter.org/index.cfm
- Math Archives Web site, http://archives.math.utk.edu/archives.html
- Free math software programs, http://members.aol.com/sth777/defaul.html
- Songs and poems for teaching math, http://mathsongs.tripod.com/
- Children's literature in the mathematics classroom, http://www.indiana.edu/~eric_rec/ieo/bibs/childmat.html

- The Math Classroom and the World Wide Web Internet ideas, http://www.mwsu.edu/~educ/coe/math/math.htm
- Math manipulative Web site for teachers, http://www.rerunbooks.com/manipulatives.html
- The GrammarKey Web site for ESOL/Math Teachers with instructional videos and software for students, http://www.grammarkey.com/

## Points to Remember

- ❏ Teachers are guided by and must adhere to both state and national standards.

- ❏ ESOL students can often excel mathematically; however, the language is a barrier to their success. Issues with verbal commands, word/text problems, and communicating with peers can lead to frustration necessitating accommodations.

- ❏ Many math manipulatives can be employed to make the learning of mathematics more concrete for the learner.

- ❏ Teaching strategies like cooperative learning; use of manipulatives; children's literature; writing/journaling; use of technology; and the use of a problem-solving approach are effective means of assisting ESOL students.

- ❏ Build on a child's prior knowledge and teach for understanding, allowing the child to communicate nonverbally and in writing.

- ❏ Special accommodations may be necessary for ESOL students in assessments or when learning mathematics.

- ❏ Teachers should use "wait-time" and patience when asking questions and working with ESOL students.

We have become a more global society and we need to make every effort to use "best practices" in the teaching of mathematics to reach all students.

# Chapter 20

## Teaching ESOL through Music, Drama, and Art

---

## KEY ISSUES

❏ How the arts are employed as a means to provide for different intelligences

❏ How the visual arts and drama are effective means of assessing students' comprehension of language and content

❏ Ways in which drama helps second language learners in the process of second language acquisition

❏ How the arts can be used to develop students' listening, speaking, reading, and writing

❏ Ways in which the arts can be context-embedded and cognitively undemanding activities for second language learners

❏ How context-embedded and cognitively undemanding activities lead to more cognitively demanding and context-reduced type activities

Mr. Jones is a veteran fifth grade teacher, but this is his first year working with ESOL students. One day he was in the teacher's lounge, lamenting his frustrations in working with this particular population. Ms. Cavazos, a first-year teacher, is in the lounge, also.

Mr. Jones:      I just don't understand it. I have been teaching my students English for three months and they still can't speak English.

Ms. Cavazos:      Have you tried doing some of the arts in your class?

Mr. Jones:      Like what?

Ms. Cavazos:      You could do music, or art, or drama…

Mr. Jones:      Do you mean this will help with their language development?

Ms. Cavazos:      Yes, and you can also assess how much English they do understand.

Mr. Jones:      Say, that's a good idea. Where did you learn that?.

Ms. Cavazos:      From my TESOL courses. The book we use for the course has a lot of great ideas.

Mr. Jones:      Maybe I can borrow your book.

Ms. Cavazos:      Sure, whenever I'm not using it myself.

This vignette represents what many teachers veteran or otherwise feel and often articulate. Most teachers want to do a good job with students, but many are confused about what to do with the ever-increasing number of second language students. While we have always had linguistic diversity in the past, we have never had the sheer numbers and the high percentage of ESOL students that we now have. Many students in the past did attend bilingual classes (up until World War I this was more prevalent than is known) and many students also dropped out and got jobs. Today's society, however, does not have as many low-skilled jobs that can be obtained without an education. Therefore, the recent research and the demands of educating an increasingly diverse population require us to change our approach to education.

With the increasing number of second language students entering our school systems it is evident that teaching students solely by traditional methods is not effective. Many ESOL teachers intuitively have tried different methods in the classroom and have discovered what works and what doesn't. These same teachers have attempted to integrate the arts into the classroom in order to facilitate students' learning of English.

In discussing ways to deepen and extend students' learning, Christison (1996) advocates using the arts. Christison stated that many of the arts cover most of the intelligences discussed by Gardner (1983). For example, the interpersonal intelligence is addressed when students collaborate on writing their own plays and acting out others' plays. The kinesthetic intelligence is addressed by role-playing; the spatial/visual by art; and the musical by singing, playing music, and listening to music.

Routman (1991) advocates using dramatic play as a way of observing the process of learning and using visual arts as a way of observing the product of learning. More and more, educators are realizing the importance of direct observation to assess, and then teach, to meet students' needs and strengths.

As Goodman, Goodman, and Flores (1979) argue, second language learners may be able to comprehend English but may not be able to produce the type of language necessary to demonstrate comprehension. Drama and the visual arts can be effective ways of assessing students' comprehension of language and content.

Nolan and Patterson (2000) discovered that using drama helped ESOL students in a variety of ways. These include: (a) students are able to address their fear of speaking English, (b) students can collaborate in meaningful ways, (c) students develop communicative awareness, (d) learning is contextualized, (e) pronunciation may be improved during drama, and (f) students acquire new vocabulary.

The arts can also be used to strengthen the ties among the four language bands: listening, speaking, reading, and writing. Hancock, Turbill, and Cambourne (1994) state that the arts can be used in conjunction with literacy to clarify ideas and make connections among reading and writing and role play, music, and art. The use of literacy-type activities can be incorporated immediately, regardless of proficiency levels.

Ovando and Collier (1985) state that music and art are parts of many oral activities and should be a regular part of the second language curriculum. Art also has the advantage of being concrete and promoting language acquisition. In addition, Ovando and Collier further state that art evokes a wide range of cognitive and emotional responses and encourages communication.

Part of this communication is using art as the basis for story-telling. This story-telling can be based on students' own art or others' art. If students are responding to art by writing, they should be allowed to write initial drafts in their first language, whenever possible. This allows students to get their ideas down on paper without having to think about vocabulary, spelling, grammar, and usage in the second language. Not all students will be literate in their first language, but those who are will find writing in their native language may allow for the fluency of ideas.

Once the ideas are written the student can transfer text to the second language. Been (1975) and Reyes (1992) advocate allowing students to write in the first language. Writing may be more fluent and of better quality in the first language than in the second. The successful writing in the first language may then act as a catalyst for successful writing in the second-language.

Hornberger (1989) states that reception and production develop along a continuum, and the view of reception preceding production exclusively is invalid. Hornberger argues that language development is contingent on both comprehensible input and comprehensible output by the second-language speaker. Permitting students to respond to language and concepts in nontraditional ways facilitates comprehensible output by students, while inviting comprehensible input by others.

Hudelson (1984) states that the four areas of language (listening, speaking, reading, and writing) are interrelated and foster one another. When students respond to literature with dramatic story-telling they incorporate all four language bands. Students write their stories, have others read it for revision and editing purposes, share their stories orally with others, and have others listen to their stories.

Cummins (1981) classifies art and music as context-embedded and cognitively undemanding. In other words, they provide students with many clues about language familiar to students, and do not require a great deal of second language usage. These types of activities are important for beginning second-language learners. In addition, these activities can be employed to teach literacy, which would be more cognitively demanding and more context-reduced. While it is important to use context-embedded, cognitively undemanding activities initially, one major goal for second language teachers is to ensure success in cognitively-demanding, context-reduced activities. To have students participate in only the former does not promote growth because eventually the activities will become too easy for students and they may become bored. On the other hand, to provide only the former too early ensures frustration because activities make little sense and are too difficult. While both (along with context-embedded, cognitively undemanding and context-reduced, cognitively demanding activities) are important to students' learning, the important thing is to match the type of activity to each student's strengths and needs.

## Music and Language Development

Music is a very effective way to motivate students while they are learning the second language. It is a way to respond to content or demonstrate understanding of content, as well as language. Students can listen to songs and demonstrate their understanding by drawing. They can also role-play songs that tell a story, such as "There Was an Old Lady Who Swallowed a Fly."

Teachers should provide tapes with lyrics after students have been introduced to songs. This will promote a print-to-speech match and promote students' sight vocabulary. Students can also write down lyrics to their favorite songs and teach them to other students.

Students can introduce a song by saying the lyrics aloud (with the lyrics written if the students can write them). If the student is unable to write the lyrics, the teacher may write them either before or after the student has introduced the song to the class. If the song lends itself to pantomime, the students should act it out as she or he introduces the song to the class. Ovando and Collier (1985) state that realia should be used whenever possible in introducing songs. They suggest responding to text by using murals, dioramas, mobiles, and collages. In addition, students can make costumes that pertain to the song being learned.

More advanced students can write a song in response to text read by them or by the teacher. Teachers can facilitate this is by playing certain songs after reading text aloud to students. For example, after reading Maurice Sendak's Where The Wild Things Are, the teacher can play the song "Wild Thing" by the Troggs. She can then ask the class why they think that particular song was chosen to represent the book. Less advanced students can choose songs to go with certain books instead of writing their own songs. Finally, the teacher can have students match song titles with books that have been read by the class.

Music can be used to teach vocabulary to ESOL students. For example, "The Hokey Pokey" can be used to teach body parts, along with verbs such as "put in," "pull out," "shake," and "turn around." The teacher starts by playing the song and modeling the movements for the students. The students should repeat the teacher's movements after each body part is introduced. The class could begin with a small number of body parts, such as five or so, and add more each week. This activity is effective when the class is studying the human body.

Students in the silent stage demonstrate understanding by using the body part as it is mentioned in the song. The teacher can ask students in the early production stage to name a body part that the teacher shows to them. A variation on this is to have the teacher use the wrong body part at times and have students correct her. A chart of the human body should be in sight so the students can check the correctness of the teacher's actions. After the students have learned a number of parts, they can then lead the game.

"Old McDonald" can be used to teach about farm animals. Students can be divided into groups to represent their assigned animal. Then they can draw masks of their animals and wear them during the song. Each group may want to make the animal's noise when it is their group's turn.

After the students have learned their songs, the teacher may want to assess their learning of the vocabulary words. One way to do this is by providing a list of words and having students cross out the one that does not belong. For example:

cow     pig     sheep     chicken     dog     egg

The most logical answer would be egg, because the other words in the list represent animals. However, the teacher should ask the students their reasons for choosing their answer, even if it is the correct answer. It is just as important to know the students' reasoning as it is to assess their choice. In addition, the teacher should also ask the students their reason for choosing an answer different from the typical/correct one. For example, if students picked "dog," their reason may be that they eat all the other items on the list but do not eat dogs. The teacher may want to give the criteria for choosing the word that does not belong, such as saying "It's the only thing on the list that does not run."

Students can also do word sorts. Closed word sorts should be done initially, because these are easier. The teacher can provide the categories and students place the vocabulary words under the proper category. Following is an example:

animals                              body parts


hand     chicken     pig     foot     head
sheep     dog     cat     arm     horse     finger

The student should place the words like this:

| animals | body parts |
|---------|------------|
| chicken | hand |
| pig | foot |
| sheep | head |
| dog | arm |
| cat | finger |
| horse | |

A variation of this is having students do an open word sort. The teacher provides the words and the students sort and then categorize the words. This should be done for more advanced students because it is more difficult.

Another way to classify words is by providing a list of words and having students choose the word that includes all the others. For example, the following can be done:

pig     cow     sheep     animals     dog

More advanced students can do analogies. One type of analogy is functional analogies, which are particularly helpful while studying body parts. An example follows:

hand: finger    as      foot:

Students can provide the word from memory or the teacher can provide them with a word bank. A variation of this is to have students choose the complementary analogy part. For example:

1. hand: finger      as            a. leg: foot

2. foot: toe      as            b. arm: hand

The student should choose "B" for number 1 because the finger is part of the hand, and the hand is part of the arm. The student should also choose "A" for number 2 because the toe is part of the foot, and the foot is part of the leg.

Another vocabulary activity that can be used with more advanced students is semantic feature analysis. The attributes are listed on the top of the page and the vocabulary words are listed on the side. The students can mark an "X" under the appropriate heading. Following is an example:

| | Barks | Has two legs | Has four legs | Gives milk | Lays eggs |
|---|---|---|---|---|---|
| chicken | | X | | | x |
| cow | | | X | x | |
| dog | X | | X | | |
| pig | | | X | | |

Music can be used to promote decoding skills. Hornsby, Sukarna, and Parry (1986) advocated using variation of text. The text can be from song lyrics that the students know. The teacher writes the lyrics on a chart or on sentence strips. For example, the teacher can write the lyrics to the song "Old McDonald Had a Farm," and point to the words as the students sing the song. When the students have finished singing, she can have students come up and point to particular words.

The next step is to insert incorrect lyrics such as "Old McDonald had a car." The students choose the word that is incorrect and provide the correct word. The students can also read the incorrect word. The teacher can provide a picture of a car if the students are unable to provide the word.

The teacher can also cover up a word and have the students predict what the word is. After the teacher uncovers the word, the students say the word. The students determine if the word makes sense and if it looks like the word provided. It is important for students to be able to see word patterns, particularly ESOL students, because they may not have the phonological sophistication to attack words the way their monolingual English-speaking peers may. Facilitating their awareness of word patterns through whole words is one way to develop phonemic awareness.

The teacher can scramble up words from a sentence and the students can arrange them correctly. In addition, the teacher can place sentences out of sequence and the students can place them in sequential order.

The teacher can also provide a word and the students choose a word from the lyrics that rhyme with it, or the teacher can have students choose a word that begins with a particular letter or begins with the same letter or sound as a particular word.

Lapp and Flood (1992) advocate the use of singing to teach syllabication by having students walk out the beat of a song, separating the words into syllables. They suggest beginning with two-syllable words and adding words with more syllables gradually. When students master words with four or five syllables, teachers should present them with words that do not have the same number of syllables, or else students will use only the predictability of the number of syllables instead of listening for the number of syllables.

Norton (1992) advocates the use of choral reading from songs or poems. Choral reading can be in the form of refrain arrangements, line-a-child or line-a-group arrangements, dialogue arrangements, cumulative arrangements, and unison arrangements.

In the refrain arrangement, the teacher sings the verse and the students sing the chorus. For example, the poem "To Market" can be sung in this type of arrangement:

| | |
|---|---|
| Teacher: | To market, to market, to buy a fat pig |
| Class: | Home again, home again, jiggety jig |
| Teacher: | To market, to market, to buy a fat hog |
| Class: | Home again, home again, jiggety jog |
| Teacher: | To market, to market, to buy a plum bun |
| Class: | Home again, home again, market is done |

In the line-a-child or line-a-group arrangement each child or group of children sings a line. For example:

| | |
|---|---|
| Group 1: | Hush-a-bye, baby, on the tree top |
| Group 2: | When the wind blows the cradle will rock |
| Group 3: | When the bough breaks the cradle will fall |
| Group 4: | Down will come baby, cradle and all |

In the dialogue arrangement, the teacher or a group sings a line and the students or another group sings the chorus. For example:

| | |
|---|---|
| Group 1: | Sing, sing, what should I sing? |
| Group 2: | Cat's run away with the string! |
| Group 1: | Do, do, what should I do? |
| Group 2: | The cat has bitten it in two. |

In the cumulative arrangement, a line or verse is sung by a group, the next line or verse is sung by that first group and joined by another group, until all the groups are singing together. For example,

| | |
|---|---|
| Group 1: | This little pig went to market |
| Groups 1 and 2: | This little pig stayed home |
| Groups 1, 2, and 3: | This little pig had roast beef |
| Groups 1, 2, 3, and 4: | This little pig had none |
| Groups 1, 2, 3, 4, and 5: | This little pig said "Wee, wee, all the way home." |

In the unison arrangement the entire class sings all the verses and choruses together. For example:

Whole class:     Humpty Dumpty sat on a wall,
Humpty Dumpty had a great fall;
All the King's horses and all the King's men
Couldn't put Humpty together again.

Cox (1999) recommends writing new lyrics to an old song. The teacher can model this. For example, the song "Twinkle, Twinkle Little Star" can be rewritten "Twinkle, Twinkle Little Bat" as in Lewis Carroll's "Alice In Wonderland":

Twinkle, twinkle little bat
How I wonder where you're at
Up above the world so high
Like a tea tray in the sky

Cox suggested using a song frame and changing nouns and verbs to create the new song. For example, the first, third, and fourth lines were changed from the original "Twinkle, twinkle little star." The students can decide if they want to change every verb and noun from each line or if they want to alternate. When they have finished their new song, students can share their songs and teach the lyrics to the rest of the class. Then songs are kept in the journals or in books for the entire class to read and sing during free reading or music time. The students can write songs based on the different arrangements already introduced.

## Drama and Language Development

Drama can be used to teach language and content. According to Pérez and Torres-Guzmán (1992) the purposes for drama are:

1.  To provide a real purpose for reading aloud and memorizing text. Instead of using round-robin oral reading, dramatic reading provides an authentic purpose for reading, along with an authentic audience.
2.  To allow students to interpret text and express themselves. This promotes divergent thinking; there is no one correct way to interpret text. In addition, students have an infinite number of response options. This allows for more creative ways of interacting with text than the traditional book report.
3.  To allow students to study dialogue form. Teachers may have to teach students how to read a text using dialogue form. Reading skits and plays aloud provides for authentic practice in reading dialogue form.
4.  To entertain others.

Cox (1999) advocated using drama in conjunction with Total Physical Response (TPR) with students in the silent stage. Some of the activities that can be used include:

1. Play "Simon Says" with body parts.
2. Play "Simon Says" with classroom objects.
3. Have students pantomime using an object and have the class guess what the object is.
4. Play "Simon Says" with students' body movements. Have students pretend to throw a ball, eat some food, etc.
5. Play "Simon Says" with sequences. The teacher acts out three small scenes out of order and students demonstrate the correct order. The teacher can then write out the correct order and re-act it.

Morrow (2001) advocates using puppets for stories that contain dialogue, especially stories that have a predictable pattern with few characters. Stories from trade books, basals, picture books, and folk tales can be included. Folk tales from the students' culture are a great source, and picture books are easily understood and applied to dramas with puppets. For example, after being introduced to "The Three Billy Goats Gruff," the students can make puppets and act out the various parts.

The first step teachers should take in using puppets is to find a familiar story or a story that is easy for the students to understand and memorize. The teacher can demonstrate how narrative in a book can be transformed to dialogue in play form. This can be done efficiently and effectively with large chart paper. The teacher can act out each part for the students and assign parts for students to memorize. After rehearsing, the students can act out the play for the teacher before performing in front of the class. Finally, the teacher can invite other classes and family members to see the puppet play.

May (1998) suggests using drama in conjunction with reading in order to extend students' understanding of literature. For example, students can pantomime a scene from a book and see if other students can figure out what they are doing and on what story they are basing the pantomime.

Students or the teacher can also introduce a new book by pantomiming a scene. After the class discusses what was pantomimed, the students may want to finish reading the book on their own. This can also be done with books the entire class is going to read. The student or teacher should introduce enough of the book to interest the class in the book but should not give away too much of the plot.

The teacher can have pairs of students who have read the same book do a mock interview of the author. Students can get information about the author from the book they have read, along with research conducted to learn more about the author's life. Once students have done research, they need to determine what information they need to share with the class. Based on this information they can write their questions and answers. Students can keep index cards with them during their mock interview but should be encouraged to use them only as prompts.

A closely related activity is for a student to pretend to be the author who is attempting to persuade a publisher to buy the book. This can be done in conjunction with having the student make a cover or advertisement for the book (which will be discussed in the visual art's section). The student playing the part of the author should include this when discussing his or her book.

If the teacher is teaching books by motifs, students can pretend to be characters from different books and have their characters talk to each other or write letters to each other. The students can talk to each other in front of the class and the class can guess what characters they are portraying. If students have their characters write to each other, the teacher can read these letters aloud to the class and they can again guess what characters are being portrayed.

Enright and McCloskey (1988) advocate ESOL students writing their own skits. The benefits are many and include all four of the language bands. They include:

1. Students get practice in writing. In addition, they acquire a sense of ownership because their own words are used.
2. Students get practice in editing scripts. Peer editing can be taught prior to this activity. In addition, the teacher can use this activity to determine mini-lessons that pertain to the script.
3. Students performing get practice in oral language. They also get authentic practice in pronunciation.
4. The audience gets practice in listening.

The teacher can have each student write a skit based on a book, but using different voices for each character. The student can hold a placard with the character's name whenever that voice is being used. A variation of this is for the student to record the skit onto tape. If the entire class has read the book the student used for the skit, the students can listen to the tape and determine who the characters are, based on the voices.

Two or more students can read the same book and write a skit based on it and present their skit to the class. They can base their skit on their favorite part of the book, or perhaps on the most important event in the book. If there is a disagreement, both students can each present their favorite part or the most important part. Afterwards, the students can discuss their reasons for choosing their scenes with the class.

After reading a book, students can write a play and change the text from narrative to dialogue form. The teacher can help scaffold this process by modeling the writing involved. The steps involved in helping transform text into play form include:

1. Modeling how to find dialogue in the original text by looking at quotation marks.

2. Modeling how to determine who is saying what. This includes the use of referents such as "he" and "she."

3. Modeling how to determine what text should be spoken by the narrator in the play and what text should be acted out by the actors. The narrator should discuss setting, introduction of characters as is necessary, and any changes in setting that may be confusing to the audience.

After doing the play, the students in the play can give the class copies. The group that did the play can then discuss the process that went into the play and what decisions were made concerning wording, acting, etc. The teacher may want to try this first with a capable group of students in order to help model it to the rest of the class.

Rhodes and Dudley-Marling (1988) suggest showing the inner thoughts of characters by having students "speak to the camera." This should probably be done only after students have had some experience performing plays and writing their own skits. The characters can discuss their motivations for doing certain things, their ambivalence about events in the play, something that has happened prior to the play's beginning in order to explain something more fully. They can also lay the foundation for a sequel.

A follow-up activity to skits and plays is to have a "quiz show" based on text. The teacher may want to ask questions the first time the game is played. Afterwards, the students can get into groups and write questions. The teacher can conference with the groups and help edit the questions to make them more comprehensible. In addition, the teacher can use the data from these conferences to do mini-lessons later.

## Art and Language Development

Teachers can use art in a variety of ways in the classroom. One way this can be accomplished is by having the teacher play tapes of various sounds and have students draw what they think it is. Teachers can also blindfold students and have them hold something, then draw what they think it is. The teacher can teach different vocabulary from this activity, such as rough, smooth, soft, etc.

Students can illustrate class events or a scene from a book or a movie. Other students can be asked to describe what the illustration is about. The student who did the drawing can tell the other students how closely they were able to describe the original intent of the drawing.

Students can also make diaramas and mobiles of real-life or story events. The mobiles and diaramas can be displayed around the room, and students can describe their own art. The other students then guess which piece of art is being described. If the students are not proficient enough in English to describe their product, the teacher may want to help them write their description and assist them in reading it aloud. A variation of this is to have the teacher read the description aloud, but only after the student has had input in writing the description.

The teacher can have pictures of things and ask questions, according to students' levels. For example, at the silent stage, the teacher can ask students to raise their hand if they think the picture represents something happy, sad, frightening, etc. The teacher may want to have a poster that depicts these different expressions. A variation of this is for students to choose the expression that goes with the picture or painting.

At the early production level, the teacher can ask yes/no, and either/or type questions. For example, the teacher can show the class a picture of some people in a restaurant eating and then ask the class if the people in the picture are having dinner or reading a book. The teacher can also ask a question that requires a "no" answer and have the students tell what is occurring in the picture or drawing. For example, the teacher can show a picture of students in class and then ask if the people are in a classroom, or show them a picture of people watching a movie and ask the class if the people in the picture are at school.

Ericson and Juliebo (1988) suggest using pictures to help students with syllabication and phonemic awareness. They suggest cutting a picture into the number of syllables a word has (car-rot) and guess what the word is. The teacher can write each syllable on the other side of the picture. Students can look for their partner, who has the other part of the picture, and then read the word.

The same procedure can be done with phonemes (c-a-t; m-oo-n). Students match the picture correctly and then look at the back to read the word. A variation of this is to cut a picture into the same number of letters that represent the word of the object or verb being depicted.

The teacher can use pictures or drawings to promote the Language Experience Approach. After examining a picture or a drawing, the students can dictate to the teacher what they see. The teacher writes the responses on the board or on chart paper. The teacher should write exactly what the students say initially and then make a revised, corrected form. This form can be called the "teacher's version." It is important for the students to see their utterances written first, so they can see the speech-to-print match immediately. The emphasis should first be on the fluency of ideas. The teacher may choose to later do mini-lessons based on the students' dictation, but not at the same time as the dictation.

The teacher can show the class a picture or drawing and students choose the correct sentence among the sentences written below it. Later, the teacher can show the same picture or drawing, but with an incorrect word, and then supply the correct word. For example, the picture may show students studying in the library. The sentence supplied to them might say "The students are eating in the library." The students need to choose "eat" as the incorrect word and give "study" as the word needed to have the sentence make sense.

If students are unable to do this, the teacher can ask them if the sentence makes sense and which word does not belong. If they are still unable to do this, the teacher can point out the incorrect word and ask what word should go in its place. If they are unable to supply the correct word, the teacher can write three or four options on the board. The teacher needs to ask the students if the word they chose makes sense within the context of the sentence. This needs to be done every time a word is chosen and not just when an incorrect word is picked.

The teacher can also use a picture or drawing and have students ask "how" and "w" questions. The teacher may want to scaffold the students' answers. For example, when asking a "where" question ("Where are the boy and girl in the picture?"), the teacher writes on the board "The boy and the girl are..."

The same procedure can be used to teach tenses. For example, the teacher can show the class a drawing and ask what the man is doing in the drawing. The teacher can model the present tense by supplying part of the answer by stating, "The man is..." The teacher can model the future tense by showing a drawing of a woman and asking what the woman will do next. The teacher supplies part of the answer by saying, "The woman is going to..." Finally, the teacher can model the past tense by showing a picture of a boy who fell down and asking the class what happened before the boy fell down. The teacher states, "Before the boy fell down..." The teacher may find it useful to write the questions, the partial answer he or she supplied, and the answer given by the students. This allows students to see and hear the language structure of the tenses, as well as how the words are spelled. Seeing the written form of the words may also add to their sight vocabulary.

Cause and effect can also be used with art. The teacher can ask the class what caused something to happen in a drawing or what will happen next. The teacher can write the answers on the chalkboard in two ways. First, she can write "The boy missed the bus because he overslept" and "Because he overslept, the boy missed the bus." The teacher can point out that the cause-effect relationship is the same regardless of which way it is written.

Hornsby, Sukarna, and Parry (1986) suggest matching illustrations of cause with illustrations of effect, or text of effect with text of cause. In addition, students can draw "bubble thoughts" of what characters may be thinking.

Students can also be encouraged to make a poster to advertise a book. When enough students make posters, the class can have an art fair, with students explaining their posters to the other students. The posters could include the setting, an important character, or an important event.

Some books lend themselves to mapmaking. For example, "The Hobbit" would be a good book for students to illustrate the path that Bilbo took on his adventures. If this book is too difficult for students, they could make a map after watching the movie version.

Picture books can be used to teach comprehension and vocabulary. The teacher can start by showing students a wordless picture book and having the class tell what is taking place. If students are able to write, they should be encouraged to write their thoughts on paper after the class discussion. The teacher may also want to use picture books that have print, but just show the pictures and have the students "tell" the teacher what the story is about. Later, students can draw their own wordless picture books. These can be kept in the classroom for others to enjoy.

Pictures can also be used to introduce a story. The teacher can show the class pictures of two events. After the teacher reads a story to the students they choose which picture goes with the story. The teacher can reread the selection, this time with students noting details that support or refute their picture choice.

Illustrations can also be used to teach figurative language. After reading a book such as "Amelia Bedilia" or any book that uses a lot of figurative language, the teacher can show the class two illustrations, one of a literal interpretation and one of a figurative interpretation. Later the teacher can ask the class which picture fits the context of the story.

## Points to Remember

❏ The arts cover many of the intelligences and are motivating for second language students.

❏ Drama, music, and the arts can be employed to assess processes and products of language. This is very important for teachers working with students whose comprehension of English may exceed their ability to produce English.

❏ The arts can be effective in assessing and extending language.

❏ The arts can be used to strengthen the ties among the four language bands; listening, speaking, reading, and writing.

❏ The arts can be used in conjunction with literacy to clarify ideas and make connections among reading and writing and role-play, music, and art. The use of literacy-type activities can be incorporated immediately, regardless of students' proficiency levels.

❏   The arts have the advantage of being concrete and promoting language acquisition. In addition, they evoke a wide range of cognitive and emotional responses and encourage communication. In addition, they are context-embedded and cognitively undemanding, which are the types of activities that promote language acquisition, especially for beginning second-language learners. Finally, and very importantly, students enjoy drama, art, and music because they are having fun while they are learning.

# Chapter 21

## Teaching Science to English Language Learners

---

### KEY ISSUES

❏ Science for all students, an imperative of the National Science Education Standards (NSES)

❏ Scientific literacy: the goal of the science education community. Engaging in scientific inquiry

❏ The importance of science learning for ESOL students

   a.  an asset in developing academic language

   b.  an asset in developing critical thinking

❏ Strategies and techniques for teaching science to second language learners

❏ Special considerations when using cooperative learning groups

## The Benefit of Science for All Students

Ms. Frank understands that science learning, when focused on the big ideas of science, will benefit children's cognitive development, lead toward the goal of scientific literacy, and improve their academic language or cognitive academic language proficiency. Maria, an English language learner (ELL) in Ms. Frank's fifth grade class functioning in the speech emergence phase of second language acquisition, Ms. Frank believes, would benefit from being in class for science instead of being in an ESOL pull out for most of the day. Ms. Frank notes that she has three other ELL students in this class, and that she regularly employs ESOL strategies. Ms. Frank feels strongly that not only do these strategies benefit her L2 students, but they aid L1 students who are struggling with academic learning. She has therefore requested that Maria stay with her for science each day. Ms. Frank knows that inquiry and guided discovery science are interesting and important for all children, and is willing to adjust her daily schedule to accommodate Maria's ESOL teacher, Ms. Ruiz. Both teachers have discussed the fact that academic language proficiency for English language learners often takes a much longer time to develop than their social language. They have seen Maria's social language improve markedly. She is now able to create sentences and communicate many of her ideas in English rather easily and clearly to others. Both teachers are aware that it is the development of academic language that is critical to future academic success for ELLs, and this development may best be accomplished in a content area class. When conferencing with Ms. Ruiz, Ms. Frank explains that science is a wonderful subject for ELLs to develop their academic language because of the experiential nature of hands-on science. The use of concrete materials used in doing science make objects and events less foreign, and students better understand what they have personally observed and investigated. Ms. Ruiz agrees that Maria will benefit from science time with Ms. Frank, and she appreciates Ms. Frank's willingness to adjust her schedule so that Maria can participate in science. Both teachers are eager to see what effect science learning will have on Maria's second language development.

# Scientific Literacy and the National Science Education Standards

The *National Science Education Standards* (NSES), under the auspices of the National Research Council (NRC, 1996) and the American Association for the Advancement of Science (AAAS, 1989), emphasize the theme of Science for All. There has been recognition that many young people exiting school have a weak knowledge of science and the scientific enterprise, are not scientifically literate, and have negative feelings about school science. The concern of scientists and science educators has expressed itself through an agenda of reform in science education (Bybee & Ben-zvi, 1998; Lee & Fradd, 1998). The publication of the NSES by the National Research Council and Project 2061 are part of that reform and emphasize that science should be active, that is, students should be doing science, with school science reflecting real science. High standards of excellence should be demanded of all students regardless of gender, race, religion, ethnicity, disability or language background (Lynch et. al, 1996). The mantra for science education reform is *Science For All*, and engaging in inquiry is recognized as the essence of science and should be reflected in the school curricula (NRC, 1996).

## Teaching Standard B

NSES: *Teachers of science guide and facilitate learning. In doing this, teachers recognize and respond to student diversity and encourage all students to participate fully in science learning* (NRC, 1996).

Scientific literacy has been a goal of science education for the past decade or longer. Although this goal seems legitimate and important, it is vague in meaning. There has not been nor is there a set definition of scientific literacy, but the National Standards now provide an indication of what scientific literacy might be. A scientifically literate student leaving high school today is an asker of questions and has the ability to find answers to those questions. This person should possess a curiosity about the natural world and be able to evaluate information based on evidence. The scientifically literate person should also be able to state a position on an issue based on the available evidence. As a result of school science, students should be able to make careful observations and record their observations into a written record. Predictions should be based on observations, and hypotheses made should be in response to questions that have arisen. Students should use the tools of science for measuring and obtaining data. They should be able to organize information into tables, graphs, or charts as documentation of findings, They should be able to analyze the data and results and draw conclusions from the findings. Developing such abilities or habits of mind would allow a person to make appropriate judgments on issues affecting their community, to evaluate environmental concerns, and to make informed decisions at the voting booth and marketplace. Dewey (1934) might have referred to this as having a "scientific attitude." Such abilities should be fostered in school science programs and represent a degree of scientific literacy.

## Inquiry: the Premier Standard

Just as Science for All is the mantra of science education and is a clear statement that no one is to be excluded, inquiry science should be the focus of learning in science.

## Content Standard A

*As a result of activities in grades K-4, 5-8, and 9-12, all students should develop abilities necessary to do scientific inquiry and an understanding about scientific inquiry. In doing this, teachers select science content and adapt and design curricula to meet the interests, knowledge, understanding, abilities and experiences of students. Inquiry into authentic questions generated from student experiences is the central strategy for teaching science.* (NRC, 1996).

Students should experience school science more like that practiced by scientists. Full inquiry, according to the standards, entails making observations, asking simple questions, carrying out an investigation to answer a question, and then communicating the results to others (NRC, 1996). The premise is that students will develop scientific ways of thinking and scientific habits of mind as well as understandings of the natural world. From the earliest grades onward, inquiry science should be in evidence in our classrooms.

This premier standard is helpful to ELL students because it is based on hands-on, minds-on experiences and questions of interest to students, and cannot be achieved by teacher lecture and textbook reading. It is modeled on scientists' ways of discovery. It must involve active investigation into questions that arise during science learning. Students should use instruments such as magnifiers, microscopes, and measuring devices to extend the senses and to garner data to support their findings. For the early grades, the NSES state that, "Types of investigations include describing objects, events, and organisms; classifying them; and doing a fair test (experimenting)." (NRC, 1996, p.123). Students in grades 5–8 can begin inquiry science with a question, collect evidence related to that question, propose an answer to the question, and share the results of their investigation with others. As students engage in inquiry science, the results of their investigations should be based on evidence from their experiments. Because of the active nature of inquiry and the experiential base of this learning, ELLs should improve in their academic content knowledge and move toward a higher level of scientific literacy. Science teachers must be aware of the level of second language development of their students, employ ESOL strategies, and keep a watchful eye on second language learners in case they need additional help or explanation. The assessment of the ELL student might be a modification of what is required for native English-speaking students (L1). "Students with limited English ability might be encouraged to use their own language as well as English and to use forms of presenting data such as pictures and graphs that require less language proficiency" (NRC, 1996, p. 37).

*Alejandro, who has just recently arrived from Colombia and knows almost no English, is sitting in a small group with language majority L1 children for science. Mr. Thomas, their third grade teacher, has asked Jaime, who is from Mexico, to join this group. Jaime, a sensitive and outgoing boy, understands and speaks English well, functioning well beyond the intermediate fluency stage. Mr. Thomas believes Jaime will be an asset to Alejandro and has asked him to be a "buddy" to Alejandro. Mr. Thomas has carefully structured this group and feels that the three other children in Alejandro's group will try to help him as they investigate during science time. Mr. Thomas believes Alejandro will benefit from science because of the experiential nature of his science teaching. He has found that with adaptations, English language fluency is not necessary for making observations, measuring, and obtaining results, as long as he does not insist on written English to record the observations. Making drawings, tables, diagrams and allowing for flexibility in the presentation of data and results are all things that ELL students can do. Mr. Thomas believes that Alejandro can succeed with assistance from him, from Jaime, and from his group.*

## A Sample Inquiry Lesson

Mr. Thomas's class has been learning about earthworms and their environment, and the children are about to investigate how earthworms move through the soil. They found out that earthworms need moist soil in which to live and that the terrarium in which they have been housed should not receive direct sunlight. They have observed the dark brown soil and found that it contains pieces of decaying vegetation. The children are able to observe earthworms in their class terrarium, and they have seen other earthworms in their school gardens and on sidewalks after a heavy rain. They 'discovered' the segments on the earthworm and hope to be able to count the segments. The children also know that there is a whole group of worms with a similar body structure, as Mr. Thomas has pictures of other types of segmented worms on the science bulletin board. The children discuss how animals such as the variety of segmented worms can live in different places (environments) and under different circumstances (environmental conditions) and still have similar body structures. They are beginning to understand the idea of classification and that these animals (segmented worms) are related because of their similarities. Mr. Thomas understands that Alejandro may not be at the same level of conceptual understanding regarding these ideas but feels Alejandro can participate in a meaningful way in the next investigation.

The children want to observe earthworms at close range because they have questions about how this animal moves through the soil. The question has come up as to whether or not an earthworm really does have "legs or feet," as some of the children have contended. Some children have read about the small appendages on the segments, but not all believe the earthworm has "feet" (setae). Each working group of children has a large deep dish with moisture and some soil in it, and they also have a hand lens. The children understand that they will have a limited time to observe their earthworm before returning it to the terrarium. They know how to care for the earthworms. They do not want the earthworms to " dry out."

The children in one group said that they had heard that the earthworm "eats" its way through the soil. This group is investigating if this is true by placing their worm in a smaller terrarium with the same soil, temperature, and other conditions. The smaller size of the terrarium, they hope, will allow them to see the earthworm moving and if it does appear to "eat the soil." Mr. Thomas believes that more questions may arise after these observations have taken place. He is focusing on the NSES Life Science Content Standard C, whereby students develop understandings of the characteristics of organisms and organisms in their environments.

Mr. Thomas will help Alejandro with the concepts *environment, organism,* and *segments*, three concepts related to the Life Science standard and his teaching unit. These three words will be the beginning of Alejandro's Personal Dictionary for science. Mr. Thomas knows he will have to use "motherese/ parentese" to a great extent when he talks with Alejandro, but he will rely on the realia of the organism and its habitat, the photographs of other segmented worms, and help from Jaime. Mr. Thomas will make clear to Alejandro that he, like the others, should make a drawing of the worm, measure it in centimeters, (the common measurement unit for students from other countries), and try to count the segments. He also has Jaime explain that the groups want to know if the earthworm really does have "feet."

Mr. Thomas has modified Alejandro's worksheet by placing the three key concept words in both English and Spanish. Jaime will further explain the words if

Alejandro appears not to understand. Besides the help that Alejandro receives from his "buddy," he can also observe the other members of his group as they look at the segments and then draw onto their diagrams. He will not be asked to write sentences about his findings, unless he can do so in Spanish. Mr. Thomas is aware of the limited nature of Alejandro's second language development at this time and hopes that Alejandro will be able to express himself in his home language (Spanish) for the present. Even if Alejandro cannot express himself well in Spanish, Mr. Thomas feels that some representation of Alejandro's understanding of the ideas will be forthcoming via his drawings and measurements. He also will monitor group interactions closely to be certain that the group is helping Alejandro in a positive manner and that Alejandro seems to be comfortable with his group mates.

## Science Teachers and their Responsibilities

The teaching of science is the focus of content-specific science teachers, but language development can be enhanced in science classrooms when science teachers provide hands-on learning opportunities as an integral part of their science instruction. With some additional teacher assistance, the implementation of appropriate ESOL strategies, and the adaptation of learning materials, second language learners can derive meaning from science instruction. Under such conditions, science provides experiential learning that can aid in the development of students' scientific conceptual understanding, and their academic language at the same time. Science class, where objects and materials are labeled and manipulated, demonstrations are clearly linked to concepts under study, and labs or activities illustrate scientific principles, providing the experiences which aid conceptual understanding for ESL students. However, it is incumbent upon science teachers to make sure that their ESL students are actively engaged and monitor their understanding regularly. The teacher should provide a variety of ways for the ELL to demonstrate his or her knowledge and understanding.

*A favorite strategy of Mr. Cooper, a sixth grade teacher, is to create a learning packet for his English language learners that is only slightly different than that of his native English speaking students. One packet on hurricanes consists of photographs of a hurricane striking the shoreline and another of coastal property and boats under siege as a hurricane moves ashore. He provides a space for writing and asks his ELL students to write words they know that are related to hurricanes, while the English speakers write what they know about hurricanes in paragraph form. He provides a space on another page for writing words that ELLs learn through the unit. Within the packet, he includes a map of the track of a recent hurricane, and asks the students to trace the path with colored markers from the coast of Africa across the Atlantic and into the waters near and around the United States. He asks them to note places that they recognize. Another page of the packet lists the categories of hurricanes and the wind velocities for each category, information on storm watch versus storm warning, and how a tropical depression is different from a hurricane. He also provides spaces for students to add drawings, which provide insight for a teacher who is trying to find ways to assess what ELLs find meaningful. Mr. Cooper feels he can gain insight into students' understanding through their drawings. Although the classroom experiences are meaningful to the ELL, they may not be able to express their understanding in traditional ways. Mr. Cooper is always ready to adapt his assessments and his teaching to accommodate his ESL students.*

*In recent years, Mr. Cooper has been able to pair one ELL with a native speaker and put them on the NOAA web site (National Oceanographic & Atmospheric Administration) which provides current information on storms and weather patterns. He may ask an English speaker to read and try to explain information on the website that a second language learner might not be able to fully understand without assistance. The use of the Internet has been helpful now that Mr. Cooper has several computers in his classroom.*

## Working with the Adolescent Learner

There are additional problems for the older ESL student who is in a regular science class. Learning science content is a challenge because of the complexity of the material and tasks performed in developing the necessary conceptual understanding. This can pose a significant problem for native speakers in science class as well. There is also the related problem of abstraction in the learning of some science content. If English language learners had science instruction before entering the United States, they often fare better than students who have their science instruction in English or in ESOL classes. Students who have had science instruction in their home countries often have an easier time in science class even when English is the medium of instruction. Science does not seem so abstract to these students. Second language learners who come from cultures where science is not a part of their schooling or where literacy and schooling are minimal are at a greater disadvantage and will probably need more assistance to understand and be successful in science classes in secondary school. Teachers should be cognizant of the fact that the acquisition of academic language may take several more years than the language exhibited by the second language learner in ordinary social conversational situations (Teenant et al., 1995).

Students may seem to be quite proficient in their everyday use of English. Their social language may be quite good, giving the impression of full comprehension of English. However, in context reduced science instruction, they may not yet have developed sufficient language proficiency to manage science content well, causing them to fall behind rather quickly. Some features of science language usage which may be difficult for an ELL are:

- Many concept words or content words in a short passage; that is the lexical density of something read or discussed in science can be very high

- Science words with very different meanings than the same word with the same spelling in everyday language. For example, mass, matter, conductor, gas (not gasoline), state

- Use of the passive voice: *The temperature of the solution was taken.* Who actually did this is left unknown to the reader or to the listener.

- Interconnected definitions and relationships and special expressions of science

When science teachers are aware of these potential difficulties, they can explain or have other students explain meanings. They can switch an explanation from the passive to the active voice to make thoughts more in line with what is familiar to the ELL. Science teachers who make science language comprehensible to an ELL also aid other students in the class who are also struggling to understand the text or terminology and to comprehend definitions and passages. In terms of lexical density (the density of content words in a passage) or where two definitions are interconnected, teachers can review words and any previously learned definitions and show how the ideas relate to each other. Creating word banks may aid students.

Demonstrations that illustrate a concept or principle are also very helpful, and make the science class interesting for all.

Teenant et al. (1995) recommend that teachers not dilute the science content for ELLs, and suggest some of the following strategies for teachers of second language learners. Recommendations include first recognizing that students' knowledge of English might not be adequate to comfortably write about the science knowledge being taught. They recommend that teachers provide opportunities for ELLs to write, phrase questions and express themselves in their first or home language. Another possibility offered by Tobin (1998) is finding other students or aides who are proficient in English and fluent in the language of the ELL. The English proficient student can aid ELLs who are uncomfortable with English in academic settings. Tobin further suggests that the learning of science could be a bilingual experience for ELLs. They can access and utilize all their knowledge and thought structures without being required to do so in English. English language learners should be able to express what they actually do know and understand in the language most comfortable for them while they are acquiring greater proficiency in English academic language fluency.

## Using and Learning About the Tools of Science

*At the beginning of the school year, Ms. Harper wants her eighth grade students to know what instruments and measuring devices they will be using during the year, what they will be used for, and how to use them. This is important for all students to know and be able to do, and essential for her ESL students. Ms. Harper has the students measure various colored liquids with graduated cylinders, beakers, and an Erlenmeyer flask. They use these devices in a variety of sizes noting the volume of liquid that each is able to measure. She has students make diagrams of each device and state what it is used for. Ms. Harper also teaches the students to light a Bunsen burner and how to set up a ring stand. She refreshes their memories about how to use a triple beam balance, a thermometer, a graduated cylinder, and a spring scale, and the purpose of each. She or another student will demonstrate how to use each instrument to L2 students. She is aware that they may not have had exposure to these instruments before. With a little extra guidance from Ms.Harper, all of the ELL students can accomplish these activities.*

*Ms. Harper expects her ELLs to measure liquid volume, determine mass and weight, and find the temperature of materials. They can write in the amounts, the units, and the names of the instruments or make a drawing of the instrument. They can write a phrase telling what the device is used for if they are able to do so. Ms. Harper has noticed that many L2 students are often very careful and accurate with their diagrams and their work. She praises the work of these students, publicly and privately, and hangs up their drawings for the class to see.*

*Ms. Harper tells her class that they will be having a quiz on which they must identify from drawings the names of the various measuring devices. They should also be able to measure various amounts of liquids with the devices and determine the mass and weight of a few objects. Ms. Harper explains to her ELL students that they, too, will have a quiz on the instruments or tools of this science classroom. She will say the name of the instrument to them, and they should draw the item and label if they can write its name. She will also give them a sheet of paper with a picture of the device on it, and they can try to tell what it is and what to do with it. Some of her ELL students will be as-*

*sessed orally and some may be able to write answers. She will be checking for recognition of the item, and for demonstration of its use, and not for spelling or writing proficiency.*

## In Already Crowded Curricula, Why Bother with Science?

In this age of testing and accountability, science learning is not always viewed as important in elementary programs. Science teaching may be subordinated to language arts and mathematics, the two areas most commonly tested at the elementary level. This is more prevalent in schools that have been labeled "low achieving." Frequently, these are the very schools that language minority students attend. In such schools, teachers may be told to not teach science (or social studies) in order to focus solely on reading, writing, and mathematics because of a belief among some administrators that this sharp focus on skill development will bring up test scores in the critical areas. No one would argue the importance of language arts and math in all children's learning. These subjects should occupy a large percentage of time in the overall elementary program. However, to eliminate content learning is a short-sighted approach. Aside from literature, what do we read about, if not the content areas? Furthermore, the children in these "low achieving schools" will have less access to and knowledge of important ideas in science, less exposure to scientific thinking, and possibly be less able to function as scientifically literate citizens in a scientifically and technologically oriented society. Furthermore, it can be argued that students' academic language may be delayed or be quite weak.

Few would argue the importance of science in everyone's life and the fact that it will become even more important in the future. Science discoveries and happenings (along with social-political events) occupy the media. Daily news reports about new medical, health and nutritional findings, about space exploration, and natural disasters capture the public's attention no matter what else may be happening. The concern for the environment and the consequences of the human impact on this planet cause many to consider solutions to a myriad of problems, and to question whether or not some policy makes sense. All of this input requires an ability to comprehend what is reported and to discern what should cause concern. Our capacity to do so depends on an understanding of scientific ideas, the scientific enterprise, and a scientific literacy. From this perspective alone, one can make a case for including science in the elementary curriculum and for developing scientific awareness at an early age.

# Older Research

It is often surprising that science is eliminated in school curricula when test scores are low, for the positive effect of hands-on, inquiry approach in science teaching has been well documented for more than 20 years. In 1977 Ruth Wellman reviewed 18 studies documenting that first-hand manipulative experiences in science enhanced children's development of process skills in grades K–3 and that this "had a positive correlation with their success in beginning language and reading achievement." In grades 4–6, she found that a strong activity-based science program had a positive effect on the development of children's language arts and reading skills. She noted the following benefits from inquiry-oriented science programs: vocabulary enrichment, increased verbal fluency and ability to think logically, improved concept formation and improved communication skills. At about the same time, Barufaldi and Swift (1977) wrote that if teachers knew the research findings that indicate "a positive relationship between children's participation in activity-centered science programs and the development of oral language skills and reading readiness," they might spend a larger proportion teaching science. Furthermore, in an in-depth review of the literature, Esler (1977) found that science activities enhance children's performance in the basics of language arts and mathematics, and are an effective means for helping children develop thinking skills.

Perhaps the most compelling reason for children learning science is their natural fascination with science. Their earliest questions are often science questions. What is more, children often behave like scientists: they want to find out. The many everyday happenings that are overlooked or taken for granted evoke curiosity and wonderment in children. However, if students are subjected to large doses of teacher talk, reading of text with emphasis on vocabulary memorization, answering questions from a book, along with traditional testing on vocabulary attainment, their interest drops off, and they lose their fascination with science. Instead, if children are given opportunities to observe simple objects, animals, or plants, investigate aspects of the conditions surrounding their observations such as conditions needed for healthy plant growth, make measurements using some of the tools of science (such as a thermometer, a balance, graduated containers, magnifying lenses and simple microscopes), and engage in investigations related to everyday occurrences, their understanding of the natural world will increase. Children who are guided and encouraged to explore and discover begin to phrase their own questions, develop hypotheses about what they observe, and develop their scientific way of thinking. Having experiences that build their knowledge structures has been shown to lead to greater language development. This is true for ELL students as well as for native English speakers.

## Cooperative Learning via Complex Instruction

*Part of their group work is based on the norm that everyone has some abilities, and none of us have all the abilities* (Cohen, 1986).

Learning science in collaborative or cooperative groups is recommended by the science education community (Lazarowitz & Lazarowitz, 1998). Lazarowitz and Lazarowitz (1998) note that cooperative learning is "the antithesis of the expository competitive classroom" and is based on a constructivist perspective toward teaching and learning. They further note that competitive methods have been fairly unsuccessful with a large segment of the general population of students, who lack positive attitudes toward science, have not realized academic science achievement, and do not have an adequate understanding of science concepts. This has been reconfirmed by the latest Third International Math & Science Study (TIMSS) of 1998 and also in 2000 with a limited number of states participating in the TIMSS. TIMSS results indicate that a number of American students from particular schools and regions do extremely well in science and math. However, the results also indicate that many more American students barely attain the mid-range of scores in this international comparison, with some groups doing poorly.

Cooperative learning is part of a constructivist perspective on learning that emphasizes collaboration, social interaction, sharing of ideas, and group efforts toward the solution of problems. Group efforts in doing projects are believed to enhance science understanding and develop meaningful learning (Cohen, 1986). Cooperative group work allows for questions to come forth that might not be addressed in more formal and traditional classroom settings, encouraging students to question and challenge each other freely (Cohen, 1991 b).

Cooperative learning groups do pose some challenges, however. Groups may reinforce negative stereotypes and allow what are perceived as "high status" students to dominate talk and action. In such situations high status students' ideas may take precedence over the ideas of "low status" students (Cohen, 1984; 1991 b). High status students, because of their popularity or position, may be able to hold sway over more scientifically grounded ideas of lower status students. The fact that they are considered smart by the group or the class may allow them to dominate talk and materials. The situation that the teacher may hope to avoid by using cooperative learning groups, namely unequal access to learning, can occur if they do not take some precautions (Cohen, 1984).

It is important that teachers consider the nature of the children with whom they place a second language learner. Teachers must know that certain partners and group members will be patient and understanding, and help the English language learner to participate in the activity as fully as possible. Positive group interdependence can encourage students to express themselves in spite of limited academic language proficiency. One way to obtain successful group work that values all voices is to train the children for the *roles* that are going to be used in the cooperative groups and to establish *norms*, a set of expected behaviors, that students will be trained and encouraged to exhibit (Cohen, 1986, 1991a, 1994). This requires time at the beginning of the school year and further reinforcement of the roles and norms throughout the school year.

Elizabeth Cohen, Rachel Lotan and a group of researchers at Stanford University developed a model and program of cooperative learning called Complex Instruction. This program is designed for heterogeneous classrooms where students are of many nationalities and ethnicities, speak many different languages, and are at various levels of cognitive development and academic performance. An elementary program for fourth and fifth graders called *Finding Out/Descubrimiento,* focuses on science and math learning. Materials are in both English and Spanish, Students work in cooperative groups and adhere to the following norms of behavior (Cohen & DeAvila, 1983):.

- No one has all of the abilities, all of us have some.
- It is your right to ask questions.
- It is your duty to answer a question.
- None of us is as smart as all of us together.

Under the Complex Instruction model, children are trained to take over many of the usual tasks of the teacher, freeing the teacher to monitor learning and cooperative behavior. As the children take over these responsibilities, the teacher can observe students at work, probe students' thoughts and understandings, encourage higher-level thinking and cooperative behavior, and suggest alternatives for the children as they work. The teacher takes the role of a facilitator, and children problem solve and investigate together as they interact in their groups. Cooperative grouping and "delegating authority" to the learners can also provide time for the teacher to assist the ELLs. This model has also been developed for use in middle schools and is specifically designed for heterogeneous classes where students work on challenging group projects (Cohen & Lotan, 1990).

*Back in Mr. Thomas's third grade classroom, each child has a diagram of an earthworm, but the class has to share the magnifying lenses and the earthworms. The children do not mind. They are accustomed to sharing materials as they work in cooperative groups. In their groups, they will discuss the differences that they may see, and know that they may need to report their findings to the class. Because the children are accustomed to working in cooperative learning groups, they observe the norms of behavior and perform their roles well. This allows Mr. Thomas time to give special attention to Alejandro.*

*Mr. Thomas realizes that Alejandro probably does not know what a magnifying lens is, nor has he had the experiences the other children in the class have had. Mr. Thomas sits by Alejandro's group, hands Alejandro a lens, and names this new tool for him, repeating the words "magnifying lens" for him clearly. He places a small clear plate containing salt crystals in front of Alejandro. Mr. Thomas knows that Alejandro knows what salt is and tells him it is salt. Alejandro has seen how the other children observe with the lenses. He begins to use his lens in the same way to observe the salt, as Mr. Thomas nods his head. Alejandro is very surprised by what he sees and becomes quite excited when he observes the tiny cubes of salt. He is amazed to see the enlargement and the detail of salt crystals. Mr. Thomas again repeats the words "magnifying lens." With gestures and careful speech he tells Alejandro that the lens magnifies and makes things seem bigger. Alejandro understands what Mr. Thomas is saying because he has observed the enlargement for himself. Mr. Thomas points to the other children and tells Alejandro to do as the other children are doing, to use his lens to observe the earthworm. Alejandro uses the lens to look at the earthworm. He understands that he too, should draw what he sees onto his earthworm diagram. Mr. Thomas asks the group to help Alejandro with any labeling that they decide is good to add to their drawings. The children have been trained to help each other and answer each other's questions before asking the teacher for help. Two of the children watch as Alejandro draws in great detail the tiny setae of the earthworm onto his diagram. After a while the group stops to look at his drawing. He has enhanced the simple drawing into a detailed reproduction of the earthworm. They are amazed at the complexity of the drawing that Alejandro has created. They realize that Alejandro has a special ability and is a careful observer. They praise his drawing. The group facilitator wants Mr. Thomas to see what Alejandro has created on his paper, and he asks him to come back to their group. Mr. Thomas is impressed and encourages Alejandro to continue and asks the children to help him label the earthworm parts. Pointing to the bulletin board, Mr. Thomas explains that he is going to put Alejandro's drawing up on the front board as a display.*

*When Alejandro is finished drawing, the children show him their drawings and the labels. They explain that each label represents a part of the worm and point to the structure on the earthworm. They indicate that Alejandro, too, should label his drawing. He repeats each word after them and copies the word from their papers onto his. He too, notices that his drawing has greater detail and is more precise than the others in his group, and he feels quite proud of his work. He sees that he can contribute and succeed in science and that there is much positive feeling in his group and in Mr. Thomas's class.*

# Helping Students Learn

The interaction of teachers with Limited English Proficient (LEP) students in the classroom is an area of concern (Verplaetse, 1998). Verplaetse found that teachers, although sympathetic to second language learners, limited the opportunities of ELLs by calling on them less frequently, asking them lower cognitive level questions, and sometimes doing work for them instead of showing them how to do it themselves. The teachers noted several things in regard to their interactions with LEP students, among them the difficulty in ascertaining what the LEP student does and does not understand. Therefore, instead of providing more think-through time, more wait time, and more questioning and restating of ideas that might scaffold the science thinking for the LEP students, they provided directives to LEP students. Instead of guiding them to think through a question or concept, they directed them in a step-wise fashion to the correct solution.

Verplaetse documented differences between the guided approach used by the teachers with majority students, and the step by step directives used with LEP students. Sympathetic teachers worried they might embarrass LEP students by asking many clarifying questions that the student may be unable to answer. The teachers then avoided asking higher cognitive level questions of the LEP student. Instead they asked simple questions or asked about procedures rather than challenging students to reconsider the concept in a different way, causing them to alter their thinking about a science idea. Many teachers seemed unaware that a student might need a lot of direct help when students' language proficiency was sufficient for them to be challenged, encouraged, redirected, or guided to consider a new idea. Some teachers were concerned with the time it took for LEP students to answer the questions posed, saying this slowed down the other students. Teachers felt a need to "cover" the curriculum. They felt that other students were in need of their time and were being deprived of access to teacher talk (Verplaetse, 1998).

A focus group of teachers seemed unaware of the longer time required for second language learners to formulate responses and the need to provide the ELL with additional wait time. It should be noted that ELLs may be unable to provide the rich expression that majority students might be capable of. The students nonetheless benefit from higher level thought, greater challenge, and listening to better English. The lack of challenge and the reluctance of science teachers to probe the understanding of their English language learners resulted in fewer questions posed by the teachers. Consequently, there were few opportunities to engage in discourse in group discussions and less need for the ELL to reason answers and think on a higher level. Verplaetse felt that teachers could alter their behaviors and, thus, enrich the opportunity of the LEP student to respond. There is a fine line between demanding too much or expecting too much of a student who is truly struggling with English and not challenging an English language learner by probing and asking thought provoking questions of a higher level. Teachers must ascertain how comfortable and how proficient a student is in English, and the ESOL teacher can aid in this determination for the teacher. Science teachers can then adjust the cognitive demands of their instruction for their ELL students. If a situation is too open ended, the ELL may feel lost or confused. If teachers spend more time with the ELL and phrase and rephrase questions that probe for understanding, it is worth the extra effort because the student gains in his or her academic language proficiency. Helping a second language learner will require some extra time on the teacher's part and the use of ESOL strategies. As mentioned earlier, cooperative group work can provide opportunities for the teacher to spend extra time with English language learners and opportunities for other students to model, discuss, aid and encourage the ELL student in learning and understanding science in a meaningful way.

## Strategies for Teaching Science to English Language Learners (ELL)

1. Use real objects or models (i.e.. model of the relationship of the sun, moon and earth), videos, Internet pictures and graphics or film, and picture books related to topics under study. When something can be seen, felt, or changed, it is more likely to be understood and remembered.

2. Emergent speakers, fluent speakers, or the teacher can read a "picture book" related to the science topic to a child functioning in the silent stage of second language acquisition.

3. Early-emergent speakers can write down all the words they can after reading from a picture book. Students in the silent stage may try to write down some words (if they have been pointed out to them). Spelling is not an issue under either set of circumstances.

4. Use cooperative learning groups.

5. Use hands-on science activities/investigations to engage students in active science learning (i.e. testing the hardness of rocks and minerals and using the MOHS scale to identify the category to which a sample belongs). A teacher-made outline of what to do and where the categories lie with pictorial representations can accompany the activity. Everyone in a group can participate in the classifying and testing activities.

6. When most children are working alone, assign a buddy to the English language learner. The buddy should want to work with the ELL and talk aloud about a science assignment.

7. Create word walls or word banks for topics under study that students can refer to for spelling and for memory jogs of particular concepts. These word walls can stay up for the entire unit and can be added to as the unit of study progresses.

8. Native English speakers and fluent English language learners can write about what they know. (i.e. Write all that you know about volcanoes and why you believe your ideas are correct. For the ELL: Write all the words you can think of related to volcanoes). The ELL could draw a volcano and label what he or she knows and possibly create phrases or short sentences about volcanoes. Use of words like magma, ash, molten, and pressure can give the teacher an idea of what the student is learning and comprehending in science and insight into the level of second language acquisition.

9. Use writing by native English speakers from the class and fluent speakers as text for English language learners. Ask fluent speakers to write text that would aid students in the early emergent stage.

10. Create a large, empty bubble diagram for early emergent students. Say words as you add them to the bubble. The ELL can also say them as well as in a choral reading. The student can keep a copy of the bubble diagram for personal reference.

11. Have linguistically advanced and native speakers create concept maps. Have the less language proficient student try to create a simpler form of a concept map. Some students find it helpful to have a fluent speaker go over the concept map and explain ideas to them.

12. Think-Pair-Share on days when the teacher does direct instruction and engages in short "teacher talks," have students listen to the teacher for 5 minutes. Then pair students and have them talk to each other about what they heard and learned. The more proficient student should explain his or her understanding first. As students develop proficiency with this technique, the time can be extended to 10 minutes with 2 minutes of talk time together. All students will find that not everyone "hears" or understands the same thing from the teacher talk.

## Points to Remember

❑ The National Science Education Standards and the reform movement in science education stress that ALL students should be learning science, including speakers of other languages.

❑ The learning of science should promote scientific literacy and greater awareness of science in the everyday life of students.

❑ Learning science enhances ESOL students' academic language, which is critical to success in secondary school.

❑ Research has shown that hands-on inquiry science has a positive effect on language and reading skills, and critical thinking is enhanced through hands-on inquiry science learning.

❑ Children have a natural fascination for science and scientific events.

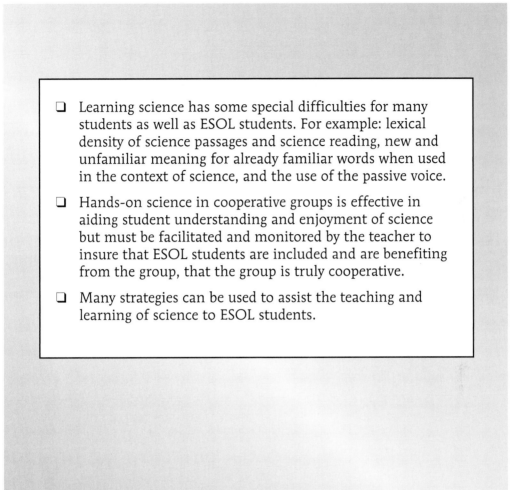

❑ Learning science has some special difficulties for many students as well as ESOL students. For example: lexical density of science passages and science reading, new and unfamiliar meaning for already familiar words when used in the context of science, and the use of the passive voice.

❑ Hands-on science in cooperative groups is effective in aiding student understanding and enjoyment of science but must be facilitated and monitored by the teacher to insure that ESOL students are included and are benefiting from the group, that the group is truly cooperative.

❑ Many strategies can be used to assist the teaching and learning of science to ESOL students.

# Chapter 22

## *Pedagogy to Teach Social Studies from a Global Perspective for English Learners*

# KEY ISSUES

❏ Challenges teachers face in teaching social studies to second language learners

❏ Employing second language acquisition techniques in teaching social studies

❏ Teaching difficult abstract, critical concepts and skills in elementary social studies instruction

❏ Integrating a global perspective in the teaching of social studies

The goal in teaching the social studies is to pose higher intellectual challenges to English language learners than those posed in other subject areas (Short, 1996; Snow & Brinton, 1997). The cognitive expectations inherent in effective social studies instruction require the development of high levels of literacy skills embedded in the understanding of abstract concepts, social science terminology, and familiarity with social studies-specific background knowledge. Further, essential elements of effective social studies instruction include higher-order thinking skills: the ability of students to collect and interpret information, draw conclusions, make generalizations and inferences, determine cause-and-effect relationships, find alternative courses of action, form hypotheses and predictions, and represent text visually (Chapin & Messick, 2002; Jarolimek, 1989; Martorella, 1998). In addition, the social studies are increasingly taught from a global perspective. Students of the twenty-first century must be equipped with the attitudes, knowledge, and skills necessary to meet the challenges of a rapidly changing, increasingly interdependent world (Anderson, 1990; Anderson et al., 1994; Cruz, 1998; Diaz, Massialas, & Xanthopoulos, 1999; Kirkwood 1995, 2001a, 2001b; Merryfield, 1990, 1997; Tye, 1992, 1999). However, many immigrant and refugee students coming to the United States have not received social studies instruction in their native country and lack requisite social studies knowledge, the ability to understand abstract concepts, and a global perspective of the world.

## The Social Studies

The field of social studies is derived from the social science disciplines of anthropology, psychology, sociology, criminology, geography, economics, political science, and history. The existing social studies curriculum in American elementary schools generally follows the expanding-communities organizational pattern (Chapin & Messick, 2000; Hanna, 1963). This approach is based on the premise that during each academic year, the learner should be introduced to an increasingly extended social environment, moving from examining self to family, community, neighborhood, nation, and the world around them. Students learn the skills to observe, record, and analyze roles of institutions and the individuals who comprise them, draw conclusions about the principles that govern them, and utilize these generalizations to gain understanding of human nature and human interactions across space and time (Martorella, 1998).

According to the National Council for the Social Studies (NCSS), the largest and most prestigious professional organization of social studies educators in the United States, the primary purpose of the social studies is to "help young people develop the ability to make informed and reasoned decisions for the public good as citizens of a culturally diverse, democratic society in an interdependent world" (1994).

## Global Perspectives

The overarching purpose of integrating a global perspective in social studies content is to develop a well-informed, competent, humanistic, and participatory citizenry in a global age. Global perspectives are designed to "cultivate in young people a perspective of the world which emphasizes the interconnections among cultures, species, and the planet" (NCSS, 1982).

Social studies taught from a global perspective emphasizes (a) the human experience is an increasingly globalized phenomenon in which people are constantly being influenced by transnational, crosscultural, multicultural, multiethnic interactions; (b) there is a variety of actors on the world stage; (c) humankind is an integral part of the world environment; (d) there are linkages among present social, political, and ecological realities and alternative futures; and (e) citizen participation in world affairs is important.

The national debate on the integration of a global perspective in American schools found expression in the publication of subject-specific standards by national professional organizations. For example, the National Council for the Accreditation of Teachers (NCATE), the American Association of Colleges for Teacher Education (AACTE), the International Global Education Commission of the Association for Supervision and Curriculum Development (ASCD), and the National Council for the Social Studies (NCSS) strongly recommended that global perspectives become an integral component in teacher education programs.

## Pedagogy

Abstract social studies concepts such as citizenship, justice, freedom, democracy, and globalization are difficult concepts for children to grasp regardless of their linguistic background. English language learners, however, face the dual problem of having to acquire the meaning of abstract concepts as well as the linguistic skills to comprehend these abstract concepts. Mehlinger (1981) suggested various hypothetical situations that can be used to engage students in discussing their views on a given concept. For example, if students are asked about the concept of justice, they have no idea of its meaning. However, if they are asked what is fair and what is not fair, they are keenly aware of their respective meanings. To elementary students, the concept of justice is synonymous with fairness (Cantoni-Harvey, 1987). This is true of native English speakers in mainstream classes. But what about the English language learners who lack the linguistic skills that are necessary to comprehend the meaning of the concept?

The following three lessons provide selected examples of teaching strategies that make social studies content, concepts, skills, and global perspective comprehensible to the English language learner.

## Lesson One

### Concept: Our World

The language of social studies content is a complex phenomenon. Second language learners of English are expected to comprehend difficult terminology, an essential skill in comprehending social studies and global education instruction. Textbooks often fail to treat key terms adequately. Frequently, only 10 words or fewer are explained for an entire chapter. Textbook glossaries only contain words highlighted in the chapters (Beck & McKeown, 1991; Brophy & Alleman, 1991; Tyson-Bernstein, 1988). Teachers cannot take for granted that second language learners possess an understanding of the meaning of key words and other difficult terminology used in social studies texts.

### Materials

Globe, wall world map, large Styrofoam balls (or inflatable beach balls), transparencies, string, glue, crayons, atlases, continent handout, enlarged continent pieces in proportion to Styrofoam or beach ball, construction paper, CD: "We Are the World"

### Teaching Episode 1

Mr. Seitz writes the content objectives of the lesson on the board with the key terminology underlined. For example, one content objective reads: Students will be able to demonstrate *latitude* and *longitude* on the world map. Mr. Seitz reads each content objective slowly and deliberately as he points to the objectives and circles each key term in different colors. Holding up a globe and turning it on its axis, Mr. Seitz informs students that the world is round. He then points to the large wall map, telling students that the world is also shown flat on maps. Geographers have created artificial lines called "latitude" and "longitude" that assist us in finding places on the world map. Mr. Seitz points out the *latitudes* and *longitudes* on the world map. He turns on the projector to show the latitude and longitude transparency.

## Latitude and Longitude

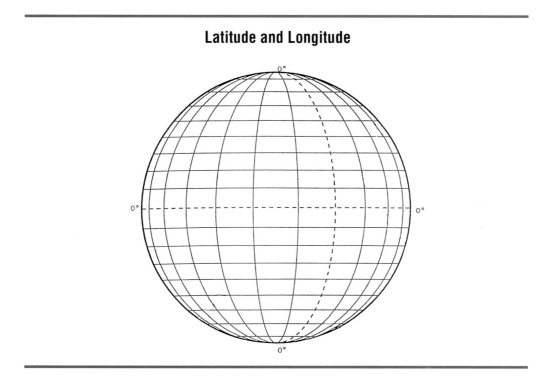

Then Mr. Seitz explains that latitude lines extend horizontally from east to west. He demonstrates their direction by extending his arms in horizontal fashion, perpendicular to his body. The longitude lines are vertical lines, extending from north to south. He stretches one hand high into the air and the other hand toward the floor. Mr. Seitz asks a native and a non-native speaker of English to come to the wall map and follow a latitude and longitude line with their finger.

Subsequently, Mr. Seitz places a blank transparency on the overhead with the heading "Geography Vocabulary." He slowly lists in printed letters the concepts of latitude and longitude. He asks students to write the terms on their vocabulary page under the heading *"Geography Vocabulary."*

Mr. Seitz continues his lesson by telling students that the most important latitude line is called the *equator,* which divides the world into two halves. He again places the latitude/longitude globe transparency on the overhead and prints "equator: on the central latitude line and thickens the existing equator line. Then he tells students that the most important longitude line, which divides the world vertically, is called the *prime meridian.* He prints "prime meridian" along the central longitude line on the same transparency and thickens the existing prime meridian line.

Then Mr. Seitz walks to the large wall map and moves his finger from east to west along the equator, slowly pronouncing the term "equator." He moves his finger slowly along the prime meridian from north to south, pronouncing the term "prime meridian." He points to zero degrees (0°) at each end of the two lines, showing his students that both the equator and the prime meridian hold a zero degree position on the world map. Mr. Seitz then places the vocabulary transparency on the overhead and slowly adds "equator" and "prime meridian" to the vocabulary list. He asks students to add the two terms to their vocabulary list. Then, Mr. Seitz asks a non-English speaker to come to the wall map to show the locations of the equator and the prime meridian. He asks, "What is the name of this latitude?" as he stretches out his arms in horizontal fashion. Mr. Seitz then reaches his right hand toward the ceiling and his left hand towards the floor, asking, "What is the name of the longitude that divides the world into two halves?"

## Teaching Episode 2

Mr. Seitz tells his students, "It is important for you to understand directions so you do not get lost when you go somewhere. There are four cardinal directions that help us find the right directions." He places the cardinal direction transparency on the overhead.

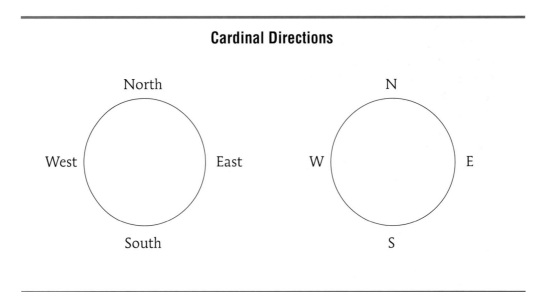

**Cardinal Directions**

Mr. Seitz states, "The cardinal directions are located on the top, bottom, left, and right sides of the world map." As he shows each direction, he state, "North is located on the top of the map. South is located on the bottom of the map. East is located to the right of the map when you stand in front of the map. And west is located on your left." As he circles the cardinal directions of the content objectives, Mr. Seitz tells his students that the directions are generally abbreviated or shortened on the map by a capital letter. He adds E next to east, W next to west, N next to north, and S next to south. He places the four letters in their proper locations on the globe. Mr. Seitz then points to each as he slowly and deliberately pronounces the terms again. He asks the class to recite the four cardinal directions as he points to them on the transparency. He then asks students to pronounce the four directions as he points to them on the wall map. He asks students to add the terms to their vocabulary list.

Mr. Seitz concludes by saying, "Here in the United States we call the four directions *north, south, east,* and *west.* In Germany, the German people call east 'Osten,' west 'Westen,' north 'Norden,' and south 'Sueden.' In Spanish-speaking countries east is called 'Este,' west is called 'Oeste,' north is called 'Norte,' and South is called 'Sur.' As you can see, people of different countries around the world use their own language in expressing the same concepts in geography."

## Teaching Episode 3

Mr. Seitz places the hemisphere transparency on the overhead.

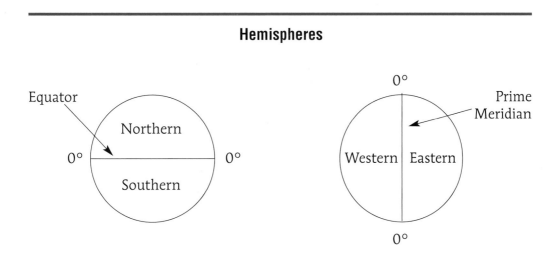

**Hemispheres**

He informs students, "Now we are going to learn that the world can be divided into four quarters or sections. The equator and prime meridian divide the world into four sections called *"hemispheres."* He points to each hemisphere as he explains that the *equator* divides the world into the *northern* and *southern* hemispheres, and the *prime meridian* divides the world into the *eastern* and *western* hemispheres. Mr. Seitz circles the terms in the content objectives listed on the board. He then walks to the wall world map and points out the northern, southern, eastern, and western hemispheres on the wall map as he repeats each concept. Then Mr. Seitz places the vocabulary transparency on the overhead and slowly adds "hemisphere," "eastern," "western," "northern," and "southern" to the existing list of terms. He asks students to add the concepts to their own list. He invites several native and non-native English speakers to come to the wall map to point out the northern, southern, eastern, and western hemispheres to the class.

## Teaching Episode 4

Mr. Seitz continues the geography lesson by telling students that most people on earth live on land. There are large pieces of land in the world that are called *continents.* They are named *Africa, Antarctica, Australia, Eurasia, North America,* and *South America.* He points out each continent on the world map as he simultaneously circles the name of each continent in the content objectives listed on the board. He then calls on several students to come up to the world map to point to each continent, asking them to state the name of each continent. Mr. Seitz asks yes/no questions as he asks students the correct name of each continent. For example, he points to Australia and ask, "Is this the continent of Africa?" The students respond, "No, it is Australia." Mr. Seitz points to North America and asks, "Is this the continent of Australia?" The students respond, "No, it is the continent of North America."

Then Mr. Seitz switches to either/or questions. For example, he asks, "Is this the continent of Antarctica or Eurasia?" as he points to Eurasia. The students respond, "Eurasia." He continues, "Is this the continent of South America or Australia?" as he points to the continent of Australia, and so on, until all continents are covered and he has received all correct answers. Then, Mr. Seitz turns on the overhead and writes "continent," "Africa," "Antarctica," "Australia," "Eurasia," "North America," and "South America" on the existing vocabulary transparency, asking students to do the same in their notebook.

Mr. Seitz asks students to form their preassigned groups of two native and two nonnative speakers of English. He places a transparency with individual continents on the overhead. (Europe and Asia are considered one continent referred to as Eurasia).

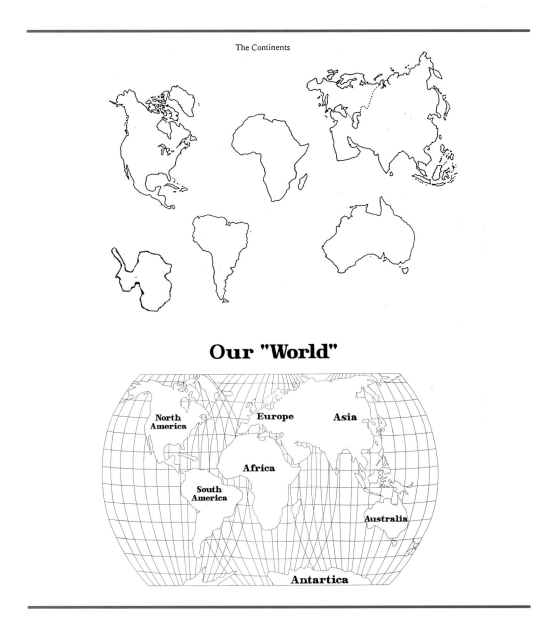

The Continents

## Our "World"

Pointing to the individual continents, Mr. Seitz asks students to cut out the six continents from the handout distributed to them, label, and color them. He calls on one group to attach the continents to the corresponding continents on the world map. He asks the remaining groups to paste the continents correctly into a round circle representing the globe on construction paper and place their world on the preassigned "geography wall."

## Teaching Episode 5

Mr. Seitz states, "Today, we have learned many geographic terms. Let's see if you have all of them written down in your vocabulary list." Mr. Seitz calls on several students to stand next to the overhead to read the terms while he indicates which ones to read. For example, the first student reads all the words that start with the letters "c" and "l." The second student will read all the continents; the third student will read the cardinal directions. Afterwards, Mr. Seitz gives directions to the class for them to read those words.

| | |
|---|---|
| geography | continent |
| latitude | Africa |
| longitude | Antarctica |
| cardinal directions | Australia |
| east (E) | Eurasia |
| west (W) | North America |
| north (N) | South America |
| south (S) | |

Mr. Seitz tells students, "We are also going to add four more geography terms to our geography vocabulary list today." He challenges the class, "What part of the world have we left out?" (oceans) "What are the names of these oceans?" (Arctic Ocean, Atlantic Ocean, Indian Ocean, and Pacific Ocean) He points to each ocean on the wall world map and repeats the name of each ocean three times. He states, "Let's add the four major oceans to our vocabulary list". He walks to the overhead and adds the names of the four oceans on the transparency as students add them to their vocabulary list.

## Teaching Episode 6

Mr. Seitz tells his students, "The next activity will complete our geography lesson. Before we do that, I want to thank you for working so hard in learning new vocabulary words in studying the geography of the world. Now, I want you to combine the geography terms learned into a final product. I want you to create your own world by using the enlarged continent pieces I have prepared for you and the Styrofoam (beach) balls. You have 30 minutes to finish this activity. Let's read together the instruction sheet that I am distributing to you now."

### Handout: Create Your Own World

Using the Styrofoam balls or inflated beach balls:

1. Cut out, color, and label the continents.
2. Paste continents in their correct location on the Styrofoam ball or inflated globe.
3. Label and color the four largest oceans.
4. Draw and label the equator and prime meridian.
5. Place a zero degree (0°) at their proper locations
6. Place the abbreviated letters of the cardinal directions in their proper locations.
7. Draw lines to divide the world into four hemispheres
8. Label the hemispheres.
9. Write your names on a paper strip and glue it on the top of your world.
10. Attach a string and hang your world from our clothesline.

Mr. Seitz walks around the classroom assisting students with their work. He plays the song, "We Are the World" as students construct "their world."

## Reflections

In this activity, students learn new knowledge directly from their teacher rather than from written text. Mr. Seitz employs several techniques to make his input comprehensible: (1) He writes the content objectives in simplified terms on the board, pronounces them orally, and highlights visually the key terms embedded in the content objectives (Echevarria, Vogt, & Short, 2000). As he demonstrates the key terms on the world map, he underlines, colors, circles, and systematically points to them. (2) He reinforces key terms by demonstrating them directly on the wall map and in hands-on activities in group settings. (3)He demonstrates the new terms visually on the transparency. Students practice the key terms orally and write them in their notebooks. (4) Mr. Seitz indirectly employs peer teaching, an often underestimated learning process in the classroom. Repetition, slow deliberate speech, reinforcement, visualization, and application in the acquisition of key social studies terminology are effective strategies in making new content comprehensible to second language learners (Morales-Jones, 2000).

### Note

Teach the lesson over a 2-day period as appropriate.

## Lesson Two

### Concept: Justice

This lesson illustrates how the social studies abstract concept of justice can be made comprehensible to second language learners. A strategy for English learners to comprehend the concept of justice is to demonstrate the unequal or disproportionate distribution of the world's resources. The pedagogy employed includes the methodology of visualization and simplification of text (Snow & Brinton, 1997). For example, a visual representation of children and two slices of a pie, a smiling child holding a large piece of pie and a child holding a smaller piece of pie provide children with a clear sense of unfairness.

The teaching of the concept of justice from a global perspective can be achieved if the teaching strategies follow the principles of global pedagogy. One element of global pedagogy is the discussion of global issues that affect other nations and their people. When the teacher moves from the concept of different pie sizes and two nameless children in an unidentified country to the unequal or disproportionate distribution of resources to people inhabiting the earth, the concept of justice acquires global properties. In the typical classroom of native speakers of English, a frequent methodology to demonstrate the worldwide, uneven distribution of resources is accomplished by having students extract specific information from the text. For English language students, the teacher makes the information comprehensible by using visuals such as graphs or charts representing the written text. This strategy simplifies length and complexity of text by reducing information to specific elements in the lesson to be learned.

## Materials

Transparency or poster: world with "baguette" of French bread, children with pies, and resources

## Teaching Episode 1

Mrs. Romanova begins her lesson by using either a transparency or poster that shows the world map and a "baguette" of bread. She informs the students, "Today's lesson addresses the abstract concept of *justice*. This concept is synonymous with fairness." She writes the concept in big letters on the board. Then, Mrs. Romanova holds up a visual representation of the two children with different pie sizes to reinforce the concept.

## Teaching Episode 2

At this point in the lesson, English language learners must first possess an understanding of the concept of *"resources"* before engaging them in further concept development (Peregoy & Boyle, 2001). Mrs. Romanova writes "resources" in huge, colorful letters on the board. She states, "We have many resources in this classroom. For example, we have books. Books are resources you can use to find information. Pencils are resources. We use pencils as a resource to help us write." Mrs. Romanova places a poster or a transparency on the overhead that shows items representing the concept of resources.

# Resources

## Teaching Episode 3

**Materials:** "Baguette" of French bread, population and resource distribution chart, large world map

Mrs. Romanova divides her class into six groups of students representing the appropriate population size of Africa, Asia, Europe, the Middle East, North America, and South America. She asks students to sit on the floor. All eyes are on her as she cuts the "baguette" of French bread into appropriate sizes equaling the resources available to them. The concept of justice is clearly demonstrated when North Americans (6% of the population and the second-smallest group of students) receive almost four times as much bread to eat (22%) as does the largest group of students representing Asia (58%) which possesses 23% of the world's resources. Mrs. Romanova asks the students in each continent group how they felt when they received their share of the bread.

## Teaching Episode 4

On an overhead or power point, Mrs. Romanova shows a graph that demonstrates the population of the continents and the unequal distribution of resources (Population Reference Bureau, Inc., 2000).

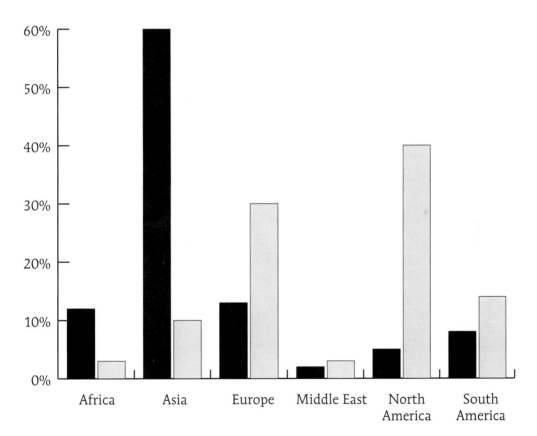

| Continent | Population | Available Resources |
|-----------|-----------|---------------------|
| Africa | 12% | 3% |
| Asia | 60% | 10% |
| Europe | 13% | 30% |
| Middle East | 2% | 3% |
| North America | 5% | 40% |
| South America | 8% | 14% |

Using the above information for reference (easier explanation), Mrs. Romanova points to the resource distributions on the graph as she explains that 12%of the world's people live in Africa but receive only 3% of the world's resources. She continues to read from the above information while pointing out on the graph transparency the percentages of the resources available to each continent. She ask, "Class, is this fair? Is this just? What happens when people do not get enough food to eat?" She continues:

- What is another name for fair? (just)
- What is another name for fairness? (justice)
- What is another name for unfair? (unjust)
- What is another name for unfairness? (injustice)

Mrs. Romanova prints the concepts in large letters on the board and asks students to copy them into their notebook.

**Note:** This activity can also be implemented with M&Ms or cookies.

## Lesson Three

### Concept: Respect for Mother Earth

The teaching of universal values is an essential element of a global education (Case, 1991; Kniep, 1987; Merryfield, 1997). Ozone depletion, global warming, hunger, poverty, overpopulation, and the spread of HIV/AIDS are problems shared by all inhabitants of earth. Universal values promote international understanding and empathy. They bond human families regardless of ability, age, class, culture, ethnicity, gender, race, or sexual orientation. English language learners and/or their parents are immigrants from many countries around the world. They share many values with Americans, such as family, education, employment, opportunities, and quality of life.

One commonality among second language learners and their native language counterparts is respecting Mother Earth. Despite advanced agricultural technology and scientific progress, the land areas of the world's continents are being increasingly depleted of precious nutrients. More and more land loses its fertility as the need for food increases with a growing world population. To respect Mother Earth is the responsibility of every individual living on earth. The concept is made comprehensible to English language learners with visual supports, gestures, guided practice, and role-play (Peregory & Boyle, 2001).

## Materials

cloth earth ball or regular globe, candle, pictures of nature, apples, plastic knives, paper plates, napkins

## Teaching Episode 1

Mrs. Chang forms students' desks into one large circle prior to students' arrival. In the middle of the circle, she places on a small table flowers, a bonsai tree, pine cones, rocks, sand, and postcards of a waterfall and mountains. After students take their seats, she holds up the earth ball and informs them, "Class, today we are learning why it is important to respect Mother Earth." She hands the earth ball to the student nearest to her and asks the student to touch it gently and then hand it to the next student, and so on. After all students have touched the earth ball, Mrs. Chang places the ball amid the display on the little table and lights a candle. The teacher then bows to the display. She walks to the board and prints "respect" in big, colorful letters. She passes out a handout to each student.

Mrs. Chang asks students to write "respect" on the blank part of the picture handout and asks the, "What does this say?" as she points to "respect" on the board. The students respond with "respect." Then, she walks to the center of the circle, smiles, and bows slowly before her students. She tells students, "I have respect for you." She smiles as she looks into her students' eyes. She states, "To respect others and their culture is a very important universal value."

## Teaching Episode 2

Mrs. Chang asks a native and a nonnative speaker of English to sit on the floor in the circle. She asks one student to hold up each item while the other student bows to the item. After each ritual, she states, "We have respect for the flowers." She continues the activity until the students have held up all items and have shown respect. Then, Mrs. Chang asks the students to stand. She holds up the earth ball and asks students to show respect for the world by bowing. Mrs. Chang asks, "What are we doing?" The students respond," Showing respect."

## Reflections

In this lesson, Mrs. Chang met four objectives that facilitated the acquisition of social studies content in comprehensible fashion for second language learners: (1) She conveyed to students that the apple simulates earth; (2) she achieved concept attainment; (3) she was able to provide understanding why it is important to respect Mother Earth; and (4) she demonstrated a global perspective by showing that Mother Earth belongs to all people of the earth and must be respected by all of them. Mrs. Chang employed pedagogy that included gestures, repetition, deliberate speech, role-play, visualization, demonstration, and active student involvement to ensure content comprehension by second language learners.

## Points to Remember

❑ Essential skills in social studies instruction include identifying basic geographic concepts on the world map, such as continents, oceans, latitude, longitude, hemispheres, and time zones.

❑ Teaching abstract concepts is a critical aspect of social studies instruction that includes concepts such as democracy, justice, and respect. These concepts require extensive visualization and repetition techniques to convey their complexity.

❑ Integration of higher-order thinking skills in social studies teaching includes collecting and interpreting information, drawing conclusions, making generalizations and inferences, determining cause-and-effect relationships, finding alternative courses of action, and forming hypotheses and making predictions.

❑ Applying a global perspective to social studies content by providing examples from other parts of the world is an essential component in learning about a rapidly changing, increasingly interdependent world.

# Chapter 23

## *Special Education and the Linguistically Diverse Student*

### KEY ISSUES

❏ Defining learning disabilities

❏ Warning signs of learning disabilities

❏ Identifying learning disabilities in second language learners

❏ Selecting and adapting materials to employ with second language learning disabled students

❏ Characteristics of gifted students

❏ Identifying second language gifted students

❏ Referral and assessment procedures for second language gifted students

❏ Challenging second language gifted students

Mrs. Killcoyne teaches in a third grade inclusive class. Her students' ability levels and learning needs are diverse. Of the 29 children enrolled in her class, three students have been identified as having learning disabilities, one student has been identified as gifted, and five students are ESL learners.

Maria, one of the ESL learners in the class, has recently moved to Florida from her native country of Brazil. Mrs. Killcoyne has noticed that despite Maria's limited proficiency with the English language, her work is consistently creative and imaginative. Maria has an intense interest in science, particularly as it relates to animals, loves to read books (written in Portuguese), has demonstrated artistic talent and excellent interpersonal skills, and learns most concepts rapidly. Maria's parents report that she spends most evenings doing her homework, reading, and writing or illustrating short stories in both English and Portuguese.

Based on Maria's learning characteristics and demonstrated ability, Mrs. Killcoyne has decided to challenge Maria by having her work in cooperative groups with high-ability learners. These groups provide many opportunities for Maria to use high-level thinking skills and nurture her artistic and creative abilities. In addition, Mrs. Killcoyne has decided to maintain an assessment portfolio of Maria's work (in both languages) that will be submitted, along with a nomination form, to begin the process of identifying Maria as a gifted student.

Another of the ESL students, Juan, has been identified as learning disabled. While Juan receives the majority of his instruction from Mrs. Killcoyne, the special education resource LD teacher comes into the general education classroom for 30 minutes a day during reading and works with Juan and the other students with learning disabilities on vocabulary and reading comprehension. Additionally, Juan leaves the general education classroom on Tuesdays and Thursdays during the language arts period to receive bilingual education services.

Although most linguistically diverse students receive their education in the general education classroom, some are referred for special education services if they appear to have special learning needs. If these linguistically diverse students are identified as disabled, gifted, or talented, they can be provided with appropriate special education services. This chapter explores the educational challenges of linguistically diverse students who may be learning disabled as well as those who may be gifted.

## Defining Learning Disabilities

Debate continues over what constitutes a learning disability and how the term should be defined. In fact, more than 40 different definitions for learning disabilities have been proposed (Heward, 2000). However, most states and school districts use either the definition as stated in the Individuals with Disabilities Education Act (IDEA, 1990) or one similar to it. According to IDEA:

> Specific learning disability means a disorder in one or more of the basic psychological processes involved in understanding or in using language, spoken or written, which may manifest itself in an imperfect ability to listen, think, speak, read, write, spell, or do mathematical calculations. The term includes such conditions as perceptual disabilities, brain injury, minimal brain dysfunction, dyslexia, and developmental aphasia. The term does not include children who have learning problems that are primarily the result of visual, hearing, or emotional disabilities, of mental retardation, of emotional disturbance, or of environmental, cultural, or economic disadvantage.

In spite of the numerous definitions, most states and school districts require that three criteria be met to be identified as learning disabled. They include: (1) a severe discrepancy between the child's intellectual ability and achievement; (2) an exclusion criterion or learning problems that cannot be explained by other disabilities or lack of opportunity to learn; and (3) a demonstrated need for special education services (Heward, 2000).

A learning disability is a perplexing condition that interferes with a person's ability to receive, process, or communicate information and affects the ability to read, write, speak, or compute math. The student may also have difficulty with concentration, attention, listening skills, and retaining information. Additionally, various disabilities are associated with learning disabilities, such as:

- Dyslexia—severe difficulty in understanding or using one or more areas of language, including listening, speaking, reading, writing, and spelling

- Dysgraphia—severe difficulty in producing handwriting that is legible and written at an age-appropriate speed
- Dyssemia—severe difficulty with signals, such as social cues
- Dyscalculia—severe difficulty in understanding and using symbols or functions needed for success in mathematics

Students can be identified as learning disabled at any age, but most are noticed during the early elementary grades. Early preschool warning signs of learning disabilities include:

- Late talking compared to other children
- Pronunciation problems
- Slow vocabulary growth, often unable to find the right word
- Difficulty rhyming words
- Trouble learning numbers, the alphabet, days of the week
- Extremely restless and easily distracted
- Trouble interacting with peers
- Poor ability to follow directions or routines (LD Online, 2000)

Warning signs of learning disabilities at the elementary school level include:

- Slow in learning the connection between letters and sounds
- Confusion of basic words (run, eat, want)
- Consistent reading and spelling errors including letter reversals (b/d), inversions (m/w), transpositions (felt/left), and substitutions (house/home)
- Transposition of number sequences and confusion of arithmetic signs
- Slow recall of facts; slow in learning new skills; heavy reliance on memorization (LD Online, 2000)

## Identification of Second Language Students with Learning Disabilities

When English is a second language, it is difficult to determine if a learning disability exists because standardized intelligence and achievement testing procedures primarily assess language. Such tests are often biased against culturally and linguistically diverse students. "On many tests, being able to answer questions correctly too often depends upon having specific culturally-based information or knowledge. If students have not been exposed to that information, then they will not be able to answer certain questions at all or will answer them in a way that is considered incorrect within the majority culture" (Waterman, 2000, p.19). This can lead to misdiagnosis that can result in false positives (students are incorrectly assessed as mildly retarded) or false negatives (students with a mild disability such as a learning disability are overlooked) (McLouglin & Lewis, 1990).

When evaluating linguistically diverse students for special education, examiners should proceed with extreme caution. The assessment process should be as free of cultural and linguistic bias as possible. Measurement devices used in the assessment process must not discriminate on the basis of race, culture, or language (McLoughlin & Lewis, 1994 in Lewis & Doorlag, 1999). Before conducting any formal testing of an LEP student who is a nonnative speaker of English, it is vital to determine the student's preferred language and to conduct a comprehensive language assessment in both English and the native language. When tests or evaluation materials are not available in the student's native language, examiners may find it necessary to use English-language instruments. This must be done with extreme caution; it is a practice fraught with the possibility of misinterpretation. Alterations such as paraphrasing instructions, providing a demonstration of how test tasks are to be performed, reading test items to the student, allowing the student to respond verbally rather than in writing, or allowing the student to use a dictionary may be used. However, if the examiner makes any such alterations, it is important that they be fully detailed in the report describing the student's test performance. Additionally, other assessment procedures such as thorough interviews and observations must also be an integral part of collecting information about the student. It may be particularly useful to gather information from the home environment, which will help the examiner in understanding the student within his or her own culture.

It is further recommended that LEP students participate in a prereferral process before decisions are made about identifying these students as learning disabled (Ortiz, 1986). The prereferral process will help "to determine if appropriate and sufficient approaches have been attempted" (Wallace, Larsen, & Elksnin, 1992, p. 467). This allows the school to adjust instruction or make other classroom modifications and see if these changes address the problem being noted. The prereferral process includes: (1) direct observation of the student in the general education classroom; (2) analyzing how the student behaves and interacts verbally in different settings; and (3) reviewing methods of instruction that are used in the general education classroom. Results should be interpreted cautiously.

# Classroom Adaptations

Most culturally and linguistically diverse students receive all or most of their instruction in general education classes. However, some of these students receive "pull-out" special education and/or bilingual services. Therefore, the four major partners involved in developing the curriculum for the student who is LEP and learning disabled are the parents, the general education teacher, the bilingual teacher, and the special education teacher. This team should undertake the following steps:

1. Meet as a team to begin the planning process. Outline planning steps.
2. Become familiar with the culture and language background of the child.
3. Become familiar with the special learning style and education needs of the child.
4. Prepare an individual instructional plan with short- and long-term goals (an IEP).
5. Develop individualized lessons and materials appropriate to the child's exceptionality.
6. Modify individualized lessons and materials using a "cultural screen" and sensitivity.
7. Refer to resource people for assistance and cooperation in instruction; coordinate services.
8. Evaluate the child's ongoing progress and develop a new IEP, materials, and so forth, as needed.
9. Start the cycle over (Collier & Kalk, 1989, p. 207).

# Selecting Materials

The following guidelines represent some of the many considerations teachers should bear in mind when evaluating, selecting, adapting, or developing materials:

1. Know the specific language abilities of each student.
2. Include appropriate cultural experiences in material adapted or developed.
3. Ensure that material progresses at a rate commensurate with student needs and abilities.

4. Document the success of selected materials.

5. Adapt only specific materials requiring modifications, and do not attempt to change too much at one time.

6. Try out different materials and adaptations until an appropriate education for each student is achieved.

7. Implement materials adaptations strategically to ensure smooth transitions into the new materials.

8. Follow some consistent format or guide when evaluating materials.

9. Be knowledgeable about particular cultures and heritages and their compatibility with selected materials.

10. Follow a well-developed process for evaluating the success of adapted or developed materials as the individual language and cultural needs of students are addressed (Hoover & Collier, 1989, p. 253).

## Adapting Materials

Several guidelines for adapting commercial materials or developing teacher-made materials are discussed in the literature (Harris & Schultz, 1986; Lewis & Doorlag, 1987; Mandell & Gold, 1984). The following list is not designed to be all-inclusive; variations may be required to meet individual needs.

1. Adjust the method of presentation or content.

2. Develop supplemental material.

3. Tape-record directions for the material.

4. Provide alternatives for responding to questions.

5. Rewrite brief sections to lower the reading level.

6. Outline the material for the student before reading a selection.

7. Reduce the number of pages or items on a page to be completed by the student.

8. Break tasks into smaller subtasks.

9. Provide additional practice to ensure mastery.

10. Substitute a similar, less complex task for a particular assignment.

11. Develop simple study guides to complement required materials.

The demographics of American schools are changing. Many students come from ethnic, racial, or linguistic backgrounds that are different from the dominant culture. Like their counterparts, linguistically diverse students will cover the spectrum in their abilities and performance. Some will be able to learn commensurate with their age and grade level, others will be below grade level and, yet, others will be advanced beyond their grade levels. The next part of this chapter addresses the special challenges that teachers will face from second language gifted students.

## The Second Language Gifted Student

Within the identified gifted population, there is well-documented concern for the underrepresentation of certain racial, ethnic, and cultural minorities. The problems of underrepresentation are further compounded for students who have not acquired proficiency in the English language. Several factors have been identified as contributing to the underrepresentation of linguistically diverse students in gifted and talented programs nationwide: (1) lack of teacher training in the identification and referral of gifted students from diverse backgrounds (Burmudez & Rakow, 1990; Frasier et al., 1995, Kitano & Espinosa, 1995; Peterson & Margolin, 1997), resulting in selective referrals; (2) methodological problems affecting assessment of bilingual children and test bias (Gonzales, Bauerle, & Felix-Holt, 1996), and (3) reliance on a deficit-based paradigm that makes recognizing linguistically diverse students' strengths and talents less likely (Frasier et al., 1995; Zappia, 1989).

## Teacher Training and Improving Recognition and Referral

The identification of gifted learners typically begins with the recognition of a student's potential followed by referral for assessment. This initial process should be nonbiased and result in a number of referrals for linguistically diverse learners in proportion to the demographics of the overall school population (Kitano & Espinosa, 1995). The literature on teacher recognition of gifted students (from all populations) suggests that without adequate training, general education teachers have difficulty identifying gifted students. When variations of linguistic and cultural backgrounds are added, the identification process becomes more problematic for untrained teachers. Recent research suggests that teachers often overlook students from linguistic and ethnic minority groups when making nominations for student participation in gifted and talented programs. Teachers use "existing ideals and moralities of the dominant culture as their guide in assessing children's giftedness" (Peterson & Margolin, 1997, p. 82).

# Referral Procedures and Assessment

The most frequently discussed reasons for the underrepresentation and limited participation of minority students and English language learners in gifted programs are related to assessment. The issue is extremely complex and centers on test bias and lack of validity in many standardized instruments for the assessment of bilingual children (Gonzales et al., 1996); differences in test performance among racial, cultural, or ethnic groups; and "effects of cultural, economic, and language differences or deprivations on the ability of minority students to achieve at levels associated with giftedness" (Frasier et al., 1997 p. 498).

Traditionally, once the gifted learner is identified by a knowledgeable adult familiar with the student (teacher, parent), a referral is then made for assessment. Specific referral procedures and assessment protocol vary from state to state and frequently within a state's school districts. Typically, assessment of the student's potential involves collecting data such as the results of intelligence tests, achievement tests, and creativity tests. Additionally, the student's work samples are reviewed along with rating scales and nomination forms completed by the student, parents, teacher, and/or peers. Once all the data are gathered and evaluated, a site-based team makes a determination regarding the student's identification as "gifted" and what kind of services will be provided (Kitano & Espinosa, 1995).

In an attempt to address identification problems and increase the participation of minority students in gifted programs, many states now advocate the use of multiple criteria, but problems remain. Frasier et al. (1997) remind us that despite these good intentions, problems in identifying gifted minority students continue to challenge educators. There is general agreement that the identification procedures of gifted language-minority students should include the use of multiple criteria. Kitano and Espinosa (1995) posit that the assessment of these students should include: (1) formal, informal, and dynamic assessment procedures that are objective and subjective, reliable, and valid for that population; (2) flexible criteria that promote inclusion versus exclusion; (3) assessment in the student's dominant language(s) by a qualified professional; and (4) a comprehensive measure of a student's abilities and performance across varied contexts. The use of portfolio and/or a case study procedure has been recommended as one way to view a holistic measure of a student's performance (Robisheaux & Banbury, 1994; Zappia, 1989). Zappia (1989) proposed that the identification and selection of gifted Hispanic students be conducted by an interdisciplinary team of professionals "committed to including greater numbers of minorities and accepting a multidimensional definition of giftedness. This team should include members who are knowledgeable in the areas of second language acquisition, bilingual education, cultural differences, and issues related to minority assessment" (p. 25).

## Identification of Gifted Second Language Students—Characteristics to Note

The identification of gifted children from culturally diverse groups is affected by a restricted definition of giftedness. The individual student's cultural values, language and ethnicity must be included and considered. Each culture brings a unique definition and value system of personality variables, cognitive attributes, and behavioral descriptions of what may be perceived as "giftedness" within the culture. In a recent study by Frasier et al. (1995), characteristics of giftedness in minority, language-minority, and economically disadvantaged populations were explored. Ten core attributes associated with giftedness were identified to provide a better basis for establishing procedures to recognize, identify, and plan educational experiences for gifted students from minority or economically disadvantaged families and areas (1995, p. 16):

1. **Motivation: Evidence of desire to learn.** Forces that initiate, direct, and sustain individual or group behavior to satisfy a need or attained goal.

2. **Communication skills: Highly expressive and effective use of words, numbers, symbols, etc.** Transmission and reception of signals or meanings through a system of symbols (codes, gestures, language, and numbers).

3. **Interest: Intense (sometimes unusual) interests.** Activities, avocations, objects, etc. that have special worth or significance and are given special attention.

4. **Problem-solving ability: Effective (often inventive) strategies for recognizing and solving problems.** Process of determining a correct sequence of alternatives leading to a desired goal or successful completion or performance of task.

5. **Imagination/Creativity: Ability to produce many ideas; highly original.** Process of forming mental images of objects, qualities, situations, or relationships, which are not immediately apparent to the senses; ability to solve problems by pursuing nontraditional patterns of thinking.

6. **Memory: Large storehouse of information on school or nonschool topics.** Exceptional ability to retain and retrieve information.

7. **Inquiry: Ability to question, experiment, explore.** Method or process of seeking knowledge, understanding, or information.

8. **Insight: Ability to grasp new concepts quickly and make connections; ability to sense deeper meanings.** Sudden discovery of the correct solution following incorrect attempts based on primary trial and error.

9. **Reasoning: Logical approaches to figuring out solutions.** Highly conscious, directed, controlled, active, intentional, forward-looking, goal-oriented thought.

10. **Humor: Ability to convey and pick up on humor well.** Ability to synthesize key ideas or problems in complex situations in a humorous way; exceptional sense of timing in words and gestures.

## Challenging the Gifted Second Language Student: Methods and Strategies

The strategies of teaching gifted students are closely aligned with best practices in TESOL theory and practice (Robisheax & Banbury, 1994). "Learning activities that establish a learning environment that promotes creativity, integration and synthesis encourages cooperation and idea exchange. In turn, cooperation and idea exchange necessitate the natural usage of language in a grammatically unstructured setting" (Robisheax & Banbury, 1994, p. 29). Kitano (1995, p. 246) recommended several general strategies for challenging the gifted second language learner:

1. Incorporating instructional strategies appropriate for the gifted, irrespective of the language of instruction (e.g., strategies that promote higher-level thinking, integration of subject-matter areas using thematic approaches, and challenging context).

2. Taking advantage of student strengths such as problem solving, creativity, and primary-language ability.

3. Demonstrating high expectation by providing a content-rich curriculum that promotes students' content mastery and provides opportunities for in-depth study.

4. Employing student-centered approaches that promote students' active involvement and engagement in learning.

5. Providing oral and written language development in English or native language throughout all aspects of instruction.

6. Valuing students' languages, cultures, and experiences and promoting their self-esteem.

While a detailed outline of the teaching models frequently used in gifted education is beyond the scope of this chapter, the reader is encouraged to explore *Teaching Models in the Education of the Gifted* by June Maker and Aleene B. Nielson (1995) and *Critical Issues in Gifted Education: Defensible Programs for Cultural and Ethnic Minorities* by June Maker and Shirley Schiever (1989) for a comprehensive review of teaching-learning models for gifted students.

Adopting broader and multidimensional perspectives of intelligence has a far-reaching impact on curriculum development and instructional strategies for all gifted learners, particularly for those with limited English proficiency. Howard Gardner's Theory of Multiple Intelligences (1993) provides an example of a broader perspective of this construct. Gardner has identified eight intelligences: verbal-linguistic, logical-mathematical, visual-spatial, musical-rhythmic, bodily-kinesthetic, naturalistic, interpersonal, and intrapersonal. There are many excellent resources available for classroom teachers that transform the multiple intelligences theory into practical classroom applications for thematic unit instruction. *The Intelligent Curriculum* by David Lazear (2000) and *Multiple Intelligences in the Classroom* by Thomas Armstrong (1994) are two such examples. Tables 23-1 and 23-2 illustrate examples of multiple intelligences (MI) thematic units appropriate for second language learners. This intermediate grade-level unit can be modified to meet the individual language and learning needs of students. The activities presented can be done individually or in cooperative groups.

## Howard Gardner's Eight Intelligences Explained

### Verbal/Linguistic

This intelligence involves the capacity to use words effectively in many forms: This might be demonstrated orally (story-teller, politician, or orator) in written form (poet, playwright, editor, or journalist).

### Visual/Spatial

Strengths in this intelligence involve the ability to perceive the visual-spatial world in an expansive manner. This intelligence involves sensitivity to color, line, shapes, form, space, and the relationships that exist among those elements.

### Logical/Mathematical

This intelligence involves the capacity to use numbers effectively, reason well, use sensitivity to logical patterns and relationships (particularly cause-and-effect and if-then relationships), understand classifications and categorization systems, and inference and hypothesis testing.

### Bodily/Kinesthetic

Strength in this intelligence is demonstrated in the ability to use one's body to express ideas and feelings (actor, mime, athlete, or dancer). This intelligence also includes abilities that involve the use of one's hands to produce or transform things (craftsperson, sculptor, mechanic, or surgeon).

### Musical/Rhythmic

This intelligence involves the capacity to work with musical forms. An individual with strengths in this intelligence would, for example, be able to perceive, discriminate, transform, and express musical forms in the ways that music critics, performers, and composers would.

### Interpersonal

Strengths in the interpersonal intelligence are reflected in the way an individual is able to perceive and make distinctions in the moods, intentions, motivations, and feelings of others. This intelligence is often associated with a "people person," one who has a capacity to "read" people and use this knowledge effectively in a number of ways.

### Intrapersonal

This intelligence revolves around self-knowledge and the ability to act adaptively with that knowledge. This intelligence includes knowing and understanding one's own strengths and limitations and having a keen awareness of one's own moods, motivations, desires, and self-image.

### Naturalistic

An individual with strengths in this intelligence is highly sensitive to and stimulated by all aspects of nature, including plants, animals, the weather, and the physical features of Earth. It includes skills such as recognizing various categories and varieties of animals, insects, plants, and flowers as well as the ability to grow things and care for and train animals.

# Table 23-1. Example of MI Thematic Unit on Cuban Culture

| Multiple Intelligences | Content Areas | | |
| --- | --- | --- | --- |
| | Language Arts | Social Studies | Math / Science |
| **Verbal-Linguistic** | Read and research the works of a contemporary Cuban author. Illustrate or translate the work to share with the class. | Create a 5-minute narrated video production promoting tourism in Cuba. | Create several mathematical word problems using Cuban demographic data. |
| **Logical-Mathematical** | Research and report the demographics of the Cuban population including average family income, educational levels, etc. | Create an annotated outline or timeline explaining Cuban history. | Compare and contrast the economy of Cuba with that of a country of your choice. |
| **Visual-Spatial** | Create a political poster or a collage of life in Cuba pre- and post-Castro. Write a narrative to explain your work. Research the works of contemporary Cuban artists---use posters and/or postcards of artist's work and present your findings to the class (written or oral report). | Create and sketch a political cartoon for a newspaper of your choice. | Design and draw to scale the perfect "raft" to be used by political refugees and explain why your raft would be superior (weight, dimensions, materials used, etc.). |
| **Musical-Rhythmic** | Research the African influence on Cuban music and prepare a written or oral report on your findings. | Research Cuban musical artists-bring samples of their music to class and share your research of their life and musical influence (written or oral report). | |
| **Bodily-Kinesthetic** | Role-play one of the works of your favorite Cuban authors. | Perform several typical Cuban dances for the class (alone or with a partner). | Investigate the math and/or science behind the construction of typical Cuban musical instruments. |
| **Naturalistic** | | Create a diorama depicting Cuba's natural resources. | Design a collage depicting Cuba's climate, wildlife, and natural habitat. Explain your collage. |
| **Interpersonal** | In a cooperative group, write a play about the life of a young Cuban child now living in Cuba. | Learn one of the typical Cuban childhood games and teach it to the class. | |
| **Intrapersonal** | Write an essay sharing your personal feelings about Cuba's political situation. OR write a "journal" of your imagined trip to the United States aboard a raft. | | |

## Table 23-2. Example of MI Thematic Unit on Mythology & Folklore: Aztec/Mexicana Creation Myths

| Multiple Intelligences | Content Areas | | |
|---|---|---|---|
| | Language Arts | Social Studies | Math / Science |
| Verbal-Linguistic | 1. Read The Creation & Legend of the Four Suns, Lacandon Creation Myth, or another Aztec legend of myth of your choice and retell the story using props. 2. In cooperative groups, write a screenplay for the myth you read. 3. Write an original myth or legend. | Compare and contrast Aztec creation myths or legends with creation myths from another culture or time period (North American Indian myths or European creation myths). Discuss or write the similarities and differences. | 1. Many of these myths and legends reference the heavenly skies and constellations. Research these constellations and share your findings in a multimedia presentation. 2. Research the astronomical differences between then and now. |
| Logical-Mathematical | | Create a timeline depicting the history of Mexico and the Mexican people. | List all the characters in the legends you researched. Create a classification system based on similarities and differences of these characters. |
| Visual-Spatial | | Research Aztec art and symbolism. Share your findings in a multimedia presentation. | Create a diagram mapping some of the constellations mentioned in the legends. |
| Musical-Rhythmic | After reading one of the myths or legends of the Aztec people, create music as a background for the story. | Research typical Mexican folk music and dance. Bring in some music to share with the class. | Identify the musical instruments depicted in Aztec art. Draw (to scale) these instruments and explain how you think they were made and what they were made from. |
| Bodily-Kinesthetic | Act out one of the legends without using words. Use music and props to help you create the scene. | Demonstrate a typical Mexican folk dance for the class. Teach your friends this dance and choreograph a performance. | |
| Naturalistic | Many of the legends use animals as part of the symbolism. List the animals used, their traits in their natural habitat, and their traits in the legend. | | |
| Interpersonal | | | |
| Intrapersonal | Reflect on the legend or myth you read. Choose one of the characters that you identify with and describe who you are. | Compare this culture's religious or spiritual beliefs to your own. | |

## Points to Remember

❏  Within the identified exceptional student population,
    there is well-documented concern for the under- or
    overrepresentation of certain racial, ethnic, and cultural
    minorities. Culturally and linguistically diverse students
    tend to be underrepresented in programs for the gifted, but
    may be overrepresented in programs for students with
    learning disabilities.

❏  One of the most frequently discussed reasons for the
    underrepresentation or overrepresentation of minority
    students in special education programs is related to
    assessment.

❏  There is general agreement that the identification
    procedures of gifted and learning disabled culturally and
    linguistically diverse students should include the use of
    multiple criteria.

❏  The identification of gifted children from culturally diverse
    groups is affected by a restricted definition of giftedness.
    The individual student's cultural values, language, and
    ethnicity must be included and considered.

❏  Teachers need to be trained in the identification and
    referral of students from culturally and linguistically
    diverse backgrounds.

❏  A much broader and multidimensional perspective of
    intelligence has far-reaching impact on curriculum
    development and instructional strategies for all learners.

❏  Teachers should make culturally sensitive adaptations to
    their instruction and materials.

# Chapter 24

## *Using Technology with English Learners*

## KEY ISSUES

- ❏ Using the Internet with English language learners
- ❏ How to teach technology effectively
- ❏ Language practice for communication
- ❏ Technology for primary grades
- ❏ Technology for intermediate grades
- ❏ Classroom resources
- ❏ Using the Internet
- ❏ Hypermedia
- ❏ Creating Web pages
- ❏ Ideas for classroom activities
- ❏ Problems to anticipate
- ❏ Interesting ESOL Websites

Mrs. Sato was excited when her school purchased new computers and she was able to network two of the new units within her classroom. She spent a great deal of time planning activities around these computers, even designing rotational activities to keep students engaged while small groups were at the computers. She was aware that many teachers used computers for drill-and-practice activities with ESOL students that required only the lower-level cognitive skills of rote memory and application. She was determined that her classes would be different. Commercial software programs designed for students learning English as a second or other language existed, but Mrs. Sato would have to find them herself and then seek funding to purchase them for her site. The task of designing computer assisted activities that would engage all class members in an equal manner would take considerable time and ingenuity and she questioned whether one teacher, with no classroom assistance, could find the time to take on this responsibility in addition to meeting other administrative expectations. She decided it would be worth the trouble to give it her best shot.

Slowinski (2000) voiced what most technology-oriented people are well aware of today; information-savvy multicultural young people hold the promise of the future in their hands, but only if schools offer them the challenge to become effective information-age workers and global citizens.

Through existing and emerging technologies, teachers are able to integrate technology and literacy to prepare students for the digital future. According to the TESOL (Teaching English to Speakers of Other Languages) Association ESL Standards, the majority of students in more than 50 U.S. cities are minorities. Technology can enhance language instruction by offering a broad range of opportunities to expand teaching and learning environments (Bush & Terry, 1997; Cummins, 1989; Dunkel, 1991; Gardner & Garcia, 1996; Little, 1996; Voller & Pickard, 1996). CALL (computer-assisted language learning) has been recognized as a valuable language learning tool for over 20 years (Dunkel, 1991; Levy, 1997) if used appropriately (Grosse & Leto, 1999). It is the responsibility of the classroom teacher to become educated in the implementation of software that will most benefit English language learners. Additionally, the educator needs to understand and "buy into" the benefits gained from making the shift from traditional textbooks that offer grammar instruction to a technology-enhanced curriculum that offers real time or virtual language instruction.

## Using Technology in Second Language Instruction

The use of technology today is apparent in a variety of media. Students are introduced to and master technology at an early age. Language is best learned by practicing in authentic contexts. Situations provided by use of the Internet offer a setting for whole language learning (Freeman & Freeman, 1992). Authentic language use, essential for second language learning (Brown, 1994; Diaz-Rico & Weed, 1995; Gass & Selinker, 1995) is accessible when children communicate with penpals and others via e-mail, dual-vision videoconferences, chat sites, Internet telephone calls, and other synchronous forms of computer technology. Typically, English learners need more interactive language practice than is offered in daily classes. By using the Internet and software programs designed for language learners, students are empowered by self-regulated, autonomous learning. They use computer-based technology to reinforce instruction and practice interactive and experiential second language learning (Cummins, 1989; Freeman & Freeman, 1992; Freire, 1970; Higgins, 1991). Overall, computer-mediated teaching by using the Web and the Internet prepares students for the information society of technology literacy, and ensures that education is more effective (Van Assche, 1998; Warschauer, 1996).

## The Teacher's Role

To be most effective in the electronic classroom, the teacher's role is manifested through a variety of formats: tutor, supervisor, teacher, assistant, and inevitably, technician (Fox, 1998). Instruction needs to be designed to interface with curriculum that is integrated and enhanced by technology (Fox, 1998) while maintaining a strong focus on literacy. In fact, technology can assist the teacher by providing software for record and grade maintenance, programs that create documents, newsletters, and flyers that depict the school's special events, and any number of published classroom materials.

Teachers must be cognizant of the responsibilities that accompany the incorporation of technology in the classroom. The teacher must be extremely well prepared for the lessons and have examined the content, site availability, and appropriateness of the language and level of difficulty involved in the task. Additionally, teachers must identify the appropriate level of student skills, actively monitor student activities, and above all, always prepare an alternate plan in anticipation of the inevitable technological glitches.

## Language Practice for Communication

Advanced use of electronic mail is one of the most effective instructional tools for language learners (Nagel, 1999). Students participate in activities that provoke collaboration with classmates, other peers, and teachers, resulting in an electronic community where learners create, analyze, and produce information (Belisle, 1996). Studies show that students who use e-mail to improve their language communication skills are more inclined to share ideas, which can develop an intimate community within the class (Lapp, 2000; Maring, Wiseman, & Meyers, 1997; Wilkins, 1991).

Through appropriate and guided Internet use, students can exchange ideas with individuals from other cultures, make new friends, and link abstract concepts with real life (Van Assche, 1998). Students engage in conversation as they exchange ideas and opinions, and express feelings and emotions, while gaining a vast resource of authentic material pertinent to other cultures (LeLoup & Ponerio, 1996). English learners can participate in multilingual communities at home and around the world, thus using English within and beyond the school setting. They share cross-cultural information with native and non-native English-speaking penpals (English being the medium) as they practice basic writing skills.

E-mail can be used as a way to have students deliver their homework assignments to the teacher. Students can surf the Interet to find sites that pertain to the content being studied and e-mail their findings to the teacher (Gibbons, 1991; Sperling, 1999). Teachers can assign a wide variety of educational tasks (Warschauer, 1999) that integrate technology with content. Students can keep vocabulary lists, summarize short stories or articles, investigate research, and do assignments on the computer. These activities encourage the students to surf the Web selectively. Remember to have the students attach a copy of the article or short story being reviewed to avoid plagiarism. To ensure Web searches are more productive, teachers should create accompanying assignments that necessitate information retrieval, such as a scavenger hunt or an information search that needs to be completed by a certain deadline. Teachers should also find and explore appropriate Websites to share with the class prior to having students surf the Web.

Overall, using e-mail and the Internet offers dynamic, open-ended, unconstrained possibilities for language teachers and students (Haworth, 1995). Electronic discussion may result in more equal classroom participation as students can work at their own pace, thus eliminating the need to prepare various lesson plans to account for disparity between higher-and lower-level verbal proficiency of students.

However, while e-mail may boost the students' ability to use complex, formal, and more sophisticated language in written electronic discussions, there can be a disadvantage to e-mail use as well (Johnson, 1991; Piper, 1986). Language without the accompanying visual cues such as facial expression, eye contact, and posture is decontextualized and as such, lacks the embedded cues that assist in deciphering meaning (Lapp, 2000).

The use of new technologies for English learners in the classroom continues to develop at a staggering speed, but fortunately, this growth is accompanied by the general desire to make language teaching more responsive to the learner's needs (Tudor, 1996).

## Technology for Primary Grades

Young English learners respond to visual and auditory stimulation, and interactive, comprehensible technology is attractive to children of any age (Ashworth & Wakefield, 1994). Cultures reflect language; the two are irrevocably intertwined (McKay & Hornberger, 1996; Romaine, 1994) and the teacher must be sensitive to the child new to the American culture. While integrating technology into the curriculum, teachers can demonstrate value for the child's culture by creating assignments that reflect interest and multicultural appreciation.

Preliterate children need exposure to written language. Several software programs exist that offer phonics instruction, such as *Rock N' Learn.* The sounds of the English alphabet are presented in isolation as well as in simple context words. Other programs such as *Kids Works, Kids Pix,* and *Roxie's ABC Fish* fascinate children because of the graphic arts, clever songs, lively music, and talking animated figures that teach vocabulary and other simple language tasks. Teachers need to screen software programs for suitability and desired objectives. Listening comprehension, pronunciation, reading, and writing are language skills that can be greatly enhanced by the interactive CD-Roms available today. With *Living books,* which are available in several languages, children can listen to stories in their native language. After understanding the theme and content, they can then listen and play the games in English using their prior knowledge to enhance comprehensible input.

## Technology for Intermediate English Learners

Intermediate learners first need to know word processing and how to manipulate the keyboard (Daiute, 1985). Knowledge of word processing in one program is easily transferred to another. Many of the e-mail activities mentioned previously are well-suited for the intermediate student, again depending upon language proficiency. Typing self-created stories, dictation, freewriting or focused freewriting, or vocabulary words are common activities for students beginning to use word processing. Later, revising, editing, spell and grammar check, and cutting and pasting will assist in speedier writing facility, thus making writing more enjoyable.

Many studies show that students who write using word processing programs develop better papers and enjoy writing more (Neu & Scarcella, 1991; Phinney, 1991).

Intermediate English learners have more facility with browsing the Web than do younger learners. Focused browsing, as assigned by the teacher, can engage students in interesting interactive activities that use authentic language in naturally occurring, pragmatic contexts. Understanding is assured by visuals, written text, and context-embedded clues. CD-ROMs, DVDs, *Encarta, National Geographic*, and other computer technology can enhance content learned in the classroom. Teachers can create and use pre-made lessons and ancillary materials to scaffold learning.

## Classroom Resources

Recommended resources needed for conducting on-line lessons include: high-speed Internet access, at least one computer per two students, a LAN (local area network), and a networked printer. Wide varieties of software and mechanical devices are available and appropriate for language learners. Some of the technological marvels that exist and are emerging daily to enhance all skill areas in language acquisition include: interactive electronic and hypermedia books with many context clues, software that functions using a language experience approach (students write at their own levels), and age and gender appropriate speech synthesizers that pronounce accurately (for listening comprehension and pronunciation practice).

## Using the Internet

Students first learn how to use the Internet for research purposes. The teacher introduces the concept of the Web, the tools used to search for information, and the differences in search engines and browsers. It is important that teachers guide students in brainstorming and concept mapping the topic before the Internet search begins. It is also helpful to identify words or phrases and synonyms to streamline searches and save time at the computer. Students become proficient using browers, such as Netscape and Explorer, moving back and forth between sites, bookmarking favorite sites, and downloading data and images. Exploring Web sites and databases also requires that students have the skills to evaluate the available information.

Teachers should distribute evaluation sheets or rubrics listing criteria the students must consider when gathering information as the task or activity is assigned. A suggestion for a beginning rubric could be:

- 20% data collection
- 20% group collaboration
- 20% written summary
- 20% class presentation
- 20% graphics and visuals

The rubric should be determined by the lesson objectives.

## Hypermedia for Constructivist Classrooms

Another valuable technological tool that students enjoy is *Hypermedia* (such as the World Wide Web) because they can receive and create a great deal of information in a fascinating manner. Using a multisensory approach, colorful graphics, sound, and video are connected by clicking links that create vibrant interactive programs (Burns, Roe, & Ross, 1999; Dillner, 1993, 1994). Students can use *Hypermedia* to author their own mini-lessons on a variety of topics, or create books, presentations, stories, games, and lessons. *Hypermedia* authoring requires students to compose text, insert graphics, and insert sound. HyperStudio, Kids Media Magic, Magic Media Slate, and MediaWeaver are other popular *Hypermedia* programs. Be aware, however, that navigating the many links used to create associations in *Hypermedia* applications may confuse the learner.

## Creating Web Pages

Tan et al. (1999) suggest that online classrooms, where students create Web pages, promote cooperative learning and creativity, and instruction is integrated with higher-level cognitive skills. Advanced classes can design a Web page using a very simple program such as *Claris HomePage,* or *FrontPage.* Students have a great opportunity to practice language and publish their writing on their Web site. Some ideas for publication include: creating an English newspaper, writing a personal opinion essay, reviewing a play, researching and writing biographies, reporting on cultural festivals from both e-mail contacts and cultural research, or simply writing a letter to friend or a business. The possibilities for incorporating technology into the multilingual classroom are endless.

## Ideas for Classroom Activities

### Activity 1: World culture reports

Each student chooses any spot on the globe for a social studies class report. Using the Internet, students need to: (1) find a map of the country; (2) investigate the area, discover, and be able to explain a traditional celebration; (3) find a picture of a native costume; (4) choose traditional, cultural foods; (5) cut and paste information into a report booklet to be shared with classmates.

### Activity 2: Using the Internet to find an online newspaper from another country.

Playing the role of the reporter/observer, students will imagine themselves as reporters and will select an issue to write about. Allow a student to interview a mock witness about a historical event and write a column to put in a mock-up paper.

## Activity 3: Creating an advertising campaign

Students choose or invent a product. Then they create an advertising campaign to sell the product and design an advertisement. The teacher initiates this activity by discussing the media and its influence over society and our images of what an ideal male or female should be. The teacher asks questions such as, "What are the messages students get through the various mediums?" Students then gather pictures and slogans from old magazines and put together a collage or poster with a written explanation of the message interpreted. They then try to sell their product to the class. Students use the Web to support their research.

## Problems to Anticipate

One of the major problems is time constraint. Students may be in departmentalized settings where time is brief. Advanced planning by the teacher should include giving instructions, offering background information to facilitate the activity, and making sure that students are always engaged and on task to make the most of a tight schedule.

Teachers may be overwhelmed with questions from students who are not familiar with the operations of the computer. One way to solve this problem is to appoint technology teams using students who have more advanced computer expertise and can be called upon to assist those less sure of the technology.

Whenever technology is used there will be some unexpected glitches. The best way to plan for these events is to have alternative activities planned.

Finally, the teacher must be familiar with the programs used by the students and realize that they might become confused in the navigation of the multitude of links. Without the teacher's advance knowledge of the equipment and program, the students with questions are at a disadvantage. Time is wasted when a teacher is unable to model the activity.

## Resources and ESOL Websites for Teachers and Students

The Internet TESOL Journal
Articles and links for teachers.
www.uoregon.edu/~call/student.html

Center for Applied Linguistics
http://www.cal.org

Hands on English (for ESL teachers and tutors of adult ESL)
http://www.4w.com.how/

National Clearinghouse for Bilingual Education (NCBE)
http://ncbe.gwu.edu/

Office of Multicultural Students Language Education (ONSLE)
(Florida DOE)
www.firn.edu/doe/bin0011/eghoc.htm

Scholastic
http://www.scholastic.com

TESOL, Inc. Home Page
www.tesol.org

Center for Research on Education, Diversity and Excellence (CREDE)
http://www.crede.ucsc.edu  and http://www.cal.org/crede

Consortium for School Networking
info@eff.org

ERIC Clearinghouse on Information and Technology
eric@ericir.syr.edu

International Society for Technology in Education
iste@oregon.uoregon.edu

Research-It: Your One-Stop Reference Desk
http://www.itools.com/
A great site to find tools to help teachers and learners and includes
    dictionary, thesaurus, maps, translator, quote reference, etc.

Books for Teaching Languages Using the Internet Linda Thalman's
    Website (useful list with annotations)
http://www.wfi.fr/volterre/biblio.html

Interactive Internet Language Learning—
http://babel.uoregon.edu/yamada/interact.html
This site offers an explanation of various modes of using the Internet
    for language learning

ESLoop—http://www.linguisticfunland.com/esloop/esloop.sites.html
A variety of sites for English language teaching and learning.

Dave's ESL Cafe—http://eslcafe.com/
Site with a huge number of links for teachers of English language
    learners

The Linguistic Funland TESL Page
This site is a resource for teachers and students and offers books,
    lessons, activities, and much more.
http://www.linguistic-funland.com/test.html

WWW Activities that Work (and Why!)
Volker Hegelheimer, Douglas Mills, Ann Salzmann
http://www.iei.uiuc.edu/resources/TESOL/WWW_activities.html

English as a Foreign Language Magazine
Great resources with jobs, activities, links and worldwide connections.
EFL Web—http://www.eflWeb.com/

Internet TESOL Journal—teaching techniques, resources, activities, etc.
http://www.aitech.ac.jp/~iteslj/

Selected links for ESL teachers. Games, activities, lessons, etc.
http://www.aitech.ac.jp/~iteslj/ESL3a.html

Selected easy to navigate sites and links for students
http://www.aitech.ac.jp/~iteslj/ESL.html

TESL Electronic Discussion Lists and Newsgroups for many topics of
    interest.
http://www.linguistic-funland.com.tesllist.html

The PuzzleMaker—Puzzles for teachers and students to make. Word
    search, cryptograms, criss-cross puzzles; enter your text and print
    out a puzzle for the classroom
http://puzzlemaker.school.discovery.com/

The Adult Education Teacher's Annotated Webliography Reviews of
    Websites for adult education and ESL
http://www2.wgbh.org/mbcweis/ltc/alri/Webliography.html

Intercultural E-Mail Classroom Connections
http://www.civilsoc.org//penpals/iecc.htm

Internet Treasure Hunts for ESL Students—A project of the Internet
    TESL journal
http://www.aitech.ac.jp/~iteslj/th/

National Clearinghouse for ESL Literacy Education—links to the ERIC
    database
http://www.sagrelto.com/elandh/Incles1.htm

Karin's ELS PartyLand —a comprehensive resource site for both teachers
    and students
http://www.eslpartyland.com/

Accents in English with eViews—Advanced listening comprehension;
    listen to native English speakers for accent and pronunciation
    practice.
http://www.eviews.net/

Randall's ESL Cyber Listening Lab—Listening skill practice.
http://www.esl.lab.com

TeachTech—A List for Technology and Language Teacher Educators
http://languagecenter.cla.umn.edu:16080/teachtech/

Web Enhanced Language Learning (WELL) Project-skills for language
    learners.
http://www.well.ac.uk/menu.html

The ESL Quiz Center
http://www.pacificnet.net/~sperling/quiz
Tests students' knowledge of verbs, prepositions, clauses, punctuation,
    etc.
**Multilevel; particularly good for lower levels**

Guide to Grammar and Writing
http://Webster.commnet.edu/HP/pages/darling/grammar.htm

The Amazing Picture Machine
http://www.ncrtec.org/picture.htm
This site offers an extensive collection of pictures for use by teachers or
   students and sample lesson plans geared towards K–12, which can
   be adapted for adults.

englishtown.com
http://www.englishtown.com
An on-line ESL community with daily lesson plans, pen-pals,
   dictionaries, and English grammar self-test, etc.

Dave's ESL Cafe
http://www.pacificnet.net/~sperling
This is one of the most comprehensive sites for ESL students and
   teachers. It includes ESL chat, discussion forums and various ESL
   links.

LinguaCenter Homepage
http://deil.lang.uiuc.edu/index2.htm
An extensive site for ESL activities with many good links for many
   levels.

Exchange Index
http://deil.lang.uiuc.edu/exchange
An online magazine where ESL students can publish their work.

## More Websites for lower levels

### Internet Skills:
The Lingua Center Search Page
http://deil.lang.uiuc.edu/Web.pages/lcsearch.html
A guide to search engines for ESL students.

ICYouSee, A Guide to the World Wide Web
http://www.ithaca.edu/library/Training/ICYouSee.html
A Critical Guide to the Web
Lesson
**Internet Search Lesson One**
**Internet Search Lesson Two**

## http://www.englishforum.com

Comprehensive Web with numerous resources for students
and teachers of English (ESL/EFL). Interactive Exercises, Message
Boards, ELT Book Catalogue, Good School Guide, Web Directory,
World News, Learning and Teaching Links, Useful Tools, and more...

Language Learning Websites on the Internet
http://www.cuhk.edu.hk/eltu/elt108/internet.html

INTERNATIONAL CENTER HOME PAGE NEWS
http://206.14.7.53/intcenter/esl2.htm
The International Center for the San Francisco Public Library: ESL
    Resources with many good links.

Frizzy University Network HomePage A site for improving grammar,
    writing, and a huge variety of other resources.
http://thecity.sfsu.edu/~funWeb

# Points to Remember

- ❑ Internet use produces learner autonomy but some initial training must take place in order to direct students to valid information for creating individual projects.

- ❑ Students must be provided with the knowledge of technology vocabulary in English so it can be used properly.

- ❑ Students must learn to evaluate Web sites and understand that any quality of material can be published on the Internet.

- ❑ Students should be taught and must understand what plagiarism is and that copyright laws must be obeyed.

- ❑ Consideration of the expense of keeping a service provider up and running must be a priority for the school.

- ❑ Teachers must be willing to shift the paradigm from the old lecture and textbook style to the new technologies.

# Appendix A

# A Rainbow of Children: A Sampler of Cultural Characteristics

The following characteristics are not comprehensive, but are general, overarching tendencies and characteristics of individuals from Spanish-speaking, Muslim, Haitian, Asian, and Native American cultures. The purpose of highlighting these cultural groups is to demonstrate the differences and similarities teachers can expect to find in today's diverse classrooms. By understanding the cultural values of their students, teachers can plan more effective instruction while incorporating a variety of techniques to address the multitude of learning styles.

## Spanish-Speaking Cultures

Spanish-speaking cultures include people from many countries (including the United States) with unique characteristics. The common thread, of course, is the fact that they all speak Spanish, albeit with varying degrees of fluency, accents, intonation, verb structures (i.e. *tú, usted,* and *vos*) and certainly different connotations for similar words. These societal variations can be likened to the differences among the United States, Great Britain, Australia, New Zealand, Canada, Jamaica, and South Africa. These countries are extremely different from one another, yet they all claim English as their native language.

Examine the following scenario and discuss the assumption made.

*Two young men are shopping in the local supermarket and are conversing in Spanish. Two American young ladies hear the gentlemen talking and say, "Those Spanish guys are handsome!"*

The statement is not negative, and the young men are speaking Spanish, but they might not be from Spain. To say an individual is Spanish is equivalent to hearing someone speak English and calling them English (from England). A Spanish speaker is often called Hispanic (traditionally associated with the Iberian Peninsula), or Latino/a (usually referring to the population from the Americas). Much debate arises with regard to this kind of labeling, but it is safe to say that being called Latino/a versus Hispanic depends on the individual's preference. Non-Hispanics probably are more familiar with the term Hispanic in reference to all Spanish-speaking individuals.

Statistics show that Spanish speakers are the fastest-growing population in the United States. The United States Bureau of the Census projected that by the year 2020, 15% of the population will be Hispanic, an increase from 9% in 1992. Many factors impact the academic and cognitive development of Spanish-speaking students, including the heritage of their families, the length of time residing in the United States, the educational level attained, and socioeconomic level reached. Carrasquillo (1991) notes that Hispanic students are diverse due to different backgrounds, but they may share general experiences through family structure, religious beliefs, and general customs. However, they are in a country that does not always value diversity, but rather appreciates uniformity through a common language, culture, and race.

The following charts are general characteristics of customs observed by Hispanic/Latinos (taken from the book *Culturegrams,* produced by Brigham Young University) as an "aid to the understanding of, feeling for, and communication with other people." Although distinct regions and countries have their own styles (e.g., in Colombia women will shake the wrist of another woman instead of shaking her hand), the general customs may be similar throughout most Spanish-speaking countries.

## Greetings

- A handshake is shared at the very least; sometimes a full embrace. It is very important to greet everyone when meeting, and say good by when leaving.

- Woman-to-woman and man-to-woman greetings are given with a kiss on the cheek, or both cheeks (Spain).

- People stand very close to each other while talking, sometimes touching a friend's clothing, hand, or arm.

- Family names and titles such as Señor (Mr.), Señora (Mrs.), or Señorita (Miss) are used to address elders or professionals. Don and Doña are used with first names to show respect.

## Gestures

- The smile is an important gesture of good will.
- Much affection is displayed publicly.
- Hand, arm, and other gestures are often used in conversation.
- People say "salud" if someone sneezes.
- People are beckoned by waving the fingers or the whole hand, with the palm down.
- It is not impolite for men to stare and make flattering remarks to women they do not know.
- Yawning is impolite because it is a sign of hunger.

## Some General Attitudes

- Individualism and personal pride are important in these societies.
- A person's appearance is extremely important.
- People strive to project an impression of affluence and social position. Styles and quality of clothing indicate status and respectability.
- People often feel it is their duty to correct or point out "errors" they see in others.
- Political power is often coveted.

## Time

- The individual is more important than schedules. Punctuality is not expected in social affairs; it is not impolite to be late, and people usually arrive late.
- If a visitor arrives unexpectedly or someone suddenly needs help, people will drop everything, regardless of how long it takes or how long someone else is kept waiting.
- Time is fluid.

## Family

- The family plays a role of utmost importance.
- Family members share good fortunes with each other.
- Although this custom is rapidly changing, the father traditionally provides for the family, while the mother is responsible for the home.
- Families often host members of the extended family for long periods.
- Traditionally men enjoy more social freedom than do women.
- Family obligations are extremely strong.

Ramirez and Casteñeda (1974) found that Hispanic students respond well to classroom strategies using techniques such as:

- Cooperative learning
- Personalized rewards
- Modeling
- Informal class discussion
- Concepts presented globally, rather than detail oriented

- Explicit classroom rules
- Personal interaction such as hugs and pats
- Humanizing the curriculum using humor, fantasy, or drama.

Other successful tactics include utilizing group projects, offering hugs and pats as personal rewards, standing closer to the students while teaching, and avoiding the use of debates (as an instructional method) and question-answer format. Short-term daily projects are more successful than long-term projects. To enhance interpersonal understanding, the teacher should stand closer to the children when teaching.

In many Hispanic cultures, religion and religious holidays pervade every segment of daily life and can even interfere with school attendance. Frequently, religious observations are linked to education and usually accompany political events. Educational systems may be more authoritative, and children wear uniforms. Students might be separated by gender and find it difficult to study with students of the opposite sex. The idea of dressing in front of peers for physical education classes may be inappropriate and misunderstood, as Hispanic students tend to be modest.

Children may be accustomed to different desk configurations in the classroom. They might have worked with partners, or groups, or sat with students in a row of attached desks. Children can become confused with democratic classroom expectations if they are accustomed to more authoritarian teachers who quickly mete out corporal punishment for transgressions and improper behavior. Educational experiences with the Socratic method, the use of audiovisual aids and laboratories, and access to special education might be foreign concepts to some children. Teaching by rote memorization, with less emphasis on critical thinking, might be what the newcomers are familiar with, so American education might appear "easier" to Hispanic students from other countries.

As with some other cultural groups, Hispanic students might be expected to lower their eyes when communicating with elders, especially when they are being reprimanded.

The classroom teacher is the main contact for the student and will provide for the needs of the student in all educational capacities. In other countries, schools do not usually have guidance counselors, special education teachers, or the PTA. Classes involving special education might be seen as an insult or retribution for wrong behavior. Most importantly, the teacher is the ultimate authority and parents are not expected to become involved other than to ensure that students complete their homework.

American teachers might be surprised to learn of the ethnocentric feelings that Hispanic groups feel for Hispanics outside their respective groups. For that reason it is important to identify individuals correctly. For example, just because someone is speaking Spanish in a place such as Miami, non-Spanish speakers should not assume they are all Cubans.

## Islamic Cultures and Speakers of Arabic

Islam, reported to be one of the fastest-growing religions in the United States and around the world, is practiced by Muslims. Many Americans consider themselves Muslims, and they are native speakers of English. Muslim students can be from any racial or ethnic background. Students from Algeria, Djiboati, Egypt, Iraq, Jordan, Kuwait, Lebanon, Libya, Mauritania, Morocco, North and South Yeman, Palestine, United Arab Emirates, Oman, Qatar, Saudi Arabia, Somalia, Sudan, Syria, Chad, and Tunisia (and other African countries) are usually Arabic speakers. Arabic is used in the Koran (Qur'an, Islam's book of scripture). However, most Muslims are not Arabic. They come from diverse countries such as Indonesia, Malaysia, Pakistan, China, Fiji, and Barbados, and do not necessarily speak Arabic.

No matter what the nationality, the Islamic follower is familiar with the Arabic language and can recite it and therefore, is subject to Arabic influence. Although Muslim students are influenced greatly by their ethnic and cultural heritage, the practices of Islamic religion often supercede cultural traits. Those individuals who follow pure Islamic tradition will demonstrate the same religious practices and observances, which means the public schools must formulate and implement policies to create a culturally sensitive academic environment.

Educators should be familiar with fundamental beliefs of Muslims and make allowances for religious holidays, days of fasting, dietary requirements, prayer time and its accompanying rituals, expressions of personal modesty, and curriculum issues. The First Amendment of the U.S. Constitution protects the religious rights of individuals, which signifies that the classroom teacher should know as much as possible to foster understanding toward the Muslim student. The fundamental religious aspects of Islam are reflected in the classroom, just as cultural aspects are. Some practices the teacher can expect are addressed in this appendix.

The Islamic perspectives highlighted in this appendix are culled from the information disseminated from the Council on American-Islamic Relations in its publication *An Educator's Guide to Islamic Religious Practices*. Also included are some general cultural characteristics as perceived by the Educational Service Staff of AFME (American Friends of the Middle East, or AMIDEAS, taken from its chapter "Cultural Clues to the Middle Eastern Student." Because of the fundamental teachings of the Koran, characteristics of different ethnic groups that practice Islam might be similar, although the cultures might be very different.

For example, Muslims from Malaysia are distinct from Muslims from Saudi Arabia, although they practice the same religion.

## Social Relationships

Manners reflect the formality of the culture, which is formal in social customs and daily routines. Respect for one another is of vital importance. Personal relationships, family, and friendship are central to life. The American ways of forming relationships quickly, but superficially, are seen as having little depth or significance. Male/female relationships are restricted and are governed by a rigid set of cultural rules. In some conservative countries, the roles of women are less prominent than those of men, as the culture is male dominated. However, in more progressive Islamic countries, women are allowed to hold high positions in public office.

## Food/Hospitality

Refreshments, even if only coffee or soft drinks, are always served when visiting. Not to offer refreshment is unthinkable.

## Fatalistic Attitudes

Life events are deigned by an omnipotent God and occur as a direct result of the will of God, without respect to the desires of man. The phrase *Inshallah* (God willing) is frequently uttered, which means the will of God will determine whatever occurs.

## Emotional Displays

Arabs generally are conservative and are not comfortable with shows of affection in public. They will not display emotion outwardly, but will wait until they are home to laugh loudly, or argue in private.

## Touch

Traditional Islamic countries like Saudi Arabia, Iraq, and Iran may find cross-gender touching inappropriate, whereas more liberal societies may be comfortable with some interaction between the sexes. Unless one is certain of the cultural mores, women are to be greeted with words because it may be inappropriate to touch them. Most Muslims avoid body contact with the opposite sex; however, men may kiss and embrace men, and women may embrace and kiss women. Men may shake hands, but the handshake should not be pulled away too quickly. Individuals may stand close to one another, and "bathe the other person in one's breath" as a way of being deeply involved with one another (Hall, 1966, p. 49). Hall also says that "Arabs look each other in the eye when talking with an intensity that makes most Americans highly uncomfortable (p 161).

## Dewariahs

Dewariahs are a place to gather to socialize and celebrate, as conversation is a tonic; however, men and women are separated from each other.

## Gifts and Invitations

If an individual admires something an Arab has, it will be given to him or her. Arabs expect to pay for meals if they invite someone to dine. Gifts given are not to be opened in front of guests. Additionally, friendship implies that favors will be done for one another, and favors are expected to be repaid reciprocally.

## Saving Face

Arabs are non-confrontational and will avoid arguments at any cost. They act humbly, are sensitive to others' feelings, and will never disgrace or embarrass others. Politeness will be shown to individuals at all times, even to one's enemy because the Koran dictates that "God loveth not the speaking ill of anyone in public." This includes writing about an individual.

## Privacy

Arabs prefer to have close personal interaction with one another and therefore have large spaces inside the home instead of walls. Physical privacy as we know it is nonexistent, and to be alone, Arabs will simply stop talking. They are very private inside their homes, and outsiders will not be invited into the home until they are very close. One can assume that an invitation into an Arab home is an honor that indicates deep friendship.

## Children and Family

The family is traditional in that the father is head of the household and the mother takes care of the children and home. Children are taught their roles early in life and are given responsibilities according to their age. The parents' word is final and elders are greatly respected. Academic choices of children will often reflect the wishes of the parents instead of their individual choice. The culture is paternalistic, and this authoritative familial pattern is evident throughout societal patterns.

## Guidelines for Educators

Since the Muslim population is growing rapidly in American public schools, teachers need to be knowledgeable about how to respect the rights and beliefs of these students. Learning about the rights of Islamic students can be accomplished by adhering to guidelines set forth by the Council of American-Islamic Relations.

### Adolescence and Gender Relations

According to Islamic rule, certain parameters regarding personal modesty are prescribed for post-pubescent boys and girls when dealing with the opposite sex. Shaking hands with the opposite sex, even if it is a teacher or administrator, for example, might be viewed as immodest, as well as co-ed physical education classes and school dances. No pressure to participate should be exhibited, nor should students be penalized for refusing to take part in these mixed gender activities.

### Physical Education

Muslim children are prohibited from uncovering their bodies and are not allowed to participate in communal showers after sports. Private showers should be available, and if the class is scheduled late in the day, students should be allowed to skip the showers altogether and wait until they get home. Physical education clothing should be modified so that the girls wear full track suits, and the boys wear knee-length shorts.

Mixed sex swimming classes are a problem for Muslim students. They should not be penalized for non-participation on religious grounds. Alternative outside certification can be an option if the school has mandatory certification.

### Muslim Holidays

The major celebrations that all Muslims celebrate are the two *Eid (holiday)* days. The first Eid day is the day after the month of Ramadan (which is marked by a month of fasting) the ninth month of the Islamic lunar calendar. The second major celebration is observed on the 10th day of the 12th Islamic month. Schools should note Muslim holidays on their calendars as the students are obliged to take at least one day off from school, which should be without penalty. However, the exact date of the Eid depends on the sighting of the new moon, which is uncertain until the night before the celebrated day.

### Dietary Requirements

Muslims are careful about food and how it is prepared because they follow Islam's Holy Scripture, which prescribes the *Halal* (permissible by Islamic law) consumption and preparation of foods. The Koran (or Qur'an) prohibits consumption of alcohol, pork (including by-products or derivatives), shellfish, and other objectionable foods such as:

Fish without fins
Pepperoni, sausage, and pork hot dogs
Bacon, alone or in foods
Animal shortening (vegetable shortening is acceptable) in breads,
    puddings, cookies, cakes, donuts, pastries, etc.
Gelatin in Jell-O, desserts, candies, marshmallows, chocolates, etc.
Lard in any form or product
Ingredients containing alcohol (vanilla extract, Dijon mustard)

School cafeteria personnel can demonstrate respect for these religious observations by highlighting their menus with a visual clue when these food items are offered.

### Personal Modesty for Men and Women

According to Islam, modesty in behavior and dress encourages value for wisdom, skills, and community contribution rather than physical attributes. Modesty, chastity, and morality are emphasized, and individuals are responsible for their deeds by the time they reach puberty.

Males are obliged to be covered from the navel to the knee, and some students cover their heads with a *kufki*. In public, females cover their heads and wear loose-fitting, nonrevealing clothing called *hijab,* or *khimar.*

Wearing a head covering is a practice misunderstood by many and may cause problems in school settings. Teachers and administrators need to protect the student's personal and religious right to wear a scarf, and should prohibit and reprimand classmates who pull or remove a Muslim girl's scarf.

### Family Life/Sex Education

Because Islam has its own specific set of teachings about human development and related issues, parents need the option to remove their children from any family life programs offered by the schools.

### Daily Prayer

Islamic believers must pray five times every day. The prayer times that fall within school hours must be observed, and students will need about 15 minutes to complete prayers. Muslims must wash their faces, hands, and feet with clean water (a restroom or any facility with running water will suffice) for about two minutes. According to the Qur'an, the individual will stand, bow, and touch the forehead to the ground and recite specific prayers. The worshiper needs a quiet, clean room where he or she will face toward Mecca (usually northeast in America). While total silence is not necessary, others should not walk in front of or interrupt the person praying. Being considerate, the other students should not interrupt the person praying unless it is an emergency. The person praying is thoroughly engaged, so he or she would probably not respond anyway.

## Fasting

In Islam, holy days and festivals are governed according to the lunar calendar, which, like the solar calendar, has 12 months. A lunar month (marked by the new crescent moon) may last only 29 days, so the lunar year is about eleven days shorter than the solar year. Muslims are required to fast in the month of Ramadan, during the ninth month of the Islamic lunar calendar.

Islam has five "pillars," which include fasting, declarations of faith, daily prayer, offering regular charity, and pilgrimage to Mecca. Fasting is to refrain from eating and drinking from break of dawn to sunset. The exact dates that determine when followers should fast change throughout the full solar year. Students who are fasting can be excused from going to the cafeteria at lunch time and from participating in strenuous physical activity. In an effort to support multiculturalism in the community, the teacher can seize this teachable moment by inviting guest speakers to teach the other students about the rituals observed in a variety of religions.

## Curriculum Issues

Muslims take issue with their portrayal as the enemy in outdated social studies texts. Negative depictions can contribute to suspicion, harassment, and violence toward followers of Islam. Textbooks should be reviewed for religious prejudice and selected under the guidance of Muslim educators to ensure that history, geography, and social studies texts offer reliable information about the tenets of Islam. One major falsehood is that "Allah" is a Muslim god, instead of the traditional Judeo-Christian God.

## School Issues

Other issues that might conflict in the traditional school setting are not saluting the flag, or refusing to recite the Pledge of Allegiance. Muslim parents may teach their children to stand up, but perhaps not salute the flag when reciting the pledge because Islam discourages acts that are irreverent to God. This is not meant to be offensive or a symbol of disrespect to the symbol of the nation.

Finally, conscientious followers of Islam might be expected to be released at midday on Friday, the day for congregational worship. This is called *Jum'ah* and it takes place at the mosque. Students might need to ask for an extended lunch period to fulfill this obligation. If many Muslim students attend the same school, the prayers can be held on school property, which is a right upheld by the Supreme Court in 1990 as the Equal Access Act.

## Suggestions for the Teacher

To embrace and enjoy interactions with new beliefs, cultures, and ideas, the Council on American-Islamic Relations offers the following suggestions for religious accommodations for Muslim students in the public schools.

■ To note pork and pork by-products in lunches, mark items with a red dot or a picture of a pig.

### Muslim holidays

■ Schedule exams and other major events around holidays.
■ Do not mark students absent.

### Ramadan fast

■ Allow students to study in the library or elsewhere during lunch.

### Physical education

■ Discuss clothing requirements with Muslim parents.
■ Reschedule classes for students who prefer same-gender exercise environment.

### Gender relations

■ Do not extend your hand first for a handshake with the opposite sex.

### Family/sex education programs

■ Allow parents reasonable time to review any material dealing with "sex education."
■ Allow children to opt-out from all or part of the family life program.

### Prayer

■ Allow Muslim students to pray in unused rooms.

### *Fairness in classroom and text preparation*

■  Check textbooks for religious biases.

■  Invite Muslim speakers to social studies and world religion classes.

## Haitian Students

The Refugee Service Center at the Center for Applied Linguistics offers current information on ethnic groups so that educators can meet the needs of their students. The information contained in this section can be accessed on the center's website at http://www.cao.org/RSC.

Haitian communities are flourishing socially, economically, and culturally in places such as South Florida, Boston, and New York. Their historical backgrounds offer richness to the multicultural fiber of the United States. Miami's Little Haiti is often the first stop for recent Haitian immigrants as they climb the ladder to self-sufficiency and eventual participation as citizens in mainstream American life.

Recent immigrants often find that they do not relate to African-Americans because the two cultures are worlds apart. Unfortunately, Haitians have been the victims of inaccurate cultural misunderstandings and negative stereotypes that have inflicted great damage upon youngsters from this culture causing them to deny their heritage. The lack of ethnic self-pride is manifested in the phenomenon of young, more assimilated Haitians claiming to be African-American, Caribbean-American, West Indians, or Haitian-Americans. They often deny that they speak Creole or claim to speak French when they cannot. Later, Haitians may assume the identity, lifestyle, language variations, and mannerisms of African-American youth to gain acceptance by their peers; hence, the rejection of the native cultures and a denial of knowledge of the native language (Portes & Rumbaut, 1996; Portes & Zhou, 1993).

The Haitian school system was modeled on the French system, which offers 14 years of education, 7 at the elementary and 7 at the secondary level, in the "elite" language of French. The system was restructured in 1978 to offer 10 years of basic education, and three years of secondary education. After much debate, and with much resistance, Haitian Creole became the language of instruction for the first four grades.

Education is highly valued and schooling is technically "free," but many Haitians do not have access to it because the poverty level is too high to afford the uniforms, books, and supplies. Consequently, the majority of the population receives little or no formal education at all. Teachers who have Haitian students in their classes must ascertain the extent of their previous educational experience. Their educational backgrounds will depend on the socioeconomic status the students encountered in Haiti.

Students from the Haitian educational system are accustomed to different educational beliefs and will exhibit behaviors that mirror those distinct values and school behaviors. As a result of different teaching and learning styles, students in Haitian schools are expected to learn more subjects in greater detail through rote learning and memorization. Haitian students will be unfamiliar with the American penchant for analysis and synthesis of material, and they will be confused by the number of correct answers possible in testing situations. Students will have to be taught explicitly how to think and discover for themselves, and exactly what is expected of them when being tested.

In Haiti, grading and testing are formal and follow strict procedures. It is more difficult to get good grades and therefore, Haitian students will place importance on studying for quizzes, tests, and making high scores.

Teacher-student relationships are formal in Haiti. The informality of teacher/student relationships in the U.S. school system may be perceived as a lack of respect for teachers. In the Haitian classroom, students are addressed by their last name. The student speaks only when asked a question, and does not look the teacher in the eye. The teacher has total authority over the class. For Haitian newcomers to the American classroom, the idea of "democracy" in the classroom is foreign and is not understood. Haitians are used to having a teacher who is feared and respected. Corporal punishment by the teacher enforces discipline and is sanctioned by the parent.

In Haiti, parent-teacher communication is formal; the only time the parent will hear from the teacher is when the student is doing wrong. This communication will result in the parent inflicting corporal punishment upon the child for committing the transgression. There is no PTA; parents are not encouraged to participate in school matters. Papers, letters, and notices are not sent home with the child; parents are expected to go to the school to pick up report cards and such. In the United States, papers are sent home from school with the child, but they might not be returned to the school because of this reason. Thus, parents who react negatively to the request for parental involvement need to be educated about what is expected of them in their new country.

In Haiti, the teacher is the absolute authority, always knows best, and is not to be questioned. Haitian children in the United States may be confused upon seeing the apparent informality of the American classroom. In trying to learn the proper classroom etiquette from their American classmates, they may inadvertently overstep their bounds. Haitian students will be unaccustomed to the "democratic" atmosphere found in the United States and need to be gently reminded of expected behavior.

Because of the poverty level in Haiti, the literacy rate is extremely low in the countryside. However, Haitians posses a rich oral tradition that includes the art of storytelling, riddles, songs, and games. As a result, they may be stronger as auditory learners rather than as visual learners.

Other points that American teachers should be aware of are:

- In Haitian schools, desks are not individualized; they are attached in rows and students sit side-by-side. Students might feel isolated when seated individually.

- Many Haitian schools are segregated by gender, and students will feel uncomfortable being in mixed classes. Additionally, the concept of playing together during physical education might be disquieting. It is culturally inappropriate for Haitian students to dress and undress in front of others, even those of the same sex. Arrangements should be made to accommodate the needs of these students.

- Haitians students might be unaccustomed to owning their own textbooks. In Haiti, they probably had to borrow a book and copy it by hand. In Haiti, audiovisual aids might be nonexistent; experiential learning is not an instructional method used; most schools have no laboratories to practice in; and learning is traditionally by rote, memorization, and recitation. Finally, due to the type of learning Haitian students are accustomed to, they are uncomfortable with and initially will resist engaging in activities that demand critical independent thinking.

- Many Haitians are religious, maintain a strong work ethic, hold deep respect for authority, and revere education, because it is a means of social mobility. Parents demand obedience from children, and children are expected to help out by translating for them, shopping, taking care of siblings, and doing other household chores. Frequent absenteeism might result as a consequence of familial expectations.

## Asian Americans

Asians are not a homogenous group. They do, however, constitute a significant minority group in the United States. Asian Americans represent many distinct subgroups who speak different languages, worship through different religions, and practice different customs and beliefs. The main groups are East Asians (Chinese, Japanese, Korean), Pacific Islanders, Southeast Asians (Thai,

Vietnamese, Cambodian, Laotian), and South Asian (Indian and Pakistani). Threads of similarities may run through the subgroups, but they all have distinct histories, origins, and cultural roots. Among these groups, differences also exist within national groups, families, and individuals themselves.

Some Asians were born in the United States, while others come from abroad. Some are affluent and come with highly developed skills while others are barely literate (Brand, 1987). Regardless of success or acculturation, many Asians are stereotyped as the "model minority" because often the Asian student is often the one who is at the head of the class and is the valedictorian at graduation. Many people believe that the Confucian ideas that stress family ideals, respect for elders, deferred gratification, and discipline, (Brand, 1987) are the reason for high educational achievement. Studies show that Asian-Americans are more likely to believe that success in life is connected to what has been studied in school.

American schooling may contradict the fundamental cultural beliefs of Asians because it emphasizes individualism and competition, while the ethnic identify of Asian children is often based on their relationship to the group and allegiance to family (Trueba & Cheng, 1993). Academic achievement and upward mobility are viewed as an obligation for the maintenance of the family, which is the responsibility of all family members (Pang, 1990).

Additionally, Asian parents teach their children to respect authority, feel responsibility for relatives, and show self-control. School failure is seen as a lack of will, and this failure can be alleviated by increasing parental restrictions. Baruth and Manning (1992) claim that Asian American children need reinforcement from the teacher, and work more efficiently in quiet, well-structured surroundings. These children appear to be more dependent, conforming, and obedient by placing the family's welfare before their own desires.

Like students from other cultures, Asians may be confused with the apparent teacher/student informality of the American classroom, and function better with structure and organization. (Baruth & Manning, 1992). Asian cultures also value the idea of humility and/or self-effacement. Children may not volunteer to participate in the classroom until specifically asked by the teacher. Drawing attention to oneself by virtue of misbehaving might cause great distress and result in "losing face" (Morrow & McBride, 1988) because children are taught to value silence, listen more than speak, speak softly, and be modest in dress and behavior (Feng, 1994).

The following suggestions are offered by Feng (1994) as a formula for teachers to address issues concerning the diversity of Asian American cultures. It should be noted, however, that these suggestions could be implemented for any ethnic group.

- Get to know the customs, values, and traditions of various cultures, and learn the conditions under which students came to the United States. Try to visit the students' homes and get to know the families.
- Learn a few words of the students' native language to set the tone for communication.
- Encourage native language use at home. Use English-proficient interpreters with parents.
- Try to learn the children's names and pronounce them correctly.
- Be careful not to encourage discord between home values and school expectations. For example, if the home expectation is conformity, don't encourage the child to challenge the teacher.
- Academic expectation should be based on ability rather than stereotypical beliefs.
- Peer tutoring can be used for children who are not yet proficient in English.
- Know who make decisions for the child and utilize the natural support system.
- Develop strong home-school links for communication.
- Avoid assumptions about children's prior knowledge and experience (e.g., not every child has experienced a birthday party).
- Discover what you can about Asian parent networks. The best way to remove a cultural barrier is to appear sincere.

## Common Characteristics of Many Asian Cultures

(from Culturegrams)

### Greetings

- Bow or nod
- Individuals do not touch each other
- Little or no public display of affection
- Stand far apart (even farther than Americans do)

### Gestures

- Smiling and laughing often indicate embarrassment
- Little or no affection is shown in public

- It is impolite to speak loudly
- Hand and arm gestures are not often used in conversation
- People's sneezes are not usually acknowledged.
- People are beckoned by waving all the fingers with the palm of the hand facing down.
- Pointing is done with the entire hand.
- Japanese say no by shaking the hand from side to side with the palm forward, and point to themselves with their pointer finger facing their nose.
- People must sit erect with both feet on the floor; it is impolite to put an ankle on the knee.
- Yawning is impolite.
- Vietnamese men do not offer to shake hands with women.

## General attitudes

- Society is group oriented.
- Loyalty is to the group, the family, and to one's superiors as opposed to personal feelings.
- Humility and self-effacing comments are normal.
- It is essential to act similar to or in harmony with the crowd.
- People strive to conform in appearance (even when wearing the latest Western styles, people must try to look like everyone else).
- Reserve and modesty must be observed at all times.
- It is important to save face at all times, for self and others.
- People will often allow others to escape potential embarrassment with dignity.
- Goals and decisions are made with the good of the group in mind, not for the personal benefit of any individual.

## Time

- Being late is impolite.
- People are prompt or a little bit early (for social as well as business affairs).

## Family

- The family is extremely important.

- The family has a strong tradition of respect and loyalty.
- There is a strong sense of family reputation and family obligation.
- Elders are highly respected.
- Many members of the extended family (particularly in-laws) live together.

## Native Americans

With over 500 Native American tribal groups, and about 2,200 different languages (Baruth & Manning, 1992), it is impossible to generalize the English language proficiency and acculturation of these populations. Language and cultural differences manifest themselves in the disparity of values found in the home and in the schools. Philips (1983) found that community norms and socialization practices influence the classroom behavior of children. By understanding the values of Native American populations, teachers can adjust classroom situations to provide optimum instructional settings.

Although many tribal groups exist, the shared characteristic of being indigenous allows for some similarities despite differences in cultural styles. Some researchers have noted that many Native American students have the tendency to be field-dependent (Baruth & Manning, 1992; Brandley, 1984; McShane & Plas, 1982; Swisher and Deyhle, 1989; Tharp, 1989) while other researchers posit that Native American students can also tend to be field-independent (1989b). Ultimately, individual characters are the deciding factor regarding field dependence and field independent learning. The behavior of Native American children reflects the values of their culture. Diaz-Rico and Weed (1995) mention a research project that took place in several Sioux classrooms where the students appeared withdrawn and silent. American teachers, who are unaccustomed to prolonged periods of silence in their verbal discourse patterns, were met with students who only gave monosyllabic or nonverbal responses when questioned. The teachers were dismayed to learn that the students were purposefully shutting them out to avoid the teacher-student learning exchange. Once they discovered that that silence was a control issue, the teachers began to involve themselves in the community and daily lives of the students. The students began to participate more when the context was changed (Dumont, 1972).

Socialization in the classroom is a direct reflection of life in the community. Teachers with typical Anglo values, expectations, and instructional methods will not be able to reach the child who prefers not to read aloud, speaks so softly that he is inaudible, and feels more comfort with a lifestyle in which only one individual is directing and controlling all activity (Philips, 1972).

Navajo children pattern their discourse after the adults in their society. Students speak at length, one at a time, while the other students wait politely until the end of the statement before beginning to speak their thoughts. Ideas are developed completely and might not have any relation to the thoughts of the previous speaker. Discourse is related to peers instead of being teacher-dominated. In this manner, the students are not silent or resentful.

Writing styles also reflect cultural values. The American culture demands a linear writing form. The thesis statement is written, and the rest of the text must provide supporting facts. This trend reflects the American culture. In Native American discussions, topics are seldom addressed directly. The listener must make his own connections after points are made indirectly. This tendency is also reflected in students' writing. Writing styles that incorporate the ways of the people will produce more success than styles based on the "foreign" style of the teacher (Scafe & Kontas, 1982).

A compilation of findings suggest the following strategies be used for developing a successful classroom for American Indian learners (Boseker, 1991; Boseker & Gordon, 1983; Gordon & Boseker, 1984; Pepper, 1976):

- Small cooperative groups and peer learning are better than traditional large class grouping and oral questions and answers. Students need to feel as though they are part of the group.

- Use learning manipulatives and incorporate activities that allow students to feel and touch to enhance learning through use of the senses. Information gained by visual, motor, tactile, spatial, perceptual, or auditory tasks/games are highly recommended.

- Use mental, non-verbal images to teach concepts rather than depending on word associations.

- Freedom of movement within the classroom is encouraged; allow students to sit on the floor, arrange desks comfortably, and permit a range of motion.

- Avoid highlighting individual students' success, accept silence, and de-emphasize competition.

- Don't use show-and-tell venues that require students to get up in front of the class and speak (Philips, 1972). Take time to let the child approach the teacher individually.

- Learning is best accomplished experientially, in natural settings, and by watching and doing instead of trial and error.

- Allow students to learn privately. Let them observe, listen, and take over parts of the task, in cooperation with and under supervision of an adult. Then let the child test himself (Diaz-Rico & Weed, 1993).

- Utilize holistic presentations, visual representations, and presentation of the whole picture before isolating skills into small segments.

- Conciseness of speech, slight variation of intonation, and limited vocal range are most valued. Silence is used for personal power, and for creating and communicating rapport with others.

- Do not force individual competition, although students may enjoy competing in teams. Emphasis should be on the group. Native American children do not want to show themselves as superior, especially if it presents someone else in a poor light (Fuller & Causaus, 1987). Harmony within the group is desirable.

- Child-rearing may be done by the extended family.

- In class, allow more response time so students can feel comfortable after considering responses. Allow them to practice their skills before expecting them to answer. Allow time for delay in responding answering questions.

- Students may ask for help silently by looking up from their work without speaking.

- Native Americans are spiritual and live in harmony with nature and natural settings. Incorporate instruction with this knowledge in mind.

- Know your Native American cultural groups and their value systems. What is innocuous to the American teacher might have deep spiritual significance for the students.

## Tips for Becoming Culturally Aware

1. Peruse the textbooks used in your classes. Note the depiction of females, males, people of color, and obvious ethnic minorities. Does it look fair to you? Be sure to make mention of inequities.

2. Be aware of the nonverbal communication you use (gestures, hand movements, body language, etc.) and focus on teaching your students what these types of communication mean.

3. Communicate respect (verbally and nonverbally) and sincere interest for your students and their cultures.

4. Look around your classroom. Make sure your class environment sends a positive, welcoming message.

5. Do all you can to encourage home/school interaction. Parents are your greatest allies and can help bridge the cultural gap. Attend cultural

celebrations in your students' community. Communicate and involve parents.

6. Be vigilant about accurate assessment. Make sure you are assessing content and not mere language ability.

7. Avoid using children as interpreters for their parents. This upsets the natural familial harmony and parental hierarchy, robbing parents of their authority.

8. Understand the struggle of conflicting home and school values. Support the parents as they try to maintain their cultural roles, values, responsibilities, and forms of discipline.

9. Encourage parents to continue to speak to their children in their rich native languages. A complete home language is a good basis for transferring knowledge to the second language.

# Appendix B

## Interesting Insights and Cultural Facts

Interesting Insights and Cultural Facts (Lip, 1985; Maple, 1971)

All cultures have beliefs that signify good and bad luck. The following are some common beliefs interesting to know and demonstrate how easily misunderstandings can occur.

# Colors

- Red ink is a death sign for Koreans. Teachers should refrain from correcting papers with red ink.

- In Afghanistan, white is a symbol of friendship for a bride and an omen of luck, harmony, and happiness for the wedding couple. In India, only an enemy would wear white to a wedding as it can bring bad luck or death to the wedding couple. Red would be a better color to wear.

- At a Chinese wedding, black or white should not be worn because both colors are associated with death.

- In China, yellow is used to mark a defective product. Green is used to indicate a product has passed inspection.

- White products cannot be sold in Hong Kong because white is associated with death.

- Yellow can have negative connotations cross culturally:
  - In American culture, yellow can mean cowardice;
  - In France, yellow is associated with being a traitor;
  - Judas is often depicted wearing yellow;
  - Nazis made Jews wear yellow stars;
  - Spanish executioners wear yellow.

- To the Chinese, a green hat connotes infidelity but the color green itself means health, prosperity, and harmony.

- Yellow flowers mean "I miss you" to Armenians, but they mean "I hate you" to Iranians. Peruvians also feel negatively about yellow flowers, as do Mexicans.

- White flowers indicate mourning for the Chinese (and other Asians), especially gladioli. Bringing white gladioli to a Chinese family would indicate a death wish for them. A little red envelope with a coin in it would mean good luck is wished.

# Numbers

■ In Mandarin and Cantonese, the word for the number 4 sounds like the word for death. Japanese and Koreans feel the same way. To have this number in an address is bad.

■ For the Chinese, numbers have positive and negative values. For example, 7 is related to the idea that ghosts return 7 days after someone dies. Positive meanings also abound; 1 is for guaranteed; 2 for easy; 3 for life; 6 for happiness; 8 for prosperity; 9 for long life. Combinations have significance also. By itself, 5 is neutral, but if it is in front of an 8, the good effect of the 8 is negated. In the Chinese culture, the fourth floor is often eliminated. Some Asian airports eliminate Gate 4.

■ Many traditional Chinese people refuse to be photographed with an uneven number of people. To have three people in a photo is the worst: it is an indicator that the person in the middle will die.

■ Phone numbers can be lucky or unlucky. Many Chinese companies moved into the San Gabriel Valley in California, which has the telephone area code 818. This combination of numbers means "prosperity guaranteed prosperity."

■ Armenians believe that an even number of flowers is unlucky. Numbers involved in funeral or death rituals are usually even in number; therefore, on happy occasions an uneven number of flowers are presented.

■ In many English-speaking cultures, the number 13 is negative. Buildings may not have a 13th floor. Many Americans will refuse to stay in a room on the 13th floor. Friday the 13th is a dreaded day.

■ Students from the Middle East, Korea, Africa, Mexico, and perhaps other countries, might bring a gift to the teacher expecting the teacher to inflate the student's grade.

# References

Abedi, J. (1999, April). NAEP math test accommodations for students with limited english proficiency. Paper presented at the Annual Meeting of the American Educational Research Association. Montreal, Quebec, Canada. (ERIC Document Reproduction Service No. ED 431787).

Ada, A. F. (1993). *Mother-tongue, literacy as a bridge between home and school cultures: The power of two languages*. New York: McGraw-Hill School Publishing.

Ada, Alma Flor, Harris, V. J., Hopkins, L. B. (1993). *A chorus of cultures: Developing literacy through multicultural poetry*. Carmel, CA: Hampton-Brown Books.

Adair, J. (1997). *Erasing the color line*. Metrowest Classroom. Middlesex News

Adams, M. J. (1990). *Beginning to read: Thinking and learning about print*. Cambridge, MA: MIT Press.

Adler, P. S. (1975). The transitional experience: An alternative view of culture shock. *Journal of Humanistic Psychology, 15*, (13), 23.

Allen, V. G. (1994). Selecting materials for the reading instruction of ESL children. In K. Spangenberg-Urbschat & R. Pritchard, (Eds.), *Kids come in all languages: Reading instruction for ESL children*. Newark, DE: International Reading Association.

American Association for the Advancement of Science. (1990). *Science for all Americans*. New York: Oxford University Press.

American Association for the Advancement of Science. (1993). *Benchmarks for scientific literacy: A project 2061 report*. New York: Oxford University Press.

American Association of Colleges of Teacher Education (AACTE). (1994). *Teacher education in global and international education: A handbook with case studies*. New York: National Council on Foreign Language and International Studies.

Anderson, A., & Lynch, T. (1988). *Listening*. Oxford, England: Oxford University Press.

Anderson, C. C., with Nicklas, S. K., & Crawford, A. R. (1994). *Global understandings: A framework for teaching and learning.* Alexandria, VA: Association for Supervision and Curriculum Development.

Anderson, L. F. (1990). A rationale for global education. In K. A. Tye (Ed.), *Global education from thought to action* (pp. 13–34). Alexandria, VA: Association for Curriculum and Supervision Development (ASCD).

Anderson, J. W. (1991). A comparison of Arab and American conceptions of effective persuasion. In L. A. Samovar & R. E. Porter (Eds.), *Intercultural communication: A reader* (pp. 96–106). Belmont, CA: Wadsworth.

Anderson, R. C., Reynolds, R. E., Schallert, D. L. & Goetz, G. T. (1977). Frameworks for comprehending discourse. *American Educational Research Journal* 14 (4): 367–381.

Anderson, R. C. & Pearson, P. R. (1988). A schema-theoretic view of basic processes in reading comprehension. In P. L. Carrell, J. Devine, & D. E. Eskey (Eds.), *Interactive approaches to second language reading,* (pp. 37–56). Cambridge, England: Cambridge University Press.

Argyle, M. (1975). *Bodily communication.* London: Methuen.

Armstrong, T. (1994). *Multiple intelligences in the classroom.* Alexandria, VA: Association for Supervision and Curriculum Development.

Asher, J. (1972). Children's first language as a model for second language learning. *The Modern Language Journal, 56,*133–39.

Asher, J. (1982). *Learning another language through actions: The complete teachers' guidebook.* Los Gatos, CA: Sky Oaks.

Asher, J. J. (1977). *Learning another language through actions.* Los Gatos, CA: Sky Oaks.

Asher, J., Kusudo, J., & de la Torre, R. (1974). Learning a second language through commands: The commands: The second field test. *The Modern Language Journal, 58,* 24–32.

Ashworth, M., & Wakefield, P. (1994). *Teaching the world's children: ESL for ages three to seven.* Markham, Ontario: Pippin.

Association for Supervision and Curriculum Development (ASCD). (1991). International Global Education Commission. Cited in S. Ramler, Global education for the 21st century. *Educational Leadership, 48(7),* 1991: 44–46

Atwater, M. M. (1994). Research on cultural diversity in the classroom. In D. L. Gabel (Ed.), *Handbook of research on science teaching and learning* (pp. 558–576).

Bachman, L. F. (1990). *Fundamental considerations in language testing.* New York: Oxford University Press.

Baker, G. (1983). *Planning and organizing for multicultural instruction.* Reading, MA: Addison-Wesley Publishing Company.

Bandouin, E. M., Bober, E. S., Clarke, M. A., Dobson, B. K., and Silberstein, S (1977). *Reader's choice: a reading skills textbook for students of English as a second language.* Ann Arbor: University of Michigan Press.

Banks, J. (1988). *Multicultural education: Theory and practice.* Boston: Allyn & Bacon.

Bareth, L. G., & Manning, M. L. (1992). *Multicultural education of children and adolescents.* Needham Heights, MA: Allyn & Bacon.

Barufaldi, J., & Swift, J. (1977). Children learning to read should experience science. *Reading Teacher,* 388–393.

Been, S. (1975). Reading in the foreign language teaching program. *TESOL Quarterly, 9,* 233–242.

Belisle, R. (1996, December). E-mail activities in the ESL writing class. *The Internet TESL Journal* (Vol. II, No. 12).

Bennett, C. I. (Ed.). (1990). *Comprehensive multicultural education: Theory and practice.* Needham Heights, MA: Allyn & Bacon.

Bennett, M. J. (1993). Towards ethnorelativism: A developmental approach to training for intercultural sensitivity. In R. Michael Paige, (ed.) *Education for the intercultural experience,* (21–71). Yarmouth, ME: Intercultural Press.

Berman, P., McLaughlin, B., McLeod, B., Minicucci, C., Nelson, B., & Woodworth, K. (1995). School reform and student diversity. In "From risk to excellence: Principles of practice". *Eric Digest* (On-line), Available: http//www.cal.org/ericcll/digest/Crede/001.htm.

Blau, E. K. (1990). The effects of syntax, speed and pauses on listening comprehension. *TESOL Quarterly, 24,* 746–753.

Blaz, D. (1999). *Foreign language teachers guide to active learning.* New York: Eye on Education, Inc.

Bloom, B. S. (Ed.). (1984). *Taxonomy of educational objectives book 1, Cognitive domain. White Plains, N.Y. Longman, 1984.*

Boseker, B.J. (1991). *Successful solutions for preventing Native American dropouts.* International Third World Studies Journal and Review, 3, 33–40.

Boseker, B. J., & Gordon, S.L. (1983). What Native Americans have taught us as teacher educators. *Journal of American Indian Education, 22,* 20–24.

Bradley, J., & Thalgott, M. (1987). Reducing reading anxiety. *Academic Therapy, 22*(4), 349–358.

Brand, D. (1987, August 31) The new whiz kids. *Time,* 130, 42–51. EJ 358-595.

Brand, D. (1987, August 3). Why Asians are going to the head of the class: Some fear colleges use quotas to limit admissions. *New York Times,* sec 12, pp. 18–23.

Brembeck, W. (1977, March) The development and teachings of a college course in intercultural communication. *Readings in intercultural communication,* Vol.2, p. 14, Pittsburgh, PA: SIETAR Publications.

Brown, G., & Yule, George. (1983). *Teaching the spoken language.* Cambridge, England: Cambridge University Press.

Brown, H. (1994). *Teaching by principles: An interactive approach language pedagogy* (3rd ed.). Englewood Cliffs, NJ: Prentice-Hall.

Buchanan, K., & Helman, M. (1993). *Reforming mathematics instruction for ESL literacy students.* National Clearinghouse for Bilingual Education.

Burmudez, A., & Rakow, S. J. (1990). Analyzing teachers' perceptions of identification procedures for gifted and talented Hispanic limited English proficient (LEP) students at risk. *The Journal of Educational Issues of Language Minority Students, 7,* 21–33

Burns, A., & Joyce, H. (1997). *Focus on speaking.* Sydney, Australia: National Center for English Language Teaching and Research.

Burns, Roe, & Ross. (1999). *Burns/Roe informal reading inventory: Preprimary to twelfth grade.* (4th ed.). Boston: Houghton Mifflin.

Bush, M. & Terry, R. M. (1997). *Technology-enhanced language learning.* Lincolnwood, IL: National Textbook.

Bybee, R. B., & Ben-Zvi, N. (1998). Science curriculum: Transforming goals to practices. In B. J. Fraser & K. Tobin (Eds.), *International handbook of science education* (pp. 487–498).

CAIR Research Center. (1997) *An educator's guide to Islamic religious practices* (2nd ed.). Washington, DC: Council on American-Islamic Relations.

California Department of Education. (1990). *Bilingual education handbook.* Sacramento, CA: California Department of Education.

Canale, M. (1983). From communicative competence to communicative language pedagogy. In J. C. Richards and R. Schmidt (Eds.), *Language and communication.* London: Longman Group Limited.

Canale, M. & Swain, M. (1980). Theoretical bases of communicative approaches to second language teaching and testing. *Applied Linguistics, 1,* 1–47.

Cantoni-Harvey, G. (1987). *Content-area language instruction: Approaches and strategies.* New York: Addison-Wesley Publishing Company, Inc.

Carger, C. L. (1997). Attending to new voices. *Educational Leadership, 54* (7), 39–45.

Carrasquillo, A. (1991). *Hispanic children and youth in the United States: A resource guide.* New York: Garland.

Carrell, P. L. (1988). Some causes of text-boundedness and schema interference in ESL reading. In P. L. Carrell, J. Devine, & D. Eskey (Eds.), *Interactive approaches to second language reading* (pp.101–113). New York: Cambridge University Press.

Carrell, P. L., & Eisterhold, J. C. (1983). From schema theory and ESL reading pedagogy. *TESOL Quarterly, 17*(4), 553–573.

Carter, R., & McCarthy, M. (1995). Grammar and spoken language. *Applied Linguistics, 16*(2), 141–158.

Case, R. (1993). Key elements of a global perspective. *Social Education, 57*(6), 318–325.

Cazden, C. (1988). *Classroom discourse.* Portsmouth, NH: Hienemann.

Chaika, E (1989). *Language, the Social Mirror* (2nd ed.) Rowley, MA: Newbury House.

Chamot, A. U., Cummins, J., Kessler, C., O'Malley, M., and Fillmore, L.W. (2001). *ESL: Accelerating English language learning* (Teacher's Ed.). New York: Longman.

Chamot, A., & O' Malley, J. (1989). The cognitive academic language learning approach. In P. Rigg and V. Allen (Eds.), *When they don't all speak English.* Urbana, IL: National Council of Teachers of English.

Chamot, A. U. & O'Malley, J. M. (1996a). The cognitive academic language learning approach: A model for linguistically diverse classrooms. *Elementary School Journal 96* (3), 259–273.

Chamot, A. U. and O'Malley, J. M. (1994). *The CALLA handbook: How to implement the cognitive academic language learning approach.* Reading, MA: Addison-Wesley.

Chapin, J. R., & Messick, R. G. (2000). *Elementary social studies: A practical guide.* New York: Addison-Wesley-Longman, Inc.

Cheng, M. H., & Banya, K. (1998). Bridging the gap between teaching style and learning. In J. Reid (Ed.) *Understanding learning styles in the second language classroom.* Englewood Cliffs, NJ: Prentice Hall.

Chitravelu, N, Sithamparam, S, & The, S. C. (1995). *ELT methodology: Principles and practice.* Shah Alam, Malaysia: Penerbit Fajar Bakti Sdn. Bhd.

Chomsky, N. (1957). *Syntactic structures.* The Hague, the Netherlands: Mouton.

Chomsky, N. (1959). *A review of Skinner's Verbal Behavior Language. 35,* 26–58.

Chomsky, N. (1969). Linguistics and philosophy. In S. Hook (Ed.) *Language and philosophy.* New York: New York University Press.

Christison, M. (1996, Autumn). Teaching and learning languages through multipleintelligences. *TESOL Journal,* 10–14.

Claire, E., & Haynes J. (1994). *Classroom teacher's ESL survival kit #1.* Englewood Cliffs, NJ: Alemany Press.

Clark, R. (1982). Theory and method in child-language research: Are we assuming too much? In S. A. Kuezaj (Ed.), *Language and development: Vol. 1. syntax and semantics* (pp. 1–36). Hillsdale, NJ: Lawrence Erlbaum.

Clay, M. (1975). *What did I write?* Auckland: Heinemann Educational Books.

Clay, M. (1979). The early detection of reading difficulties. In S. F. Peregoy and O. F. Boyle *Reading, Writing, and Learning in ESL: A resource book for K–12 teachers.* New York: Addison Wesley Longman.

Clay, M. (1982). *Observing young readers: Selected Papers.* Portsmouth, NH: Heinemann.

Cohen, A. (1990). *Language learning: Insights for learners, teachers, and researchers.* Boston, MA: Hienle & Hienle.

Cohen, A. (1996). Developing the ability to perform speech acts. *Studies in Second Language Acquisition, 18*(2), 253–267.

Cohen, A., Glasman, H., Rosenbaum-Cohen, P. R., Ferrara, J., & Fine, J. (1979). Reading for specialized purposes: Discourse analysis and the use of student informants. *TESOL Quarterly*, 13: 551–564.

Cohen, E. G. (1984). Talking and working together: Status interaction and learning. In P. Peterson & L. C. Wilkinson (Eds.), *Instructional groups in the classroom: Organization and Processes*. New York: Academic Press.

Cohen, E. G. (1986). *Designing group work: Strategies for heterogeneous classrooms*. New York: Teachers College Press, Columbia University.

Cohen, E. G. (1991a, April). *Classroom management and complex instruction.* Paper presented at the American Educational Research Association, Chicago, IL.

Cohen, E. G. (1991b). From theory to practice: The development of an applied research program. In J. Berger & M. Zelditch (Eds.), *Theoretical research programs* (pp. 1–56). Stanford, CA: Stanford University Press.

Cohen, E. G. (1991c, December). *Teaching in the heterogeneous classroom.* Paper presented at the International Association of Intercultural Education, Vancouver, British Columbia.

Cohen, E. G., & DeAvila, E. (1983). *Learning to think in math and science: Improving local education for minority children*. Stanford, CA: Stanford University Press.

Cohen, E. G., & Lotan, R. A. (1990). *Untracking the middle school: Curriculum, instructional strategies, and access*. Proposal to the Carnegie Corporation, New York.

Cohen, M. D., & Tellez, K. (1994). Implementing cooperative learning for language minority students. *Bilingual Education, 18*, 1–19.

Collier, C., & Kalk, M. (1989). Bilingual special education curriculum development. In L. M. Baca & H. T. Cervantes (Eds.), *The bilingual special education interface* (pp. 257–290). Columbus, OH: Merrill.

Collier, V. P. (1995). *Promoting academic success in ESL students: Understanding second language acquisition for school.* Elizabeth, N.J: New Jersey Teachers of English to Speakers of Other Languages-Bilingual Educators.

Connor, U. (1987). Argumentative patterns in student essays; Cross-cultural differences. In Connor & Kaplan (Eds.),*Writing across languages: Analysis of L2 text.* Reading, MA: Addison-Wesley.

Cornet, C. E. (1983) *What you should know about teaching and learning styles.* Bloomington, IN: Phi Delta Kappa Education Foundation.

Cox, B.G., and Ramirez, M. (19 81). Cognitive styles: Implications for multiethnic education. In J. Banks (Ed.), *Education in the 80's: Implications for multiethnic education.* Washington, DC: National Education Association.

Cox, C. (1999). *Teaching language arts: A student- and response-centered classroom.* Boston: Allyn & Bacon.

Cox, C. & Many, J. E. (1992). Towards an understanding of the aesthetic stance towards literature. *Language Arts, 66:287–294.*

Crandall, J. A. (1987). *ESL through content-area instruction: Mathematics, science, social studies.* Englewood Cliffs, NJ: Prentice Hall, Inc.

Crandall, J. (1994, January). Content-centered language learning. *Eric Digest* (On-line), http//www.cal.org/ericcll/digest/crede/001.html

Crew, A. (1977). *Experiential learning: Theory and practical applications in secondary schools.* (Eric Document Reproduction Services No. ED256523).

Cruz, B. C. (1998, November). Global education in the middle school curriculum: An interdisciplinary perspective. *Middle School Journal.*

CultureGrams. (2002). *Standard edition.* Orem, UT.

Cummins, J. (1980). The construct of language proficiency in bilingual education. In J. E. Alatis (Ed.), *Georgetown University roundtable on language and linguistics* (pp. 76–93). Washington DC: Georgetown University Press.

Cummins, J. (1981). The role of primary language development in promoting educational success for language minority students. *Schooling and language minority students: A theoretical framework.* Sacramento: California State Department of Education.

Cummins, J. (1989). *Empowering minority students.* Sacramento, CA: CABE.

Curt, C. J. (1976). *Teacher training pack for a course on cultural awareness.* Fall River, MA: National Assessment and Dissemination Center for Bilingual Education.

Curtain, H., & Pesola, C. A. (1994). *Languages and children, Making the match.* New York: Longman Publishing Group.

Daiute, C. (1985). *Writing and computers.* Reading, MA: Addison-Wesley.

Dale, T., & Cuevas, G. (1992). Integrating mathematics and language learning. In P. Richard-Amato & M. Snow (Eds.), *The multicultural classroom.* White Plains, NY: Longman.

Dalton, S. (1989). *Teachers as assessors and assisters: Institutional constraints on interpersonal relationships.* Paper presented at the meeting of the American Educational Research Association, San Francisco, CA.

Dewey, J. (1934). The supreme intellectual obligation. *Science Education, 18,* 1–4.

Dias, P. (1990). A literacy -response respective on teaching reading comprehension. In D. Bogdan & S. B. Straw (Eds.). *Beyond communication: Reading comprehension and criticism* (pp. 283–299).

Diaz, C. (1989). Hispanic cultures and cognitive styles: Implications for teachers. *Multicultural Leader, 2(4),* 1–4.

Diaz, C. F., Massialas, B. G., & Xanthopoulos, J. A. (1999).*Global perspectives for educators.* Boston: Allyn & Bacon.

Diaz-Rico, L. T. & Weed, K. Z. (1995). *The crosscultural, language, and academic development handbook: A complete K–12 reference guide.* Boston: Allyn & Bacon.

Dillner, M. (1993/1994). Using hypermedia to enhance content area instruction. *Journal of Reading, 37(94),* 260–270.

Dulay, H., Burt, M., & Krashen, S. (1982). *Language two.* Oxford, England: Oxford University

Dumont, R. (1972). Learning English and how to be silent: Studies in Sioux and Cherokee classrooms. In C. Cazden, V. John, & D. Hymes (Eds.), *Functions of language in the classroom.* New York: Teachers College Press.

Dunkel, P. (1986). Developing listening fluency in L2: Theoretical principles and pedagogical considerations. *The Modern Language Journal, 70(2),* 99–106.

Dunkel, P. (1991). Listening in the native and second/foreign language: Toward an integration of research and practice. *TESOL Quarterly, 25(3),* 431–457.

Dunkel, P. (Ed.). (1991). *Computer-assisted language learning and testing: Research and issues and practice.* New York: Newbury House.

Dunn, R. S. & Dunn, K. J. (1979). Learning styles/teaching styles: Should they...can they...be matched? *Educational Leadership, 36*, 238–244.

Dunn, R. S., & Griggs, S. A. (1995). *Multiculturalism and learning styles: Teaching and counseling adolescents.* Westport, CT: Praeger.

Echevarria, J., Vogt, M. E., & Short, D. J. (2000). *Making content comprehensible for English language learners.* Needham Heights, MA: Allyn & Bacon.

Ehrman, M. E., & Oxford, R. (1995). Cognition plus: Correlates of language learning success. *Modern Language Journal 79*(1), 67–89.

Elbow, P. (1973) *Writing without teachers.* London: Macmillan Education.

Ellis, R. (1993). The structural syllabus and second language acquisition. *TESOL Quarterly, 27*, 91–113.

Emig, J. (1977). Writing as a mode of learning. *College composition and communication, 28*, 122–128.

Enright, D., & McCloskey, M. (1988). *Integrating English: Developing English language and literacy in the multilingual classroom.* Reading, MA: Addison-Wesley Publishing.

Ericson, L., & Juliebo, M. (1988). *The phonological awareness handbook for kindergarten and primary teachers.* Newark, DE: International Reading Association.

Eskey, D. E. (1973). A model program for teaching advanced reading to students of English as a second language. *Language Learning 23*(4), 169–184.

Esler, W. K. (1977). *Teaching elementary school science.* Belmont, CA: Wadsworth, pp. 4–12.

Felder, R. M., & Henriques, E.R. (1995). Learning and teaching styles in foreign and second language acquisition. *Foreign Language Annals, 28*(1), 21–31.

Feng, J. (1994). Asian-American children: What teachers should know. *ERIC Digest*, Champaign, IL: Clearinghouse on Elementary and Early Childhood Education. (On-line) Available:http://ericps.ed.uiuc.edu/eece pubs.

Ferreiro, Teberosky, (1982). *Literacy before schooling.* (K. Castro, Trans.). Exeter, NH: Heinemann.

Finnocchiaro, M., & Brumfit, C. (1983). *The functional-notional approach: From theory to practice.* New York: Oxford University Press.

Fishman, M. (1980). We all make the same mistakes: A comparative study of native and non-native errors in taking dictation. *Research in Language Testing.* (J. W. Oller, Jr. & K. Perkins, Eds.). Rowley, MA.: Newbury House.

Florida Department of Education. (1996). *Performance standards for teachers of English for speakers of other languages.* Tallahassee: Florida Department of Education.

Flower, L. & Hayes, J. (1980). A cognitive process theory of writing. *College composition and communication, 31*(4): 365–387.

Fox, G. (1998, September). The Internet: Making it work in the ESL classroom. *The Internet TESL Journal*, Vol. IV, No. 9. http://www.aitech.ac.jp/~iteslj/Articles/Fox-Internet.html

Frasier, M., Hunsaker, S. L., Jongyeun, L., Mitchell, S., Cramond, B., Krisel, S., Garcia, J. H., Martin, D., Frank, E., & Vernon, S. F. (1995). *Core attributes of giftedness: A foundation for recognizing the gifted potential of minority and economically disadvantaged students* (Report No.RM-95210). Storrs, CT: National Research Center on the Gifted and Talented. (ERIC Document Reproduction Service No. ED 402 703).

Freeman, T. S. & Freeman, D. E. (1992). *Whole language for second language learners.* Portsmouth, NH: Heinemann.

Freeman, T. S. and Freeman, D. E. (1998). *ESL/EFL Teaching Principles for Success.* Portsmouth, NH: Heinemann.

Freire, P. (1970). *Pedagogy of the oppressed.* New York: Continuum.

Friedman, T. L. (1999). *The lexus and the olive tree.* New York: Farrar, Strauss and Giroux.

Gardner, D., & Garcia, R. B. (1996). Interactive video as self-access support for language learning

Gardner, H. (1983). *Frames of mind: The theory of multiple intelligences.* New York: Basic Books.

Gardner, H. (1993). *Multiple intelligences: The theory in practice.* New York: Basic Books.

Garrison, L. (1997). Making the NCTM's standards work for emergent English speakers. *Teaching Children Mathematics, 4*(3), 132–138.

Gass, S., & Selinker, L. (1995). *SLA: An introduction*. Mahwah, NJ: Lawrence Erlbaum.

Genese, F. (1995, December). Integrating language and content: Lessons from Immersion. *Eric Digest* (On-line), Available: http://www.cal.org/ericcll/digest/ncrcds05.html.

Gibbons, P. (1991). *Learning to learn in a second language*. Portsmouth, NH: Heinemann.

Gillian, Brown. (1977). *Listening to spoken English*. New York: Longman.

Gollnick, D. M., & and Chin, P. C. (1998). *Multicultural education in a pluralistic society* (5th ed.). Englewood Cliffs, NJ: Prentice Hall.

Gonzalez, F. (1978). *Mexican American culture in the bilingual education classroom*. Unpublished doctoral dissertation, The University of Texas, Austin.

Gonzales, V., Bauerle, P., & Felix-Holt, M. (1996). Theoretical and practical implications of assessing cognitive and language development in bilingual children with qualitative methods. *The Bilingual Research Journal, 20*(1), 93–131.

Goodenough, W. H. (1981). *Language, culture, and society*. New York: Cambridge University Press.

Goodman, K. (1988). The reading process. In P. L. Carrell, J. Devine, & D. E. Eskey (Eds.) *Interactive approaches to second language reading* (pp. 11–21). Cambridge, England: Cambridge University Press.

Goodman, K. S., Goodman, Y. & Flores, B. (1979). *Reading in the bilingual classroom: Literacy and biliteracy*. Rosslyn, VA: National Clearinghouse for Bilingual Education.

Gordon, A. (2001) *How to cope with culture shock*. Unpublished manuscript.

Gordon, S. L., & Boseker, B. J. (1984). Enriching education for Indian and non-Indian students. *Journal of Thought, 19*, 143–148.

Grabe, W. (1991). Current developments in Second Language Reading. *TESOL Quarterly, 25*(3), 375–405.

Grabe, W., & Kaplan, R. B. (1997). *Theory and practice of writing*. London: Longman.

Graves, K. (1996). *Teachers as course developers*. England: Cambridge Press.

Griffiths, R. (1992). Speech rate and listening comprehension: Further evidence of the relationship. *TESOL Quarterly, 26*, 385–391.

Grosse, C. U. & Leto, L. J. (1999). Virtual communication and networking in distance learning. *TESOL Matters, 9*(1), 1–7.

Hall, E. T. (1961). *The silent language.* New York: Fawcett.

Hall, E. T. (1966). *The hidden dimension.* New York: Doubleday.

Hall, E. T. (1976). *Beyond culture.* New York: Anchor Press/Doubleday.

Hall, E. T. (1983). *The Dance of Life: The other dimension of time.* Garden City, N.J.: Anchor Press/Doubleday.

Hancock, J., Turbill, J., & Cambourne, B. (1994). Assessment and evaluation of literacy learning". In S. Valencia, E. Hiebert, & P. Afflerbach (Eds.) *Authentic reading assessment: Practices and possibilities.* Newark, DE: International Reading Association.

Hancock, M. (1997). Behind classroom code-switching: layering and language choice in L2 learner interaction. *TESOL Quarterly 31* (2) 217–235.

Hanna, P. R. (1963). Revising the social studies: What is needed? *Social Education, 27*, 190–196.

Hanvey, R. G. (1976). *An attainable global perspective.* New York, NY: The American Forum for Global Education.

Harmer, J. (1991). *The practice of English language teaching* (Chapter 12: Planning). Harlow, UK: Longman.

Harmer, J. (1998). *How to teach English.* (Chapter 12: Planning). Harlow, UK: Longman.

Harris, W. J., & Shultz, P. N. B. (1986). *The special education resource program: Rationale and implementation.* Columbus, OH: Merrill.

Harrow, A. J. (1977) *Taxonomy of the Psychomotor Domain.* New York: Longman.

Harste, J., Woodward, V., & Burke, C. (1984). *Language Stories and Literacy lessons.* Portsmouth, NH: Heinemann.

Heald-Taylor, G. (1991). *Whole language strategies for ESL students.* San Diego, CA: Dormac, Inc.

Hegelsen, M. (1993). *Find the Mistakes in New Ways in Teaching Reading,* Richard R. Day (Ed.). Bloomington, IL: Pantagraph Printing.

Heward, W. L. (2000). *Exceptional children: An introduction to special education.* (6th Ed.). New Jersey: Prentice Hall.

Higgins, J. (1991). *Fuel for learning: The neglected element in textbooks and CALL.* Paper presented at TESOL, New York, NY.

Hoover, J. J., & Collier, C. (1989). Methods and materials for bilingual special education. In L. M. Baca & H. T. Cervantes (Eds.), *The bilingual special education interface* (pp. 231–255). Columbus, OH: Merrill.

Hornberger, N. (1989). Continua of biliteracy. *Review of Educational Research, 59*(3), 271–296.

Hornsby, D., Sukarna, D., & Parry, J. (1986). *Read on: A conference approach to reading.* Portsmouth, NH: Heinemann.

Horowitz, D.(1988). To see our text as others see it: Toward a social sense of coherence. *JALT Journal, 10*(2): 91–100.

Hosenfeld, C. (1984). Case studies of ninth grade readers. In J. C. Alderson & A. H. Urquhart (Eds.), *Reading in a foreign language,* pp. 231–244. New York: Longman.

Hudelson, S. (1984). Kan yu ret an rayt en ingles: Children become literate in English as a second language. *TESOL Quarterly, 18,* 221–238.

Hudelson, S. (1986). ESL children's writing: What we've learned, what we're learning. In P. Rigg & D.S. Enright (Eds.). *Children and ESL: Integrating perspectives* (p. 23–54). Washington, DC: Teachers of English to speakers of Other Languages.

Hudelson, S. (1989a). *Write on. Children writing in ESL.* Englewood Cliffs, NJ: Prentice-Hall.

Hudelson, S. (1989b). "Teaching" English through content-area activities. In P. Rigg & V. G. Allen (Eds.) *When they don't all speak English: Integrating the ESL student into the regular classroom.* Urbana, IL: National Council for Teachers of English.

Hudelson, S (1994). Literacy development of second language children. In Fred Genesse (Ed.) *Educating Second Language Children,* New York: Cambridge University Press, 129–158.

Individuals with Disabilities Education Act of 1990, (Pub.L. No. 101-476), 20 U.S.C. Chapter 33,§ 1400–1485.

Intercultural Development Research Association (IDRA). (1995). Math and Science. IDRA Focus. *IDRA Newsletter, 22*(2). San Antonio, Texas: Author.

Jarolimek, J. (1989). In search of a scope and sequence for social studies. *Social Education. 53*(6), 376–385.

Jarvis J. & Robinson, M. (1997). Analyzing educational discourse: An exploratory study of teacher response and support to pupils' learning. *Applied Linguistics 18* (2), 212–228.

Jensen, L. (2001) "Planning Lessons". In Celce-Murcia, Marianne (Ed.) *Teaching English as a Second or Foreign Language* (3rd Ed.) Heinle & Heinle, Boston, MA.

Johns, A. M. (1991). *Insights into the reading-writing relationship.* Paper presented at the California TESOL Conference (CATESOL), Santa Clara.

Johnson, D. M. (1991). Second language and content learning with computers: Research in the role of social factors. In P. Dunkel, (Ed.), *Computer-assisted language learning and testing: research issues and practice,* pp 61–83. New York: Newbury House

Johnson, D. W. and Johnson, R. T. (1993). Encouraging thinking through constructive controversy. *Enhancing thinking through cooperative thinking.* New York: Teachers College Press.

Juffer, K.A. (1984) *ISECSI, Bulletin of International Interchanges , 21,* 16–28.

Kagan, S. (1989). *Cooperative learning: Resources for teachers.* San Juan Capistrano, CA: Resources for Teachers.

Kagan, S. (1995). "We can talk: Cooperative learning in the elementary ESL classroom". *Eric Digest* (On-line), Available: eric@cal.org.

Kagan, S. (1997). *Cooperative Learning.* San Clemente, California: Kagan Cooperative Learning.

Kaplan, R. B.(1990). Writing in a multilingual/multicultural context: What's contrastive  rhetoric all about? *Writing instructor, 10*(1): 7–17.

Kelch, Ken. (1985). "Modified Input as an Aid to Comprehend." *Studies in Second Language Acquisition, 7,* 81–89.

Kessler, C., & Quinn, M. E. (1987). ESL and science learning. In J. Crandall (Ed.), *ESL through content-area instruction: Mathematics, science, social studies* (pp. 55–88). Englewood Cliffs, NJ: Prentice Hall.

King, P. E. & Behnke, R. R. (1989). The Effect of Time-Compressed Speech on Comprehensive, Interpretive, and Short-Term Listening. *Human Communication Research, 15*, 428–41.

Kirkwood, T. F. (1995). Teaching from a global perspective: A case study of three high school social studies teachers. *International Dissertation Abstracts.* Miami, Florida: Florida International University.

Kirkwood, T. F. (2001a). Our global age requires global education: Clarifying definitional ambiguities. *The Social Studies. 92*(1):10–15.

Kirkwood, T. F. (2001b). Preparing teachers to teach from a global perspective. The Delta Kappa Gamma Bulletin. 67(2):5-12.

Kitano M., & Espinosa, R. (1995). Language diversity and giftedness: Working with gifted English language learners. *Journal of the Education for the Gifted,* 18 (3), 234–254.

Kluckholn, J.F., & Strodtbeck, F. (1960). *Variations in value orientations.* New York: Peterson.

Kniep, W. M. (1987). *Next steps in global education: A handbook for curriculum development.* New York: American Forum.

Knopp, C. (1994). Workshop handout. In H. Curtain and C. A. Pesola, *Language and children, Making the match.* New York: Longman Publishing Group.

Kohls, R. (1984). *Survival Kit for Overseas Living.* Chicago: Intercultural Press,

Kohlsl, L. R. (2001) *Survival Kit for Overseas Living.* (4th edition). Yarmouth, ME: Intercultural Press.

Kramsch, C. J. (1993). *Content and culture in language teaching.* Oxford: Oxford University Press.

Kramsch, C. J. (1998) Language and culture. *Oxford introductions to language study.* Oxford: Oxford University Press.

Krashen, S. (1981a). *Second Language Acquisition and Second Language Learning.* Oxford: Pergamon Press.

Krashen, S. (1981b). Bilingual education and second language acquisition theory. In California State Department of Education (Ed.). *Schooling and language minority Students: A theoretical framework.* Los Angeles: Evaluation, Dissemination and Assessment Center, California State University.

Krashen, S. (1982). *Principles and practices in second language acquisition.* Oxford: Pergamon Press.

Krashen, S. (1985). *The input hypothesis: Issues and implications.* New York: Longman.

Kratwohl, D. R., Bloom, B. S., and Masia, B. B. (1964) *Taxonomy of Educational Goals,* Handbook 2, Affective Domain. New York: David McKay.

Kroeber, A. & Kluckhohn, C. (Eds.) (1952) *Culture: A Critical Review of Concepts and Definitions.*

Lang, F. K. (1995). Math power for all students? Toward equity issues for students of color. *Culture and Difference: Critical Perspectives on the Bicultural Experience in the United States.* Edited by Darder, A., 106–126. Westport, Connecticutt: Bergin and Garvey.

Lapp, D., & Flood, J. (1992). *Teaching reading to every child.* New York: Macmillan.

Lapp, S. (2001). Using e-mail dialogue to generate communication in an English as a second language classroom. *The Australian journal of language and literacy, 23,* 1, 50–62.

Lara-Alecio, R. (1996, April). *A three year study of a new pedagogical theory/model in a bilingual education program using mathematics as a vehicle of instruction.* Paper presented at the Annual Meeting of the American Educational Research Association. (ERIC Document Reproduction Service Nol ED 398735).

Larsen-Freeman, D. (1997). Grammar and its teaching: Challenging the myths. *ERIC Digest* (On-line), Available: http://www.cal.org/ericcll/digest/larsen01.html

Laudin, Tika (Ed.) *ESL, English as a second language-Methodology and curriculum development in second language instruction.* No.1, second language acquisition [video-recording] Louisiana Public Broadcasting, Lincoln, Nebraska: GPN Distributor (1991)

Lazarowitz, R. & Hertz-Lazarowitz, R. (1998). Cooperative learning in the science curriculum. In B. J. Fraser & K. G. Tobin (Eds.), *International handbook of science education* (Chapter 4.2, pp. 449–469).

Lazear, D. (2000). *The intelligent curriculum.* Tucson: Arizona: Zephyr Press.

Ldonline.org/ld_indepth/resource-guide.html

Lee, O., & Fradd, S.H. (1998). Science for all, including students from non-English-language backgrounds. *Educational Researcher, 27*, 12–20.

Lennerberg, E. (1967). *Biological foundations of language.* New York: John Wiley & Sons.

Levy, M. (1997). *Computer-assisted language learning.* Oxford: Clarendon Press.

Lewis, R. B., & Doorlag, D. H. (1987). *Teaching special students in the mainstream.* Columbus, OH: Merrill.

Lewis, R. B. & Doorlag, D. J. (1999). *Teaching special students in general education classrooms.* (5th edition). New Jersey: Prentice-Hall, Inc.

Lip, E. 1985. *Chinese Beliefs and Superstitions.* Singapore: Graham Brash.

Little, P. (1996). Freedom to learn and compulsion to interact: Promoting learner autonomy through the use of information systems and information technologies. In R. Pemberton et al. (Eds.), *Taking control: Autonomy in language learning* (pp. 203–218). Hong Kong: Hong Kong University Press.

Louie, A. (1982). *Yeh-Shen: A Cinderella story from China.* New York: Philomel.

Lund R. J. (1990). A taxonomy for teaching second language listening. *Foreign Language Annals, 23*, 105–115.

Lynch, S., Atwater, M., Cawley, J., Eccles, J., Lee, O., Marrett, C., Rojas-Medlin, D., Secada, W. Stefanivh, G. & Willetto, A., (1996). *An equity blueprint for Project 2061.* Washington, DC: AAAS.

Maker, J. C. & Nielson, A. B. (1995). *Teaching models in education of the gifted* (2nd ed.).Texas: Pro-Ed.

Maker, J. C., & Schiever, S. W. (1989). *Critical issues in gifted education: Defensible programs for cultural and ethnic minorities.* Austin: Pro-Ed

Mandell, C. J., & Gold, V. (1984). *Teaching handicapped students.* St. Paul, MN: West.

Maple, E. 1971. *Superstition and the superstitious.* New York: A. S. Barnes and Co.

Maring, G., Wiseman, B., & Meyers, K. (1997). Using the worldwide Web to build learning communities; Writing for a genuine purpose. *Journal of adolescent and adult literacy, 41*, 3, 196–207.

Markham, P. L. (1988). Gender differences and the perceived expertness of the speaker as factors in ESL Listening Recall. *TESOL Quarterly 22*, 397–406.

Marshall, C. (1991). Teachers' learning styles: How they affect student learning. *The Clearing House 64*, (4), 225–226.

Martorella, P. H. (1998). *Social studies for elementary school children: Developing young citizens.* Upper Saddle River, NJ: Prentice-Hall, Inc.

Mauranen, A. (1994). Two discourse worlds. *Finlance, 13*, 1–40.

May, F. (1998). *Reading as communication: To help children read and write.* UpperSaddle River, NJ: Merrill/Prentice Hall.

McCloskey, M. L. (1992). Turn on units: English as a second language content area curriculum in math, science, and computer science for grades K–6. *Teaching Guides.* Georgia State Board of Education, Atlanta, GA. (ERIC Document Reproduction Service No. ED 347090)

McKay, S., & Hornberger, N. H. (Eds.) (1996). *Sociolinguists and language and language teaching.* Oxford: Oxford University Press.

McLaughlin, B. (1987). Reading in a second language. Studies of adult and child Learners. In S.R. Goldman & H.T. Trueba (Eds.), *Becoming literate in English as a second language*, pp. 57–70. Norwood, NJ: Ablex.

McLoughlin, J. A. & Lewis, R. B. (1990). *Assessing special students* (3rd edition). New York: Macmillan Publishing Company.

McNeil, J. (1992). *Reading Comprehension* (3rd edition). New York: Harper Collins

McTighe, J. (1992). Graphic Organizers: Collaborative Links to better thinking. In Neil Davison and Toni Worsham (Eds.) *Enhancing thinking through collaborative learning*, New York: Teachers College Press of Columbia University.

Mehlinger, H. D.(Ed), (1981). *UNESCO handbook for the teaching of social studies.* UNESCO: 146–148.

Merryfield, M. M. (1990). *Teaching about the world: Teacher education programs with a global perspective.* Columbus, OH: Mershon Center. The Ohio State University.

Merryfield, M. M. (1997). *A framework for teacher education. Preparing teachers to teach global perspectives: A handbook for teacher educators,* edited by M. M. Merryfield, E. Jarchow & S. Pickert. Thousand Oaks, CA: Corwin Press, Inc.: 1–24.

Meyer, B. J. F., Brandt, D. M. & Bluth, G. J. (1980). Use of top-level structure in text: Key for reading comprehension of ninth grade students. *Reading Research Quarterly, 16,* 72–103.

Miranda, A. O., & Matheny, K.B. (2000) Socio-psychological predictors of acculturative stress among Latino adults. *Journal of Mental Health Counseling, 22*(4), 306–317.

Miranda, A. O. & Umhoefer, D.L. (1998). Depression and social interest differences between Latinos in dissimilar acculturation stages. *Journal of Mental Health Counseling, 20,* 159–171.

Moore, C. G. (1994). Research in Native American mathematics education. *For the Learning of Mathematics.* 14(2), 9–14.

Morgan, S. & Ariza, E. (2002). *Critical thinking in teacher education: Challenging learning styles literature reviews.* Unpublished paper.

Morrow, L.M. (1983). Home and school correlates of early interest in literature. *Journal of Educational Research, 76*: 24-30 in Peregory, S.F. & Boyle, O.F. (2001). *Reading, Writing, & Learning in ESL: A resource book K-12 teachers.* (3rd ED.). New York, NY: Addison Wesley Longman, Inc.

Morrow, L.M. (1993). Literacy development in the early years: Helping children read and write, (2nd) ed.). Boston: Allyn & Bacon in Peregory, S.F. & Boyle, O.F. (2001). Reading, Writing, & Learning in ESL: A resource book K-12 teachers. (3rd ED.). New York, NY: Addison Wesley Longman, Inc.

Morrow, L. (2001) *Literacy Development In The Early Years.* Boston: Allyn and Bacon.

Moskowitz, G. (1978). *Caring and sharing in the foreign language class.* Cambridge, MA: Newbury House.

Nagel, P. S. (1999). E-mail in the virtual ESL/EFL classroom. *The Internet TESL Journal.* (On-line), Available: http://www.aitech.ac.jp/~iteslj/Articles/Nagel-Email.htm.

Nagy, W. E., Herman, P. A., & Anderson, R.C. (1985). Learning words from context. *Reading Research Quarterly, 20* (2), 233–253.

Nation, I. S. P. (1990). *Teaching and learning vocabulary*. New York: Newbury House/Harper & Row.

National Council for Accreditation of Teacher Education (NCATE), (1994). *NCATE standards*. Washington, DC: Author.

National Council for the Social Studies (NCSS), (1994). *Curriculum standards for social studies: Expectations of excellence*. Washington, DC: Author.

National Council for the Social Studies (NCSS), (1994). *Expectations of excellence: Curriculum standards*. Washington, DC: Author.

National Council for the Social Studies (NCSS), (1982). *Position statement on global education*. Washington, DC: Author.

National Council of Teachers of Mathematics (NCTM). (1989). *Curriculum and evaluation standards for school mathematics*. Reston, VA: Author.

National Council of Teachers of Mathematics (NCTM). (2000). *Principles and Standards for School Mathematics*. Reston, VA.

National Research Council. (1996). *National science education standards*. Washington, DC: National Academy Press.

Nelson, S., Gallagher, J., & Coleman, M. (1993). Cooperative learning from two different perspectives. *Roper Review, 16,* 117–121.

Neu, J., & Scarcella, R. (1991). Word processing in the ESL writing classroom: A survey of student activities. In P. Dunkel (Ed.) *Computer-assisted language learning and testing: Research issues and practice*. (pp. 169–188). New York: Newbury House.

Nieto, Sonia. (1996). *Affirming diversity: The sociopolitical context for multicultural education*. White Plains, NY: Longman.

Nolan, R., & Patterson, R. (2000). Curtains, lights: Using skits to teach English to Spanish-speaking adolescents and adults. *Journal of Adolescent & Adult Literacy, 44,* (1), 6–14.

Nolan, R.W. (1990). Culture shock and cross-cultural adaptation or I was ok until I got here. *Practicing Anthropology, 12,* (4), 2–20.

Norton, D. (1992). *The impact of literature-based reading*. New York: Merrill.

Nunan, D., & Miller, L. (Eds.). (1995). *New ways in teaching listening*. Alexandria, VA: Teachers of English to Speakers of Other Languages. (ERIC Document Reproduction Service No. ED 388 054).

Nutall, C. (1982). *Teaching reading skills in a foreign language*. London: Heinemann.

Oberg, Kelvero. (1960). Cultural shock: Adjustment to new cultural environments. *Practical Anthropology, 7*, 177–182

Ogbu, J. (1988) Cultural diversity and human development. In D.T. Slaughter (Ed.) *Black children and poverty. A developmental perspective* (pp. 11–28). San Francisco: Jossey-Boss.)

O'Malley, J. M., Chamot, A., Stewner-Manzanares, G., Kupper, & Russo, R. (1985). Learning strategy applications with students of English as a second language. *TESOL Quarterly. 19*(3), 557–584.

O'Malley. J. M. and Chamot, A. U. (1990). *Learning strategies in second language acquisition*. New York: Cambridge University Press.

O'Malley, J. M. and Pierce, L. V.(1996). *Authentic assessment for English language learners: Practical approaches for teachers*. Addison Wesley Publishing Co.

Ortiz, T. (1986). Characteristics of limited English proficient Hispanic students served in programs for the learning disabled: Implications for policy and practice (Part II). *Bilingual Special Education Newsletter,* University of Texas at Austin, Vol. IV.

Ovando, C. & Collier, V. (1985). *Bilingual and ESL classrooms: Teaching in multicultural contexts*. New York: McGraw-Hill.

Oxford, R., & and Erhman, M. E. (1995). Adults' language learning strategies in an intensive foreign language program in the United States. *System, 23*(3), 359–386.

Oxford, R., Ehrman, M. E., & Lavine, R. Z. (1991). Style wars: Teacher-student style conflicts in the language classroom. In S. Magnan (Ed.), *Challenges in the 1990's for College Foreign Language Programs* (pp.1–25). Boston: Heinle & Heinle.

Padilla, A. M. (1980). The role of cultural awareness and ethnic loyalty in acculturation. In A.M. Padilla (Ed.), *Acculturation: Theory, models, and some new findings* (pp. 47–84). Boulder, CO: Westview Press.

Paige, R. M. (1993b). On the nature of intercultural experiences and intercultural education. In R.M. Paige (Ed), *Education for the intercultural experience*. Yarmouth, MW: Intercultural Press, 169–199.

Pajares, F. M. (1992). Teacher's beliefs and educational research: Cleaning up a messy construct. *Review of Educational Research, 62*(3), 307–322.

Pang, V. O. (1990, Fall). Asian-American children: A diverse population. *The Education Forum, 55*(1), 49–66.

Pepper, F.C. (1976). Teaching the American Indian child in mainstream settings. In R. L. Jones (Ed.) *Mainstreaming and the minority child* (pp. 133–158). Reston, VA: Council for Exceptional Children.

Peregory, S. & Boyle, O. (1990). Kindergarteners write! Emergent literacy of Mexican  American children in a two-way Spanish immersion program. *Journal of the Association of Mexican American Educators,* 6–18.

Peregory, S. and Boyle, O. (1993). *Reading, writing & learning in ESL: A resource book for K–8 teachers.* New York: Longman.

Peregoy, S. F. & Boyle, O. F. (2001). *Reading, writing, & learning in ESL: A resource book for K–12 teachers.* (3rd ed.). New York: Addison Wesley Longman, Inc.

Pérez, B. & Torres-Guzmán, M. (1992). *Learning in two worlds: An integrated Spanish/English biliteracy approach.* New York: Longman.

Perkins (1992). *Smart Schools.* New York: Free Press.

Peterson, B. (1992). Selecting books for beginning readers. In D. E. DeFord, G. S. Pinnell, & C. Lyons (Eds.), *Bridges to literacy.* Portsmouth, NH: Heinemann.

Peterson, J. S., & Margolin, L. (1997). Naming gifted children: An example of unintended "reproduction". *Journal for the Education of the Gifted, 21* (1), 82–100.

Philips, S. U. (1983). *The Invisible Culture: Communication in classroom and community on the Warm Springs Indian Reservation.* White Plains, NY: Longman.

Phinney, M. (1991). Computer-assisted writing and writing apprehension in ESL students. In P. Dunkel (Ed.) *Computer-assisted language learning and testing: Research issues and practice* (pp. 189–204.) New York: Newbury House.

Piaget, J. (1963). *The language and thought of the child.* New York: W.W. Norton.

Piper, W. (1976). *The Little Engine That Could*. Putman Publishing Group.

Population Reference Bureau, Inc., (1998). *Population and food supply percentages*. Washington, DC: Author.

Portes, A., & Rumbaut, R. G. (1996). *Immigrant America* (2nd ed.) Berkeley, CA: University of California Press.

Portes, A. & Stepnick, A. (1993). *City on the edge: The transformation of Miami*. Berkeley, CA: University of California Press.

Portes, A., & Zhou, M. (1993). The new second generation: Segmented assimilation and its variants among post-1965 immigrant youth. *Annals of the American Academy of Political and Social science, 53*, 74–98.

Raines, S. & Isbell, R. (1994). *Stories: Children's literature in early education*. Albany, NY: Delmar.

Ramirez, M., & Castañeda, A. (1974). *Cultural democracy, bicognitive development and education*, p. 169–170. New York: Academic Press.

Read, C. (1971). Pre-school children's knowledge of English phonology. *Harvard Educational Review, 41*, 1–34.

Reid, J. (1987). The perceptual learning style preferences of ESL students. *TESOL Quarterly, 21* (1), 87–111.

Reid, J. (1995). Preface. In J. Reid (Ed.), *Learning Styles in the ESL/EFL Classroom* (pp.ix–xvii). Boston: Heinle & Heinle.

Reid, Joy M. (1993). *Teaching ESL writing*. Englewood Cliff, NJ: Prentice Hall Regents.

Reyes, M. (1992). Challenging venerable assumptions: Literacy instruction for linguistically different students. *Harvard Educational Review, 62* (4) 427–446.

Rhodes, L., & Dudley-Marling, C. (1988). *Readers and writers with a difference: A holistic approach to teaching learning disabled and remedial students*. Portsmouth, NH: Heinemann.

Richard-Amato, P. (1989). *Making it happen: Interaction in the second language classroom*. White Plains, NY: Longman.

Richards, J., & Rodgers, T. (1986). *Approaches and methods in language teaching: A description and analysis*. New York: Cambridge University Press.

Rief, L. (1990). Finding the value of evaluation: self-assessment in a middle school classroom. *Educational Leadership, 47*(6): 24–29.

Rivers, W. M. (1981). *Teaching foreign language skills* (2nd ed.). Chicago: University of Chicago Press.

Robb, L. (1999). *A basic vocabulary strategy to boost comprehension and reading comprehension.* Scholastic Professional Book

Roberts, P.L. and Kellough, R.D. (2000). *A guide for developing interdisciplinary thematic units.* ( 2nd edition). Upper Saddle River, NJ: Merrill Prentice-Hall.

Robisheaux, J. A. & Banbury, M. M. (1994, September–October). Students who don't fit the mold. *Gifted Child Today Magazine, 17*(4) 28–31.

Romaine, S. (1994). *Language in society: An introduction.* Oxford: Oxford University Press.

Rosenblatt, L. M. (1978). *The reader, the text, the poem.* Carbondale, IL: Southern Illinois University Press.

Rosenblatt, L. M. (1991). Literature —S.O.S.! *Language Arts, 68,* 444–448.

Rosenblatt, L. M. (1994). The traditional theory of reading and writing. In R.B. Ruddell, M.R. Rudell, & H. Singer (eds.) *Theoretical models and processes of reading* (4th ed.), pp. 1057–1092). Newark, DE: International Reading association.

Routman, R. (1991). *Invitations.* Portsmouth, N.H. : Heinemann.

Rubin, J. (1994). A review of second language listening comprehension research. *The Modern Language Journal. 78*(2), 199–221.

Rubin, J. (1995). The contribution of video to the development of competence in listening. In D. Mendelsohn & J. Rubin (Eds.), *A guide for the teaching of listening* (pp. 151–165). San Diego: Dominie Press.

Samson, M., Allen, R., & Sampson, M. (1990). *Pathways to literacy.* Chicago: Holt, Rinehart, & Winston.

Samuels, S.J. (1994). Toward a theory of automatic information processing in reading revisited. In R.B. Ruddell, M.R. Rudell, & H. Singer (eds.) *Theoretical models and processes of reading* (4th ed.), pp. 816–837. Newark, DE: International reading association.

Samuels, S. J. & Kamil, M.L. (1988). Models of the reading process. In P.L. Carrell, J. Devine, & D. E. Eskey (Eds.) *Interactive Approaches to Second Language Reading*, (pp. 22–37). Cambridge: Cambridge University Press.

Saravia-Shore, M., & Arvizu, S. F. (1992). Introduction to cross-cultural literacy: An anthropological approach to dealing with diversity. In M. Saravia-Shore & S. F. Arvizu (Eds.), *Cross-cultural literacy: Ethnographies of communication in multiethnic classrooms* (pp. xv–xxxviii). New York: Garland Publishing.

Saville-Troike, M. (1973). Reading and the audiolingual method. *TESOL Quarterly 7*(4): 395–405.

Saville-Troike, M. (1978). *A guide to culture in the classroom*. Rosslyn, VA: National Clearinghouse for Bilingual Education.

Savington, S. (1983). *Communicative Competence: Theory and Practice*. Reading, MA: Addison-Wesley Publishing Co.

Scafe, M., & Kontas, G. (1982). Classroom implication of culturally defined organizational patterns in speeches by Native Americans. In F. Barkin, E. Brandt, & J. Orstein-Galicia (Eds.), *Bilingualism and language contact: Spanish, English, and Native American languages*. New York: Teachers College Press.

Shohamy, E., & Inbar, O. (1991). Validation of Listening Comprehension Tests: The Effect of Text and Question Type. *Language Testing.* 8: 23–40.

Short, D. (1994). *Integrating language and culture in middle school American History Classes* (Educational practice Rep. No.*). Santa Cruz, CA and Washington, DC: National Center for Research on Culture Diversity and Second Language Learning.

Short, D. J.(1996). *Integrating language and culture in the social studies*. Final report submitted to the Office of Educational Research and Improvement. US. Department of Education. Washington, DC: Center for Applied Linguistics.

Skinner, B.F. (1957). *Verbal Behavior*. New York: Appleton-Century-Crafts.

Slowinski, J. (2000, January). Breaking the Language Barrier: How technology can enhance multilingual communication. *Electronic School* (On-line), Available: http://www.electronicschool.com/2000/01/0100f3.html.

Smalley, R. L. & Hank, M. R. (1992). College teachers. In A. K. Koshi, Ed., *Discoveries: Reading, Thinking, Writing* (pp. 125–127). Boston: Heinle & Heinle.

Smalley, W. A. (1963). "Culture shock, language shock and the shock of self-discovery. *Practical Anthropology,* 10, 45–56.

Smith, Frank (1988). *Understanding reading: A psycholinguistic analysis of reading and learning to read.* Hillsdale, NJ: Lawrence Elbaum.

Snow, M. A. & Brinton, D. M. (1997). *The content-based classroom: Perspectives on integrating language and content.* White Plains, NY: Addison Wesley Longman, Inc.

Solomon, I.D. (1996). Workshops on a multicultural curriculum: issues and caveats. *Education, 117,*1,81-84.

Spanos, G., Rhodes, N: Dale, T. & Crandall, J. (1998) Linguistic features of Mathematical problem-solving Insights and Applications. In J. P. Mestre and R. R. Cocking (Ed) *Linguistic and culture influences on learning mathematics* (pp. 221–240). Hillsdale, N.J. Lawrence Erlbaum.

Sperling, D. (1999). *Dave Sperling's Internet guide for English language teachers.* Burlingame, CA.: Alta.

Spiedel, G.E.(1987). Language differences in the classroom : Two approaches for developing language skills in dialect-speaking children. In E. Okaar (ED), *Socioculture perspectives of language acquisition and multi-legalism.* Tubingen, Germany: Gunter Narr.

Stewig, J. (1981). Choral speaking. Who has the time? Why take the time? *Childhood Education, 58* (1), 25–29.

Sulzby, E. (1985). Children's emergent reading of favorite storybooks. *Reading Research Quarterly, 20*: 458–481.

Swisher, K. & and Deyhle, D. (1989, August). The styles of learning are different, but teaching is just the same: Suggestions for teachers of American Indian youth. *Journal of American Indian Education,* 1–14.

Sysoyer, P.V. (2000, March). " Developing an English for specific purposes course using a learner centered approach: A Russian experience." *The Internet TESL Journal,* Vol. VI, No. 3 (On-line), Available: http://www.aitech.ac.jp/~iteslj/techniques/sysoyev-ESP.htm.

Tan, G., Gallo, P. B., Jacobs, G. M., Kim-Eng Lee, C. (1999, August) Using cooperative learning to integrate thinking and information technology in a content-based writing lesson. *The Internet TESL Journal,* Vol. V, No. 8. (On-line), Available: http://www.aitech.ac.jp/~iteslj/techniques/Tan-Cooperative.htm.

Tannen, D. (1990a). Culturally compatible education: A formula for designing effective classrooms. In H. Trueba, G. Spindler, & L. Spindler (ed), *What do anthropologists have to say about dropouts?* New York: Falmer Press.

Tannen, D. (1990b). *You Just Don't Understand: Women and Men in Conversations.* New York: Morrow.

Tarkington, K. (1996). The rationale for experiential/participatory learning. *Working Papers in Early Childhood Development,* 16. Available from the Bernard von Leer Foundation, Communications Section, P.O. Box 92334, 2508 EH The Hague, The Netherlands.

Tauroza, S. & Allison, D. (1990). Speech rates in British. *Applied Linguistics, 11,* 90–105.

Taylor, B.M. (1980). Children's memory for expository text after reading. *Reading Research Quarterly, 15,* 399–411.

Taylor, D. and Dorsey-Gaines, C.(1988). *Growing up literate: learning from inner city families.* Portsmouth, NH: Heinemann.

Teachers of English to Speakers of Other Languages, Inc. (1991). *ESL Standards for Pre-K-12* [Brochure]. Alexandria, Virginia.

Teenant, A., Bernhardt, E. B., Rodriquez-Munoz, M. & Aiello, M. (1995). *Bringing science & second language learning together: What every teacher needs to know.* National Center for Science Teaching & Learning, Columbus, OH.

Terrell, T. D. (1977). A natural approach to second language acquisition and learning. *The Modern Language Journal, 66,* 121–32.

Terrell, T. (1981). The natural approach in bilingual education. In *Schooling and language minority students: A theoretical framework.* Los Angeles: Evaluation, Dissemination and Assessment Center, California State University, Los Angeles.

Tharp, R. (1989a). Culturally compatible education: A formula for designing effective classrooms. In H. Trueba, G. Spindler, & L. Spindler (Eds.), *What do anthropologists have to say about dropouts?* New York: Falmer Press.

Tharp, R. (1989b, February). Psychocultural variables and constants: Effects on teaching and learning in schools. *American Psychologist, 44*(2), 349–359.

Tiedt, P. L. & Tiedt (1998). *Multicultural teaching: A handbook of activities, information, and resources* (5th ed.) Boston: Allyn and Bacon.

Tierney, R. J., Carter, M. A. & Desai, L. E. (1991). *Portfolio assessment in the reading-writing classroom.* Norwood, MA: Christopher-Gordon.

Tierney, R. J. & Gee, M. (1990). Reading comprehension. In D. Bogdan & S.B. Straw (Eds.), *Beyond communication: Reading comprehension and criticism,* pp. 167–196. Portsmouth, NH: Boynton/Cook and Heinemann.

Tijanero, J. and Calderon, M. (1988). Language Experience Approach Plus. *Journal of Educational Issues of Language Minority Students, 2:*31–45.

Tobin, K. (1998) Issues and trends in the teaching of science. In B. J. Fraser & K. Tobin (Eds.) *International handbook of science education* (pp. 129–151). Great Britain: Kluwer Academic Publishers.

Tobin, K., Tippins, D. & Gallard, A. J. (1994). Research on instructional strategies for teaching science. In D. L. Gabel (Ed.) *Handbook of research on science teaching and learning* (pp. 45–93).

Trueba, H. T., &. Cheng, L. (1993). *Myth or Reality: Adaptive Strategies of Asian Americans in California.* Bristol, PA: Palmer Press.

Tudor, I. (1996). *Learner-centeredness as language education.* Cambridge, University Press

Tye, B. B. & Tye, K. A. (1992). *Global education: A study of school change.* Albany, NY: State University of New York Press.

Tye, K. A. (1999). *Global education: A worldwide movement.* Orange, CA: Independence Press.

Ur, P. (1996). *A course in language teaching: Practice and theory.* Cambridge: Cambridge University Press.

Valdez-Pierce, L. and O'Malley, M. J. (1993, Spring). Performance and portfolio assessment for language minority students. *NCBE Program Information Guide Series,* Number 9, (On-line) Available: http://www.ncbe.gwu.edu/ncbepubs/pigs/pig9.htm.

Verplaetse, L. S. (1998). How content teachers interact with English langauge learners. *Tesol Journal Autumn,* pp. 24–28.

Voller, P. & Pickard, V. (1996). Conversation exchange. A way towards autonomous language learning. In R. Pemberton et al. (Eds.), *Taking control: Autonomy in language learning* (pp. 115–132). Hong Kong University Press.

Voss, B. (1979). Hesitation Phenomena as Sources of Perceptual Errors for Non-Native Speakers. *Language and Speech 22*: 129–44.

Vygotsky, L.S. (1962). *Thought and language.* Cambridge, MA: MIT Press.

Vygotsky, L.S. (1978). *Mind in society: The development of higher psychological process.* Cambridge, MA: Harvard University Press.

Vygostky, L.S. (1987). The development of scientific concepts in childhood. In R.F. Rieber & A.S. Carton (Eds.) (N. Mink, trans.) *The collected works of L.S. Vygostky,* vol.1 pp. 167–241.

Wallace, G., Larsen, S.C., & Elksnin, L.K. (1992). *Educational assessment of learning problems: Testing for teaching.* Boston: Allyn and Bacon.

Wallner, A (1994. *Betsy Ross.* Carmel, CA: Hampton-Brown Books.

Walter, T. (1995). *English Learner Achievement Project (ELAP) training handbook.* San Diego: San Diego City schools.

Walter, T. (1996). *Amazing English!* Addison Wesley.

Warschauer, M. (1996). *E-mail for English teaching: Bringing the Internet and computer learning networks into the language classroom.* Burlingame, CA: Alta.

Waterman, B. (2000). Assessing children for the presence of a disability. National Information Center for Children and Youth with Disabilities News Digest, Vol 4. (On-line), Available: http://www.ldonline.org/ld_indepth/assessment/assess-nichcy.html.

Wax, R. H. (1976) Ogala Sioux Dropouts and Their Problems with Educators. In Joan I. Roberts and Sherrie K. Akinsanya, (Eds.), *Schooling in the Cultural Context,* 216–26. New York: David McKay

Wellman, R. (1978). Science: a basic for language & reading development. In M. B. Rowe (Ed.) *What research says to the science teacher.* (pp. 1–12). NSTA Arlington, VA.

Whorf, B. L. (1956). *Language, thought and reality.* Cambridge, MA: The MIT Press.

Widdowson, H.G. (1978). *Teaching language as communication.* London: Oxford University Press.

Wilkins, H. (1991). Computer talk: Long distance conversations by computer. *Written Communication, 8,* 1, 56–77.

Witkins, H. A., (1967). A cognitive style approach to cross-cultural research. *International Journal of Psychology, 2,* 233–250.

Wright, A. (1999). *Pictures for language learning* (8th ed.). Cambridge, England: Cambridge University Press.

Wright, (1987). *Roles of teachers and learners.* Oxford: Oxford University Press.

Zappia, I. A. (1989). Identification of gifted Hispanic students: A multidimensional view. In C. J. Maker and S. W. Schiever (Eds.), *Critical Issues in gifted education* (pp.19–26). Austin: Pro-ed.

Zemelman, S., Daniels, H., & Hyde, A. (1998). *Best practice: New standards for teaching and learning in America's school* (2nd ed.). Portsmouth, NH: Heinemann.

Zero Population Growth Bureau, Inc. (2000). *Facts and statistics.* Washington, DC.: Author

# Index